T5-AGL-606

The Early Modern Englishwoman: A Facsimile Library of Essential Works

Series I

Printed Writings, 1500–1640: Part 2

Volume 12

Protestant Translators: Anne Lock Prowse and Elizabeth Russell

Advisory Board:

Margaret J.M. Ezell
Texas A & M University

Elaine Hobby
Loughborough University

Suzanne W. Hull
The Huntington Library

Barbara K. Lewalski
Harvard University

Stephen Orgel
Stanford University

Ellen Rosand
Yale University

Mary Beth Rose
University of Illinois, Chicago

Hilda L. Smith
University of Cincinnati

Retha M. Warnicke
Arizona State University

Georgianna Ziegler
The Folger Shakespeare Library

The Early Modern Englishwoman:
A Facsimile Library of Essential Works

Series I

Printed Writings, 1500–1640: Part 2

Volume 12

Protestant Translators:
Anne Lock Prowse and Elizabeth Russell

Selected and Introduced by
Elaine V. Beilin

General Editors
Betty S. Travitsky and Patrick Cullen

Ashgate

Aldershot • Burlington USA • Singapore • Sydney

The Introductory Note copyright © Elaine V. Beilin 2001

All rights reserved. No part of this publication may be reproduced, stored in a retrieval system, or transmitted in any form or by any means, electronic, mechanical, photocopying, recording, or otherwise without the prior permission of the publisher.

Published by
Ashgate Publishing Limited
Gower House
Croft Road
Aldershot
Hants GU11 3HR
England

Ashgate Publishing Company
131 Main Street
Burlington, VT 05401-5600 USA

BS
1515.4
.P7613
2001

Ashgate website: http://www.ashgate.com

British Library Cataloguing-in-Publication Data
Prowse, Anne Lock
The early modern Englishwoman : a facsimile library of essential works.
Part 2: Printed writings, 1500–1640: Vol. 12: Protestant translators
1. English literature – Early modern, 1500–1700 2. English literature – Women authors 3. Women – England – History – Renaissance, 1450–1600 – Sources 4. Women – England – History – Modern period, 1600– – Sources 5. Women – Literary collections
I. Title II. Russell, Elizabeth III. Travitsky, Betty S.
IV. Cullen, Patrick Colborn, V. Beilin, Elaine V.,
VI. Calvin, Jean, 1509–1564. Sermons upon the song that Ezechias made … VII. Taffin, Jean. Of the markes of the children of God, and of their comforts in afflictions
VIII. Ponet, John. Way of reconciliation of a good and learned man …
820.8'09287

Library of Congress Cataloging-in-Publication Data
The early modern Englishwoman: a facsimile library of essential works. Part 2. Printed Writings 1500–1640 / general editors, Betty S. Travitsky and Patrick Cullen.

See page vi for complete CIP Block 99–55939

The woodcut reproduced on the title page and on the case is from the title page of Margaret Roper's trans. of [Desiderius Erasmus] *A Devout Treatise upon the Pater Noster* (circa 1524).

ISBN 1 84014 225 1

Printed in Great Britain by Antony Rowe Ltd, Chippenham, Wiltshire.

CONTENTS

Library of Congress Cataloging-in-Publication Data
Protestant translators : Anne Lock Prowse and Elizabeth Russell / selected and introduced by Elaine V. Beilin.
p. cm. -- (The early modern Englishwoman. Printed writings, 1500-1640, Part 2 ; v. 12)
Contents: Sermons of John Calvin, upon the songe that Ezechias made after he had bene sicke, and afflicted by the hand of God, conteyned in the 38. chapiter of Esay / Anne Lock Prowse, translator ; A meditation of a penitent sinner / [attributed to] Anne Lock Prowse -- Of the markes of the children of God, and of their comforts in afflictions / Jean Taffin ; Anne Lock Prowse, translator -- A way of reconciliation of a good and learned man touching the trueth, nature, and substance of the body and blood of Christ in the sacrament / Bishop John Ponet ; Elizabeth Russell, translator.
ISBN 1-84014-225-1
1. Bible. O.T. Isaiah XXXVIII--Sermons. 2. Sermons, French--Translations into English. 3. Christian poetry, English. 4. Suffering--Religious aspects--Reformed Church. 5. Lord's Supper--Reformed Church. 6. Reformed Church--Doctrines. I. Prowse, Anne. II. Russell, Elizabeth Cooke Hoby, Lady, ca. 1540-1609. III. Beilin, Elaine V. IV. Calvin, Jean, 1509-1564. Sermons of John Calvin, upon the songe that Ezechias made after he had bene sicke, and afflicted by the hand of God, conteyned in the 38. chapiter of Esay. V. Prowse, Anne. Meditation of a penitent sinner. VI. Taffin, Jean, 1529-1602. Des marques des enfans de Dieu et des consolations en leurs afflictions. English. VII. Ponet, John, 1516?-1556. Diallacticon viri boni et literati, de veritate, natura, atque substantia corporis et sanguinis Christi in Eucharistia. English. VIII. Series.

BS1515.4.P7613 2000
230'.42--dc21

99-55939

PREFACE
BY THE GENERAL EDITORS

Until very recently, scholars of the early modern period have assumed that there were no Judith Shakespeares in early modern England. Much of the energy of the current generation of scholars has been devoted to constructing a history of early modern England that takes into account what women actually wrote, what women actually read, and what women actually did. In so doing the masculinist representation of early modern women, both in their own time and ours, is deconstructed. The study of early modern women has thus become one of the most important—indeed perhaps the most important—means for the rewriting of early modern history.

The Early Modern Englishwoman: A Facsimile Library of Essential Works is one of the developments of this energetic reappraisal of the period. As the names on our advisory board and our list of editors testify, it has been the beneficiary of scholarship in the field, and we hope it will also be an essential part of that scholarship's continuing momentum.

The Early Modern Englishwoman is designed to make available a comprehensive and focused collection of writings in English from 1500 to 1750, both by women and for and about them. The three series of *Printed Writings* (1500–1640, 1641–1700, and 1701–1750), provide a comprehensive if not entirely complete collection of the separately published writings by women. In reprinting these writings we intend to remedy one of the major obstacles to the advancement of feminist criticism of the early modern period, namely the limited availability of the very texts upon which the field is based. The volumes in the facsimile library reproduce carefully chosen copies of these texts, incorporating significant variants (usually in appendices). Each text is preceded by a short introduction providing an overview of the life and work of a writer along with a survey of important scholarship. These works, we strongly believe, deserve a large readership—of historians, literary critics, feminist critics, and non-specialist readers.

The Early Modern Englishwoman also includes separate facsimile series of *Essential Works for the Study of Early Modern Women* and of *Manuscript Writings*. These facsimile series are complemented by *The Early Modern Englishwoman 1500–1750: Contemporary Editions*. Also under our general editorship, this series will include both old-spelling and modernized editions of works by and about women and gender in early modern England.

New York City
2001

INTRODUCTORY NOTE

As writers strongly committed to the Reformation, Anne Lock Prowse and Elizabeth Russell translated works which they believed were doctrinally useful to their Protestant readers. Anne Lock Prowse (1534-after 1590?) published two translations: as 'A.L.', she translated *Sermons of John Calvin, upon the songe that Ezechias made after he had bene sicke* (1560), and as Anne Prowse, she translated *Of the markes of the children of God* by Jean Taffin (1590). The sonnet sequence, *A meditation of a penitent sinner*, which is appended to the translation of Calvin, and the poem following the translation of Taffin, 'The necessitie and benefite of Affliction', have also been attributed to her. Each of these works centres on the struggle of the faithful with adversity, a theme strongly identified with nonconformist ideology. Elizabeth Russell translated Bishop John Ponet's *A Way of Reconciliation of a good and learned man, touching the Trueth, Nature, and Substance of the Body and Blood of Christ in the Sacrament* (1605), a work arguing for the resolution of conflicts within the Reformed Church over the doctrine of the Eucharist.

Anne Lock Prowse

Anne Lock Prowse was the daughter of Stephen Vaughan, a London merchant and royal agent with Reformist leanings, and Margaret Guinet (or Gwynnethe), whom her husband described before her early death in 1544 as 'witty and housewifely' (Richardson, 1953, p. 85n). Anne Vaughan's stepmother was Margery Brinklow, widow of Henry Brinklow who wrote *The Complaynt of Roderyck Mors*, a strongly Protestant polemic. By 1553, Anne Vaughan had married the first of her three husbands, Henry Lock, a Protestant mercer and neighbour from the parish of St Mary Bow. The Locks' strong religious commitment is indicated by their friendship with John Knox, who lived with them in London in 1553. Anne Lock corresponded with Knox from 1556 to 1562 while he lived in Geneva and Scotland; fourteen letters from Knox to Lock are printed in Laing's edition of Knox's *Works*. At Knox's urging, in May 1557 Lock journeyed to Geneva with her two infants, Harry and Anne; her daughter died soon after she reached Geneva. (Harry was the Henry Lok [1553–1608?] who wrote *Ecclesiasticus ... in English Poesie* and two hundred sonnets in *Sundrie Sonets of Christian Passions*.) Some time during the next two years, Lock translated four sermons that Calvin preached in 1557 on the song of Hezekiah from Isaiah 38; her work was published in 1560 after her return to London as *Sermons of John Calvin, upon the songe that Ezechias made after he had bene sicke*.

Widowed in 1571, in the next year Lock married Edward Dering, the noted puritan preacher. Dering was at the forefront of religious controversy in the early 1570s, his patrons and correspondents including the Cooke sisters, particularly Katherine Cooke Killigrew. That Anne Lock Dering was herself linked with this circle is suggested by one of her husband's letters (Collinson, 1965, p. 284) and by the inclusion of her brief Latin dedicatory verse with the Cooke sisters' dedications to the Earl of Leicester in Bartholo Sylva's *Il Giardino Cosmografico* (Schleiner, 1994, p. 40). Edward Dering died of tuberculosis in June 1576. Before 1583, Anne Lock Dering married Richard Prowse, a draper of Exeter who served as mayor of the city three times and as a Member of Parliament in 1584. As Knox's old friend and correspondent, Anne Prowse was the dedicatee of John Field's edition of *A Notable and comfortable exposition of M. John Knoxes, upon the fourth of Mathew* (1583), published by Thomas Man, who also published her translation from Jean Taffin, *Of the marks of the children of God*, in 1590. In 1589, Man had published *The French Historie* by Anne Dowriche, one of Prowse's family connections who lived near Exeter; the strong puritan ideology of both writers raises the possibility that they belonged to the same local nonconformist circle.

Sermons of John Calvin, upon the songe that Ezechias made after he had bene sicke, and afflicted by the hand of God, conteyned in the 38. Chapiter of Esay; A meditation of a penitent sinner (1560)

Lock translated Calvin's four sermons from French, dedicating the work to Katharine, Duchess of Suffolk, the notable Protestant patron who had recently returned from exile. The dedication may indicate an acquaintance, as suggested by Lock's praise of the 'godly conversation that I have sene in you', and a recognition of the duchess' financial patronage of Lock's Reformist publisher, John Day. His publication of Lock's translation of Calvin's sermons and the appended sonnet sequence, *A meditation of a penitent sinner: Written in maner of a paraphrase upon the 51. Psalme of David*, continues his and the duchess' Reformist agenda, now newly stimulated by Elizabeth's accession. Hannay finds that Lock worked from a manuscript of Calvin's sermons (Hannay, 1992, p. 22); Felch finds that the prose text of Psalm 51 in the margin of the sonnets 'is Lock's own original translation' based on 'the Gallican version of the Latin psalms' (Felch, 1999, lvi–lvii).

The authorship and provenance of *A meditation of a penitent sinner*, a sequence of twenty-six sonnets, are somewhat clouded by the headnote which precedes it [on sig. A]. The identities of the 'I' who added the meditation and 'my friend' who delivered it are unknown, although it is possible that John Day the printer wrote the heading to indicate that Lock gave him the sonnets; it is also possible that Lock wrote the note to attribute the sonnets to her friend, John Knox, or that she was masking her own authorship. On the basis of internal parallels between the sonnets and the dedication to the Duchess of Suffolk, signed 'A. L.', and to Lock's second translation which also concludes with verses, a likely attribution of the *Meditation* to Lock may be made (Woods, 1992, pp. 137–38; Hannay, 1993, pp. 21–2; Felch, 1999, liii–liv). The *Meditation* appears to be the first sonnet sequence written in English (Roche, 1989, pp. 154–55).

STC lists two copies from the edition of 1560 (*STC* 4450), one in the British Library and one in the Folger Shakespeare Library. Felch argues that the Folger copy contains corrections overseen by Lock (Felch, 1997, lxxi–lxxvii). The British Library copy bears the inscription on the flyleaf, 'Liber Henrici Lock ex dono Annae uxoris suae. 1559' ('Henry Lock's book, a gift of his wife Anne'). Although the family name appears elsewhere as 'Lok' and 'Locke', the choice of 'Lock' in the present volume follows the spelling in this inscription. The present edition is a facsimile of the Folger Library copy, except that sig. F3v, where twenty-five non-consecutive lines were printed upside down, has been replaced by the signature from the British Library copy. Signature C2 is misnumbered as B2, and pages 65–93 (sigs. F1–G7) are misnumbered as 50–79. In the section of misnumbered pages, there are omitted numbers (55, 59, 63, 66), two pages numbered 61 and two pages numbered 65. John Day published the work again in 1574, but the British Library copy, the only copy listed in *STC*, was destroyed in World War II.

Of the markes of the children of God, and of their comforts in afflictions (1590)

Anne Lock Prowse's translation of Jean (or John) Taffin's French treatise carried on her work for the cause of continued reformation. Taffin (1529–1602), a Calvinist minister who studied at Geneva at approximately the same time as Anne Lock's residence there in the late 1550s, served as an advisor and pastor in the court of William of Nassau in the 1570s and as minister of the Walloon churches of Anvers and Harlem. The first edition of *Des marques des enfans de Dieu et des consolations en leurs afflictions* appeared in 1586; the editions published after 1588 were revised and expanded by the author. An anonymous translation, *The tokens of the children of God, and comfortes in their afflyctions*, was entered in the Stationers' Register to Edward Aggas on 30 October 1587. *Of the markes of the children of God, and of their comforts in afflictions*, translated by Anne Prowse (*STC* 23652), was entered in the Stationers' Register to Thomas Man on 26 March 1590. The popularity of this translation is suggested by further editions of 1591, 1597, 1599, 1608, 1609, 1615 and 1634. Variations among editions include orthographical changes, corrections, and some minor alterations (Felch, 1999, lxxxi–lxxxvi).

As before, Prowse dedicates her work to an influential 'godly' patron, Anne Russell Dudley, the Countess of Warwick. White argues that Taffin's exhortation to the faithful to persevere in troubled times and to welcome their adversity as a sign of righteousness reflects the embattled spirit of the English puritan movement at the end of the 1580s (1999, pp. 382–4). The appended poem, 'The necessitie and benefite of Affliction', may reasonably be attributed to Prowse; it is written in common meter with alternating rhymes and continues the themes of the prose treatise. The present edition is a facsimile of the Huntington Library copy which is an excellent copy.

I am grateful to Susan Felch for her generous assistance with Anne Lock's texts.

Elizabeth Russell

Elizabeth Cooke Hoby Russell (1528–1609), elegist, translator, and patron, joined her sisters, Mildred Cooke Burghley, Anne Cooke Bacon, and Katherine Cooke Killigrew, in their active support of the English Reformation. The daughter of the Reformist educator and court official, Sir Anthony Cooke, and Anne Fitzwilliam Cooke, she was educated with her sisters in Latin, Greek, and modern languages.

The earliest remains of Russell's work consist of over eighty lines in English and Latin on the tomb of her first husband, Sir Thomas Hoby (1530–1566), and his half-brother, Sir Philip, in the church at Bisham, Berkshire. When her two young daughters died in 1571, she wrote the brief elegy inscribed on their tomb. She also wrote verses for the tomb of her sister, Katherine Killigrew; and Greek and Latin verses for the tomb in Westminster Abbey of her second husband, John Lord Russell (Schleiner, 1994, pp. 46–51, Appendix 2). Many of Russell's letters to her brother-in-law, William Cecil, Lord Burghley and to his son, Sir Robert Cecil, are extant; she wrote to request their aid and influence in both legal and familial affairs (Wilson, 1970, pp. 13–40, 225–37; Lamb, 1985, pp. 121–24). She built her own monument in Bisham Church, depicting herself surrounded by her descendants.

Russell translated Bishop John Ponet's Latin *Diallacticon viri boni et literati, de veritate, natura, atque substantia corporis et sanguinis Christi in eucharistia* as *A Way of Reconciliation of a good and learned man, touching the Trueth, Nature, and Substance of the Body and Blood of Christ in the Sacrament.* In the dedication to her daughter, Anne Herbert, she refers to the work as her 'last legacie'. In 1605, Russell was in her late seventies and wanted to see her translation in print, 'fearing lest after my death it should be Printed according to the humors of other, and would be wrong of the dead, who in his life approved my Translation with his owne allowance'. It is possible that Ponet, who died in 1556, may have approved the translation; or, the approval may have come from Russell's father, Sir Anthony Cooke, who died in 1576 and who had himself published Ponet's Latin original in Strasbourg in 1557. A French translation of Ponet, to which Russell refers in her dedication, appeared in 1566. It is also possible that the translation belongs to the time of her first marriage to Sir Thomas Hoby who apparently shared her commitment to the Reformation and her interest in translation; before their marriage, he had translated Martin Bucer's *Gratulation ... unto the Churche of England for the restitution of Christes Religion* (1549) and, later, Castiglione's *The Courtier* (1561).

A Way of Reconciliation attempts to mediate the profound conflict over the doctrine of the Eucharist, one that continued to divide the Reformed church. Ponet uses historical scholarship to argue that the disputants possess common beliefs despite their disagreements. By translating Ponet, Russell contributed a significant polemic to the English Church, thus joining the efforts of her sister, Lady Anne Bacon, who translated Bishop John Jewel's Latin treatise as *An Apologie or aunswer in defence of the Church of England* (1564).

STC lists one edition of *A Way of Reconciliation* (21456). The present edition is a facsimile of the copy in the Folger Library.

Editions

STC 4450 (Calvin), 23652 (Taffin), 21456 (Ponet)

Lok, Anne (1990), *A Meditation of a Penitent Sinner: Written in maner of a Paraphrase upon the 51. Psalme of David*, Brown University Women Writers Project

Locke, Anne (1997), *A Meditation of a Penitent Sinner: Anne Locke's Sonnet Sequence*, Kel Morin-Parsons (ed.), Waterloo, Ontario: North Waterloo Academic Press

Lock, Anne Vaughan (1999), *The Collected Works of Anne Vaughan Lock*, Susan Felch (ed.), Tempe, Arizona: Arizona Center for Medieval and Renaissance Studies in conjunction with Renaissance English Text Society

References

Anne Lock Prowse

Collinson, Patrick (1965), 'The Role of Women in the English Reformation Illustrated by the Life and Friendships of Anne Locke', *Studies in Church History* 2: 258–72; reprinted in *Godly People: Essays on English Protestantism and Puritanism*, London: The Hambledon Press, 1983: 273–87

Felch, Susan (1999), 'Introduction' in *The Collected Works of Anne Vaughan Lock*, Tempe, Arizona: Arizona Center for Medieval and Renaissance Studies in conjunction with Renaissance English Text Society

Hannay, Margaret (1992), '"Strengthning the walles of … Ierusalem": Anne Vaughan Lok's Dedication to the Countess of Warwick', *ANQ* 5: 71–75

— (1993), '"Unlock my lipps": the *Miserere mei Deus* of Anne Vaughan Lok and Mary Sidney Herbert, Countess of Pembroke' in Brink, Jean R. (ed.), *Privileging Gender in Early Modern England, Sixteenth Century Essays and Studies* 23: 19–36

Huttar, Charles A. (1998), 'Translating French Proverbs and Idioms: Anne Locke's Renderings from Calvin', *Modern Philology* 96: 158–83

Richardson, W. C. (1953), *Stephen Vaughan: Financial Agent of Henry VIII*, Baton Rouge: Louisiana State University Press

Roche, Thomas P. (1989), *Petrarch and the English Sonnet Sequences*, New York: AMS Press

Schleiner, Louise (1994), *Tudor & Stuart Women Writers*, Bloomington and Indianapolis: Indiana University Press

Spiller, Michael R. G. (1997), 'A literary "first": the sonnet sequence of Anne Locke (1560)', *Renaissance Studies* 11: 41–55

White, Micheline (1998), Cunning in Controversies: Protestant Women and Religious and Literary Debates 1580–1615, Dissertation, Loyola University of Chicago

White, Micheline (1999), 'Renaissance Englishwoman and Religious Translations: The Case of Anne Lock's *Of the markes of the children of God*', *English Literary Renaissance* 29: 375–400

Woods, Susanne (1992), 'The Body Penitent: A 1560 Calvinist Sonnet Sequence', *ANQ* 5: 137–40

Elizabeth Russell

STC 21456

Ballard, George (1752), Ruth Perry (ed.), 1985, *Memoirs of Several Ladies of Great Britain*, Detroit: Wayne State University Press

Farber, Elizabeth (1977), *The Letters of Lady Elizabeth Russell 1540–1609*, Dissertation, Columbia University

Lamb, Mary Ellen (1985), 'The Cooke Sisters: Attitudes toward Learned Women in the Renaissance', in Hannay, Margaret (ed.), *Silent But for the Word: Tudor Women as Patrons, Translators, and Writers of Religious Works*, Kent, Ohio: The Kent State University Press

McIntosh, Marjorie Keniston (1975), 'Sir Anthony Cooke: Tudor Humanist, Educator, and Religious Reformer', *Proceedings of the American Philosophical Society*, 119: 233–250

Reges, Reginae, Nobiles, et Alii in Ecclesia Collegiata B. Petri Westmonasterii sepulti ... (1606), London. *STC* 4518

Schleiner, Louise (1994), *Tudor & Stuart Women Writers*, Bloomington and Indianapolis: Indiana University Press

Wilson, Violet (1924), *Society Women of Shakespeare's Time*, London: John Lane. Reprint 1970, Port Washington, NY, London: Kennikat Press

ELAINE V. BEILIN

Sermons of John Calvin, upon the songe that Ezechias made after he had bene sicke, and afflicted by the hand of God, conteyned in the 38. Chapiter of Esay; A meditation of a penitent sinner (*STC* 4450) is reproduced here, by agreement, from the copy at the Folger Shakespeare Library. The size of the text-block is 105 × 61 mm.

SERMONS OF JOHN CALVIN, VPON THE SONGE that Ezechias made after he had bene sicke, and afflicted by the hand of God,

conteyned in the 38. Chapiter of Esay.

¶ Translated out of Frenche into Englishe.

1560.

☞ Newly set fourth and allowed, accordyng to the order appointed in the Quenes Maiesties Iniunctions.

¶ Imprinted at London, ouer Aldersgate, by John Day.
And are there to be solde at his shoppe vnder the Gate.

¶ Cum Gratia & priuilegio Regiæ maiestatis.

TO THE RIGHT HONORABLE, AND Christian Princesse, the Lady Katharine, Duchesse of Suffolke.

T often falleth out in experience (my gracious & singular good Lady) that some men beynge oppressed with pouertie, tossed with worldlye aduersitye, tourmented with payne, sorenes, & sicknes of body, and other suche cōmon matters of griefe, as the world counteth miseries & euils: Yet hauing theyr myndes armed & fournished with prepared patience, and defence of inward vnderstandyng, all these calamities can not so farre preuaile, as to make them fall, nor yet once stoupe into the state of men to be accompted miserable: but they beare them with suche constaunce, as if suche afflictions were not of such nature as other commonly do fele them, or as if those men were suche vpon whome those troubles coulde not worke theyr naturall propertie. On th'other side we se some that flowyng in earthly wealth & suffisance, free from *fortunes crueltie, healthy in bodye, and euery waye to the worldes seming blessed: yet with mynde not well instructed, or with conscience not well quieted, euen vpon such small chaunces as other can lightly beare, are vexed aboue measure with reasonlesse extremitie. Wherby appeareth that the greues of body and calamities of fortune do so farre onely extende, to afflict, or make a man miserable, as they approch to touch the mind, & assaile the soule. Which proueth that the peines and diseases of minde & soule are not only the most greuous, & most daungerous, but also they onely are peinfull & perillous, and those of the body & fortune are such as the mynde vseth, and maketh them. So as to a sicke stomacke of mynde, all bodylie matters of delite and worldely pleasures are lothesome and displeasant, as on th'other side the power of a healthy soule easely digesteth and gathereth good nouriture of the hard peines, and bitter tormentes of the body and fortune. He then, that cureth the sicke minde, or preserueth it from disease, cureth or preserueth not onely minde, but bodye also: and deserueth so much more praise and thanke, than the bodies Physiciõ, as the soule excelleth the bodie,*

and

and as the curing, or preseruation of them both is to be preferred before the cure of the bodye alone. But we se dayly, when skilfull men by arte, or honest neyghbours hauyng gathered vnderstandyng of some specyall dysease & the healing therof by theyr owne experiment, do applie their knowledge to the restoring of health of any mans body in any corporall sicknesse, howe thankfully it is taken, howe muche the releued patient accompteth him selfe boūd to him by meane of whose aide and ministration he findeth him self holpen or eased. What then deserueth he, that teacheth such a receipt, wherby health both of body and mynde is preserued, & wherby if health be appaired, it may be restored, yea whereby sicknes and common miseries continuyng shall not haue so muche power to trouble a man as to make him sicke, or miserable? This receipte God the heauenly Physitian hath taught, his most excellēt Apothecarie master Iohn Caluine hath compounded, & I your graces most bounden & humble haue put into an Englishe box, & do present vnto you. My thākes are takē away & drowned by the greate excesse of ductie that I owe you: Master Caluine thinketh his paynes re-

compensed if your grace or any Christian take profit of it: bicause how much soeuer is spent, his store is neuerthelesse. And for God, recompensed he can not be: but how he is continually to be thanked, your graces profession of his worde, your abidyng in the same, the godly conuersation that I haue sene in you, do proue that your selfe do better vnderstand & practise than I can admonishe you.

And that you maye be assured, that this kinde of medicine is not hurtfull: two moste excellent kinges, Ezechias and Dauid, beside an infinite numbre haue tasted the lyke before you, and haue founde health therin, such healthe as hathe cured them for euer, and not as common or naturall reasons of Philosophie doe cure a sicke or soore mynde, which with easie and weake not well drawynge or cleansinge plasters, so ouerheale the wounde that it festreth and breaketh oute afreshe wyth renewed and doublye encreased danger.

Suche remedye as here is conteined can no Philosopher, no Infidele, no Papist minister. For what perfite helpe can they geue to a dyseased mynde, that vnderstande not, or be-

leue

leue not the onely thyng that muste of nedefull necessitie be put into all medicines that maye serue for a tourmented soule, that is to say, the determined prouidence of almyghtie God, whiche ordreth and disposeth all thynges to the best to them that truste in him?

This Physicke resteth onely amonge trewe beleuyng Christians, who are perswaded that whatsoeuer betideth vnto vs, his hie wisdom that sent it, and that seeth all thynges, sent it of hys good pleasure and decreed purpose, and that for oure benefite if we loue and beleue hym, thoughe oure weake vnderstandynge knoweth not howe it shoulde be profitable, but naturally iudgeth it hurtefull and vnpleasaunt. And necessarye it was that he whiche by vnderstandynge of Godes hatred of synne and felynge of hys iustice, is subiect to fall into the moste perillous peine and tourment of conflicte with sinne and desperation, shoulde by conceyuynge of Godes mercy, and beleuyng of his prouidence, haue helpe of the moste and onely perfect and effectuallye working medicine.

But in heauye case is he, that beynge

afflicted with that daungerous disease of the felyng of Gods wrath kindled against him, hath not the cõserue of belefe of Gods prouidẽce remainyng with him, or beyng ministred to him either for feblenesse of stomack can not receiue and brooke it, or his oppressed appetite beyng ouerwhelmed with grosse faithlesse and papisticall humors can not abide the tast of it. Wo is (I say) to them: for theyr disease is daungerous and hard to be cured. For when the wretched man findyng all helpe of man not able to vphold him from perishing, being striken with the mightie hande of God, feleth him selfe vnable to stande, no soundnes in his bodye, no strẽgth in his limmes, no helpe of nature to resist the violence of that disease that Gods displeasure hath laide vpon him, seeth no signe of Gods grace in his soule, but the depe woundes that Gods anger hath left in his cõscience, perceiueth no token to argue him th'elect of God and partaker of the death of his Sauiour, hearyng pronounced that the soule which sinneth shall die, knowyng him selfe to haue sinned, & felyng him selfe dying: alas what helpe remaineth in this extremitie? If we thinke the helpe of papistes, to begge and borrowe others Virgins

gins

gins oyle that haue none to spare, to bye the superfluous workes of those men that say they haue done more than suffiseth to satisfie Gods lawe and to deserue theyr owne saluation, to appease God with suche extraordinarie deuised seruice as he neuer commaunded, and such like vnholsome stuffe as papisticall soulesleaers haue ministred to Christian patientes: If (I say) we thinke these good & sufficient medicines: alas, we do nothinge therby, but plant vntrew securitie, promise health, & performe death: the pāges wherof whē the deceiued sick man feleth, he to late espieth the falshod of the murtherous Physiciā. The pore damned soule in Hell tourmented with the lamentable peines that turmoile him, from whome God the onely author of ioy and comfort is absent, perceiueth to late howe wandring the wrong way from heauen, he is fallen into Hell. That selly wretche flamyng in the infernall fire feleth, alas, to late that thei which gaue him mans medicines to drincke, haue slayne his soule: they which taught him to trust of saluation by mā̄s deuises haue set his burnyng hert in that place of flames, where th'euerlasting Chaos suffreth no droppe of Godes mercye to descende: they

which

which taught him to seeke health any other where thā in the determined purpose of God, that hath sent his own sonne for our redēptiō, haue spoiled him of all benefit of redemption. He feleth at length all to late howe by faulte of ill diet and throughe poisonous potions which his iguoraunt corrupted and traiterous Physicion suffered him to vse, and bad him to take, he lieth dead eternally.

But on th'other side, when the beleuynge Christian falleth (as God hathe made none to stande wherby they should not nede his mercye to raise them when they are fallen) he knoweth whither to reache his hande to be raised vp againe: beyng stong with the stinge of the scorpion he knoweth howe with oyle of the same scorpion to be healed agayne: beyng wounded with the iustice of God that hateth sinne, he knoweth howe with the mercy of the same God that pardoneth sinne to haue hys peine asswaged and hurt amended. He knoweth that whome God hath from eternitie appointed to liue, shal neuer die, howsoeuer sicknesse threaten: no misery, no tentation, no perill shall auaile to his euerlasting ouerthrowe. He knoweth that his safetie is much more surely

rely reposed in Gods moste stedfast and vnchangeable purpose, and in the most strong & almightye hande of the alknowynge and alworking God, than in the wauering will and feble weaknes of man. This healeth the Christians sicknes, this preserueth him from death, this maketh him to liue for euer. This medicine is in this litle boke brought frō the plentifull shop & storehouse of Gods holye testamēt, where Gods euerabiding purpose frō beyond beginning is setfourth, to the euerlasting saluatiō of some, & eternall cōfusion of other. Beside that, this boke hath not only the medicine, but also an example of the nature of the disease, & the meane how to vse & apply the medicine to thē that be so diseased. For when a man languishing in corporall sicknes, heareth his neighboure reporte vnto him, or himselfe hathe before time sene in an other the same cause of sicknes, the same maner of fits, passiōs, alteratiōs, & in euery point the same qualities of sicknes, & the same dispositiō of body that he knoweth & feleth in him self: it geueth him assurāce, & maketh him to know that he is sick of the same disease that th'other was: wherby knowing howe th'other was healed, what diet *he kept, what Physicke he toke, he doeth with the greater boldnes, confidence of mynde, and desire, call for, taste, and gredely receyue that healthfull & lifefull medicine wherby he saw and knew his neighbour healed, and with the greater care kepeth the same diet wherewith he saw & knew th'other preserued. So here this good soules Physiciā hath brought you where you maye se lyinge before youre face the good king Ezechias, somtime chillinge and chattering with colde, somtime languishing & meltyng away with heate, nowe fresing, now fryeng, nowe specheleße, nowe crying out, with other suche piteous panges & paßions wrought in his tender afflicted spirit, by giltie consciēce of his owne fault, by terrible consideration of Gods iustice, by cruell assaultes of the tyrannous enemie of mans saluation, vexynge hym in muche more lamentable wise than any bodely feuer can worke, or bodyly fleshe can suffer. On th'other side for his helpe, you se him sometyme throwe vp his gastly eyen, starynge wyth horrour, and scant discernynge for peine and for want of the lyuely moisture to fede the brightnes of theyr sight. You se him sometyme yeldyngly stretch oute, sometyme struglinglye throwe his weakned legges not able to susteîn his feble body: sometime he casteth abrode, or holdeth vp his white & blodles hand toward the place whether his soule longeth: sometyme with fallyng chappes, he breatheth out vnperfect soũdes, gasping rather thã calling for mercy & helpe. These thinges being here laid open to sight and remainyng in remembraunce, (as the horrour and piteous spectacle can not suffre it to fall out of a Christian tender minde) if we feele oure selues in like anguishe, we finde that the disease is the same that Ezechias had, and so by conuenience of reason muste by the same meane be healed. Thẽ behoueth vs to remember or to be infourmed by oure diligent Physitian or charitable neighbour, howe we sawe Ezechias healed, whome we imagine in this Boke to see, both dying, reuiued, and walking after health recouered. There we se the heauẽly Physician anoynt him with the merciful Samaritãs oyle, purge the oppressing humors with true repentaũce, strengthen his stomack with the holsome conserue of Gods eternall decree, and expell his disease, and set hym on foote with assured faith of Gods mercy, and staieng his yet vnstedy pace & foltring legges*

with

with the swete promyses of Gods almyghtye goodnes. So learne we what Physicians helpe we shall vse: and this medicine beyng offered vs, we are bolde to take it, bycause we knowe it wyll heale vs. And beyng healed, knowyng and hearyng it confessed, that sinne was the cause and nourishement of Ezechias disease, we learne a newe diet, and to fede as Ezechias his Physician and oures apointeth, absteinyng from thinges hurtfull taking things healthfull as he prescribeth. So doth the Christiā atteine his health, so beynge attemed he preserueth it for euer. And as it is true that seconde & returned sicknesses by surfit or misdemenour are most cruell and daungerous, so holdeth he yet this also for trueth, that to this Physiciā with this medicine, no disease neuer so long rooted, neuer so oft retourned, is vncurable. Beyng then thus muche beholden to this Physician we must nedes confesse that we owe vnto him our life and health, & all that we be or haue. And for his faithful minister master Caluine, I beseche your grace wyth me, to wishe hym Gods benefit of eternall happie life for his rewarde, euen as I wishe your grace continuall health of life and soule for your preseruation,

no

not onely for this newe yeare, but also for the tyme that shall excede all extent of yeares, besechinge you to accepte bothe my worke and prayer.

Concernyng my translation of this boke, it may please you to vnderstand that I haue rēdred it so nere as I possibly might, to the very wordes of his text, and that in so plaine Englishe as I could expresse: Suche as it is, I beseche your grace to take it good parte.

Your graces humble

A. L.

☞ *The writinge of Ezechia kinge of Iuda, when he had bene sicke, and was recouered of his sicknes. I said in the cuttyng shorte of my daies, I shall go downe to the gates of the graue. I haue sought the residue of my yeares, I sayd I shall not see the Lorde, the Lorde in the land of the liuing. I shall not beholde man any more, nor those that dwell in the world. My life is withdrawen, and is chaunged like a shepeherdes lodge.*

As the name of God is immortall, and we oughte to trauaill that they which come after vs, do cal vpon it, and that it be honored and glorified in all times: So is it not enoughe, that during oure lyfe, we endeuor oure selues to honor God: but as I haue said before, our care should extende it selfe to the time to come, to the end we may haue in store some continuyng seede of religion, in suche sort as the trueth of God may neuer be abolished. But speacilly they whom God hath ordeined in anye estate to guide other, ought therfore so much the more to applie them selues vnto it. As also we se that S. Peter declaryng his ende to be nere, and that he should depart out of this worlde: addeth 2.Pet.5.

that somuch as he possibly may, he woulde make the doctrine whiche he preached, to remayne alwayes in force and memory, that mē might take profit after his death. Behold now wherfore Ezechias was not cōtented to make this protestation whiche we reade here, with his mouth, but wold also wryte it, that to the ende of the worlde men might knowe how he had ben vexed in hys affliction, and that the same myght serue for doctrine to all the worlde: so as at this day we may take profyt thereof.

He sayth expressely that this wrytinge was made after he was recouered. For oftentimes when we ar touched eyther with sicknes or anye other rod of God, we make protestations enow, but we do nothing els but shake our eares (as the prouerbe is) when we ar escaped, & we by and by forget al those thinges which we made a shew as if we knewe. But here it is shewed vs that the kinge Ezechias beinge recouered, forgat not the correction whiche he had receiued at the hand of god, nether the anguishes which he felt, but minded to make a memoriall of the whole, that those which come after might be enstructed therby.

But it appereth at the first shew that this writing serueth not for any instruction of them that shold rede it, but shold rather be an offēse. For we see the outragious passions of a man as it were rauished in minde which so abhorreth death, that he thought all to be lost when god shold take him out of the worlde, and in this we see nothing but the sinne of infidelitie. He tormenteth and rageth with him self (as it semeth) with a rebelling, vncomcomely for a seruāt of god: to be short it appeareth that we can gather nothing of this song, but ỳ al the faithe whiche Ezechias had was only in hys prosperitie and quiet, & also that he gaue the bridle to much vnto him selfe in his heauinesse, in so muche that he complayned of god, as we see that he compared him to a Lyon. But whē all shal be wel cōsidered, we shal see that there is no instruction better or more profitable for vs than this. For when we shal haue well examined al that is in vs, then we shall knowe that the same is also propre vnto our selues.

But first let vs note how the good king Ezechias did not here set fourthe his owne vertues to be praised of the world, for he might haue kept in silēce that which he hath declared of his owne waywardnesse, & in place therof he mought haue spoken of hys request made to God, and the constance of his faythe: So then he sayth not that he was of valiant courage, that he ouercame al tentations without any stoppe or strife, he sayth not that he had a faith so stedfaste that it nothing troubled him to be corrected of ỳ hand of god: nothing of al thys. what then? we see a poore man tormēted euen to the extremitye, and so striken downe, that he wiste not what myghte become of hym. We se a mā astonished with feare of the wrath of God, lokyng on nothyng but his own affliction. Then seyng Ezechias doeth discouer him selfe, and sticketh not to confesse his owne faultes, in this we perceiue that he was not led of ambitiō, nether of any vaine glory to be praised of mē, or to get reputatiō, but he rather was willing him self to be cōfoūded & shame, ỳ god might be glorified.

What is then his purpose? It is in one parte to make vs know howe he had bene afflicted then, when he thought that God was against him: and moreouer that therin men might know somuche the more howe great the goodnes of God was, when he receiued him to mercy, and woulde not forsake him in necessitie.

We haue then to beholde here, as in a loking glasse, our owne wekenes, to the ende that euery man may prepare himselfe against the time when his faith shalbe proued as the fayth of Ezechias was, and when God shall shew vs some tokens of his wrath, so as if then we seme in maner destroyed, yet we cease not therfore to truste that God will geue to vs an end of our troubles, as he did to this good king. Next to this, that we may learne to geue al praise of our safetie to the mercy of God, knowledging that so sone as he forsaketh vs, we are vtterly vndone, and that then we become more then miserable.

And nowe we see howe, and wherfore the good king Ezechias was thus tourmented, that is, because he sawe death so nere at hande. It semeth at the first face, that suche passion besemeth not a faithful mā. Trew it is that of nature death is dreadfull to vs al. For there is no man but (as they saye) desireth to be, and in death we thinke that we perishe, ẏ we be broughte to nought, and cease to be. Thus of nature we flie frō & abhorre death, and therfore also S. Paule saith in the v.

2. Cor. 5 chapter of the seconde epistle to the Corinthians, that we do not desire to be vnclothed of this body for it is impossible for man to desire to change his estate

estate. I meane as concernynge thys lyfe. And those that do kyll them selues haue no natural affection, but the Deuil so carrieth them away that they are altogether blinded. And suche are to be reckened as vnnaturall monsters, in whom al the order of nature is changed. To be short it is most assured that death shalbe alwaye to vs terrible, and not onely because we are enclined to desire to to lyue, but also for so muche as God hath lefte a certeine marke, in suche sorte that the Heathen thẽ selues & the vnfaithfull are constrained to fele that death is a curse of God, which was prõũced vpon Adam, and al his linage. For asmuch then, as death is come vpon the world by sinne, & that it is a witnes of the wrath of God, that by it we are as it were cast of from him, banished from his kingdome (which is the kingdome of life) it must nedes be, although we haue no light of faith neyther euer had any one word of doctrine, that this be imprinted in our mindes, that it is naturallye vnpleasant vnto vs. Behold then by what meanes we are brought to flie death, & to withdrawe our selues from it so muche as we possibly maye. Fyrst bicause we are desirous to be: secondly for that we conceyue death to be a certeine signe of Gods wrath: yea althoughe we harde therof no certaine instruction, yet God hath printed a certaine naturall instinction and feling therof within oure hertes. Yet notwithstandynge it is also trew that the faithfull do ouercome those feares, and do prepare them selues to die when it pleaseth God, but not (as the place speaketh whiche we haue alledged out of S. Paule) in suche sort that thei simply & without other cōsideratiō desire to die, for ẏ wer ẏ doing of mē in desperatiō, but thei prepare thē selues, forasmuch as thei know, ẏ after they haue bene vnclothed they shalbe clothed againe, ẏ this body which is but a ruinous lodgyng, is nothing but rottēnes, & ẏ they shalbe restored to ẏ kingdō of god. For asmuch as thē we behold this hope ẏ is geuē vs, thus we ouercome the feares of deth. Besid this on ẏ other side, we know ẏ our lord Jesus Christ hath repared this desolatiō & ruine ẏ fel vpō vs by ẏ sinne of our father Adā. So bycause we take hold of life in the middest of deth, ẏ maketh vs ẏ we are not afraid to widraw our selues hēce whē god calleth vs to him, for we know ẏ death is but a passage to life. moreouer we know what is our true being: It is not to dwel in this world, for this is but a thorow fare, & we must alwai haue in remēbrāce, ẏ which is spokē ẏ god placeth men here onely to manage thē, & to make thē to fetch their cōpasses (as thei say) & sodenly to turne againe. Thē whē we are taught ẏ our life is nothing els but a course, & the the world is but a shadow, which passeth & vanisheth awai: we know ẏ our true beyng, & our permanēt estate is in heuē, & not here by low. Thus se we how we ought not to flie deth: but (ẏ more is) we haue occasiō to desire it, bicause on the one side we ar fraile, & being holden vnder the bondage of sin, we se so mani corruptiōs in our selues ẏ it is wofull, & when we desire to serue God we draw vp our legs, & whē we lift vp one fote thinking to set forward one step, we slip backward, & oft it cōmeth to passe ẏ we stūble or fall. Se now how iust a cause we haue to lamēt our life, not in wey of despeir, but bicause we ought to hate & ab

horre sin, We ought also todesire god to drawe vs
out of this so miserable captiuitie wherin we ar,
as s. Paul sheweth vs exãple. He cõfesseth him Rom.7.
self to be vnhappy, bicause he dwelleth in his bodi
as a prison. He asketh howe he shalbe deliuered.
On the other side, we know ỹ we ought to desire 2.Cor.5.
death ỹ more ỹ we might come nere to our God.
For (as it is saide in this place ỹ we haue alled=
ged) while we liue by faith we are as it were ab=
sent frõ God. Thẽ, where is our felicitie & per=
fect ioye? but in this ỹ we cleaue to oure God in
perfectiõ. For asmuch thẽ, as by death we come
nere to him, it is a thing to vs happy, and whiche
ought to make vs ioyfull. And therfore he saieth
in the first chap. to the Philip. that as touchinge Philip.1.
him self, it should be more auãtage to him to die
then to liue, & although his life was profitable to
the church, yet in hauing no other regard, but to
his own person, he was desirous to be drawẽ a=
way frõ this place by low: mark thẽ what ought
to be ỹ affectiõ of ỹ faithful. Now let vs come to
king Ezechias. It semeth ỹ he had lost al maner
tast of ỹ goodnes of God, ỹ he knew nothing of ỹ
resurrectiõ, ỹ he was ignorãt ỹ he shold be resto=
red by meane of ỹ redemer, he conceiued nothing
but the wrath & curse of God: wher is his faith?
where is his obeidiẽce? wher is this cõsolatiõ of
the holy Gost, & this ioy inestimable, whiche we
ought to receiue whẽ God certifieth vs of ỹ loue
which he beareth vs? In dede if he had had this
perswasiõ deply roted in hĩ, ỹ he was one of ỹ chil
drẽ of god: doth not ỹ adoptiõ brĩg ỹ iheritãce? to
what end hath god chosẽ vs for his childrẽ, but ỹ
we shold be partakers of ỹ heuẽly life wherunto
he guideth vs? but we se none of al this in Ezec.

It semeth thē that he was altogether distraught from sense and reason, that he hath forgottē God: that all the good doctrine that euer he heard before is vtterly blotted oute, and that he thinketh no more of it. These thinges at the firste shew, seme very straunge. Trew it is that at that time he had no suche reuelation of the heauenly life, as we haue at this day by the gospel. But yet Ezechias and all the other holy kinges and Prophetes, and all the rest of the faithfull dyd well conceiue that God had not chosen them in vaine. For
Math.22 though this sētēce of our lord Iesus Christ was not pronoūced, yet was it engraued in the herts of all the faithfull that God is not the God of the dead. All they then that are cōprised in the number of his people haue bene assured to haue an abidyng life, and that shall endure for euer. And on the other side it is said that God calleth him selfe the God of Abraham, of Isaac and of Iacob long after their death. It must nedes be thē that they then lyued. So therefore the faithfull haue this assurāce that God did not nourishe them in this world as brute beastes, but he gaue them a certeine taste of hys goodnes, vntyll suche time as they myght haue full enioyinge thereof after
Num.23 their death. Euen Balaam himselfe whiche neuer knew any thing of the lawe, yet he failed not to say: I wishe my soule to dye the death of the righteous, and my end to be such as theirs shalbe. He desireth to ioyne him selfe with the race of Abraham, and yet he was a wicked & refused man And who maketh him to speake thus? euē this, that he is there as vpon the racke, & God wringeth

geth out of him this confession. Now if Balaam which was possessed of the Deuill, and gaue oute his tonge to hyre, to curse the people of God, hath bene constreined to say thus, what shall we think of them that had trewlye profyted in the lawe of God? But howsoeuer it be, trew it is that thold fathers had not so cleare and manifest knowlerge of the heauenlye life as we haue at this daye in the Gospell, and in dede the same was reserued vntill the coimming of our Lorde Iesus Christ. And with good reason: for we haue a good gage of our life in our sauiour Iesus Christ, in that he is risen againe, and that it was not for him selfe alone but for all his body. This is the full assuraunce that God hath geuen in the parson of our Lorde Iesus Christ, that we passe through this world to come to the life that lasteth euer. The auncient fathers came not to suche degree, they were not so auauinsed. But howesoeuer it were it is so that the tast which they had of the heauēlye life so suffised them, that they rendred them selues peaseably to God. And we reade not that they were greatly tourmented in theyr death, as whan Abraham departed, he made not lamentations, wayling and complaintes, as the King Ezechias did: but he was fylled and satisfyed wyth lyfe, saieth the scripture. In like maner was it of Isaac and Iacob, who rendring the lastē groane saith: I wyll put my truste in thy saluation, my God. Thoughe Iesus Christ had not yet appered vnto the world, yet Iacob had in him selfe a stedfast and vndoubted hope, and made him selfe as sure of his saluation, as if he held it in his hād.

Gene. 25. 35. 49.

So then we see that the holy fathers were not in doubt or suche mistrust, that they did not alwayes aspire vnto the heauēly life, but that it was their chiefe desire to atteine thereunto.

Now let vs retourne to the king Ezechias. We must conclude that he had some speciall reason in him selfe, why he so complayned of death, which we shall better see in the person of Dauid.
Psalm.6. Dauid is sometimes in suche anguyshes that he
Psalm.30. crieth, alas my God, who is he that shal acknowledge thee in death? And when I shalbe a poore rotten carion, what profite shalt thou haue? whē thou shalt haue brought me into ashes, what is it
1.Reg.2 that thou shalt haue gained? He made there hys
1.Par.29. cōplaints, neuertheles in the end he dyed peaseably. For no man saw that he was so passioned in his departyng, but that he rendred him self mildly into the handes of God. Howe came it then to passe that he wrote thus? It is bicause he cōceiued the wrath of God, whether it were in sickenes, or in any other affliction, and that is asmuch as if the very hels were presently set before him. The affliction then that he conceyued, was not of symple death, but ẏ God gaue him some signe that he punished him bicause of his sinnes. Now seyng ẏ we se this same disputatiō in the parson of Dauid, it shalbe easy for vs to cōclud touching the king Ezechias ẏ he was also greuously vexed in his death, but that was not for that he was loth to depart out of this worlde, neither that he was tourmented as the poore Infidels whiche aspire not to a better life, which are also as it wer drowned in theyr delites, and bringe them selues an slepe in such sort that they set nothynge by the hea-

heauenly life. We see that Ezechias was not so striken downe, and yet he thought that God was against him, as we shall se yet more largely. And in dede it was not without cause that the Prophet Esay was sente vnto him, for he was as a Heralde of armes, to make him defiaunce, and to declare vnto him: Beholde God is thine enemy: thou muste susteine his extreme rigour, for thou haste offended him. When Ezechias heard that, he had no regard to ẏ simple death, by the which he muste of necessitie passe, but he hathe an other ende of consideration, ẏ he should be cut of from the worlde as an accursed creature, as one vnworthy, whō the earth should beare. And when God stroke him, that gaue a tokē to him that the land should be made desolate, for he knewe what should be the estate of the people: he sawe that all should be destroyed after his death, yf God dyd not remedi it by miracles. And he thought thus: My death shall not be onely to sende me into the throte of hell, but it shall be to bringe a generall ouerflowyng ouer all, so that in all the land there shalbe nothing but desolation. Shall the seruice of God then be throwen dowen, and shall al this be cast vpon my neck bicause I haue offended my God? Alas, and what shall this be? Let vs not nowe thinke it straunge if Ezechias speake thus as we heare, but let vs hold this alway that it is not the simple death whiche dyd affraye him so. What then? the wrath of God, when he behelde his sinnes, and that God toke away from him all fauor of his goodnes, & turned his back vnto him as if he had sene him armed against him, & lifted vp his arme, as if he would bring him to nought.

When

When Ezechias sawe that, he was so confouded that his mouth was stopped, & not without cause.

Nowe this is right worthy to be noted, for there are many blockish persons (and the mooste part) which feare death, but it is not because they fele the curse of God appeare to them. It is true as we haue saide before, that God leaueth alway this point in the conscience of man, but they haue not all alike consideration therof. Wherfore is it then that death is dreadfull vnto them? bycause euery one will say, I desire to be. Truely when they speake in this maner it is as much as if they said I would be a calfe, or an asse, or a dogge, for the beyng of brute beastes is in this world, & the beynge of men where is it, but in this that they are ioyned to theyr God? But now we are as it were in prison, for in steade that this world shold haue bene vnto vs as an earthlye paradise (if we had continued in the obeidience of God) now we are as in a straunge countrey, wherein we be as lockt vp and banished. It is trew that yet we se many times some, yea many trackes of the goodnes of God, but how so euer it be, yet we do but languish here. But there are but few that know this. So much ye more the ought we to note wel this doctrine, which I haue here before touched; that is to wit, that both in death, and in all other afflictions we are more accombred and troubled with the wrath of God than with the euyll that we can fele. If one be afflicted with pouertie, so that he hath hunger and thirst, an other be stricken with sicknes and suffer great tourmentes, another be persecuted of men so as he hathe no time of rest, and more if in the end death come before oure eyes, we oughte to knowe that there is nothing so muche to be feared as the wrathe and vengeaunce of God. But men do cleane contrary. And this marke, why I haue sayde that we must note this doctrine the better: because a man may se that the pore sicke persones, and they that are afflicted, in what sort soeuer it be, wyll crye Alas, one wyll cry the armes, another wyll crye the legges, the one here, the other there: but yet they come neuer to the grounde of the euill. And that procedeth of the leprosie that is in vs. For we are so dull witted that we can not atteine to know the iudgemēt of God. So much the more ought we to lerne whē we shalbe beatē with such roddes as I haue sayd to make vs loke vpon the cause whence this euill procedeth: which is, that God will haue vs to fele our sinnes, and that he sommoneth vs to the ende that we shoulde there come as it were before oure iudge, and that we should not come there with sleyghtes and meanes of excuse, but with franke and free confession, and that the same be not only made wyth mouth, or assent by writyng, but that we be woūded euē to the bottome of the herte, felynge what it is to haue done agaynst the will of oure God, to haue styrred him vp against vs, & to haue made warre against his iustice. This is it that we haue to holde in minde when we see that the kyng Ezechias was in such extremitie of anguish, bycause God dyd punishe him for his sinnes.

Yea and this we ought to marke well, that

though

though before he haue protested that he had walked in puritie and vprightnesse of lyfe, and that he had studied all hys lyfe long to obey and please God, neuerthelesse he resteth not his mind vpon his vertues, nor hys owne merites, he entreth not into plea wyth God, for he seeth well that all that coulde nothynge profite him nor brynge hym any relefe. Therfore he setteth not fourthe what his lyfe hathe ben, but he knowlegeth that rightfullye he is afflicted.

So then we learne, when it shall please God to correcte with his roddes, not to grudge at it, as if he did vs wronge, as if he had no regarde to oure merites, or as yf he vsed greater sharpnes wyth vs than we had deserued. Let al such blasphemies be beaten down, and let vs confesse that he hath iust cause to punishe vs, yea not only to expulse vs out of the worlde, but also to throwe vs downe into the gulfe of hell. See then howe we deserue to bee ordred yf wee looke vpon all our owne lyfe.

Moreouer let vs not thynke it straunge that god sendeth vs afflictions whiche seme greuous and sharpe vnto vs, seing wee see that Ezechias hathe walked before vs to shewe vs the waye. Men when they haue had any good affectiõ and desyre to serue god, do muche maruell yf god punishe them more then the wicked, and they suppose that they haue lost theyr labour. This tentacion is to cõmõ, as we see, that euẽ Dauid was also tormented with it when he saith: what meaneth this? for I see the despisers of God prosper and be in iolitie, and make theyr triumphes, and in the meane time I do nothinge but sup vp the

drynke

drynke of sorrow, frō the euening to the morrowe I haue no reste. It semeth then that it is tyme lost to serue God: Behold how at the extremitie he is beatē downe, yf God by his wonderfull vertue had not upholden him. And because the lyke maye come unto us, let us make us a buckler of the example that is here set before us of the kinge Ezechias: for wee haue seen here before howe he had framed all hys lyfe to the law of God: he had a zele which is not to be founde in manye people, to purge al hys land of all superstitions and ydolatries: many alarumes were stirred up agaynst hym, to make him somwhat to reuolte: but that nothyng stayed hym but that he set up the trewe and pure religyon, & in his priuate lyfe he sought nothing but that god might be glorifyed in, and through all: and yet loke how God cōmeth to assayle him: yea, and that of a straunge fashion, for he is as a lyon that breaketh his bones: So whē we see that Ezechias, is thus handled, ought not we to learne to beare pacientlye the corrections that God shall sende us. Loe this is it that wee haue to conceiue of this place.

Now to the rest of the passions that Ezechias endureth, and although he slipt here of the henges yet stil in the middest therof he declareth the loue that he had to God, and that he desyred not thys present life after the maner of them that are therein become brutish, and whiche seke for nothynge but to eate and drynke, and know not for what ende they are created, but onlye to pastime here for a whyle. But Ezechias sheweth well that hee was guyded by an other spirite. He sayeth:

I haue

I haue sayd in the cutting short of my dayes. I shall go down to the gates of the graue, I shall not se anye more the Lorde: euen the Lorde. He speaketh here of his lyfe, that it shalbe cut of in the middes of his course: But yet he sheweth that he desireth not here to liue to be at his ease. He was a kinge, and might haue fared well, he moughte haue had greate store of delicates, and pleasures in this world, shortly he myghte haue made him selfe dronk with al sortes of thinges of delite. He mourneth not for want of all these: but he saieth, that he shall no more see the Lorde, and he is not contented to haue pronounced this word once, but he repeteth it againe to expresse a greater vehemencie: The Lord, euen the Lord, saith he: By this he sheweth that he desireth not so much his life, as to exercise him selfe here beneth to knowe that God was his father, and to confirme him selfe more and more in that faith.

Let vs then marke well wherunto oure lyfe is to be directed, that is, that we should perceiue that God alreadye in part sheweth him selfe a father toward vs. I graunt it trewe (as I haue alreadye said) that we ar absent from him, for our saluation lieth in faithe and hope, it is hydden and we see it not with naturall sense. Yet in the meane while God faileth not to sēd down certein beames hither by lowe to lighten vs so, as we be guided to the hope of the life euerlasting and perceiue that God is not so farre estraunged frō vs, but that yet he stretcheth fourth his hand hether by lowe to haue care of vs, and to shewe vs by experience

experience that he hath vs in his safekeping. For when the sunne riseth in the mornynge, se we not what a fatherly care God hath for vs? After whē it goeth downe at euenyng, see we not that God hath an eye to our weekenes, that we maye haue rest, and be somewhat releued? Doth not God then in so hydyng the sunne in the nyghte tyme, shew him selfe our father? Further, when we se the earth bring forth her frutes for our nourishement: when we se the raynes and all the chaunges, and alterations that are in nature: in all this perceiue we not that God hath his hād stretched out to draw vs alway vnto him, and howe he already sheweth him self a liberall father vnto vs, and that we enioy the temporall benefites which he doth for vs, to the ende that by this meane we may be drawen vp hyer, that is to say, to knowe that he hath adopted and made vs his chyldren, that we may come to the fulnes of ioye and of all felicitie, when we shalbe fully ioyned with hym? Beholde nowe wherunto we ought to applie all our life, if we wyll not that the same be accursed, and that as many yeares, monthes, dayes, houres, and minutes as we haue lyued here by low, all the same be put together in accompte, for euer to encrese, and enflame the vengeance of God vpon vs. And therfore let vs know that we ought here to study vpon the workes of God. For euen therfore also are we set in this worlde, and therefore in the v. chapter, when the Prophete mynded to rebuke the Iewes of a certeine vile brutishnes. They haue not (saieth he) beholden the workes of God. He speaketh of theyr dronkennesse, of theyr gluttony, and of theyr dissolute li- *Esay. 5.*

nes, but the lump that maketh vp the heape of euell is this, that they haue not beholden the workes of God. So nowe the good kyng Ezechias sheweth vs, that it were better for vs all to haue died before we had bene borne, and that the earth should haue gaped whan we came out of our mothers wombe, to swallow vs, thā to liue here bylowe, if it were not for thys, that we do here alreadie see oure God: not that we haue a perfecte sighte. But first he sheweth himselfe vnto vs by his worde, which is the trew lokyng glasse. And next, we haue aboue and beneath so manye signes of his presence, and of the fatherly care whiche he hath for vs, that if we be not to much dulwitted, and altogether vnfornisshed of vnderstandynge and reason, we must nedes see hym. For all the world is as a liuely image, wherein God setteth fourth vnto vs his vertue and highnes.

Moreouer, this that we are gouerned vnder his hand, is a more familiar witnes of his iustice, of his grace and of his mercy. Let vs then learne to lyue to this ende, to practise our selues to worship God as him that hath created and fashioned vs. Next, that we beare to him honor and reuerence as to our father, and that in the tastinge of good things (which he nowe dealeth among vs) we maye be confyrmed in the fayth of the heauenly lyfe. And further, for asmuch as he vouchsafeth to extende his prouidence euen hyther bylow, for this entent to gouerne vs in this transitory and fraile life, that we doubt not, when we shal come vnto him, that then we shal beholde face to face that, whiche we nowe see darkely and in

a small

a small portion.

And so the kynge Ezechias remitteth all to God, as if he shold say: Alas it is true that I am here, as to beholde clearly the graces of God. But nowe I see that all this is as it were plucked from me: For it semeth that God is mynded to spoile me of all that he hath geuen me before: and now there resteth no more for me but to despayre, for as muche as he hathe geuen ouer and forsaken me. He hath sent his prophete with this message, that I am vndone. Alas, and when I perceiue no more signe of the goodnes of my god, neyther that he extendeth this strength to comfort me in my afflictions: no not when I am in the anguishes of death: Lo is not this a wofull thing that our Lorde hath forsaken me there, and that I am cut of from him? Nowe of this we haue to gather, that be it in life, be it in death, this grace onely shoulde alwaye suffice vs: that is to say, that God geueth vs the felynge of his goodnes. And whē he sheweth vs that he is fauourable vnto vs, let vs go on boldely, and if we lāguish in this life, let vs leaue it patiently. Trewe it is that we may well grone & sigh that we are captiues, in this prison of sin: & besid ẏ we may also bewaile seing these afflictions ẏ God doth send thē vpon vs. And yet oughte we not to cease alwayes to blesse the name of God, and to reioyse in the myddest of all our sorowes. When we shal fele that he wyll be oure father, and that he wyll knowe vs for his children, in death we shall beholde euerlastyng lyfe, whiche shall make vs forget all lamentations, so as we shall no more say: Alas what shall I do?

Howe shall I behaue my selfe? Whither shal I go? We shal cut of all these thinges, and we shall saye no more: Shall I drinke no more? shall I eate no more? For such is the maner of brut beastes. But now I se that my God draweth neare vnto me, I go nowe to throwe my selfe downe before him, I go to yeld my self into his handes, and to ioyne my self with him, as with mine own father. When (I saye) we shalbe thus dispo-

Psalm. 31. ted, we may say with Dauid, Lord I commende

Luke. 23. my spirite vnto thee. Dauid sayd this during his life, but our Lord Iesus Christ sheweth vs that we must so say when God draweth vs out of this world. And last of all, when we thinke vpon all the benefites of god, let vs learne to glorifie him, as these be thynges inseparable. Accordynge then as God maketh vs partakers of his graces & that already in part he sheweth vs y^t al our felicitie is to be of the cōpany of his children, so ought euery one of vs to endeuor to honor him as oure

Ionas. 2. father. This was the cause why Ionas beynge drawen out of the whales throte, saith: I shall blesse my God. He saith not, I shall lyue to eate and drinke: But I shall come to the temple the sanctuarie of my God, & there I wyll geue him prayse for thys redemption, that is to wytte, for that he hath plucked me back from the deth. Beholde now what it is that we haue to do.

Psalm. 90 Nowe concernynge that whiche Ezechias speaketh of the cuttynge shorte of his dayes, he speaketh as hauing respect to the naturall course of mans life wherof is made mention in the song of Moyses, for he began to reigne at the age of .xv. yeares. In the xiiii. yere of his raigne, Hie-

rusalem

rusalem was beseged, and then he fell into thys sicknes, as we se. Thus was he xxxix. yeres old. Nowe he saieth that his life is cut short, bicause he is not come to old age. Trew it is ỹ Moyses speaketh of the frailtie of men, and saith: What are men? After that God hathe let them walcke here their dayes, then they are gone againe. And in dede when man commeth to lx. yeares, he is al decaied, and if ye adde x. yeares more, there is nothing but lothsomnes and werines, he is nothing but a burden unprofitable, and life it selfe is combersom unto him. He sheweth thẽ that this life beyng short and fraile, ought not to holde us. But howsoever it were, this kyng Ezechias was as in the flowre of hys age, he was not yet come to the age of xl. yeares. And in this respect he saith that God hath cut shorte his dayes, not that we have any tyme determined. For do not children die sometimes before they come into this world, and so sone as they be come, doth not death already besege thẽ? But he was not yet come to that old age, which is accordingto the ordinary course of mans life. Ezechias than beholdeth this: and above all thinges hath his eies fastened upõ this message of the Prophet Esay, that is, that God hath punished him bicause of his sinnes. And it is asmuch as if he should say talking to him selfe. I see well that God wyll not leave thee in thys world, for the assault is very violẽt. And wherof commeth that, but of thy offences and sinnes: as we shall see that he addeth afterwarde. It is true that he attributeth al unto God as unto his judge, but he toke the faulte upon his owne person, confessyng him selfe onely to be culpable. Loe

howe

howe he vnderstandeth that his dayes were cut short.

When he saith *that he shall come to the gates of the graue, that he shall se no more the lyuing:*

That was bicause he shoulde be conuersant no more amonge men, to exercise him selfe in the seruice of God. But nowe this is not without cause that in it also he conceyued the wrathe of God. Althoughe he were subiecte to dwell as it were confusely myngled amonge manye rascalles, as in dede there were many Hypocrits in Juda, and many wicked and dissolute persons mockers of God, and of his law. And among the Heathen there was nothing els but vngodlines, and rebellion. Now when Ezechias saw that, I knowe nowe (sayeth he) that I am vnworthye to dwell vpon the earth, because these tarry styll in the world, and God hath cut me of, yea with a strong hand, as if he would come armed to make open warre against me as my enemye.

Then when Ezechias had suche imaginations, it is not to be maruepled thoughe he made suche complaintes. But howsoeuer it were, all commeth to this end that God did persecute him. This same was to him a burden so heauy that he as it were foltred vnder it. So muche the better oughte we to note thys doctrine, that if God at any tyme shall afflict vs, more hardelye than we woulde that he should, we shoulde not cease for all that to acknowledge that he loueth vs, and that this perswasion which we shall haue of hys

hys goodnes should make vs to ouercome al temtations which otherwyse myght ouerthrow vs.

Furthermore, if he reproue vs, and cause vs to feele our synnes: that we runne vnto hym, and take the condemnation vpon vs: For we shall gayne nothynge by all oure startynge hoales: yf we wyll pleade, of necessitie the case muste passe wyth hym. Then when we see that God is iuste in punisshynge vs for oure synnes, let vs come wyth head bowed downe, that we maye be releued by hys mercye: and let vs haue no other confidence, nor truste of saluation, but in thys that it pleaseth him in the name of oure sauioure Jesus Christ, to receaue vs to mercye, for as muche as in vs there is nothyng but cursednes.

Nowe let vs throwe oure selues downe before the maiestie of our good God, in the acknowledgynge of oure synnes, besechynge hym, that more and more, he wyll make vs to feele them, and that he wyll in suche sorte cleanse vs from all oure fylthynesse, that we beynge perfectly awaked from oure dull drowsinesse, maye grone and sobbe: not onelye for the miseryes that we see in the world throughe our synnes: but also bycause we cease not so muche as in vs lyeth, more and more to augement the same.

And yet alwaye lette vs runne to oure God, and although it semeth that he persecuteth vs, and that hys hande be verye roughe and dreadfull vnto vs, yet let vs not cease to approche vnto hym, and magnifie hys goodnesse: beynge verye well assured that it shall farre, surmonte and excede all oure faultes and offences.

And though we fele no rigour in him, yet neuertheles let vs acknowledge that it is much better for vs to draw home to his house, and vnder his safegarde, than to runne away from hym as wretched desperyng persons, & let vs beseche him to geue, not onely vnto vs this grace, but also to all peoples.

¶ C.

☞ *My lyfe is withdrawen, it is chaunged as a shepeherds lodge. I haue cut of my dayes as a weauer, he hathe oppressed me with sicknes. From mornyng vntill night thou shalt consume me. I made rekenyng to go vntill morning, but he hath brused my bones as a Lion. Thou shalt destroy me from morning to night, and shalt make an ende of me. I chattered like a Crane, and swalow, & mourned like a Doue, my eyes wer lift vp on high, and they failed me. Trouble oppresseth me, Lord refresch me. What shall I say, it is he that hath spoken it, and it is he also who hath done it.*

Ezechias continuynge the matter whiche yester daye was entreated of, sayeth here that hys lyfe was chāged as a shepherdes lodge. By this similitude he sheweth that there is no reste in the life of man, which he had proued in him selfe, for as much as he was as it were at rest, & in one moment God toke him oute of this worlde. When we make a comparison of our bodies with our houses where we are lodged, it is likely that the bodye of man which is more than the house, shoulde haue some rest: For what is ẏ house, but a place for the bodye,

Math.6. dye to resort vnto? For they are builded for the vse of men. He then whiche dwelleth in any buildynge, ought to be preferred to the house, as the bodye to the gowne, and other garmentes. But Ezechias saith here, that he dwelt in thys world as a shepcherd: who hath his litle cottage which he draweth and carieth hyther, and thether. He speaketh after the custome of that countrey, bycause men there kepe theyr foldes, and a shepeharde wyll cary hys lodgyng as easely as a man would cary any lyght thyng: he sheweth them in summe, that his life was none other thing then a wanderyng, and that God chaunged him by and by. He speaketh after the opinion whiche he had conceaued: for he was as it wer vpon the brinke of the pit. And in dede it was necessarye, that he should dispose him selfe to die seyng God had sent him suche a message as is saide. To be shorte he speaketh as if the thing wer already come. Now afterwarde he commeth to the cause of his sicknes, and confesseth that he is culpable. He saith that he him selfe had cut of his daies: euen as a weauer hauyng a pece of clothe vpon his Loome should cut it all of. I may not then (sayeth Ezechias) accuse any parson: for this euyll oughte to be imputed to me onely: for I haue prouoked the wrath of God, and haue depriued my selfe of hys blessyng, therfore muste I nowe blame my selfe of all this.

Nowe thoughe he do speake here but of one man alone, yet we haue thereby a good admonition of the shortnesse of oure owne lyfe also. Trueth it is, that it is a thynge well ynoughe knowen vnto vs, and yet we do verye seldome thyncke of it. For althoughe we do confesse thys present lyfe to be nothyng els but a shadowe: yet are we so wrapped therein that no man thinketh vpon any other thinge, but to make prouision for a hundreth yeres. And to be short, it semeth that we should neuer depart from this world, we are so occupied on things of the world. So much the more then ought we to call that to mynde which the scripture sheweth vs of the frailtie of our life, as S. Paule also saith that now we are lodged in a cabine: the body of a mā is not a house worthy to be called a goodly dwellyng, or buyldyng: for in it is nothing but trāsitory, wherfore let vs mourne waytyng tyll we may be fully restored, and let vs not be tyed so to this world but that alwaies we may be goyng forward. For the vnfaithful how so euer it be, they shall come to theyr ende: but by no meanes come they neare vnto God, but rather they are settled in this worlde, and in the steade of goynge forewarde, they do drowne them selues more depelye in it. Let vs then learne to goe forwarde, that is to saye, let vs learne to be so dysposed to folowe God when he calleth vs, that death maye neuer come to vs before his time. 2. Corin. 5.

Touchyng this that Ezechias saieth, that he was cause of his owne euil, let vs also practise well this doctrine. So ofte, and when soeuer it shall please God to afflicte vs, we se that we are gyuen to murmurynges: and although it be so that wee bee founde gyltye of oure

faultes

faultes, yet cease we not to vexe our selues, as yf God passed measure. So then, that we may confesse with a true humilitie that God doth punish vs iustly in all thafflictions which he sendeth vs, let vs saye after the maner of Ezechias: it is I that am cause of this euill.

It is true that by and by he attributeth that to God: but they both agre very wel, to wyt, that man be authour of al the miseries ẏ he endureth, and that God neuertheles worketh as a Judge. For when an euill doer shalbe punished, he ought not to complaine of his Judge: but rather for as muche as he seeth him selfe to haue offended the lawes he should condempne him selfe, and also he should know that God by thauctoritie of iustice brought him to that iust punishment, euē so must we do: that is to say, that fyrste we acknowledge that if God do afflicte vs, it is not bycause he taketh pleasure in tourmēting vs: but that he must rewarde vs as we haue deserued, though he yet he hath not altogether regarde to our offences: For what a thinge shoulde that be? we shoulde be an hūdred thousand times ouerwhelmed if he wold vse rigour towardes vs: but accordynge to that, which he knoweth to be good for vs, he chasteneth vs, although we haue our mouth alwayes closed, and that no murmuryng escape thereout.

And nowe to the rest, whan we shall knowe that we haue prouoked his angre, let vs vnderstande that we may not go fourther than our selues, to say who is ẏ cause of this? but let vs simplie accuse our selues. Lo now in sūme what we haue to learne of this matter. Now it foloweth, *From the morninge to the nyghte, thou shalte bringe me to naught.*

In which wordes Ezechias sheweth howe horrible the displeasure of God is, for he meaneth that god nede not deuise this policie, or that, whẽ he would be reuenged on mẽ: but if he speake the worde, the thinge shall forthwith be done. To be short he sheweth here what the power of God is, on the one side, and what the frailtie of man is on the other side. And that is to pull out of vs al the folish imaginations that we conceiue, in making our selues beleue that we may escape his handes. And we se howe men drawe backe alwaies: and although God handle them streighly, they think they may finde some way howe to flee from hym. To be shorte, we thrust out time with oure sholders (as the prouerbe is) and promise our selues, leysure enoughe, and though the corde be straite, yet we conceiue still some vaine hope. And what is ẏ cause therof: that we haue not respect to our frailtie: for there is no minut of tyme, when deth threatenneth vs not: And if we are now standing vpright, at the turning of a hande, behold we are fallen. On the other side we are ignoraunt of the infinite power of God: For if he do but once laye his hande vpon vs, he nede not do it the seconde time, it shall suffice that he onely blow on vs, and loe, we shall be broughte to nothinge. It is not without a cause that Ezechias sayeth here, that *from morning tyll night, he shalbe brought to naught.*

For we heare also that we are not sustained, but in this that God geueth vs strength: but if he withdraw his spirite, it must nedes come to passe that we beyng troubled, must immediatly fayle. *Psal. 104.*

But

But if he shewe him selfe to be againste vs, and that he persecuteth vs, then must we be yet more striken downe.

Folowynge then the admonition of Ezechias, let vs after consider howe feble we are, and let vs acknowledge what we be of oure selues: To witte, that every minute God susteineth vs: but that death neuertheles besegeth vs, and that it neede not make any great assaute to ouerthrow vs: for one blast onely were ynoughe. And loe streight waies we shold be withered like grasse: as we shall se in the fourtie Chapter of Esay.

Esay. 40.

Moreouer let vs acknowledge what the wrathe of God is when it is armed agaynst vs. For God is not lyke vnto creatures, so that he shoulde nede to arme him selfe, and to make great preparatiō, for so sone as he speketh the word, we shall fourthwyth be destroied by his only word. Seynge it is so then, let vs learne to walcke in carefulnesse, commyttynge oure lyues into hys handes, and let vs knowe that we are nothynge at all, but in so muche as we haue oure beynge in in him: And so muche rest as it pleased hym to geue vs, let vs attribute it whollye to his grace, and so when he prolongeth our life: for we should be as men without strength, yf he would shewe but one onely droppe of his power agaynste vs.

Note then what we haue to marke vpon thys place, where he sayeth:

From mornynge vntyll nyght.

Now he addeth that *he chattered as a Crane or as a swallowe*, *and that he mourned like a Doue.*

Wherin

Wherin he meaneth that anguishe helde him in locked in suche sorte, that he had not so muche as a word fre to expresse hys passyons. If a man crye and lament, and make hys complaintes, and declare hys euyll, it is then to be sayde that he is sore troubled: but when a man is so striken down that he can not declare what he ayleth, when he stammereth so in him selfe, that he can not draw forth one onely worde to declare howe vehement hys passyon is: when he nowe sygheth, nowe bryngeth forth halfe a worde, and the rest kepte in, as if one had his throte locked vp: thys is a greate extremitie. Ezechias then sayeth that he was so. Now there is no doubt, but that he had hys respecte vnto God cheifely: As if he shoulde saye, that menne perceaued well ynoughe the heauynesse that he was in: But whan that he woulde frame anye request vnto God, he was as it were dombe, & that on the one syde the sicknesse troubled hym, and yet he coulde not plainelye expresse what he ayled: so that he was in two extremities. Thone, yͤ he was in such sort locked vp within, yͭ with great payne could he fetch out any cōplaint. Theother yͭ he was oppressed wͭ so vehement passyons, that he wyste no wheare to begynne to make his Prayer. But thys maye be thoughte very straunge, that Ezechias who before had in him selfe so greate strength, shoulde now be so faint harted yea, as it were brought, to naught: but that was because he had a spirituall conflict, felynge his sinnes, and knowynge that God was his iudge: for (as we touched yesterday) this trouble surmounteth all the other.

It

It is very likely that Ezechias had an extreme paine, wherwith he was throughly strike͞ down: And also it may be coniectured that it was some burnyng pestilence. Beholde then that his paine was great in it selfe: but that was nothing in co͞parison of the conceiuing of Gods wrath, whe͞ he behelde his sinnes, and knewe God to be armed against him as his aduersary, and that it was he that persecuted him. This was it that in suche sorte affraied him: And in dede, whan a man is brought to that point, all his courage and iolytie must of necessitie faile: for what is the constancie of a man to stande against the wrath of God? It must nedes be more then a frensie and mad rage, when a man wyll thinke to do so. It is true that a man may be constant to indure afflictions when God shall sende them: but how? so farre forth as he shall be strengthened of God. Agayne if men trouble or molest one, he will co͞sider that he hath to do w͞ creatures: if he suffer any trouble, well, he biteth on the bridle: but whe͞ God summoneth vs to appeare, and maketh vs to fele that we are giltie before him, and that presently we must render an accompt, that our sinnes threaten vs, and that in the meane time we perceiue eternal death to abide vs: there (as I haue saide) can we not thinke that we haue any strength to make oure partye good, except we were more then in a mad rage. Let vs not then think straunge if Ezechias be so stricken downe, for he hathe not to do wyth resistyng sorowe, neyther with withstandyng iniuries done vnto him on mens behalfe: neyther bowyng down his sholders to endure any affliction, but he hath to fight agaynst God.

And

and howe could he perfourme that? than must he nedes be as a water that is powred out and spilt. See nowe what is the cause that he could frame no maner of complaint to expresse his griefe, and yet could he neuer kepe silence. Se also why Dauid sayde that sumtymes he helde his peace, and by and by after he set on crying and roring out, & Psal.23.
yet felt no release. We se that the passiõs of Dauid were like to these of the good king Ezechias: as in dede he also addeth that his synnes troubled hym, and that he was affrayed of the wrath of God, he kept not then any certain rule or measure, but sumtyme he caste out sighes, he lyfte vp him selfe, and anone after he was so caste downe that he could not recouer his breath, and yet styll the payne continewed. And in an other place he Psal.39.
saith ỹ he held his peace as if he had bene bridled, & had concluded in hym self to vtter not one word more: no (saith he) I wyll be as a dome creature, I wyll not speake, I wyll not brynge forthe one syllable: yet notwithstanding (saith he) I felt the griefe increase, and kindle more and more, euen as a fyre that is long kept very close, if it be opened then the strength encreaseth & sheweth greater force, and breaketh out in a flame, so Dauid protesteth that in his anguishe, when he had determined to kepe silence and to say neuer a word, euen then was he deceaued, and shewed all that was hyden in his harte, although it were not by wordes well ordred and placed. And to be short, they that knowe in deede what the wrathe of God is, wyll speake and crye, and yet they know not on whiche side to begin: and again when they holde their peace they wote not why they doe it:

but they ar alway in anguish. And we se a notable exāple of al thes things in ẏ good king Ezechias.

It is trew that God doth not examine al mē a lyke with suche extremitie: for if he exercise vs it shalbe according to our weaknes: he seeth that we shall not be able to endure suche tormoiles and assualtes. He spareth vs thē: but whē it shall please him to proue vs in such sorte as we reade here in the example of kyng Ezechias: We muste then be armed with this doctrine. This it is then that we haue to beare away. Now to the rest: let vs lerne what is al the constantie of men. They may well shewe some token of valiantnes when God doth not shew forth his force against them, but so sone as he shall call vs to accompt, thē nedes must all that lustines whiche we thynke that we haue within vs, droupe and vanishe awaye. This is it that we must practise for our instruction to learne true humilitie, for we know that men do cōmonly rest in theyr owne presumption and trust in them selues. And what is the cause of that? but for that euery man hath an eye to his felow, and therefore think we our selues to be strōgly fournished. But we ought to lift vp our wit to God, for there shold we finde, that so sone as he setteth vpon vs we become as nothynge. Let vs then learne to knowe what it is to plonge our selues downe to the bottome in one minute, so sone as God maketh vs to fele his wrath: Let vs also learne that until we be spoiled of all cōfidence in our selues, we can not be set in ẏ array of right humilitie. For so long as mē haue any opiniō of thēselues, & think ẏ they cā do this or ẏ, it is certaine ẏ they robbe god of ẏ which belōgeth vnto him, & so whē they lift vp thēselues without stay to rest vpō, it is to breake theyr own neckes. This it is thē ẏ we haue to hold in memori ry, that all the imagination of mē when they trust in their own strengthes is nothing but a dreame, bicause they loke not vpō God, & do not there stay themselues, ẏ they mighte be spoiled of all vayne ouerweening of thē selues. Nowe when we heare speake of such a chattering, & that Ezechia cōfes-seth ẏ he could not bring forth one word, but ẏ he stāmered, not wottyng what to say: let vs knowe that whē our Lord shal presse vs in such sort that we ar not able to frame one request, or to haue one formall prayer, the gate yet shall not be locked against vs, but ẏ we maye haue accesse vnto him: Which I speak bicause this tentation is very dāgerous. It is true that if we perceiue not in oure selues a zele to pray vnto God, & also a disposition to way depely the promises whiche he geueth vs, to take boldnes to approche vnto him, ẏ ought to displease vs, & we oughte to thinke ẏ we are farre frō him on our behalfe: but yet we must ouercome this tentatiō. Thē when a man shall fele himself in suche troble ẏ he can not bring forth one worde to pray to God, that he shalbe there throwē down & that he shal not know at what end to begin, yet must he pray how so euer it be, & in what sort: at ẏ least, let vs chatter, ẏ is to say, let vs cast forth grones & sighes, which may shew some excessiue passiō, as if we wer euē there vpō ẏ rack, & God heareth euē those groninges: as also we se ẏ S. Paule saith, ẏ the holy gost moueth vs to vnspekable grones, such as can not be expressed. Therefore if one would make an arte of Rethorick of ẏ praiers of ẏ faithful, it is a great abuse: for our lord hūbleth vs to this end, ẏ we shold not imagine to obteine any thing at his hāds by any fair tale: he had rather ẏ we were so confused, ẏ we had not only one word Rome. 8.

a right in oure praiers, but that nowe we shoulde cast out puffynges, and blowinges, and anon that we should abide styll with silence: alas my God, alas what shal I do? and when we shall mourne so, that we should be so wrapped in, and tangled, that there should neither be begynnynge nor ending. Thē when we shalbe brought to that point, our lord knoweth this kind of lāguage, although we vnderstande it not, and although our perplexities hinder vs, that we can not bringe forthe one perfect sentence, so that men also vnderstande not what we would say: yet God (as we haue said before) wyll heare vs well ynoughe. Se then what we haue to learne at this time: that if troubles oppresse vs, so that Sathan by meanes therof go about to exclud vs that we shold not pray to God, but ẏ we should be as it were afraied of hym, yet let vs not cease to presēt vnto god these gronings, although they be cōfuse. Now Ezech. after saith: *That he made rekening vntill euening, & that God brake all his bones, as yf he were in the throte, and betwene the clawes of a Lyon.*

In saying that he made reckening vntil night, he meaneth that he cast his accōpt, well then I will se what will happen betwene this and nyght: but (saith he) the euill encreased: for I knew not yet sufficiently the terrible & dredfull mighte of God, when he setteth him selfe agaynst a pore creature. Now then we haue yet to lerne, that by the word of God, we haue bene taughte what is his force, and that we haue also fealte it by experience, although we conceaue thereof but a portion onely. For God shall exalt him selfe in suche sorte, as we shall perceiue that all that we thoughte of hym before was but a smal shadow. So thē let vs lerne to cōsider what is ẏ power of God, & therunto to applie al our wit & studies, & to be desirously minded to walke in his feare, & to dread his maiestye, knowing ẏ he doth let vs fele but asmal tast of his strength. For if he would lay hard to our charge, we should finde ẏ whiche we before thought was as a farre of, & as it were in a dreame. This was it that the good kyng Ezechias ment to expresse, that we should learne by his exāple not to recken without our hoste, but ẏ we should know ẏ marueilous are the iudgementes of God, & the corrections which he sendeth to punish the sins of men, and ẏ then we should thinke that we haue not yet cōprehēded all, for our capacitie is to sclēder. But that we are guided vnto it a farre of, ẏ is to saye, that if so be, ẏ when God doth chastise and correct vs, we be forthwith taken with feare, & thoughe we be dull witted, yet he maketh vs to fele what and how mighty is his maiestie, we may imagine that it is a hundred thousand times more thā our spirites can conceaue, and that therby we may be alway so muche the more styrred vp to feare him.

Now as to the similitud of the Lyon, it semeth that Ezechias doth here a wrong to God, for this is not to speake of him with suche reuerence as he deserueth to compare hym to a cruell beast, ẏ deuoureth, bruseth, destroieth, teareth & breaketh al. *Esay. 103.* And we know ẏ the scripture preacheth vnto vs of God, cleane cōtrary thereunto, ẏ is to say, that he is kind, pitiful, pacient, ful of mercy, ful of equitie & mildnes: briefly that he beareth such loue to men, ẏ he desireth nothing but to handle thē deintely as his owne children. Seyng thē it is so that

God declareth himself to be suche a one, it semeth that Ezechias speaketh blasphemy in comparing him to a lion: But the good kinge meant not here to protest against God: but onely he hath declared his passions, & he did it not to preache hys own praises, as we haue already sene, but he had rather to receaue this shame, euē to ẏ ende of the world, ẏ men might know what his frailtie was, & that we should haue such instruction thereby as might profit vs. And thus Ezechias hath not spared himself, but hath set him self out vnto vs for an exāple ẏ we might se how he was takē with feare & therby learne our selues to feare God, & also to arme vs wt his promises whē we shal come in such troubles, to thend ẏ we may cōtinew to cal vpon him: & though we faile in al this, & become altogether cōfused, yet let vs still hold this point to offer our selues to god, to sēd forth vnto him our sighes & groninges. And this is it ẏ we haue hereby to learne. Now is it not wout cause ẏ Ezechias cōpareth God to a liō, for (as we haue sene before) al the peines ẏ we shal fele in our bodies, & al ẏ greues ẏ we may cōceiue are nothing in cōparison of this cōceuing of the wrath of god, & this is ẏ cause ẏ we say ẏ the spirituall battailes are much more hard thā al other tētations ẏ we can haue. We cal spiritual battails, whē god cōpelleth vs to cast an eye vnto our sinnes, & on the other sid so awaketh vs ẏ he maketh vs haue in mynd what his wrath is, & to cōceue ẏ he is our iudg, & ẏ we be sūmoned to appere before him, to render accōpte. This is a battel which we cal spiritual, which is much more heauy, & much more terrible thē all the sorrowes, anguishes, feares, tormēts, doubts & perplexities ẏ we may haue as in the world. Nowe when we shalbe come thus farre, we may not maruel if god be vnto vs as a liō, as to ẏ we fele of him, for thys word is not here spoken as touchinge the nature of God. And when he hath thus turmented the king Ezechias, it is not for ẏ he hath forgottē his goodnes & mercy, which on thotherside he sheweth vnto him. But it was nedefull ẏ Ezechias should first know himself to be in the hāds of God, as betwene the pawes, & in the throte of a liō, & so must it be that we come to the same point as I haue already saide, for otherwise God can not winne vs. There is suche an arrogancye in vs ẏ we alwaye think our selues to be strong & mightie, & that we can neuer be beaten down but with a great thonder and lightening. And forasmuch as we can not magnifie the power of God as it ought to be, we talk of it, & we think somwhat of it, but we do not geue vnto it an infinite greatnes so as we be rauished when we think of it, & so as it occupie all our senses in such sort as it ought. It behoueth therfore ẏ our lord do (as a man wold say) trāsfigure him self, ẏ is to say, make himself terrible more thā all ẏ lions in the world, & that he declare himselfe vnto vs & such a power ẏ we be vtterly afraid & all, euē as if we espied a hūdred deathes. For the wrath of god is not only to make vs die: but we se the gulfes of hell opē whē god sheweth himself as our iudge. It is therfore no maruel if we be thē so astonished, as if a liō shoulde teare vs in peces betwene his pawes, & break our bones & his teth, & if we cōceiue such horror whē god is agaīst vs: frō hēce thē procede al these cōplaints ẏ we see in the Psalmes. They ẏ ar not exercised in these batails & perplexities, think ẏ Dauid meant to make his trouble greater thā it was, or they thinke it likely that he was very delycate: but when we come to the profe, we fele ẏ there is not one word to much for the stormes that the faythfull fele when God searcheth them earnestly and to the quicke, surmount al that may be expressed with mouth. Let vs not thinke then that this similitude that is here put forth by the kyng Ezechias is superfluous, for we shall finde the maiestie of God a great deale more dreadefull then all the woordes here conteined can expresse, when it shall please hym to call vs to accompt, and make vs fele that he is a iudge: for if the mountayns tremble before him and melt away, howe may we that are nothynge stande before hym? So then let vs note wel whē somtime god taketh frō vs ẏ tast of his goodnes, & we shall thynk our selues to be cut of from his kyngdome, and perceyue nothing but our sinnes whiche are as great heapes of wood to kindle the fire of his wrath, and when we cōsider only that forasmuche as he is almyghty, it must nedes bee that he stryke vs with lyghtninge & ouerwhelme vs. When we fele these thynges we must nedes be altogether oppressed vntyll he releue vs. And in dede in one minute of tyme we shall be plunged euen to the depth of hell, were it not that he helde vs fast by the hand, and that we were after a secrete maner stayed by hym, although we see not howe. Loe this is a doctrine whiche ought to serue vs on the one side to humble vs that we may forget all the strengthe whiche men thynke to haue in them selues, and reste our selues vpon the maiestie of God, and that we bee altogether throwen downe vnder that maiestie, and yet neuerthelesse that we may knowe the ende and necessitie that we haue of hym to vpholde vs, euen after an incomprehensible maner. And when we

shall

shall thinke that he hath altogether forsaken and forgotten vs, let vs be assured that yet he wyll holde vs by the hande, we shall not perceiue it, but yet he wyll doe it. and we can neuer get out of suche a maze vnlesse by his infinite mercye he drawe vs out: as it is certaine that Ezechias had neuer bene releued, if God by his holy spirit had not susteined hym within, and enlyghtened hym whyle he was in these great troubles. Now after he hath so sayde, he added. Lorde, the payne vexeth me sore, comfort thou me. But what shall I say? It is he that hath done it euē as he hath sayde it. Here Ezechias confesseth in summe that (as touching him self) he is vanquished, and that there is no remedy without God helpe, and set hym selfe as pledge. The word that he vseth signifieth some time to answer for, which mē terme to be suretie, it may then be thus expressed. Lord be thou my suretie in this extremitie, for I can no more. Thou seest that there is no more power in me, then must thou aunswere as suertie for me in my place. And this worde also is often among the complaintes of Job. But it signifieth also to refreshe, and all come to one point, to wit; as we haue touched before, that Ezechias knew that he had no strength and that he must e nedes perishe as touching him selfe: as if a man should declare that he hath nothing to satisfie his creditour that which he oweth, he commeth then to God for refuge. Nowe haue we here yet an other good admonition whiche is that we can not call vpon god as we ought except we be led to this reasō to make our selues as nothing. For while mē kepe I wote not what remnant, it is sure that they shall shal neuer cal vpon God but by halfes. We must then be so brought in subiection that being altogether stripped naked of our selues, our folly may constrayne vs to seke in God that whiche wanteth in our selues. Loe this is one thing to be noted: Yet in the meane time we are aduertised not to be discouraged when God shal so haue spoyled vs that we shalbe voide of all strength. For we may yet moue our matter vnto hym folowynge the steppes of Ezechias. Lord I can no more, so I beseche thee that thou wylt ease me. Loe this it is that we haue to learne of this place. But it is true that we are not alway pressed as Ezechias was, but howe soeuer it be, though the constraint be not so violent, yet ought we to be spoyled and voide of all false perswasion of our owne strength that God may be glorified as he is worthy. And in the meane tyme as I haue sayde, let vs followe with our prayers and requestes vnto God, though we be so vanquyshed that we haue not one whit of strengthe in vs, let vs neuertheles haue our recourse to our God, & he shall geue vs that whiche we want, for asmuche as in hym lieth all the fulnesse of good thynges.

Nowe he further addeth, and what shall I saye? for he that hath spoken hath also done it. Here some thynke that Ezechias woulde nowe reioyse felyng the delyueraunce whiche God had sent hym that he breaketh all his complayntes whiche he vsed, and that now he hath his mouth open to confesse the goodnesse of God. But the naturall meanyng of the text beareth it not. Rather Ezechias breaketh his matter to shewe the anguishe whiche suffered hym not to continue as he would gladly haue done. And we see manye suche examples in all the Psalmes where there is some declaration of the chastisementes whiche God sent eyther to Dauid or to his other seruauntes. Then when God hath so sharply afflicted his people, ther haue bene such like requestes as nowe and then the faythefull enterlace alwayes, I wote not howe, as if they were vtterly cast awaye. So doth Ezechias now. And there is an example verye lyke in the nyne and thirtye Psalme, whiche we haue already alledged. For there Dauid also acknowlegeth that he had to do with God. It was then muche to knowe that men persecuted hym, but when he sawe the hand of God to be against hym, I maye not (sayd he) come to plede here, nor to pursue actions, there is nothyng better for me than vtterly to kepe silēce and take the condemnaciō vpon me. And in Iob we see many suche lyke complayntes. Nowe let vs come to the meaning of Ezechias. What shal I say? it is he whiche hath sayd and he also hath done it. He lamented not as they whiche founde no hope, for suche people wyll crye alas, but all their sighes vanishe awaye on the ayre. Contrariwyse Ezechias sheweth vs here that if we wyll haue God to heare vs, we must open all our passions and sorowes before hym, that we may be vnburthened, as it is said in the Psalme. Ezechias hetherto hath folowed this order, y^t is that he hath opened al his perplexities and cares whiche he endured as if he layde them abrode rounde about God. But now he reproueth hym selfe. Alas sayeth he: what shold I doe? for it is God hymselfe whiche hath sayde it and done it. Psal. 39.

He hath

He hath sent me this message by his Prophet, that there was no hope of life, it is then in vaine that I pray vnto hym. What shall I auayle the in all my prayers? what shal I do? And I wote not whether he will haue pitie on me. We se now howe Ezechias outraged against him selfe. It is true that suche disputacion proceded of infidelitie, but it is necessary that there should be infidelitie in vs to the ende that our fayth might the better be proued. Yet this is not ment to speake properly that we shoulde be infideles, when we are so tossed with vnquietnes, but that we haue a feble faith & that our Lorde exercise vs in suche maner that we in the meane tyme maye knowe what we are, and that without him we should be a hũdred thousand times vãquished euery houre. Lo in effect what Ezechias ment to declare here. What shall I say? For I fele not that the prayer and entreating whiche I can make, doth profit me, and why? God afflicteth me and I fele no maner of ease. I am afrayd to present my selfe before him. Yet neuertheles I truste that my request shall not be reiected of hym, although that I knowe for a truthe that when he speaketh by the mouthe of his Prophet, he hathe forthwith stretched out his hande, and I fele by profe that thys message is not as a threateninge of lyttle chyldren, but that God hath published and proclaymed warre against me, whiche he hath done as it were with fyre and bloud, and it appeareth that there is no more remedy.

Nowe haue we here a good place to shewe vs that we ought to despise Sathan and al vnfaithfulnes, when we haue to doe with prayinge to

God,

God, so that when we shall haue a hūdreth thousand disputacions, yet we shall not let to cōclude, so it is that I shall ouercome all maner of lettes in the strengthe of my God, and I will seke him although he repulse me, & though it appeare that he hath an hundred armies to thruste me far frō hym, yet wyll I come vnto hym. Thus haue I tolde you howe we ought to be armed when we are to praye vnto God. For as we haue nede in all extremities to runne vnto our God, so must we knowe that Sathan applieth all his power to stoppe vs that we haue no accesse vnto God. And there is none of the faythfull whiche doeth not fele this more than he would desire. But in the meane tyme let vs lerne to know the sicknes, that in nede we may take such remedy as is here geuen vs of God. When then the deuill shall set before vs: What shouldest thou doe to praye to God? And what thinkest thou that in so greate wretchednesse as thou felest in thy selfe, he wyll ayde thee? And what thinkest thou myserable creature? to whome preparest thou to go? Is it not God himselfe that doth persecute thee? But let vs passe forwarde, this notwithstanding, and force our selues to breake through al stayes, treadyng vnder foote suche wandryng discourses.

Moreouer it chaunceth that being yet in some rest if we lift vp our wit to God, by and by this cometh in our fantasie. Alas what are we? that we dare to approche vnto God? Howe ofte haue we offended him? And hereupon we sometyme conclude to holde vs there still. But yet such disputacions are very ill, and they are euen so many blasphemies, if God would lay thē to our charge,

as when

as when we make questiō or doubte whether we be hearde or no, certayne it is that this is a deadly offence, and if God dyd not upholde us in our feblenesse, we coulde not but bee drowned. But howesoeuer it be, after we haue bene condempned, after we haue felte that our spirite is wrapped in many dispayres, and that we are in a maze: Yet for all that let us take good courage, and after we haue sayde, alas what shall I doe? let us breake that stroke and saye: I muste yet pray and seke for my God. And why? for he hath sayde that he wyll heare them that seeke unto hym, euen from the depest bottomes. Now then loe, this is the fit tyme when I must goe to him. This it is that we haue to learne of this doctrine of Ezechias, when we see these broken unprofit tales, and that he hath chattred, and we see hys passions so excessiue that they torment hym. Let us knowe that it was Gods pleasure to shewe here a mirrour wherein we myght beholde our owne feblenesse and the temtations whereunto we are subiect, that we shold fight against them, and styll to followe on tyll we fele the relefe that he doth promyse us, euen as we shall fele in dede, so that we haue a true continuaunce and faile not by our owne slacknesse and slouthfulnesse in the mydwaye.

Nowe let us throwe oure selues downe before the maiestie of our good God, acknoweledging our faultes, praying hym, that more and more he wyll make us to fele them, untyll suche tyme as we be utterly spoyled. And though he haue alway muche to reproue in us: Yet let us neuer cesse to hope in his mercy, and that he wyll

make

make vs so to taste the same in the name of oure Lorde Jesus Christe, that it may geue vs a true patience in all our afflictions, and that we maye be so holden in his obedience that we desire nothyng but to offre our selues vnto hym and by hym to bee throughly sanctified.
And that not only he graunt
this grace vnto vs, but
also to all peoples
and nations.
(.·.)

☞ *What shall I saye? he who hath sayde it hath also done it. I wyll walke leasurly all the dayes of my lyfe in the bitternes of my soule. Lorde, to all those that shall lyue hereafter, the life of my spirite shall be notable among them, in that thou hast cast me in a slepe, and hast reuiued me. Behold in my prosperitie the bitternes was bytter vnto me: And thou hast loued my soule, to drawe it out of the graue, because thou hast cast my sinnes behynd thy back.*

WE haue already herebefore declared that the good kyng Ezechias complaynyng that it is God that persecuteth him, is more confused for that, than if he had all the men in the worlde his ennemies, and if they all had conspired to tormente him, as of truthe it is a case muche harder & that ought to amase vs more without comparison if God lyft vp him selfe against vs, than if all creatures did make warre vpō vs. Behold then the cause why Ezechias standeth cōfused and in trouble, because he well feleth that the thinge whiche God declared vnto him by his Prophet Esaye, is nowe fulfilled in hym, and this it is that moste toucheth vs to the quicke when we make comparison, betwene the worde of God and that which

which we fele of his iudgements. If God did simply but strike vs, we might wel be throwen down wythall: but when he addeth also his word to reproue vs, to make vs know that it is he that doth chastise vs, yea and that for our sinnes, lo this is a cause of muche greater confusion. Expresly then Ezechias saieth: According as he hath spoken he hath also done it, and therfore he doeth thereupon conclude that he hath nothing to replie agaynst it. For if we had to do wt men, we might well make our complaintes againste them, but when we are to accuse God, the case must passe on his side. We may pleade for a tyme, but he shall alway be iustified, when we shalbe condemned. Therfore it is first tyme to thinke to amend our harme when we shall not escape condenation before God, but when we desire to stande in oure owne defence, and vse murmuryng and complaint, all this doth nothing but enforce our euyl, euen so farre as to drown vs altogether. And therfore let vs kepe oure mouthe close as it is sayd in Iob: for that is it whiche the good kyng Ezechias meant in this place.

Nowe further he saieth: *That all the tyme of his lyfe he wyll walke in feare, & go on easily or softly as a man whose pride is abated, & draweth his legges after him. Yea in the bitternes of his soule.*

Here Ezechias declareth that God hathe so engraued in hym the felyng of this correction, and hath so printed it in his hert, that the remembrãce therof shall neuer be blotted out. It maye manye tymes come to passe (and we finde it in profe ofter

 than

than we nede) that when God presseth vs, we be altogether astonished, & then we grone, & if we be to cõfesse our faultes & humilitie, it is maruell to here vs. Brifly we be not niggardly in wordes, ether to shew ỹ greatnes of our grief, or to declare our faults, or to blesse the name of god. But we do nothing but shake our eares by & by after, & by the next morow after god hath geuẽ vs release or rest, we think no more of it. Lo in what sort men be, & howe they seke God (as it is sayd vnto the Prophet) while he doth draw them vnto him by force, then they cal vpon him, and confesse the det as we haue said, but so soone as God spareth them, they are as they were before, they lift vp theyr heades like stagges, they do nothinge but reioyse, where before they were so striken down as nothing cold be more, their face was all amazed with feare, shortlye, there was euen nowe nothinge but sorrow, and fourthwith they make great chere, they retourne to theyr delites, and (that more is) they fare as if they meant to despise God openlye. We se then this inconstancie, this chaunge, this lightnes in maner in all men. On the contrary side Ezechias saith here that it is not only for the tyme present that he knoweth that God hath chastised him, but for so long as he shal liue in this world he shall alwaye haue minde of the correction that he hathe receaued, and he shall goe as wyth a tremblynge pace, for the worde whiche he vseth, doeth some tyme signifie to go softely, and sometyme to remoue. Nowe in effecte, he meaneth to saye that he shall neuer haue stedfast pace, but he shall be so muche enfebled, that he shall be as a man drawen out of the ditch, or as he that hath a long time ben sicke, he doeth with great paine drawe his legges after him, and though he shewe him selfe abroade in the stretes yet men see well that, that is all he can do, & when he standeth vp he semeth styll readie to reele and stagger. Nowe see we in a summe what Ezechias meant to say. Hereby we are put in remembraunce not to thinke straunge if God somtime afflict vs more rigorously than we wold. For we haue not sufficiently profited by his roddes vntyll we be truely humbled for all oure lyfe after. Who is he that shall find thys in hym selfe? Let euery one nowe looke, if a moneth after that God hath shewed him mercy he hathe reknowleged his faultes and tremble therat. But contrariwise (as I haue already saide) we seeke nothinge but to blot out all remembraunce of them, for we thinke it to be matter that moueth melancholie. Sithe then we so easily forget the roddes of God, let vs not maruell if after we haue bene once chastised he returne againe the seconde tune and shew him selfe so sharpe that we shall not knowe where to become. Wherfore behold what we haue to do: that is, that during the corrections, and when we be in trouble we beare patiently the rigour of god, knowynge that it is not without cause that he vseth so excedyng great sharpenes against vs, and that it is bicause he knoweth we haue nede of it: take this for one note. And also for another note, that we endeuour to awake, bycause of the great slouthfulnesse that is in vs, for we are so sluggishe and so coolde, that it is a pitie to see. Let vs then durynge the tyme of oure affliction thyncke vpon all oure offences, that we may haue a felynge and conceauynge thereof engraued euen in the bottome of our herts, & when God hath deliuered vs,

Let vs styll thinke vpon it, and let not the feling of our euill be only for one day or for a small space, but as we praye God to supporte vs, and to geue vs leisure to blesse his name and to reioyse in him, let vs so do it that he be not compelled cōtinually to stryke vs lyke asses, seing our carelesnesse and the slownesse that is in vs. Let vs preuente the roddes of God vnlesse we wyl haue them always tyed at our backes. And nowe lette vs note that Ezechias trembled in suche sorte, that he cessed not to be holden vp by the hande of God, and to seke for comforte in God, knowyng well that he was mercifull vnto hym. But these two thinges agree well, that on the one side the faithful are alwayes in care fearing to stomble the seconde and thirde tyme when they haue once paste a deadlye fall. And yet neuerthelesse they take courage and trust in God to walke frely, for as muche as they knowe that he wyll neuer fayle them. Loe this it is ẏ we haue to practise, on the one side to thinke vpon our sinnes and offences, and to be moued with horrour, seing that we haue deserued ẏ God shoulde set him selfe against vs, and that this do so cut vs that it make vs to walke tremblyngly, & as scant able to goe. Loe howe we oughte to bee throwen downe and humbled vnder the hande of God. For there is no question hereof beynge to wylde, but rather we must knowe that the chiefe vertue of the faithfull when God doth afflict and punish them is to be as brought to naught, & yet alwaye drawynge our legges after vs to goe on our pace sithe it pleaseth God to shewe vs mercy. And that we know, that though we haue offēded him, yet he will alway continue his goodnes to-

warde

warde vs, he wil geue vs courage, and that therfore on the other side we become fresh agayne. Lo this is the summe that we haue here to learne of Ezechias.

After he addeth that the bitternes became to him bitter in his prosperitie. Here he enforceth ŷ euill that he hath felt, because he was sodenly taken with it, whē he thought he was at rest & free from affliction. As on the other side we see that ŷ thing whiche is forseen farre of, may be more patiently suffred. For what is the cause that discourageth vs when we are in afflictiō, but that euery one during his prosperitie maketh him selfe beleue that all shal go wel. If a man did thinke of the death of his father, or of his wife, or of his childrē, if he did think that his own life were subiect to calamities, it is certain that he woulde be prepared with defense against all temtations, so as he wold not be found so amased when they come vpon him. But because euery mā deceiueth him self in vaine hope, that is it that troubleth vs out of measure, when our Lorde sendeth any aduersitie. Nowe Ezechias confesseth that it is so chaunced vnto him, and for this cause he sayeth that hys griefe hath bene so much the more bitter for that it happened vnto him in his prosperitie. For we haue seene here before, howe God afflicted hym euen to the extremitie, that is to wete, when he was spoyled of his Realme, and that al his lande was wasted by his ennemies. He was beseged in the town of hierusalem, there he was brought vnder, there they mocked hym; there they spake of hym all shame and reproche that was possible, yea, euen the name of God was vilanouslye blasphemed. Lo thus was Ezechias all confused. Here- vpon God deliuered him miraculously, euen as if he had come downe from heauen to succour hym. He seing that disconfiture so great whiche was done by the hande of the aungel, reioysed, and not without good reason, for God gaue him cause ha- uing declared suche a signe of fauour toward him, as if he had reformed all the worlde at his desyre. But there was a fault, wher soeuer it was, that is that he thinketh no more of his affliction passed, & resteth him to muche, that is to say, he becometh careles and negligēt. Lo herfore nowe he saith that his sorowe is come vpon him in his peace and in his prosperitie. Nowe here we haue a very profi- table warning, that is to say, when we know the graces of God, we must so reioyse that yet we for get not the tyme passed, and that for the tyme to come we alwayes haue our estate before our eyes, that is to say, that with the turning of a hand our lyfe shalbe turned into death, our light into dar- kenesse, as we see the dyuerse chaunges in thys frayle life. Briefly let vs so magnifie the goodnes of God, when he assureth vs that he wil maintein vs in peace and at rest, that in the meane tyme we still consider what our frailtie is, and let vs not be dasled when God shall blesse vs and sende vs all after our desire, let not that (I saye) make vs fal to muche on slepe, but let euery man make him selfe ready when it shal please him to sende vs any chaunge to receiue alwayes in feare, in humilitie, and in all pacience that whiche he wyll sende vs. If we doe so, we shall not finde the hand of God so greuous nor so heauy vpon vs as we are wont to do. But whē we ar to sound on slepe, although we knowe the grace of God, wherof we presently reioyse, he must awake vs, yea and pluck vs hard by the eare, yea and laye great strypes vpon vs. *Psalm.30.* And here we haue one example in the kyng Ezechias, as we haue also an other in Dauid. For in the. xxx. Psalme he confesseth that he was so dronke that felicitie had made hym to forget hys estate. I haue sayde in myne abundance, I shall no more be shaken. And how so? Dauid had had so many prickes to pricke hym forwarde, he had bene exercised so many wayes to haue alwaies in mynde what the life of man was, and he did profit right well therin, for he had bene a long tyme as in the shadow of death. He had bene persecuted of the people, being prysoner among his ennemies, and hauing no minute of rest. Then when God had set hym on the roiall seate, he concluded that he shoulde neuer stomble, and that he should therein remaine peasable. If Dauid hauinge the spirit of God in suche excellence as we know, hauing had so many profes that he was altogether rauished vnto God, yet neuerthelesse hath so forgot him self: what shal become of vs? After he addeth. It was of thy free goodnesse that I was vpholden O Lorde, thou hast establyshed me as on a mountaine, but thou turnedst thy face, and lo I was troubled. Thus sheweth he his vnthankfulnes in that. For although he had not altogether forgot the blessing which he had receiued of ꝥ hād of God, yet is it so that he did not thinke vpō this, god hath deliuered me once ꝥ I shold alway haue my recourse vnto him: knowing ꝥ my life hāgeth as by a thred except ꝥ stay of it be on his goodnesse, & that frō minute to minute he worketh, cōfessing that by and by I should perysshe if he continued not still to ayde me. Dauid thought not vpon this, and he knewe also that he had fayled, and so he addeth after. Lorde thou hast hyd thy face and behold I was troubled. So is it of Ezechias, he was in peace, and loe sodeinly God wou͂ded hym so that the stripe was deadly, & he coulde not cõceiue any thing but such an astonishment as if God had striken him with lightning from heauen. Therfore of necessitie must it be that he receiued a terrible bitternesse.

Nowe let vs applie this doctrine to our profit, and let vs not stay till God make vs with force of strypes to know our infirmitie. But whyle he doth yet spare vs and whyle he hathe pitie of our feblenesse, let vs not cesse to thynke of hym, and let vs feare hym, keping our selues hid as it were vnder his wynges, knowynge that we can not stand one minute without his ayde. To the rest, if sometime we be ouertaken, let vs know it was because we were to fast a slepe.

He addeth a lytle after that God hath deliuered his soule, but he vseth a maner of spech which emporteth more. He sayth thou hast loued my soule, or thou hast had thy good pleasure in it to plucke it back from the graue. By this circumstance he magnifieth the goodnesse of God so much ye more for that he is come to seke hym euen to the graue. For if God doe holde vs styll in our estate, I graunt we therby knowe that we are beholding to him, but therin we knowlege it but very coldly. But if he deliuer vs from death, then we better perceiue howe good he is, for that in suche extremitie he as it were cometh downe vnto vs.

For

For it semeth unto us that we are not much bou͂d unto God, if he preserue us in this life, bicause we take that to be but as an order of nature. True it is that the more he spareth us so muche the more we ought to fele his fatherlye goodnes, but we do it not, and so by reason of our dulnes it is become nedefull that God work of another fashion. Now then as I haue already sayde, if that God plucke us out of the graue, and that we haue bene as forsaken for a time, that it semed we were cut of from al hope, that euen men disdaigned to loke upon us as if we were pore rotten carrions, if in this case God haue pitie upon us, in this he sheweth us so much greater brightnesse to se his mercye, and so much more we haue occasio͂ to acknowledge what and howe infinite his bountye is, in this that god hath so plucked us backe from the death. Lo, this it is that Ezechias meant to say.

Lord (saith he) thou hast loued my soule: And how so? was there any thing in it that might moue God to loue it. Alas, no: for it was nothinge but shadow, a dead thing. I was (saith he) at the graue, and then thou declaredst thy loue towarde me, when then we shalbe altogether disfigured, & that God neuertheles wyll vouchsafe to caste eye upon us, and to haue care of us, in this we ought much more to be enflamed to blesse his name, and to geue him such praise as doth here the good king Ezechias. Behold the͂ in a summe what we haue to learne of this place: that is, for asmuch as God seeth that we are not touched enoughe with the good thinges that he hathe done for us, nor wyth his graces, and that it is nedefull that we be so striken downe, and in suche extremitie that there

be

be in vs no more hope of life, that when we shalbe as forsaken of him and of men, he maye then take vs to mercy. Thus are we earnestly touched and made to geue him thankes, knowyng that he saw nothing in vs but miseries when he shewed hys mercy vpon vs.

Now he saieth also on the other side: Lorde, they that shall lyue after, shall know that the lyfe of my spirite hath bene prolonged. This place bicause of the shortnes therof is darke, for it is not a sentence layd out at length, but they are as it wer broken wordes. He saieth in summe: Lorde they shall liue amonges them, and in them all the lyfe of my spirite, thou hast cast me on slepe, and thou hast reuiued me. Bicause he speaketh not here of the yeres in the beginning of the verse, that is the cause of the shortnes. But when we loke nearer, we shall finde that Ezechias meant to say that the miracle whiche had bene done vpon his persone shuld be knowē not only for a dai, but also after his decease. Some men do expound it, ẏ God shall also prolonge the life of other: but that exposition is not to purpose. For Ezechias meant to saye, that this was not a cōmon or ordinary benefit, but rather he hath felt that God hath wrought wyth him after an extraordinary fashiō. Hereunto tendeth his porpose, ẏ this miracle of God shal neuer be put vnder fote, but thoughe he be dead, yet we shall still talk of it. Before he said I shal remember all the time of my lyfe howe I haue bene chastised, & I shall fele the strokes: for I yet go staggering with all, Now he stretcheth forther & largelier ẏ which he saide before, that is to saye, that not onely he him self shalbe humbled before God, but

but also all the world shall haue occasion to saye: Behold here an act worthy of perpetuall memory that god hath done for a mā. For we ought to desire ÿ all the good thinges ÿ God bestoweth vpon vs, be also knowen of other, that they maye take ensample therof, & that they maye serue for theyr edification. And we se whē Dauid wold be heard in his requestes, he addeth commonly this reason, that euery man shall thinke of it, ÿ the good shalbe edified, & the wicked confounded. Lord (saith he) whē men shal se that thou so assistest thine, al they that call vpon thee shall reioyce, & shalbe so muche more cōfirmed in waitynge for the like: & also the wicked shalbe cōfoūded & though they now mock at the trust ÿ I haue in thee, seyng ÿ thou hast afflicted me, if they knowe ÿ I haue not bene disapointed when I haue had my recourse vnto thee, they shalbe abashed. Thus much then saith Ezechias, now ÿ this miracle of God shall profit not onely him but also other, as a thing knowen & notorious to all. And after he amplifieth it, saying ÿ it shall not be for a smal time, but also after his decease. For asmuch as his lif hath ben so prolōged, it shall be talked of for euer. For (saieth he) thou hast cast me on slepe. This worde to caste on slepe emporteth ÿ he was as it were in the graue, & after was reuiued. As in dede this miracle is euen yet at this day celebrate in ÿ church of god, & shal be to thend of ÿ world. So thē we se ÿ it hath not only profited one person alone, but hath bene a cōfirmation generally to all ÿ faithful, in this ÿ they waite for God, to haue pitie vpon them in theyr necessitie to succor them, and though he do not prolong theyr life in such sort yet ÿ he shall kepe them to the ende, and that if he se them striken downe, he shall lift them vp againe, he shall geue thẽ some token of his pitie, so that in life and deth they shall fele him alway theyr sauiour, and shall know that they haue not bene forsaken nor geuẽ ouer of him. Loe wherunto this song is profitable, & to what intent it was made.

Nowe ought we to haue suche like affection, as Ezechias had, to endeuour so much as shall lye in vs that the graces of God may be knowen of al the world, although they specially perteine to vs. For when God doeth good to euery one of vs, we ought not onely in secrete to thank him, feling our selues bound vnto him, but to endeuour to publish the same, that other may be confirmed and hope in God, seyng such a profe of his goodnes to thẽ that call vpon him: and that praise may be geuen hym in common as S. Paule saith, when the faithful shall all together praise God, that he hath bene deliuered, and that this geuynge of thanckes shall geue suche a sounde, that this shalbe a cause why God shall alwaye deliuer him so muche the more that praises may be giuẽ to him by many. I grãt we oft do publish such graces of God as we haue felt, but many do it by ambition and hipocrisie, for makynge a shewe to magnifie the name of God, they draw a part of the praise to them selues. Let vs beware of that, and let vs haue an vpright and pure affection, so as euery one may learne to loke vnto God, and to haue his hope wholy staied vpon him, and let vs haue this zele and this feruent desire that all creatures beare vs company when we are to blesse the name of God.

Moreouer when God shall as it were haue

striken

striken vs dead, and reuiued vs by his grace, let this so much ỹ more moue vs to praise him. Ther is not so smale a benefit that deserueth not thankes, and when we shall applie all oure wittes to thanke God onely for this that he nourisheth vs, yet can we not aquite our selues of the hundreth part of our det. But if God vse a more excellent maner to declare his fauour toward vs, and that the good thinges which he doeth for vs, are as it were wonderfull and incomprehensible of men, our bond encreseth so much the more, and we haue so much the lesse excuse if we be not then enflamed to praise him with full mouth, and to preache euerye where the goodnes that he hathe made vs to feele.

After this Ezechias addeth that God hathe cast his sinnes behynd his backe. Here he leadeth vs back to that we saw before, that is, that al ỹ he endured was but the payment that was due vnto him for his faultes. And that nowe this that god hath bene mercifull vnto him, is for that he hathe hidden and buried his offences which brought all the euyll vpon him. This sentence is worthye to be well noted. For (as we haue before declared) although we knowe well that aduersities happen not vnto vs by chaunce, but that it is the hande of God that stryketh vs, yet so it is that we can not come to the true cause as we ought. And that is partly bicause euery one doeth flatter him selfe in his owne faultes, and partly also bicause we entre not in iudgement or examination of our owne life to knowe whether it hathe bene well orderd: for wyllingly we are very lothe to be disquieted. And yet must we come vnto it, for that is ỹ true signe of repentance when men of them selues search the depth of their sinnes, and tarry not till God force them vnto it, but they present thẽ selues vnto him they sommon them selues so as they nede neyther sargeant nor officer, but they examine themselues and say: Alas, how haue I lyued? how stande I with God? When men of their own mynde enter into this triall, in this thei declare that God hath touched thẽ by his holy spirite. But this is a rare thing as I haue sayde, on the one syde hipocrisie stoppeth vs that we examine not our owne faultes, and that we discouer them not, seking always to flee from the shame and to hide our owne cuyl: yea and we say that the euill is wel, and we make our selues beleue that we haue not offended God, or at least we make our faultes lesse as if thei wer nothynge, and as if we neded but only wype our mouthes. Loe howe we are caried away by pride and ambition that is roted in our nature whẽ we come not rightly to God in knowledging what we are. On the other part we are desirous to flee from sorowe, as naturally it is a thyng that greueth vs. Now there is no sorow so great as whẽ we thinke that God is our iudge, and that we ar euill doers before hym, for there we fele ẏ whiche before hath bene sayde, that he breaketh our bones as a Lyon: the wrathe of God is so terrible a thyng that it is no maruell though we flee from it. And yet is this a faulte, for we oughte not to make our selues lyke to them that are so blockish that they wyll in no case thynke vpon that which they haue deserued of God, that is the punishmẽt wherof they ar worthy. For this cause we ought so muche the more to note thys doctrine where

Ezechias

Ezechias leadeth vs by his example to knowe our synnes, so ofte as the Lorde doth rygorouslye handle vs, that we may not only knowe that it is his hand which afflicted vs, but also that then he serueth his processe vpon vs, and accuseth vs of the synnes that we haue committed, and bicause we would not of our owne mynde come to haue our cause tryed before hym, and to aske hym pardon that he is dryuen to drawe vs thereunto by force. This is the firste thynge that we haue to learne of this place.

The seconde point is that when God withdraweth his hande which he had heuyly layde vpon vs, that is a token that he is mercifull vnto vs, & that he wyll no more laye our synnes vnto our charge. True it is that somtime God after that he hath afflicted the wicked and reproued, leaueth them there and they ware lustier than they were before as I haue already sayd. But here Ezechias sheweth how we ought to fele the goodnesse of God when he sendeth vs any release, whē he releueth vs of any sicknesse, whē he delivereth vs from any daunger, when he comforteth vs in povertie, when we haue bene in trouble and sorrowe and he draweth vs out. If then we be sad and sorrowefull, it is not enough for vs to fele the euyll, but we oughte to looke vnto the principall cause & to come to the originall spring therof. So when a litle babe crieth, so sone as the teate is geuen him he is appeased. And why? he sucketh & is content, for he hath no vnderstādīg to go further than to his own hūger, he knoweth not whence ẏ meat cometh, he hath no skil to thanke her ẏ gaue him his substāce, for he hath neither wit nor reson

But

But whan a man of the age of discretion shall see his father angry with him, and shall here him say to hym: away villein, get the out of my house: it is certaine that this sorrowe more perceth hym to the quicke to be thus cast of by his father than to endure hunger or thirste, & all the pouerties that it is possible to thinke on. But if the father afterwarde doe pardon hym at the request of his frendes, or for that he seeth his sonne to be sory that he hath offended hym, & sayth vnto hym, come home againe and dyne with me, if that childe haue any reason he wyll not so muche esteme his dyner as that he is returned into the fauour and loue of his father, so as he had rather to fast and to abide hūger and thirst than euer to geue occasion to his father for to caste hym of agayne, & is a greate deale more glad that his father hath forgeuen hym than of eating and drinking his fill.

Nowe let vs applie this to our vse. The moste part are as litle chyldren: if God be quickely appeased with them and plucke backe his hande, so as they haue no more outwarde occasion to be sorrowefull: by and by they ware ioyfull, and praysed be God (say they) which hath holpē me out of this sicknes: but in saying praysed be God they thinke not vpon hym: they enter not into examination of their sinnes, thei loke not vpō the cause why God afflicted them, and so sone as they be cōforted they doe not acknowledge that it is because God loueth them and is fauourable to them: And yet thereunto ought all their ioy to be applied and not to say behold my myrth is returned. He that hath bene in any daunger, if he see himself deliuered, he reioyseth that he is no more in tormēt as he was,

but in

but in the meane time doth he loke vpon the principall benefit and soueraigne felicitie of men, to be reconciled vnto God? No, that cometh not in his mynde. So muche the more ought we to take holde of this doctrine, where Ezechias sayth not only, I am nowe vp on foote agayne, and it hathe pleased God to releue me, my life is prolonged, as he hath sayde before: but he resteth all vpon thys: God hath pardoned me my faultes, he hath taken me to mercie, he layeth not to my charge the offẽces that I haue committed, he hath so forgeuen me that nowe he is well pleased with me, he will no more call me to'accõpt as my iudge, for he hath forgotten all my sinnes and hath cast them behind his back. Loe this it is wherunto Ezechias leadeth vs by his example.

So, as oft as we shalbe afflicted by the hand of God, let vs learne to entre into examinatiõ of our owne sinnes: and when we praye God to delyuer vs, let vs not set the cart before the horse, but let vs pray him to take vs to his mercy. And though we haue deserued a thousande moe afflictiõs thã he maketh vs to endur e, let vs praye that yet he cesse not to be mercifull vnto vs: and whẽ he hath set vs vp againe, let vs geue hym prayses not only for the good that he hath done vs touching our bodies, but for that whiche is muche more to bee estemed, that he hath forgotten all our offences & so is agreed agayne wt vs that he accepteth vs as his owne chyldren, because he tourneth his face from our sinnes, for whyle God loketh vpon our sinnes he can not loke vpon vs but with indignation, and he doth but abhorre vs.

Then that God may loke vpon vs with a mer-

 cifull

tifull and fauourable face, it must firste be that he forget our sinnes, and thinke no more on them. True it is that when we so speake, it is after the maner of men, for we know that all is present before God. But when we say that he muste forget our sinnes and loke no more on them, that is to expresse that he cal vs not to accompt, but loue vs as well as if we neuer had offended him.

Moreouer by this fashion of spech that Ezechias vseth, we se what is the remission of our sinnes, that is, that God cast them behind his back, and cast them there in suche sorte that he punishe them no more, nor aske vengeaunce on them. And this is worthy to be noted: For the deuill alwaye trauaileth to darken this doctrine bicause it is the principall point of oure saluation, and as it is shewed vs in holy scripture, there is no other righteousnes nor holynes, but this fre forgeuenes of sinnes. Happie is the man (saith Dauid) whose sinnes are pardoned. Saint Paule saieth that hereby we see what is our rightcousnes, and that Dauid hath made a briefe summe therof.

For this cause the deuill hath alwaye trauailed by suttle meanes to tourne men from this that they may not knowe what nede they haue of thys forgeuenes of sinnes, as in the Popes church we partly see they say it is not but with penance and confession, and beside that, that we muste bringe some recompence, and if God pardon vs the fault yet that he reserueth the punishment as a iudge. And that this should be a derogation to his maiestie, if we should say that he wholly and fully pardoneth, and they saye that he muste nedes shewe alwaye some rigor with his mercy, & that otherwyse

wyse it were to spoyle hym of his nature: Lo e howe the Papistes haue treated of the remission of sinnes, so that if a man should say vnto thē that God pardoneth oure sinnes of his mere goodnes, this shold be to them as a blasphemi, for (say they) we must make satisfactiō. And what is ẏ ŏworks aboue measure, which we do more thā god cōmādeth vs in his law. It is certain ẏ these are detestable sayings. But howsoeuer it be ẏ pore world hath bin so made drōk & such sorceries. So much ẏ more thē must we note this place wher it is said that God in receiuyng vs to mercy, will entre no more into accōpt with vs, as Ezechias saith here.

Thou haste caste my sinnes behinde thy backe.

It is true that God hath neither backe nor stomack. For we know that his offence is infinite & spirituall: but he vseth thys similitude to signifie that he pardoneth our sinnes like as whē it is said that he casteth thē to the bottom of the sea, ẏ is as much as if he would haue no more remembrance of them nor would haue them more spokē or made mention of. We see then in summe when God receiueth vs in such sort ẏ he is at one with vs, that it is not onely to pardon vs the fault as the Papistes haue imagined & inagled wout reason, but it is to thende that we maye fele his fauor euerye way, and that he wyll persecute vs no more. And in stede that we were afflicted of his hande, and in stede of ẏ he gaue vs by it a testimony of his wrath that contrariwise he maketh vs to know ẏ he taketh vs for his childrē, & that he wil vse vs gētlye shewing the loue ẏ he beareth vs. Lo here in sum what Ezechias meant to say, vsing this maner of spech ẏ god had cast al his sinnes behind his back.

Now true it is that many tymes though God doth pardon vs our faultes yet he wyl not cesse to chastise vs, as it happened to Dauid: but that shal not be but for our commoditie and profit, to thend that we may walke so muche the more warely in tyme to come. I sayde euen nowe that God sendeth his punishement in suche sorte that there remaineth alway some marke to put vs in mynde. Then God wyll surely punyshe vs although he be mercifull vnto vs. But these two thynges are not contrariant, that is, to cast our sinnes behynd his back, and to receyue vs by and by to mercye & make vs prosper by his blessynge, and yet in the meane tyme not to nourishe vs in our idlenesse, but to awake vs & make vs fele some signe of his wrath to preuēt vs. Yet neuertheles if he meane to declare vnto vs fully the remission of our synnes, he will geue vs oftentymes outwarde signes, that is to saye he wyll geue vs suche a tast of his goodnesse that we may perceiue assuredly that he hathe shewed mercy vnto vs, and that it is impossible that he shoulde vse vs with suche gentlenesse and fauour, except he wold examine our sinnes no more, and that he fully and perfectly acquiteth vs, and that he requireth nothing but that we should walke with him as being made at one and truly reconciled vnto his maiestie. Loe thus God declareth vnto vs the remissiō of our sinnes not only by his worde or inwardlye by his holy spirit, but also by the frutes, that is to say, when by his blessing he maketh vs to prosper, and whē he handleth vs so fauourably that we are compelled to confesse in our own conscience that he vseth a fatherly bountie toward vs.

Then

Then when we shall haue these signes, let vs conclude boldly that God hath pardoned our sinnes and that he hath cast them behinde his back, neuer to examine or thinke of them any more. So then so ofte as we shalbe afflicted of the hande of God, let vs remembre that he hath shewed hym selfe good not only to those whome he hath taken out of this world wher they somtime haue endured strong & greuous afflictions, but that he hath also pardoned their sinnes, and let vs knowe that he wyll vse the same goodnesse toward vs. And in doing this let vs learne to humble our selues hereafter. Moreouer the grace of God shall so muche the more brightlye shyne, as he shall not onlye handle vs with all fauour touching our bodies, but also in this that he woulde not haue respect vnto oure sinnes, and wyll shewe vs that although we did prouoke his wrath and gaue him occasion alwaye to forsake vs in our myseries, yet he wyl not handle vs with rigour but that he wil drawe vs vnto hym by his infinite mercye and goodnesse.

Now let vs throwe our selues downe before the maiestie, of our good God, acknowledging our faultes, beseching him that more and more he will make vs to fele them, and that it may be to humble vs in suche sorte that comming vnto hym we may bryng only a pure and simple cõfession of our sinnes, and that in the meane tyme he geue vs suche tast of his goodnesse that we maye not cesse to runne vnto hym although our consciences doe reproue and cõdempne vs, that we may embrace his grace whiche he hath promysed in the name of our Lord Jesus Christe, and as oft as he maketh vs to fele it by experience that we may learn to turne it to our profite, and that we may be so armed against all tentations, that we maye neuer sinke downe vnder the burden, how heauy or troublesome soeuer it be. And that he wyll not only graunt vnto vs that grace, but also to all peoples. &c.

For the graue shall not singe of the, and the dead shall not praise the, nether shall they that are brought down into the pitte waite for thy truthe. The lyuing, the lyuing shall sing of the, as I do this day: the father shall make thy truthe knowen to his children. The Lorde it is that saueth me: we wyll sing a song in the temple of the Lorde all the dayes of our lyfe. And Esai, commaunded, that one shold take a cluster of figges, and make a plaister of them to lay vpon the sore, and he shoulde be whole. Then sayd Ezechias, what signe shall I haue that I shall goe vp into the house of the Lorde?

It is certaine that if our lyfe were ordered as it ought to be, we shoulde alway shoote at this principall marke, to honour God so longe as we be in this worlde. And good reason it is y^t we applie all our studie therunto seing that without ende and ceassing we proue the gracious good dedes that he doth vs. For this cause nowe Ezechias after that he hath knowledged that god prolonged his life, and hath geuen him a profe to witnesse his singular loue toward him, sayth y^t with so muche more courage he wil magnifie the name of

God to cõfesse the receit of so great a benefit. And expresly he sayth that this shall not only be whyle he is in the worlde that he will trauayle to haue the name of God blessed, but he wil endeuour also for his successours that it may for euer be knowē howe God hath wrought for him. Finally for cõclusion he saith that there is no sauiour but God: and if men rest them selues vpon hym their saluation shalbe certain and infallible.

But it may seme straunge that he sayeth that ÿ death nor yet the graue shall not be to prayse god, for it semeth that he accompted vpõ and knoweth no other goodnesse of God but whē he preserueth men in this frayle life. In dede if we loke not but here belowe, our faith shalbe but weake. And we knowe that we lyue to no other purpose but to tast in part the goodnesse of God, to the ende we may be drawen vp hier and altogether rauished to the heauenly lyfe. It semeth then that Ezechias is to muche geuen to the worlde, and that he hath no conceiuing of the spirituall kyngdome of God. For in saying that the graue can not praise God, nor they ÿ be dead, it semeth that he hathe no other regarde but to this present lyfe. And we knowe that it is sayde in the first place, that God wil be glorified as wel in our death as in our life. And S. Paul for the same cause sayeth, that he careth not whether he lyue or die, so the glorye of God might be alway auaunced. There appeareth to be great diuersitie betwene S. Paul and Ezechias, for the one fleeth and abhorreth death, alleging that those whiche are departed shall not prayse God, the other saith it is to me al one whether I lyue or dye, for God shall alwaye be glorified in fied in me. If we beholde the estate of those that are departed in that, that they are drawen oute of this world, and that God hath taken them nerer to him, it is likely that they shold be better disposed, & more chearfull to blesse his name. Fourthly we be here heauely loden in this prison of oure body, we can not half (as a man may say) opē our mouth to praise God, we goe not with a free courage nor with so vehement feruor of zele, as were requisite: now the dead are not so encombred, they are not absent from God as we are (as S. Paule speaketh in the seconde to the Corinthians) they may then so muche the better agree with the angeles of paradise in this melodie. And we knowe what is said of the angels (as it is to be sene in the vi. Cha. of Esay) that without ceasing they cry, blessed be the Lorde of hostes, the holy, the holy, the holy. Then as farre as we may iudge, those whom God hathe drawen out of this transitorye life, ought to be more readye to prayse hys name. But let vs firste marke that Ezechias here had respect to the cause why God placed vs in thys world, and wherfore he kepeth vs therin. He asketh not any reward of vs. He is not lyke vnto a man that setteth seruauntes in his house: for that wer to emprow his lands, & make profite therof, nether is he like vnto a great prince which requireth to haue manye subiectes, for that he is to be maintened and succoured by them when he hathe nede. But God seketh no auauntage by vs, as he hathe no nede: Onely he will that we do homage to hym for all the benefites ẏ he geueth vs. For all our life ought to be applied to this marke, (as euen now we haue touched) ẏ we blesse god, 2. Cor. 5.

and render witnes that his benefits were not cast away vpon vs as they should be if we were lyke dōme men. Lo this it is that we haue to obserue, that Ezechias (in sayinge that the lyuynge shall praise God) meant to note, that men peruert the order of nature whē they apply not themselues to praise God, and that theyr vnthankfulnes is by no meanes excusable, when they bury the graces of God and put them in obliuion. Seyng it is so thē that our Lord requireth of vs nothyng but ŷ hys name be glorified in the world, it is not to be merueyled that Ezechias saieth: the liuing, the lyuing shall praise God.

We must also note what difference is betwene the state of the liuing and of the dead. Though the dead praise god, yet we can not iudge nor imagine that they assemble after our maner to shewe an agrement of theyr fayth. Eche one of them cā right well praise God by him selfe, & yet it meaneth not that they ar gathered together in one body, as we are nowe, for the scripture saith nothing thereof. And we maye not forge fantasies of oure owne braine as we thinke good. For we know that god reserueth this perfection to the latter day that we should be all vnited and in suche sort ioyned vnto our God that his glory should fullye shine in vs. For as muche then as they whiche are departed haue not suche a manner of exercysinge them selues in the praysynge of God as we, therefore it is said that, that is a thynge properly perteynyng to vs that be lyuyng.

But there is yet more. For Ezechias speaketh not here simply of death as we haue touched alreadye, but he setteth oute hys death to be suche as if he had bene cut of from the Churche of God, and from all hope of saluation, when this iudgement was come to be executed, or as if he had bene before hys Iudge: Then Ezechias prepared not him selfe to dye, as by nature we can not flee thys necessitie: but he had thys testymonye of Godes wrath, wherewith he was so feared as if all were lost to hym. Nowe we knowe that no man can synge the prayses of God excepte he haue occasion and matter. For whan oure Lorde sheweth vs a terrible countenaunce, oure mouthes are stopped, we are fylled wyth suche anguisshe, that it is impossible for vs to blesse hym. Rather contrariwise there shall be nothynge but gnashynge of teethe, when the wrath of God shall so astonishe vs. Loe thus stoode Ezechias. On the other syde, when God sheweth hym selfe mercyfull towarde vs, and vttereth some signe of hys fauor toward vs, he openeth oure mouthes, as it is sayde in the li. Psalme. Lorde thou haste opened my mouth: therefore wyll I synge thy songes. And in other places. Lorde thou haste put a newe songe in my mouthe, by thys the Prophete signyfieth when God maketh them ioyfull for theyr delyueraunce frome some euyll, that by thys meane, he styrreth them vp to synge hys songes, and to blesse hys name, and to be myndefull of hys benefytes. *Psal. 51. Psal. 40.*

So then, when we conceaue nothynge but altogether terrour in God, we are in a swounde, and then the gate is shutte so that we can not prayse God. So Ezechias in this place, sayinge that the dead shall not praise god, meaneth not generallye all those that departe oute of this transitorye lyfe, but

but those whiche are as it were cut of from God, and are confounded with his wrath, who also tast not his goodnes any maner of way, & are made naked and estranged from all hope of healthe. It is then impossible that such should praise God.

There is yet another point to note. For when the faithfull are holden downe & oppressed wyth any distresse, they se nothing but theyr own grief, and euery man hath experience of this in him selfe to much. When any euyll hath cast vs downe altogether, we can not applie oure selues to anye other thing, for we are there holdē fast as in a streight prison. So was Ezechias, as also it is said in the lxxxviii. Psalme. That the state of those that are dead, is a land of forgetfulnes: men knowe not there what God is. This semeth to be a blasphemie. But these maners of spech procede of the vnskilfulnes and weakenes of men, that is bicause they can not withdraw them selues to iudge with a setled sence, & to haue a well framed and ordered knowledge. But the trouble so vexeth & carieth them awaye that they speake as at randon & confuselp. Behold, Iob saieth that men beyng taken out of this world haue no more carefulnesse, but euery one is at rest, as if there were a confuse mixture, that the master & the verlet were all one, and that the tyrant shoulde cause no more terror. He speaketh of the state of those that are departed, as if death should destroy all thinges. Yet he had not such opinion, but it was bicause that his sorow suffred him not to speak as a mā at rest. For he was tossed with such vnquietnes that his words wādred. So may we think of Ezechias. He speaketh not of the estate & condition of those that are departed

Iob. 3.

parted as the scripture teacheth vs, and why? his heauines, & the horrour whiche he had conceiued bare rule ouer him in suche sorte that he wiste not where he was: it is true y^t this is not for excuse.

And thus therfore oure Lorde geueth vs mirrours of our frailenes when we see that the moste holy, & most perfect speak so. Yet in ye meane time God supported Ezechias, because the principall thing remained with him styll, as we haue alreadye sene, that he tended to this mark to glorifie the name of God, for he had rather die a hundred tymes than to be one minute in this world prophaninge by vnthankfulnes the benefites that God hath done for him. Lo than Ezechias kepeth this rule that men ought not to desire to liue one daye but to that end that God might be glorified in it. But in the meane time this y^t he was tossed with so great troubles that he could not orderly speake as he ought, proceded of his weakenes, whiche God holdeth for excused and supporteth. For it is not a disobediēce, though we haue many ranging wordes in our prayer. It is true that we oughte alway to frame our selfes to his rule, which is geuen vs, to thend that euery man pray to God, not at aduenture, and after his own fansie. But howsoeuer it be, we shall haue measurable sorowes, & complaintes in vs, and it behoueth that god haue pitie of vs in this behalfe. Loe in a summe what we haue to learne, that aboue all, while we lyue, we alway tend to this ende that God be honored. For therfore it is he y^t hath set vs in this worlde, to that end it is that he hath chosen vs to be of his flok, to wete, that we might be assembled to singe his prayses with one accorde.

And

And we see this yet better in the 115. Psalme, where is a lyke sentence. And it is not one man that speaketh, but the whole body of the Churche of the faithfull, which say that one can not prayse God in death, but we that lyue (say they) vnto the ende shall confesse that god hathe preserued vs. There it is signified vnto vs that God wil alway kepe his church, and that he will haue some people remaining vnto the ende of the worlde. Why? bicause he wyll be knowen the father and sauiour among men. And although it be not of the greater multitud, yet wil he haue some company that shal praise him. So then let vs learn to exercise our selues in blessynge the name of God while he kepeth vs here below, and while we be nourished by his liberalytie, and while (whiche more is) he calleth vs vnto him to tend alway to the hope of the eternall heritage. Sithe then it is so, let vs applie all our study therunto, yea all the daies of oure lyfe. If we do otherwise, it wer better for vs that our mothers had bene deliuered of vs before our time, or that the earth had gaped to swallow vs vp, thā to be here gluttons, as brute beastes, and to continue vnthankfull for so manye benefites as God hath geuen vs, and that his praise shoulde be buried by vs. Take this for a note.

The residue: Let vs alwaye be ready folowyng the example of S. Paule, to glorifie God, be it by life, be it by death. If at any tyme we be in trouble as the good kynge Ezechias was, let vs know that all our sorowes, complaintes and groninges, oughte to be suspicious vnto vs, bycause we can not kepe measure by reason of the fraltie

So

that is in vs.

So that this which is sayd here, The dead shall not prayse God, may not be drawen of vs for a cōsequent profe, to pleade wyth God when it shall please him to call vs vnto him. Let vs not make this excuse vnder pretext of Ezechias, or Dauid who spake so in the vi. Psalme, or of all the people as we shall aledge. For there was excesse, bycause as well Dauid as Ezechias, and generally al the Churche then when a horrible dissipation was neare tempted as if god wold reiect them, and vtterly disclaime in them, and woulde haue no more to do with them. As they then were pulled backe from God, so were they abasshed. And no maruell. Let vs not therfore make therof a rule, as if we might do the like: but let it serue to make vs knowe our own weakenes. Moreouer although God do support vs, yet let vs not please our selues in suche a vyce. Loe this it is that we haue to learne.

Nowe we are taughte for as muche as God hath made vs to feie his graces, to haue our herts set at large, and our mouthes opened to blesse hys name. And on the other side that we can not pronounce one worde to his prayse, whiche procedeth from a good hartie affectiō, except we be throughly perswaded in this, that God is mercyfull vnto vs, & that we vse to our profit the benefits which we receaue of his hande.

As touchinge the firste pointe, let euerye one learne to styrre vp him selfe accordynge to that whiche he receyueth of the graces of God, for the number is infinite.

There

There is none of vs when he shall duely consider him selfe, but ought to be rauished as it is saide in the xl. Psalme, that if we wyll number the testimonies that God hathe geuen vs of the fatherlye care which he hath for vs, and of his mercye, they are mo than the heares of our head, and we shalbe therat as it were astonyshed. But accordynge as God setteth fourth the richesse of his goodnes toward euery one of vs, let vs be so muche the more moued to blesse his name, & let euery one exercise and pricke him selfe forward vnto that. Lo this is in summe that whiche we haue to marke vpon this place.

Now on the other side, let vs confesse that our lyfe is cursed if we gluttonously deuoure the good thinges that God geueth vs and do not therin behold his goodnes. For we vnchristianly abuse all that which was apointed for our vse and saluation vnlesse we be brought to this point that God sheweth him selfe a very father vnto vs, and that by all meanes of gentlenesse he draweth vs vnto him, that we should not doubt that he taketh vs for his children. And in this also we see how miserable is the state of Papistes, for they will not assure them selues of the goodnes of God, but saye that alwaies we must be in doubt of it. And so all theyr prayeng and thankesgeuyng to God, is nothing but Hipocrisie and faining. For we can not call vpon the name of God but with affiaunce, we can not praise his name except we know that he is fauourable vnto vs. Then they are altogether excluded. Let vs learn then that we can neuer offer to God a sacrifice of thākesgeuing which he esteemeth and setteth by, and that we can neuer attein to the right scope of oure life, vnlesse we be fullye perswaded of his goodnes. And so as ofte as we thinke vpon all the graces and benefites of God: let this come into our minde, that God doth confirme and ratifie vnto vs his adopsion to the ende that we maye not doubte that he compteth vs as his children, and that we freely call vpon him as our father: Lo in a summe what we haue to learn of this place.

Nowe we must also note this which Ezechias saieth. The lyuing, the lyuing shal prayse the? Yea the father shall declare to his childrē thy vertue. He had said before that the dead shalnot wait any more for the truth of God, that is to say, they shall haue no hope. And in this we see that which I haue touched, that Ezechias speaketh not indifferently of all these whom God hath taken out of this world. For it is certeine that the faithfull do waite vpon the truth of God. When Iacob yeldyng vp his spirite, saide: I wyll waite for the saluation of the Lorde. He saide not that for one minute, but he declared and protested that he had this assurance imprinted in his hert, which shold neuer be pulled out, so ẏ though he passed through a hundred deathes yet alway this treasure should remayne with him. Nowe then the saintes and faythful although God called thē out of the world ceased not alway to nourishe the hope of the resurrection, and of this felicitie which is promised thē. But Ezechias speaketh of the departed, whiche are as it were banished and estraūged altogether from the kyngdome of God whome also he forsaketh. Now, he was euen in the same estate in his own cōceit vntil god cōforted him by his prophet.

For ŷ messag which was sēt to him, was to shew that God was his enemy, and that he came as his aduersary with armed hande against him. Than was Ezechias driuen to remayne confounded. Then it is not without a cause that he saide, that those which are departed, waite not for the truth of God, that is to say, that they ar altogether shut out frō the promisses, so as they are no more of the number of his children.

But nowe he saieth that the lyuinge whiche tast the goodnes of God, shall cause theyr children to knowledge hys truth. Nowe here we se again how God shalbe duely praised and honored amōg vs, that is, when a man shall knowe that he is faithfull to all his owne, that he neuer forsaketh them, but that his helpe is ready for them in their necessitie, and that they shall neuer be disapointed which leane vnto him. Lo this is the true substaunce of Gods praise. So in a summe we se that it is nothing but falshede and lies when men shal pray vnto God, and shall make as thoughe they gaue thankes vnto him, & in the meane time they are not instructed of the loue ŷ God beareth them nor certified of theyr saluation, and shall knowe of no promise. Then when that wanteth, it is certaine that all theyr prayses of God, whiche maye be sounded in the mouthes of men, are but winde, and smoke. Wyll we then prayse God as it aperteyneth, in suche maner as he alloweth the sacrifices whiche we shall offer vnto hym of praise, and thankes geuinge? Let vs profit in his word, lette vs knowe what it is, to truste in hym, which we canne not doe tyll he declared hys good wyll

towardes

towarde vs, and haue certyfyed vs that he hathe receaued vs, ẏ we may freiy come vnto hym, and that we shal neuer be forsakē, so we fle vnto him. If we haue not suche an instruction, we can neuer pronounce one worde of Goddes prayses as we oughte. Loe hereunto it is to be applyed, that Ezechias sayeth here, that the father shall make knowen vnto hys chyldren the treweth of God.

Moreouer, where as he sayeth, that the dead can not wayte for it, nor leane vnto it. Lette vs knowe, that for as muche as God declareth hymselfe mercyfull and lyberall vnto vs, that is alwaye the more to confyrme oure hoope: That we shoulde take so muche the more courage to runne vnto hym, and not to doubte that he hathe hys hande alwaye readye to helpe vs at neade.

Howe then shall we vse the graces of God as we oughte? When we shall be alwaye confyrmed more and more in the faythe, when we canne dyspyse all temptations, when we canne resolue oure selues, that in callynge vpon God, we oughte in no wyse to feare the losse of oure laboure, for as muche as oure hope shall neuer be confounded.

When then we shall be well satisfyed in thys so as we maye fyghte agaynste Sathan, to beate backe all temptations, beholde howe we maye wyselye applye the benefytes of God to oure own vse, and howe wee maye take profyte of theym: Loe in a summe what wee haue heare to learne.

Moreouer, when he speaketh howe fathers ought to behaue them selues towarde theyr chyldren we haue to gather in generall (as hath bene said here before) ỷ it is not ynough ỷ we procure that god be glorified during our life, but we ought to desire as his name is immortall so that frō age to age it may be honored, & that those which shall come after vs, may kepe ỷ pure religiō, & that the seruice of God may neuer fall in decaye. That it maye be folowed and aduaunced alwaye and that the goodnes of God maye be euery where magnified. They that haue childrē, let them knowe that God hath committed them incharge to thē, & that they must rendre an accompt if they bestow not al trauaill to teache them to serue God. For when it is sayd that the father shall shewe to his childrē the truth of god, we must alwai come to this end. Why? to this ende that the children may trust in him, that they may call vpon him, that they maye geue to him the prayse of all good thynges, ỷ they may dedicate & cōsecrate thē selues wholy to him, & to his obediēce. Thē if fathers wil discharg thē selues of theyr duties, let them knowe that this is the principall heritage that they ought to leaue to theyr children. But if they heape vp goods & yet geue them the bridle when they shall see them dissolute, mischieuous, wicked despisers of God. Wo be to them in that they shall take peine to aduance them in this world: for they lift them vp very hye to make them break theyr neckes, & theyr fal shall be more deadly when they shal haue store of goodes: and yet in the meane tyme they shall despyse God in his doctrine, there confusion shalbe more hor-

horrible, bicause theyr vnthankfulnes shalbe lesse excusable. Let the fathers then thinke better of this thē they haue bene accustomed, that is to say, when God geueth them children, he bindeth them to this charge, that they endeuor so much ẏ more, that they may be instructed in his truth, so long as as they lyue, as also we se thexample geuen vs in Abraham, which is the father of the faithful. For when God meant to shewe that Abraham would gouerne his house, as appertened: Shall I hyde from my seruaunt Abraham (saith he) that which I haue to do? No. Lo howe God maketh hym selfe familiar with him. For (saicth he) he shal instructe his children in my statutes, in my lawes, & in my ordinances: Lo, this is the marke whereby the faithfull are knowen frō the despisers of God. If then we will be numbred in the church, let vs folow this zele, and this affection of Abrahā, that euery one accordynge to the familie that he hath, trauaile that God be honoured in it, and that hys truth be alway knowen euen to the ende.

Nowe for conclusion Ezechias saicth: The Lorde it is that shall saue me. This worde doeth emport that he despiseth and throweth awaye all other safegarde, as if he should saye, there is none but God. He might haue said: The Lord hath saued me. He might haue said: I hold my life of him and of his mere grace. But he goeth further, as if he meant here to mainteine the honor of God, and to beate down all the affiances that men conceiue in theyr fantasie. For we are wonte to make our discourses when we mynde to mainteine oure selues, and when we seke to be assured, we take this meane, and that meane.

Nowe Ezechias forsaketh all and declareth that there is none but God, and that he it is whom we ought to go vnto.

True it is that God suffreth vs to vse all the meanes that he offreth vs, and he hathe ordeyned them for that vse, but yet he wyll not that his glorye be darkened, as it is no reason it shoulde be. Neuertheles men be so wicked and froward, that alway they take occasion to minishe the glorye of God vnder this coloure that he helpeth them by his creatures. If God hath not bene content only to make vs fele his owne vertue, but also applieth al his creatures to our vse we ought to be so much the more styrred to prayse him. But cleane contrary, we robbe him of his right, we forsake him, and fasten our affiaunce here, and there, and we thinke that oure saluation procedeth from thys thing and from that. Lo how God is defrauded of his ryght. So much the more ought we to marke this that is here sayd by Ezechias. The Lorde it is that saueth vs. That is, thoughe the Lorde do stretch his hande vnto vs, and geueth vs wherewith to be mainteined, yet let vs confesse that he is the fountain, and let the riuer that floweth frō him vnto vs, not hinder vs to knowe whence the riuer commeth. Let vs then tende alway to thys welspring that God be glorified, and that he kepe his owne wholy: and after, when we are made naked of all other meanes, let vs say: the Lord alone shall suffise. And for this cause saith Dauid. The mercye of God is more worth than all lyues, not meanyng that the lyfe of men is not of the mercye of God, but he sheweth ȳ men ought not to be fast bound here beneth, ꝯ that they are become brutish

when

when they thinke to preserue, mainteine, or warrant them selfes by this, or that mercy, & that they ought aboue all thinges to preferre the only goodnes of God and to rest in the same. So then beholde here a saying of great doctrine, if we cā haue skil to take profite therof. Let vs then folowe the example of Ezechias, and when God hath succored vs at our nede: let vs geue him the prayse for our life confessinge ŷ there is none but he alone to saue vs. Herunto he addeth againe. And we wyll singe our songes all the dayes of our life in ŷ house of the Lord. Here he repeteth agayne the saying that he spake before, that is, that he will employe all the residue of the life that god hath geuē him to make to God acknowledgement therof, that he might not be foūd vnthākful. For as I haue said it were better that we had neuer bene borne, than to enioy ŷ good things that God hath done for vs, and yet to haue oure mouth close and to thinke no more vpon him. Let vs then note well that thys repetion is not superfluous when Ezechias saieth so manye times that sith his lyfe is prolonged, he wyll be so muche the more styred to prayse God. Take this for one note.

Now, he furder sheweth that this shal not be for a sodein braide, as many can wel praise God ŵ a merely vehement affection, when they haue had profe of his goodnes, but that droupeth awaye by and by, and the memory is lost of it, & they thynke that it is enough ŷ at one time they haue testified ŷ thei thāk God for the good ŷ thei haue receiued. But Ezechias sheweth vs ŷ we ought to cōtinue therin ŵ a true perseuerāce, for we are beholdē to god no more for one day of our life thā for another

It

It must therfore be fully dedicate & auowed vnto him. So seyng the slouthfulnes and coldnes that is in vs, let vs learn to styrre vp our selues when we shall fele that oure zele waxeth colde for feare lest it be wholy quenched. Let vs awake. How? If I haue once or twise reknowledged the grace of God. What is that? must it be now forgotten? And if I blesse the name of God duringe one moneth, a yere. or two, or thre: And now I think no more of it. To what purpose shal ẏ serue me? but to make me so much ẏ more giltie of hipocrisie, & to shew ẏ ther was nothing but a fire of stubble, that there is no constancie nor stedfastnes. If then we beholde well the example of this good kynge, we shall euerye one be the more pricked forwarde, to fede our selues no more in this idlenes whiche is naturall vnto vs, and whereunto we be to muche enclined.

When he sayeth, In the house of the Lorde. He meaneth not that the prayses of God shoulde be enclosed within the tēple, for euery man in hys owne house maye and ought to praise God. But Ezechias sheweth that it is not ynoughe that he prayseth God in secrete, but that he wyll styrre vp other, to haue more companye. He speaketh here of a solemne sacrifice of praise which he wil make to God in a great assemblie. And for this same cause our Lorde hathe wylled his to gather together. For he was able ynough to haue taught thē perticulerly if he would, & to saye: Let euery man prayse me in his chāber. But his pleasure is that there be this policie, that we be knit together in one body, that we call vpon him with one mouth, and that we make confession of our faythe with one

accord:

accord. And why so? True it is, that firste we see that it behoueth that all oure senses be applied to glorifie him, but there is also a seconde point, that euery one styrre vp other as we haue nede, for there is none of vs that feleth him self disposed to praise God, but he hathe yet a pricke forwarde when he shall see the company of the faithfull, and example shewed him. For asmuche therfore as this doeth styrre vs vp, God willeth that openly and in common we sing his praises. And for this cause Ezechias saieth expresly that he will go to the temple of the Lorde to prayse and blesse his name, as we se also that Jonas dyd the lyke. He speaketh of house of the Lorde, and why? not (as I said) that the praises of the Lorde are there shut vp & hiddē but for that the people there assemble together, & for that he knew that this should bring more profite because there shoulde be some that shoulde be styrred vp by his example. Lo in a sum the songe of Ezechias. *Ionas.2.*

Now in the end it is here recited that ỹ Prophet Esay commaunded to make him a plaster of figges vpon his wounde, wherby it is likely that it was a pestilence which he had. And after he by and by addeth ỹ Ezechias also demaūdeth a token which is graunted him, as we se when the sonne was drawē back of his course vpon the diall of Achas. A man mighte here moue a question, whether thys playster were for medicine, or a token that the Prophet gaue him. And it semeth that if it had ben for medicine, it should haue diminished the glory of God, for it behoued that Ezechias life should be miraculous. Why did he not then heale him without any meane? But when all shalbe

well

wel considered, the signe or miracle that was geuen to Ezechias whē the sonne stayed his course, and when the shadowe of the dyall was drawen back so many degrees, was sufficient, and toke awaye all doubt. Moreouer although Ezechias used this plaister it is not therfore to be saide that his healyng was naturally wrought, for sith God had chaunged the order of the heauen, and shewed a witnesse so euident that this proceded from his hande, and that it was an extraordinary benefite, we ought to content our selues with that, and we see many times that God is serued with his creatures and yet he hath sufficientlye declared that it was his owne power only.

They whiche thinke that Ezechias rather had this plaister as a sacrament to confirme hym, doe thinke that the figges would more haue hurt his wounde than helped it. But a man maye make a compound of them to ripe a sore, and that is commonly knowen. True it is that God somtime geueth signes that seme cleane contrary, and that is to drawe us the more to him, to make us forsake our owne fantasies and hold us content with that whiche he hath spoken. As how? God promiseth that the worlde shall neuer be destroyed with water, and what signe geueth he therof? a signe that naturally threateneth us raine. When we see the rainbowe, what token is it? it is such a drawyng together of waters, that maketh seme we shall all be ouerwhelmed and the earth shal perysshe. And how so? This signe is geuen us of God to make us know that therth shal neuer be destroied with ouerflowynge of water. Yea but it is to make us learne to stay upon his truthe and to stoppe our

eyes

eyes against all the rest, and against al that we cõceiue in our selues, and that the truthe of God be of so sufficient credit with vs, that we receiue it without gainsaying. So thē God worketh wel in suche sorte: but as to this place, we maye rather iudge that the Prophet to asswage the griefe of Ezechias gaue hym thys remedye, lyke to a fyre that burneth a man. And so when GOD hadde prolonged the lyfe to this good kynge, he would yet of abundant grace adde this goodnesse also, that the paine should be mitigate. Then the prophet gaue him this as it wer an ouerplus that God had not only prolonged his life, but also wold not haue him endure so muche or suffer the tormentes whiche he felt before.

Thus behold howe in all and euery waye God hath declareth him selfe pitiful towarde this good king, how he would shewe him selfe pacified altogether after that he had vsed suche roughnes toward him and had stretched out his arme as if he wold haue altogether ouerwhelmed him, but this meaneth not ỹ God doth ỹ very same to euery one of his children, to the ende ỹ we shold not aske that in one minut of time God make vs glad after he hath drawen vs out of the graue and hath geuen vs throughlye to content vs, but that it maye be his pleasure by litle and lytle to geue vs ease of all our greues, in the meane time lette vs be content with this.

And in dede we may gather that God hetherto hath wrought by degrees in Ezechias: for this miracle was done since the shadow of the sonne was drawen back, and the message of prolonging his lyfe was geuen him by the prophet.

It semeth thē that Ezechias was altogether deliuered, and yet this plaister was also requisite. So then whē our lord after he hath geuē vs anye ease in oure trouble shall leaue some remnaunt of peine: let not that trouble vs, nether let vs be wery of bearyng his correction, vntill he haue healed vs altogether.

Nowe we haue to declare why Ezechias demaunded a signe, for although it wer of wekenes yet God heard him in suche a request, and herein we se howe louynge God is towarde vs, when he doeth not onely graunt the requestes whiche we make of a pure and right affection: but also though there be some infirmitie mingled withall, and that we bear passions somwhat excessiue, yet God hath pitie on vs in this point. Certaine it is that Ezechias when he had perfect faith he was content to haue heard the word from the mouth of the Prophet. Then when he saieth alas shall I not haue some signe: herin he sheweth that he geueth not ful and perfect faith to the word of God. But yet he confesseth his fault, and in confessyng it, he asketh remedy: & of whō? of God him self. Then whē we shalbe so encombred, fyrst let vs acknowledge our owne pouertie and let vs not go aboute to excuse the euell, but let vs take vpon vs the sentence of condemnation willyngly. If then we aske of God to helpe it by his goodnes, he wyll succor vs, and heare our requestes.

It is true that it becōmeth not vs to require a signe or miracle when we thinke good, for as it hath bene declared in that place wher the prophet euen nowe made mention of the signe. Ezechias had a speciall motion vnto it, as Gedeon also had: Iudi. 6.

Let

Let vs leaue that to ẏ good pleasure of God, whē we know our infirmitie, & pray him to helpe, and to confirme vs to the ende we may be fullye satisfied in his worde. Lo then how we muste go forward, and in this doyng we shall fele that this is not written onely for the parson of the kyng Ezechias, but that God would geue it for a common instruction to all his church, that in oure troubles when we shalbe come to the extremitie: yea, to the bottome of hell, we may yet know that we ought to haue our refuge to him that hath called vs, and handled vs so gently, hopinge that he wyll shewe fourthe his strength towarde vs, althoughe for a time it be farre from vs, and that we se no signe of it, & so that he will geue vs mater to glorifie him, and also we are taughte to applye all oure lyfe to to blesse the name of God, and to sing his prayses accordyng as we haue experience of his goodnesse towarde vs.

Now let vs throwe downe our selues before the maiestie of our good God, in acknowledgyng of our faultes, praying him, that more and more, he wyll make vs to feale them, and that this may be to beate vs altogether downe, and humble vs before him ẏ we may fight with the vyces which make warre against vs, knowyng that our Lord hath ordeyned vs to this conflict, till we be fullye renewed and clothed with his iustice, & that there may be no stoppe to let vs frō the obedience of his good will, and that he graunt this grace not onely vnto vs, but to all peopes and nations, &c.

A MEDITATION OF A PENITENT SINNER: VVRITTEN IN MANER OF A *Paraphrase vpon the* 51. Psalme of Dauid.

¶ I haue added this meditation folowyng vnto the ende of this boke, not as parcell of maister Caluines worke, but for that it well agreeth with the same argument, and was deliuered me by my frend with whom I knew I might be so bolde to vse & publishe it as pleased me.

¶ The preface, expressing the passioned minde of the penitent sinner.

The hainous gylt of my forsaken ghost
So threates, alas, vnto my febled sprite
Deserued death, and (that me greueth most)
Still stand so fixt before my dasled sight
The lothesome filthe of my disteined life,
The mighty wrath of myne offended Lorde,
My Lord whos wrath is sharper than the knife,
And deper woundes than dobleedged sworde,
That, as the dimmed and fordulled eyen
Full fraught with teares & more & more opprest
With growing streames of the distilled bryne
Sent from the fornace of a grefefull brest,
Can not enioy the comfort of the light,
Nor finde the waye wherin to walke aright:

So I blinde wretch, whome Gods enflamed ire
With pearcing stroke hath throwne vnto ẏ groũd,
Amidde my sinnes still groueling in the myre,
Finde not the way that other oft haue found,
Whome cherefull glimse of gods abounding grace
Hath oft releued and oft with shyning light
Hath brought to ioy out of the vgglye place,
Where I in darke of euerlasting night
Bewayle my woefull and vnhappy case,
And fret my dyeng soule with gnawing paine.
Yet blinde, alas, I groape about for grace.
While blinde for grace I groape about in vaine,
My fainting breath I gather vp and straine,
Mercie, mercie to crye and crye againe.

But mercy while I sound with shreking crye
For graūt of grace and pardon while I pray,
Euen then despeir before my ruthefull eye
Spredes forth my sinne & shame, & semes to saye
In vaine thou brayest forth thy bootlesse noyse
To him for mercy, O refused wight,
That heares not the forsaken sinners voice.
Thy reprobate and foreordeined sprite,
For damned vessell of his heauie wrath,
(As selfe witnes of thy beknowyng hart,
And secrete gilt of thine owne conscience saith)
Of his swete promises can claime no part:
But thee, caytif, deserued curse doeth draw
To hell, by iustice, for offended law.

This horror whē my trēbling soule doth heare,
When markes and tokens of the reprobate,
My growing sinnes, of grace my senslesse cheare,
Enforce the profe of euerlastyng hate,
That I conceiue the heauens king to beare
Against my sinfull and forsaken ghost:
As in the throte of hell, I quake for feare,
And then in present perill to be lost
(Although by conscience wanteth to replye,
But with remorse enforcing myne offence,
Doth argue vaine my not auailyng crye)
With woefull sighes and bitter penitense
To him from whom the endlesse mercy flowes
I cry for mercy to releue my woes.

And then not daring with presuming eye
Once to beholde the angry heauens face,
From troubled sprite I send confused crye,
To craue the crummes of all sufficing grace.

With

With foltring knee I fallyng to the ground,
Bendyng my yelding handes to heauens throne,
Poure forth my piteous plaint & woefull sound,
With smoking sighes, & oft repeted grone,
Before the Lord, the Lord, whom synner I,
I cursed wretch, I haue offended so,
That dredyng, in his wrekefull wrath to dye,
And damned downe to depth of hell to go,
Thus tost with panges and passions of despeir,
Thus craue I mercy with repentant chere.

A Meditation of à penitent sinner, vpon the 51. Psalme.

Haue mercie vpon me (o God) after thy great merci

Haue mercy, God, for thy great mercies sake.
O God: my God, vnto my shame I say,
Beynge fled from thee, so as I dred to take
Thy name in wretched mouth, and feare to pray
Or aske the mercy that I haue abusde.
But, God of mercy, let me come to thee:
Not for iustice, that iustly am accusde:
Which selfe word Iustice so amaseth me,
That scarce I dare thy mercy sound againe.
But mercie, Lord, yet suffer me to craue.
Mercie is thine: Let me not crye in vaine,
Thy great mercie for my great fault to haue.
Haue mercie, God, pitie my penitence
With greater mercie than my great offence.

And according vnto the multitude of thy mer-

My many sinnes in nomber are encreast,
With weight wherof in sea of depe despeire
My sinking soule is now so sore opprest,
That now in peril and in present fere,
I crye: susteine me, Lord, and Lord I pray,
With endlesse nomber of thy mercies take
The endlesse nomber of my sinnes away.

So

So by thy mercie, for thy mercies sake,
Rue on me, Lord, releue me with thy grace.
My sinne is cause that I so nede to haue
Thy mercies ayde in my so woefull case:
My synne is cause that scarce I dare to craue
Thy mercie manyfolde, whiche onely may
Releue my soule, and take my sinnes away.

cies do away myne offences.

So foule is sinne and lothesome in thy sighte,
So foule with sinne I see my selfe to be,
That til from sinne I may be washed white,
So foule I dare not, Lord, approche to thee.
Ofte hath thy mercie washed me before,
Thou madest me cleane: but I am foule againe.
Yet washe me Lord againe, and washe me more.
Washe me, O Lord, and do away the staine
Of vggly sinnes that in my soule appere.
Let flow thy plētuous streames of clensing grace.
Washe me againe, yea washe me euery where,
Bothe leprous bodie and defiled face.
Yea washe me all, for I am all vncleane,
And from my sin, Lord, cleanse me ones againe.

Wash me yet more from my wickednes, and clense me from my sinne.

Haue mercie, Lord, haue mercie: for I know
How muche I nede thy mercie in this case.
The horror of my gilt doth dayly growe,
And growing weares my feble hope of grace.
I fele and suffer in my thralled brest
Secret remorse and gnawing of my hart.
I fele my sinne, my sinne that hath opprest
My soule with sorrow and surmounting smart.
Drawe me to mercie: for so oft as I

For I knowledge my wickednes, and my sinne is euer before me.

Presume

Presume to mercy to direct my sight,
My Chaos and my heape of sinne doth lie,
Betwene me and thy mercies shining light.
What euer way I gaze about for grace,
My filth and fault are euer in my face.

Againste thee onelye haue I sinned, & don euill in thy sight.

Graunt thou me mercy, Lord: thee thee alone
I haue offended, and offendyng thee,
For mercy loe, how I do lye and grone.
Thou with allpearcing eye beheldest me,
Without regard that sinned in thy sight.
Beholde againe, how now my spirite it rues,
And wailes the tyme, when I with foule delight
Thy swete forbearing mercy did abuse.
My cruell conscience with sharpned knife
Doth splat my ripped hert, and layes abrode
The lothesome secretes of my filthy life,
And spredes them forth before the face of God.
Whō shame frō dede shamelesse cold not restrain,
Shame for my dede is added to my paine.

That thou mightest be founde iust in thy sayinges, and maiest ouer come when thou art iudged.

But mercy Lord, O Lord some pitie take,
Withdraw my soule from the deserued hell,
O Lord of glory, for thy glories sake:
That I may saued of thy mercy tell,
And shew how thou, which mercy hast behight
To sighyng sinners, that haue broke thy lawes,
Performest mercy: so as in the sight
Of them that iudge the iustice of thy cause
Thou onely iust be demed, and no moe,
The worldes vniustice wholy to confound:
That damning me to depth of during woe
Iust in thy iudgement shouldest thou be found:
And from deserued flames releuyng me

Iust

Iust in thy mercy mayst thou also be.

For lo, in sinne, Lord, I begotten was,
With sede and shape my sinne I toke also,
Sinne is my nature and my kinde alas,
In sinne my mother me conceiued: Lo
I am but sinne, and sinfull ought to dye,
Dye in his wrath that hath forbydden sinne.
Such bloome and frute loe sinne doth multiplie,
Such was my roote, such is my iuyse within.
I plead not this as to excuse my blame,
On kynde or parentes myne owne gilt to lay:
But by disclosing of my sinne, my shame,
And nede of helpe, the plainer to displaye
Thy mightie mercy, if with plenteous grace
My plenteous sinnes it please thee to deface.

For loe, I was shapen in wickednes, and in sinne my mother cōceiued me.

Thou louest simple sooth, not hidden face
With trutheles visour of deceiuing showe.
Lo simplie, Lord, I do confesse my case,
And simplie craue thy mercy in my woe.
This secrete wisedom hast thou graunted me,
To se my sinnes, & whence my sinnes do growe:
This hidden knowledge haue I learnd of thee,
To fele my sinnes, and howe my sinnes do flowe
With such excesse, that with vnfained hert,
Dreding to drowne, my Lorde, lo howe I flee,
Simply with teares bewailyng my desert,
Releued simply by thy hand to be.
Thou louest truth, thou taughtest me the same.
Helpe, Lord of truth, for glory of thy name.

But lo, thou haste loued trueth, the hidden and secrete thinges of thy wisedome thou haste opened vnto me.

With swete Hysope besprinkle thou my sprite:
Not such hysope, nor so besprinkle me,

Sprinkle

me, Lorde, with hisope and I shal-be cleane: washe me and I shal-be whiter then snow.

As law vnperfect shade of perfect lyght
Did vse as an apointed signe to be
Foreshewing figure of thy grace behight,
With death and bloodshed of thine only sonne,
The swete hysope, cleanse me defyled wyght.
Sprinkle my soule. And when thou so haste done,
Bedeawd with droppes of mercy and of grace,
I shalbe cleane as cleansed of my synne.
Ah wash me, Lord: for I am foule alas:
That only canst, Lord, wash me well within.
Wash me, O Lord: when I am washed soe,
I shalbe whiter than the whitest snowe.

Thou shalt make me beare ioye and glad-nesse, ad the bones which thou hast broken shal reioyse

Long haue I heard, & yet I heare the soundes
Of dredfull threates and thonders of the law,
Which Eccho of my gylty minde resoundes,
And with redoubled horror doth so draw
My listening soule from mercies gentle voice,
That louder, Lorde, I am constraynde to call:
Lorde, pearce myne eares, & make me to reioyse,
When I shall heare, and when thy mercy shall
Sounde in my hart the gospell of thy grace.
Then shalt thou geue my hearing ioy againe,
The ioy that onely may releue my case.
And then my broosed bones, that thou with paine
Hast made to weake my febled corps to beare,
Shall leape for ioy, to shewe myne inward chere.

Turne a-way thy face from my sinnes, and do a-

Loke on me, Lord: though trēbling I beknowe,
That sight of sinne so sore offendeth thee,
That seing sinne, how it doth ouerflowe
My whelmed soule, thou canst not loke on me,
But with disdaine, with horror and despite.
Loke on me, Lord: but loke not on my sinne.

Not

Not that I hope to hyde it from thy sight,
Which seest me all without and eke within.
But so remoue it from thy wrathfull eye,
And from the iustice of thyne angry face,
That thou impute it not. Looke not how I
Am foule by sinne: but make me by thy grace
Pure in thy mercies sight, and, Lord, I pray,
That hatest sinne, wipe all my sinnes away.

way all my misdedes.

Sinne and despeir haue so possest my hart,
And hold my captiue soule in such restraint,
As of thy mercies I can fele no part,
But still in languor do I lye and faint.
Create a new pure hart within my brest:
Myne eld can hold no liquour of thy grace.
My feble faith with heauy lode opprest
Staggring doth scarcely creepe a reeling pace,
And fallen it is to faint to rise againe.
Renew, O Lord, in me a constant sprite,
That stayde with mercy may my soule susteine,
A sprite so setled and so firmely pight
Within my bowells, that it neuer moue,
But still vphold thassurance of thy loue.

Create a cleane hart within me, O God: and renew a stedfast spirit within my bowels.

Loe prostrate, Lorde, before thy face I lye,
With sighes depe drawne depe sorow to expresse.
O Lord of mercie, mercie do I crye:
Dryue me not from thy face in my distresse,
Thy face of mercie and of swete relefe,
The face that fedes angels with onely sight,
The face of comfort in extremest grefe.
Take not away the succour of thy sprite,
Thy holy sprite, which is myne onely stay,
The stay that when despeir assaileth me,

Cast me not away from thy face, and take not thy holy spirit from me.

In

In faintest hope yet moueth me to pray,
To pray for mercy, and to pray to thee.
Lord, cast me not from presence of thy face,
Nor take from me the spirite of thy grace.

Restore to me the comforte of thy sauing helpe, & stablishe me with thy free spirit.

But render me my wonted ioyes againe,
Which sinne hath reft, and planted in theyr place
Doubt of thy mercy ground of all my paine.
The tast, that thy loue whilome did embrace
My chearfull soule, the signes that dyd assure
My felyng ghost of fauor in thy sight,
Are fled from me, and wretched I endure
Senslesse of grace the absence of thy sprite.
Restore my ioyes, and make me fele againe
The swete retorne of grace that I haue lost,
That I may hope I pray not all in vayne.
With thy free sprite confirme my feble ghost,
To hold my faith from ruine and decay
With fast affiance and assured stay.

I shal teach thy waies vnto the wicked, & sinnes shall be tourned vnto thee.

Lord, of thy mercy if thou me withdraw
From gaping throte of depe deuouring hell,
Loe, I shall preach the iustice of thy law:
By mercy saued, thy mercy shall I tell.
The wicked I wyll teache thyne only way,
Thy wayes to take, and mans deuise to flee,
And suche as lewd delight hath ledde astray,
To rue theyr errour and returne to thee.
So shall the proofe of myne example preache
The bitter frute of lust and foule delight:
So shall my pardon by thy mercy teache
The way to finde swete mercy in thy sight.
Haue mercy, Lorde, in me example make
Of lawe and mercy, for thy mercies sake.

O God, God of my health, my sauing God,
Haue mercy Lord, and shew thy might to saue.
Assoile me, God, from gilt of giltlesse blod,
And eke from sinne that I ingrowyng haue
By fleshe and bloud and by corrupted kinde.
Upon my bloud and soule extende not, Lorde,
Uengeance for bloud, but mercy let me finde,
And strike me not with thy reuengyng sworde.
So, Lord, my ioying tong shall talke thy praise,
Thy name my mouth shall vtter in delight,
My voice shall sounde thy iustice, and thy waies,
Thy waies to iustifie thy sinfull wight.
God of my health, from bloud I saued so
Shall spred thy prayse for all the world to know.

Deliuer me from bloud o God, God of my helth & my tong shall ioyfully talke of thy iustice.

Lo straining crampe of colde despeir againe
In feble brest doth pinche my pinyng hart,
So as in greatest nede to cry and plaine
My speache doth faile to vtter thee my smart.
Refreshe my yeldyng hert, with warming grace,
And loose my speche, and make me call to thee.
Lord open thou my lippes to shewe my case,
My Lord, for mercy Loe to thee I flee.
I can not pray without thy mouyng ayde,
Ne can I ryse, ne can I stande alone.
Lord, make me pray, & grãt whẽ I haue praide.
Lord loose my lippes, I may expresse my mone,
And findyng grace with open mouth I may
Thy mercies praise, and holy name display.

Lord, open thou my lippes, and my mouth shal shewe thy praise.

Thy mercies praise, in stede of sacrifice,
With thankfull minde so shall I yeld to thee.
For if it were delitefull in thine eyes,
Whereby mought thy wrath appeased be,

If thou haddest desired sacri-

Of

fice, I wold haue geuen thou delytest not in burnt offringes.

Of cattell slayne and burnt with sacred flame
Up to the heauen the vaprie smoke to send:
Of giltlesse beastes, to purge my gilt and blame,
On altars broylde the sauour shold ascend,
To pease thy wrath. But thy swete sonne alone,
With one sufficing sacrifice for all
Appeaseth thee, and maketh the at one
With sinfull man, and hath repaird our fall.
That sacred hoste is euer in thine eyes.
The praise of that I yeld for sacrifice.

The sacrifice to God is a trobled spirit: a broken and an humbled hart, o god, thou wilt not despise.

I yeld my self, I offer vp my ghoste,
My slayne delightes, my dyeng hart to thee.
To God a trobled sprite is pleasing hoste.
My trobled sprite doth drede like him to be,
In whome tastlesse languor with lingring paine
Hath febled so the starued appetite,
That foode to late is offred all in vaine,
To holde in fainting corps the fleing sprite.
My pining soule for famine of thy grace
So feares alas the faintnesse of my faithe.
I offre vp my trobled sprite: alas,
My trobled sprite refuse not in thy wrathe.
Such offring likes thee, ne wilt thou despise
The broken humbled hart in angry wise.

Shew fauour, o lord in thy good will vnto Sion, that th walles.

Shew mercie, Lord, not vnto me alone:
But stretch thy fauor and thy pleased will,
To sprede thy bountie and thy grace vpon
Sion, for Sion is thy holly hyll:
That thy Hierusalem with mighty wall
May be enclosed vnder thy defense,
And bylded so that it may neuer fall
By myning fraude or mighty violence.

Defende

Defend thy chirch, Lord, and aduaunce it so,
So in despite of tyrannie to stand.
That trēbling at thy power the world may know
It is vpholden by thy mighty hand:
That Sion and Hierusalem may be
A safe abode for them that honor thee.

of Hierusalem may be bylded.

Then on thy hill, and in thy walled towne,
Thou shalt receaue the pleasing sacrifice.
The brute shall of thy praised name resoune
In thankfull mouthes, and then with gentle eyes
Thou shalt behold vpon thine altar lye
Many a yelden host of humbled hart,
And round about then shall thy people crye:
We praise thee. God our God: thou onely art
The God of might, of mercie, and of grace.
That I then, Lorde, may also honor thee,
Releue my sorow, and my sinnes deface:
Be, Lord of mercie, mercifull to me:
Restore my feling of thy grace againe:
Assure my soule. I craue it not in vaine.

Then shalt thou accept the sacrifice of righteousnesse, burnt offringes and oblations. then shall they offre yonge bullockes vpon thine altare.

FINIS.

Of the markes of the children of God, and of their comforts in afflictions (*STC* 23652) is reproduced here, by agreement, from the copy at the Huntington Library. The size of the text-block is 119 × 56 mm.

Page 73: The word under the blot is 'that'.

OF
The markes of the chil-*dren of God, and of their* comforts in afflictions.

To the faithfull of the Low Countrie.

By Iohn Taffin.

Ouerseene againe and augmented by the Author, and translated out of French *by* Anne Prowse.

Rom 8.16.

The spirit beareth witnes to our spirit that we are the sonnes of God. If we be sonnes, then are we also heires, the heires of God and ioynt heires with Christ: so that we suffer together that we also may be glorified together.

AT LONDON,
Printed by *Thomas Orwin,*
for *Thomas Man.*
1590.

To the right Honorable *and vertuous Ladie, The* Countesse of War-*wicke.*

FOrasmuch as it hath pleased almightie God of his infinite goodnesse, to giue vnto the glorious Gospell of his eternall sonne, so long & prosperous successe in this our Countrie; it is now time (right Honorable and my verie good Ladie) for euerie one that is a true professor of the same, all carnall perswasions of humane reason deluding the soule being set aside, to prepare our selues to the day of trial. For although it pleaseth God sometimes, for the gathering of his Church, to giue vnto it as it were *Halcyon* daies: yet common it is not, that it should any long time continue in rest and pleasure. Nay, by the word of GOD wee know, & by experience sometimes of our selues (her Maiesties royall person not excepted) and now of our neighbours round about vs we see, that the Church of God in this world, as it euer hath bin, so must it euer be vnder the crosse. And therefore if wee will bee compted of the Church indeede, and glorie in that excellent name of a Christian, let vs knowe assuredlie, that vnto vs, euen vnto vs (that haue so long liued in rest and pleasure, if wee be the children of God) in some sort and measure a triall must come. For, if God chastise euerie sonne whom he receiueth, and euery member of Christes body must be fashioned like vnto the head, if the afflictions of this world are manifest tokens to the children of God, of his fauour and loue towards them, and sure pledges of their adoptiõ: how can we looke, or how can we desire to bee exempted

ted from this common condition of God his owne children and houshold? To this end therefore (right Honorable Ladie) I haue translated this little booke, first to admonish some (who for lacke of experience, neuer feeling other daies than these full of peace and quietnes) that they learne to applie vnto themselues whatsoeuer they heare or reade of the triall of GOD his children, least falselie imagining it to appertaine either to the times that are past, or to other Nations, it fall sodainlie vpon them as a theefe in the night, & they be destitute of all hope and comfort. Secondlie, to awake others abounding both in knowledge and other graces, whom notwithstanding, satan (by the deceaueable lusts & vaine pleasures of this wicked world) hath so rockt a sleepe, that they seeme almost, as they that are diseased with the Lethargie, to haue forgottē both themselues, their holie calling and profession. Last of all, to comfort an other sort, whome it hath pleased GOD so to presse downe with sorrowes, and to exercise with the continuall afflictions and calamities of this mortall life, as no times seeming fauourable vnto thē, they can scarse receiue the words of any comfort. And because your Honor hath been of long time, not onlie a professour, but also a louer of the trueth, whom the Lord (exalting to an higher place of dignitie than many other) hath set vp, as it were a light vpō an high candlesticke, to giue light vnto manie, I haue especiallie dedicated vnto your Honour this my poore trauaile, humblie beseeching the Lord to make it no lesse comfortable to your Honour, and to those that shall reade it, than it hath been vnto me who haue translated it. Euerie one in his calling is bound to doo somewhat

what

what to the furtherance of the holie building; but because great things by reason of my sex, I may not doo, and that which I may, I ought to doo, I haue according to my duetie, brought my poore basket of stones to the strengthning of the walles of that Ierusalem, whereof (by grace) wee are all both Citizens and members. And now to returne to those whō experience hath not yet taught, and whom prosperitie will not suffer to awake: I earnestlie beseech them both in the Lord, no longer to deceiue themselues with vaine imaginations, neither to suffer their hearts so to be tied to earthlie vanities, that they should despise or neglect those things that cā truely make them happie indeed. When it shall please GOD to open their eyes to discerne betweene heauenlie and earthly, betweene things transitorie, and things euerlasting, I know they will of themselues bee ashamed of this their negligence. For what are all the pleasant things of this world, which most bewitch the minds of men, if they be compared with heauenlie and eternall things? If statelie & sumptuous buildings do delight; what building is so statelie and glorious as newe Ierusalem? If riches; what so rich as that, whose pauemēt is of pure gold, whose foundations and walls of precious stones, & gates of orient pearles? If friends, kinsfolke and neighbours; what Citie so replenished as this, where God himselfe in his Maiestie, Iesus Christ the head of the Church in his glorie, & all the holie Angels, Patriarchs, Prophets, Apostles and Martirs do dwel together in happinesse for euer? If honor; what honor comparable to this, to be the seruant and child of so mightie a King, and heire of so glorious a kingdome; where neither

time

time doth consume, nor enuie depriue of honour, nor power of aduersarie spoyle of glorie, that is endles & incōprehensible? If then there be no comparison betweene things heauenlie and things that are earthlie, and no man can attaine to the things that are heauenlie, but by the same way that Christ himselfe attained vnto them; which was by the crosse: why (casting off all impediments that presseth downe) doo we not runne on our course with cherefulnes and hope, hauing Christ so mightie a King, for our Captaine & guide, who (as the Apostle saith) for the glorie that was set before him, indured the crosse, and despising the shame, sitteth now at the right hand of the throne of God? How slowe and dull of heart are wee, if as *Esau*, (who for a messe of pottage sold his birthright) wee are contented for a small and short pleasure in this wic-

ked

ked world, to leese that incomparable and euerlasting glorie, which Christ the sonne of GOD with so great a price hath purchased for vs. The Lord giue vs wisedome to vnderstand, & grace to heare his voice while it is saide to day, that when daies and nights & times shall cease, wee may (without time) enter into his ioye and rest which neuer shall haue end. The Lord euer preserue your Honor; and adde vnto a multitude of happie yeares spent in his feare, a continuall increase of al spiritual graces to his glorie, and your endles comfort.

Your Honors in the Lord

most humble *A.P.*

To the faithfull of the Low Countrie.

T is not without reason (right deare and worship-full bretheren) that the Church of Christ is called militant vpon earth: and compared as well to a woman in trauaile of child from the beginning of the world, as to a ship vpon the sea tossed with tempests, and to a field tilled, vpon which the plowe is drawne to cut it. The present estate of the Church exercised by so manie dissipations, assailed so mightelie by continuall warres (the mother and nurse of all calamities) and afflicted by reuolts, by Libertines, by people prophane, and by so many heretiques, is to vs a liuelie mirrour, a manifest seale, and an example good to be marked. Now, as the infirmitie of the flesh which dieth not in the verie children of God, but at their death, taketh from thence, and from other matter, occasion of temptations most dangerous, and many assaults: so the bounden

due-

duetie & affection which I beare towards you, driueth me to testifie vnto you the feruent desire which I feele continuallie in my heart, of your comfort, constancie and perseuerance in the way of saluation. For this cause it is that in my voiage frō Germanie *I made this little treatise* Of the markes of the children of God, & of their consolations in their afflictions: *the which (being GOD be thanked returned) I was willing, with the aduise of my brethren and fellowes in the holie Ministerie, to put to light & dedicate vnto you, to the end that reading it you might knowe and feele more and more the incomprehensible grace of GOD towards you, by the testimonies of your adoption, and the full assurance of the certaintie of it: and that in the middest of your so long and heauie afflictions, you might bee partakers of the vnspeakable comforts which GOD setteth forth to his children in his word: whereby also you feeling your selues truelie happie, you maie constantlie perseuer in his holie trueth and obedience of his will, aspiring with contētment and ioy of the holie Ghost to the inioying of that kingdome of glorie, the right*

and

and possession whereof is purchased for you, and kept in your head Iesus Christ. Finalie, I pray God with all my heart to shewe me this fauour, that this my little labour may bee acceptable vnto you, and that it will please him to blesse it, by the efficacie of his holie spirit, to your comfort and saluation, and to the aduancement of the Kingdome of our Lord Iesus Christ: Harlem *15. September 1586.*

Your humble brother and seruant in Christ:

Iohn Taffin Minister of the holie Gospell in the French Church at *Harlem*.

The matters that are handled *in this Treatise.*

10 Of

OF

Of the markes of the chil- dren of God, and of their *consolations in their afflictions.*

To the faithfull of the Low Countrie.

Of the great and incomprehensible felicitie of the euerlasting life promised to the children of God.

Cap. 1.

SAint *Paul* hath verie aptlie set forth vnto vs the incomprehensible excellencie of the felicitie of the childrẽ of GOD, saying, *That the eye hath not seene, the eare hath not heard, neither hath it entred into the heart of man, what things God hath prepared for those that loue him.* According to this sentence, Saint *Augustine*, tending to the same butt, saith of the

1.Cor.2.9.

Aug. Enarrat. 2. Psal. 26. Tom. 8. goodnes of grace: *Let your hearts goe beyond all that you are able to comprehend, and stay not your selues at the greatnes and excellencie of it which you imagine: but say, yet this is not it; for if it were it, it could not enter into thy thought and heart.* This happines then cannot bee comprehended by vs according to the greatnes and excellencie of it, 2. Cor. 5. 1. so long as wee dwell in these earthlie 1. Cor. 13. 9 mansions, where we knowe God but in part and darkly. Notwithstanding, seeing the same Apostle addeth, that 1. Cor. 13. 12. the holie Ghost who searcheth the most deep things of God, hath giuen 1. Cor 2. 10. vs some reuelation: Seeing also he praied to God for the *Ephesians*; That Ephe. 1. 18. he would open the eyes of their vnderstanding, that they might knowe, what is the hope of their vocation, and what are the riches of the glorie of his inheritance among the Saints: we should be too vnthankful to God, and enemies of our owne comfort, if wee should make curtesie or refuse to vnderstād that, which it pleaseth him to reueale vnto vs by his word. Now,

in

in it this felicitie is oftentimes signified by the promise of life euerlasting, and, not without reason. For in our felicitie, two poynts may and ought speciallie to bee considered: first, the greatnes and excellencie of the good thing: secondlie, the long continuance and surenes of it. Now, both the one and the other is noted by these words, *life euerlasting*: For by life is signified the greatnes of the felicitie, and by euerlasting, the infinite length of it. As touching life, wee may consider three degrees as wel in the bodie, as speciallie in the soule. The first degree of life as touching the soule, is ment by this peace of conscience, and ioy of the holie Ghost which wee receiue and feele, being reconciled to God in Iesus Christ. And this peace and beginning of life, surmounteth al vnderstanding, as Saint *Paule* doth witnes, & God his children doo feele. And indeed it is a thing rauishing our soules with ioye vnspeakable, when GOD maketh the brightnes of his face to shine vpon vs: As also *Dauid*

Life euerlasting comprehendeth the felicitie of the childrē of God.

Three degrees of life to the body and to the soule.

The first degree of life.

Rom. 5. 1.

Philip. 4. 7.

Psalm.80. sheweth, whẽ he asketh so oft of God this grace, for a full measure of all felicitie. As touching the bodie, the first degree of life lieth in this, that the afflictions of it be not onlie mitigated, & made light by this life of the soule reconciled to God, and feeling ioye
Rom.8.27. through the brightnes of his counte-
Heb.12.6. nance, but also are conuerted (being the fruits of the loue of God towards vs) into saluation and glorie. The se-
The second degree of life. cond degree of life may bee considered in the seperation of the soule and the bodie, the which improperlie (as touching the faithful) is called death. For euen as touching our bodies, although they goe to rot in the earth, yet being then deliuered, and free from all sicknes, from hunger, thirst, heate, cold, and from a thousand other torments, which of their nature are a kind of death, they goe to rest in
Esay.57.1. their beds, as *Esai* saith; and being deliuered from their labours and tra-
Apoca.14.13. uailes, they are blessed, as Saint *Iohn* saith. And this rest proceeding from the fauour of God, cannot properlie

be

be called death, but is to them a kind of life. But speciallie the soule thẽ entreth into the possesion of the second degree of life. For being deliuered from the bodie, she is carried vp by the Angels into the bosome of *Abraham*, and into Paradise with Iesus Christ, exempted then from ignorance, from incredulitie, frõ mistrust, from couetousnes, ambition, enuie, hatred, feare, terrour, lustes, and from all other pasions, vices and corruptions which are deadlie in thẽ, which also bring forth the fruites of death. And contrariwise, is then fully sanctified, victorious, and assured against Satan, Hell, sinne and all other enemies: waiting after that, with great ioye, for the accomplishment of her glorie in the resurrection of her bodie. The third degre, shall bee at the glorious comming of Iesus Christ, when our bodies being awaked out of their sleepe, they shall rise againe all renued, bodies incorruptible, spirituall and immortall, yea fashioned like to the image of the glorious bo-

Luk. 16.22. Luk. 23.43

The third degree of life.

1. Cor. 15. 42.

Philip. 3.21

die of Iesus Christ: And so being ioy-
1.Thess.4. ned together againe to their soules,
17. they shall be together caught vp into
Ephe.4.10. the clowdes before our Lord Iesus
Ioh.14.2.
Ioh.17.24. Christ in the ayre, and exalted aboue
all the heauens, into the house of God
1.Thess.4. our father. Then also shall be the ac-
17. complishmēt of the life of our soules
reunited to their bodies, being together where Iesus Christ is, and with
him, as members of his bodie, his
brethren, and his spouse, vnited to
him, & by him, to God the fountaine
of life. And by this vnion inioying a
communitie in all his goods, and of
1.Pet.1.4. this incorruptible inheritance, which
can neither faile nor fade away, reserued for vs in heauen. Then shall God
Reue.21.4. wipe all teares from our eyes, & death
shall be no more, neither shal there be
any sorrow, crie or trauaile any more.
All these old things shall be gone a-
way: God shall make all things new.
Reue.7.14. Then shall we be before the throne of
God, and shall serue him night and
day in his Temple, and shall be led by
the Lambe to the liuing fountaines
of

of waters. Then shall be the day of our Reue.19.7.
mariage with the Lambe, when being
clothed with pure & bright raiments,
wee shall sit at his mariage banquet.
Then shal we be like vnto the Angels.
If our bodies shall shine then as the Matth.22.
Sunne, what shall the brightnes of 30.
our soules be? Then our pilgrimage Matth.13.
being finished, we shall be indeed the 43.
citizens of this heauenlie and holie Bern. meditation. 9.
Ierusalem, which shall bee all of pure
gold like vnto the cleere glasse: ha- Reue 21.
uing the foundations of the wall gar- 18.
nished with pretious stones: whereof also the twelue gates, are twelue
pearles: which hath no need of the
Sunne, nor of the Moone to shine in
it, because the brightnes of God shall
be the light of it, and the Lambe him
selfe shall be the candle of it. O how
happie shall the citizens be, that shall
liue in such a Citie? See then what
good things are signified by life euerlasting, and the three degrees of it.
But Saint *Paul* lifteth vs vp yet higher
into the contemplation of this life
which wee shall inioy after the resur-

 rection.

1.Cor.15. rection. Then, saith Saint *Paule*, Iesus
24. Christ shall giue vp his kingdome vnto God his father, as if he should say: Father, behold those whom thou hast giuen to me before the foundation of the world: they were lost, & thou diddest send me to saue them: I haue redeemed them with my bloud; thou hast appoynted me King ouer them: they are my kingdome which I haue gotten, and which I haue so guided and gouerned, that hauing sanctified and deliuered them from all their enemies, I haue brought, giuen and presented thē vnto thee, that hauing as touching my selfe, accomplished the worke & charge which thou haddest enioyned me, frō this time forth, thou maiest be king raigning immediatlie in them, and filling them with all happines and glorie. Then shall there be no creature either in heauen or in earth, that shall haue any domination or Lordship. There shall bee
1.Cor.15. neither King nor Prince, neither Ma-
28. ster nor Lord. There shall bee neither father, mother, husband nor wife.

There

There shall be neither Prophet, Doctor, Minister nor Pastour. There shall be neither riches, nor estates. All the enemies also of Iesus Christ shall bee destroyed for euermore, death being swallowed vp into victorie, and Satan with his angels, and all the reprobate being cast into the bottomlesse pit. Contrariwise, the Elect being fullie sanctified, shall bee lifted vp both in bodie & soule aboue all the heauens. The worke of Christ shall be finished. And all being done. The verie same offices which Christ hath receiued, & shall exercise for the accomplishment of our saluation, to be a King, a Priest, and a Prophet, and to sit at the right hand of God, shall cease, but so, as the fruites and the incomprehensible benefits gotten by thē vnto the church, shal euer abide to his euerlasting glorie. But what shall that be then? God the Father, the Sonne, and the Holie ghost, one onlie God shall be immediatlie all thinges, both in this man Christ, and in all vs the members of his bodie. The Godhead (I say) shall

Reue.21.6.

be

be in the man Iesus Christ and in vs, King, Prince, father, riches, life and glorie. To be short, all things, & such a heape of happines and felicitie, that as sundrie vessels cast into the sea are full of water, so as they can neither want, nor haue more: So this sea of Diuinitie being all things in vs al, we shall be filled and satisfied with life & glorie, so as we can neither want, nor receiue more. Then shall we not onlie

Psal.34.9. tast how sweete our God shall be, but we shall be filled and throughlie satisfied with his sweetnes most won-

Cipri. de asce. Christi 1.Cor.15. 28. derfull. Then shall the sonne himselfe be subiect to the father, to wit, as touching his humanitie: but that shall be for the increase of his glorie, and our felicitie. For the sonne of man a-

August. lib. 80. *quaest.* 69. *& lib. de trinit.* 1. *cap.* 8. biding still vnited to the sonne of God, and then ceasing the gouernement which he shall haue vntill the resurrection, God shall in such sort be in this sonne of man, and in vs, that the maiestie and brightnes of the diuinitie then raigning immediatlie, shall cause the difference between the

diui-

diuinitie of Christ, and his humane Ihe.17.22.
nature subiect vnto it to appeare. But Phil.2.7.
as the principall glorie of the sonne of man, is to be vnited vnto the sonne of God in one person, and that this his diuinitie shall be for the most part as it were, hid vntil that day, and that then it shall bee fullie reuealed: how much more the diuine maiestie of the sonne of God, shall cause the subiection of the sonne of man to appeare, so much the greater shall appeare the glorie of this sonne of man vnited in one person to the Godhead then raigning in his full maiestie and glorie. As (if a mā may find any thing neuer so little to represent this high mysterie) wee may consider, that the felicitie and glorie of the brethren of Gen.47.
Ioseph was so much the greater, that by the greatnes of *Ioseph*, exalted to the gouernment of *Ægypt*, they were subiect vnto him, and there appeared a great difference between *Ioseph* and his brethren, not by the diminishing of them, but by the increasing of *Ioseph*, his brethren hauing this happi-

nes

nes and honor, to be the brethren of *Ioseph*, ſo much more great and honorable, by how much, the greatnes of the maieſtie & glorie of *Ioseph*, made their ſubiection more to appeare. And this is it that may in ſome ſort be noted in the church. For although that now, her ſubiection and the difference appeare betweene her, gathered and compoſed of ſinfull men, hauing their ſanctification and their life of their head Ieſus Chriſt: and betweene him verie GOD, and perfect man ſitting at the right hand of God the father almightie: yet as then, the more great the glorie of Chriſt ſhall appeare, ſhewing himſelfe immediatlie with his diuine maieſtie in his brightnes: ſo much the more clearelie ſhall the ſubiection and difference of the Church appeare, not by diminiſhing the happines and glorie of it, but by the increaſe of the glory of her head, brother and bridegrome: The Church hauing this happines & honor, to be, and ſtil to abide vnited vnto Chriſt, making with her this new

man

man, whereof Saint *Paule* ſpeaketh, Ephe.2.15.
yea ſo much the more happie & glorious, by how much the excellencie
of the maieſtie and glorie of Chriſt,
the ſonne of man with vs, ſhall exceed
in greatnes, being vnited to the ſonne
of God, ſhining then with the Father
and the Holie ghoſt, one onlie GOD
in his diuine maieſtie. Hereof alſo it
followeth, that our chiefe felicitie
ſhalbe to behold this glorie of Chriſt.
And indeed this is that benefite and
happines which he asked for vs of
God his father, ſaying: Father, my
deſire for thoſe whome thou haſt gi- Ioh.17.24.
uen me, is, that they bee where I am,
and that they may ſee my glorie. And
what glorie? That we ſhould ſee him, 1.Ioh.3.2.
as he ſhall bee in maieſtie incomprehenſible as touching his Godhead,
and conſequentlie in ſoueraigne glorie as touching his humanitie vnited
to this diuine maieſtie. Behold alſo
how this ſhall be accompliſhed which
is written, that wee ſhall ſee God face 1.Cor.13.
to face for the accompliſhmēt of our 12.
felicitie. Which that we may the better

Ioh.15.11. ter comprehend, we must finallie con-
Ioh.16.24. clude, that the fruit thereof, shall bee
Matth.25. this, ioy full and perfect, which Christ
21. hath promised vs, promising further, to make vs enter into the ioye of our Lord. Saint *Augustine* in a certaine meditation (which is inded both holie and heauenlie) sheweth verie excellentlie, how great this our ioy shall be, and that ioy of our Lord which we shall enter into. Hauing discoursed of the euerlasting felicitie of the children of God, thus he saith. O heart humane, poore & needy, O hart exercised with miseries, & almost cōsumed of thē, what should thy ioy be, if thou haddest the full inioying of the aboūdāce of these good things? Aske of thy soule if thou were capable of the ioy, which thou shouldest feele of one such felicitie. But if besides, any other whō thou louest as thy selfe, should inioye the same happines with thee, surelie this superabounding ioy which thou shouldest feele of thine own happines, should it not be twise doubled, for the glorie & the ioy of him whō thou lo-

Aug. in manuel. cap. 35.

uest

uest as thy self, & for whose happines, thou shouldest bee as ioyfull as for thine owne happines? Now, if there were two, three, yea a great nūber inioying the same happines with thee, whom also thou louedst as thy selfe, thou shouldest feele as much ioy for the happines of each of them, as for thine owne happines. What then shall be in this perfect charitie, when wee shall loue all the blessed angels, and all the elect, louing euerie each one of them euen as our selues, and being no lesse ioyfull of the felicitie of each of them, than of our owne? Surelie if neuer a one of the elect shall be capable of his owne ioy for the greatnes of it, how shall he bee capable of so manie ioyes for the happines of so manie of the elect, for whom he shall feele as much ioy, as for his owne? Loe what it is Saint *Augustine* saith. But yet how much shall this ioy be augmented for the happines, felicitie and glorie of this elect of God, in whome wee our selues haue been elected, who hauing died for the elect, shall sanctifie, pre-

serue

serue and lift them vp into heauen to the inioying of this felicitie? who is not onlie man holie and iust, but also true God, especiallie beholding him in his glorie, to bee vnited in one person to the Godhead then shining in his Maiestie. Surelie if wee, louing other elect as our selues, should haue as much ioy of the happines of each of them, as of our own, what shall be the ioy that we shall receiue of the happines and glorie of this soueraigne Elect Iesus Christ, whom by good right we should loue more than our selues? See then more than a sea of ioy proceeding from the happines of the seruants of God. Let vs now vnderstand the great deapth of ioy which we shall feele, entering into the ioye of our Lord. The cause why wee should loue

Bernard in tract. de diligendo deo.

God (saith Saint *Bernard*) is God him selfe. And the measure which wee ought to keepe in this loue, is to loue him without measure, and so, infinitlie. But according to that wee knowe

1. Cor. 13. 12.

him, we loue him. But now we knowe him, but in part, and as it were in

darknes; euen so very little and obscure is the loue which we beare him. But when wee shall knowe him as he is, wee shall loue him according as he is. What shall our loue bee towards him then, when Iesus Christ hauing 1.Cor.15.24.
giuen ouer his kingdome to God his Father, God the Father, the Sonne, and the Holie ghost one onlie God, 1.Cor.15.28.
shall bee all things, in this man Iesus Christ, and in vs? and when wee shall knowe him as hee is, beholding the brightnes of his face, and his Godhead then raigning immediatly in vs, & filling vs with all happines? Without doubt this contemplation of the glory of the diuine maiestie shal bring forth in vs an infinite loue towards God. Now (to returne to the meditation of Saint *Augustine*) if according to that we loue each one, wee should reioyce of his happines. Then as in this blessed felicitie each one of vs shall loue God without comparison, more than himselfe, and more than all the Angels and elect with vs: so shall we feele more ioy without com-

parison of the blessednes and glorie of God, than of our owne, or of al the Angels and the elect with vs. And if then wee shall loue God with all our heart, with all our soule, with all our vnderstanding: yet so as al our hart, al our vnderstanding, and all our soule shall not be capable of the excellencie of this loue: Surelie wee shall so feele ioy with all our heart, with all our vnderstanding, and with all our soule, as yet all our heart, al our vnderstanding and all our soule shall not bee able to comprehend the fulnes of this ioye. Howsoeuer it bee then, that this full ioy, yea more than full, through the greatnes of it (whereof all our hearr, all our vnderstanding, & all our soule shall not be capable) cannot enter into vs: It shall remaine that we, (filled with the sea of ioye of the felicitie of the Angels, and of all the elect) shall enter into this great deapth of ioye proceeding from the contemplation of the glorie of our God. And this shalbe the ioy of the Lord, into which
Matth.25.21. all his faithfull seruants shall enter.

Now,

Now, when this felicitie so great, and ioy incomprehensible, shall indure so manie yeares as there bee drops of water in the sea, or graines of sand in the whole earth, yet should not this be a perfect happines. For howsoeuer the continuance shall seeme to vs infinite, yet the end will once come. And indeed the drops of water, and the graines of the sand are numbred before God. But this our felicitie and ioy shal last without end. Such shall bee the life euerlasting: As also Saint *John* saith, we shall raigne in heauen world without end. We shall bee the kingdome of that immortall king whom *Esai* calleth the father of eternitie, who hath promised life and immortalitie to those that shall beleeue the Gospell. Also death shall then bee swallowed vp into victorie. The author and prince of life, hauing vanquished the diuell, who had the rule ouer death, shall make vs partakers of the life that is euerlasting. And as we shall be vnited to the fountaine of life, so shall it run in vs eternallie.

Of the eternitie of the life to come

Apoc.22.5.
1.Tim.1.17.
Esai.9.6.
2.Tim.1.10.
1.Cor.15.45.
Act.3.15.
Heb.2.14.
Apoc.21,6

For as the fountain of this life which we shall inioy, hath no beginning, so the life that proceedeth from it, shall haue no end. The mercie of GOD (saith S.*Bernard*) is from eternitie to eternitie vppon those that feare him; from eternitie, because of the predestination; to eternitie, because of the glorification: The one hath no beginning, the other hath no ending. This therefore shall be a happines incomprehensible for the greatnes, and infinite for the eternitie of it. Behold
Ioh.16.22. also how we shall then inioy a ful and perfect ioy, which shal neuer be taken away from vs. Now, this life is promised and assured to all the children of God, in as much as they are heires of
Rom.8.17. God the fountaine of life, & coheires
Psal.36.10. and members of Iesus Christ, who is
Ioh.14.6. the way, the trueth, and the life: who
Ioh.3.15. also hath so oftē protested, that who-
Ioh.6. soeuer beleeueth in him, he hath life euerlasting. Let vs conclude then, that the children of God are truelie and onlie blessed, being assured to inioye this great and incomprehēsible hap-

pine

pines of life euerlasting, which is purchased, promised, and kept for them in Iesus Christ our Lord.

How we shall knowe that we are the children of God.

Cap. 2.

OF this conclusion it followeth, that there is no greater ioy or contentmēt in this present life, or any thing more sure or more necessarie for the happie ouercomming the difficulties of it, thā to knowe and feele that wee are the children of God. For this foundation being laid, wee ought to bee assured that whatsoeuer shall happen vnto vs, can bee none other than the blessing of a father, and so consequentlie a meane, aide, and way disposed by his prouidence, either to leade vs vnto life euerlasting, or to increase our glorie in it. True it is, that GOD onelie knoweth his owne, whom hee hath 2. Tim. 2. 19.

chosen before the foundation of the world to bee his children. Yet there are two principall meanes by which he giueth vs to vnderstand who are his children: the one is outward, by markes visible vnto men: the other is inward by testimonies, which he that is the child of GOD feeleth in himselfe. The outward marke lieth in this, that we be mēbers of the church of Christ. Now, wee call that the church of Christ, in which the word of God is trulie preached, the Sacramēts are purelie ministred, and one onelie God is called vpon in the name of his onelie sonne Iesus Christ. First, this Church is often called the kingdome of heauen, because that by it, wee enter in thether; so that it is (as it were) the suburbs or the gate of it. Whereof it followeth, that being the true members of the Church, we are in the way and forwardnes to enter, & make our abode in heauen. It is also called the house of God, to giue vs to vnderstand, that those that abide there, are by good right accompted the childrē

2. markes of our adoption.

Of the outward mark

Matth. 13.

Mat. 21. 13.

Ephe. 2. 19.

and houſehold of God. Furthermore, when after wee haue proteſted in our Creede, that wee beleeue the holie Church vniuerſall, we adde the communion of Saints, the forgiuenes of ſinnes, the riſing againe of the bodie, and the life euerlaſting: is not this to aſſure vs that thoſe that are the members of the Church, haue a communitie in all theſe treaſures and goods of it, and conſequently that they are the children of God, and inheritours of euerlaſting life? According vnto this S. *Luke* alſo ſaith reſolutlie, that God ioyned vnto the Church thoſe that ſhould be ſaued. The which is confirmed by the Prophet *Ioel* ſaying, that there ſhall be ſaluation in Sion. And S. *Paule* himſelfe ſticketh not at all, to call thoſe that are the members of the Church, the elect of God. But yet ſo much the more to reſolue vs, let vs conſider the marks of the true church touched here before. The firſt is, the pure preaching of the word of God. Now, Ieſus Chriſt ſaith, my ſheepe heare my voyce, and they follow me:

Act.2.47.

Ioel.2.32.

1.Theſ.1.4

Ioh.10.27.

shewing thereby very manifestly, that
this is one marke to bee the child of
Ioh.8.47. God, to heare the voyce of his sonne
Iesus Christ: As also he saith in ano-
2.Cor.5.18 ther place, that he that is of God, hea-
Ephe.6.15. reth the voyce of God. And indeed,
Act.14.3. Act.20.32. seeing that the preaching of the Go-
Act.13.26. spell is called the ministerie of recon-
Act 5.20. ciliation, the Gospell of peace, the
Phil.2.15. word of grace, of saluation and of life,
(as without doubt, God by the mini-
sterie of his word, presenteth Reconciliation, peace, grace, saluation and
life): So they that are the members
of the Church, heare and receiue the
word, shew therein, that they are partakers of all these benefites, and consequentlie, the children of God. The
second mark of the Church consisteth
in the Sacraments of Baptisme and of
the Lords supper. As touching Baptisme, it is a seale & sure warrant that
Act.22.5. the sinnes of those that receiue it are
Rom.6.4. washed away by the bloud of Christ:
Tit.3.5. that they are ingrafted and incorpo-
Gal.3.27. rate into his death and resurrection:
that they are regenerate, & that they
haue

haue put on Iesus Christ. Whereof it followeth, as S. *Paule* affirmeth, that they are the children of God. The like assurance of our adoption is giuen vs in the Lords supper. For if the bread and the cup, which are giuen to the members of the Church, are the communion of the bodie and of the bloud of Iesus Christ: it followeth that in this communió of Christ, they haue the foode and life of their soules. And that consequentlie, as the children of GOD, they shall obtaine life euerlasting, according to the protestation of Christ. He that eateth my flesh, and drinketh my bloud, he hath euerlasting life. The third marke of the Church of God, is the inuocation of the name of God, in the name of that onlie one Iesus Christ. Now, as all the seruice of God is oftentimes signified by this inuocation: So Saint *Luke* noteth the faithful and children of God by this description, that they call vpon the name of the Lord. As on the contrarie side, it is said of the reprobate, that they do not call vpon the

Gal. 3. 26.

1. Cor. 10. 16.

Ioh. 6. 54.

Psal. 14 4.
Gen. 12. 7.
Act. 2. 21.
Act. 9. 14.

Psal. 14. 4.

the name of God. And indeede when
the members of the Church ioyne
together and lift vp their praiers vnto
Matth.6 9. God, saying: Our Father which art in
heauen: and so calling him father, by
the commandement of Christ, they
may well assure themselues that God
doth acknowledge them for his children, and that he wil make them feele
the fruit of their praiers, according to
the promise of Christ, that whatsoe-
Mat.18.19. uer they shall with one consent aske
of GOD, it shall bee giuen them. By
this that is aboue said, it manifestlie
appeareth, how euerie member of the
Church may and ought to assure him
selfe to be the child of God, and to acknowledge all other members of the
Church with him in like manner to
be the children of God. If any alledge
that we may thus accompt such a one
for the child of God, who possiblie
is an hypocrite, and may after shewe
himselfe a reprobate, we answere, that
such discourses are contrarie to charitie, so much recommended vnto vs
1.Cor.13. by Saint *Paule*, noting amongst other
pro-

properties of charitie, that she thinketh not euill, or is not suspitious, but that she beleeueth all things, and hopeth all things. Wee ought then to hold the members of the Church, for the children of GOD. vntill that departing from it, or discouering their hypocrisie, they shewe themselues reprobates. Furthermore, as GOD would that al those to whō he vouchsafeth to bee father, should acknowledge the Church for their mother: so let vs not doubt, but being borne againe, and nourished in the Church our mother, we may call God our father, and abiding vnited to the familie of the mother, let vs not doubt but that wee bee the heires of the father. Thus much for the outward markes.

Now let vs come to the inwarde markes. As to the blind and deaffe the opening of their eyes and eares is needfull, clearelie to see and heare the voyce of him that speaketh: So being of our owne nature both blind and deaffe as touching vnderstanding, the holie spirit is hee, that openeth our eyes

Of the inward marke of our adoption.

eyes and eares,to comprehend the reuelation of our adoption,and to feele
in our harts the aſſurance of it,ingen-
dring in vs faith, which is as it were
the hand, by which wee apprehend
this great benefite : whereof alſo the
fruites and effects as well of the holie
ghoſt dwelling in vs, as of the faith
that is in vs, are the principall & moſt
aſſured markes,to giue vs knowledge
of our adoption. According where-
Rom.8.16. vnto,Saint *Paule* ſaith,that the Holie
ghoſt giueth teſtimonie to our ſpirits
that we are the children of God,ſo as
hauing receiued this ſpirit of adoption,wee crie with all aſſurance,Abba
1.Ioh.3.24 father.This is it alſo which S.*Iohn* teacheth vs,ſaying:we know that he abi-
deth in vs,by the ſpirit which he hath
1.Ioh.4.13 giuen vs. Alſo,By this we knowe that
we dwell in him,and he in vs, becauſe
he hath giuen of his ſpirit vnto vs. In
like manner the Apoſtle S. *Paule* af-
Rom.5.1. firmeth, that by the peace and quietnes which we feele in our conſciences
before GOD in the free forgiuenes
of our ſinnes by the bloud of Ieſus
Chriſt,

Christ, we shewe and prooue that wee are iustified by faith, and so the children of God. Wherein to confirme vs, he saith in another place, that after wee haue beleeued, wee are sealed by the holie spirit of promise, which is the earnest penie of our inheritance, Ephe.1.13. vntill the redemption of the possession purchased to the praise of his glorie. First he sheweth there, that faith is as it were the seale whereby the Holie ghost imprinteth in our hearts for our assurance, that wee are the children of God. Furthermore, as in a thing that is bought there is somtimes giuen an earnest penie, to wit, some part of the monie agreed on, as well for the beginning of the paimēt, as by consequent, for the assurance that the bargaine shall be held firme: so the holie ghost, who by faith ingēdreth peace and ioye in the hearts of the faithfull, is the earnest penie, assuring vs, by this beginning, of the spirituall blessings which God promiseth to his children, that he holdeth vs for his possession, purchased to the praise

of

of his glorie, and that at the length he will gather vs into the full inioying of the inheritãce of heauen. Hereunto it is alſo, that that goodly gradatiõ leadeth vs, which is propoſed of the ſame
Rom.8.28. Apoſtle, ſaying: Thoſe whõ God hath before knowne, thoſe hee hath alſo predeſtinate to be made like vnto the image of Ieſus Chriſt: and thoſe whõ he hath predeſtinate, he hath alſo called, and thoſe whom he hath called, he hath alſo iuſtified: and thoſe whõ he hath iuſtified, thoſe he hath alſo glorified. For all will confeſſe, that thoſe that are elected and predeſtinated to be made like vnto the image of Ieſus Chriſt, are the children of God, as alſo they, who in his eternall counſel and decree are glorified. Now they, who being lightened with the knowledge of the Goſpell, beleeue that their ſinnes are waſhed away by the bloud of Ieſus Chriſt through his ſatiſfaction, and ſo are called and iuſtified, are elected and glorified before God, as S. *Paule* teacheth here: it followeth then, that they are the chil-

dren

dren of God. And this is so certaine, that the Apostle, opposing the will & power of GOD, against all impediments, addeth: If GOD bee on our side, who shall bee against vs? S. *Bernard* teacheth the selfe same thing verie aptlie, saying: we are certain of the power of God to saue vs: but what shall we say of his will? who is he that knoweth whether he bee worthie of hate or of loue? who is he that hath knowne the will of the Lord? or who hath bin his counseller? It behoueth that herein faith helpe vs, and that trueth succour vs. That that, which is hid concerning vs in the heart of the father, may bee reuealed vnto vs by the spirit, and his spirit testifying vnto vs, may perswade vs that wee are the childrē of God; that he perswade it vs, I say, in calling and iustifying vs freelie by faith, which is as it were a meane or passage from the predestination of GOD to the glorie of the life euerlasting. The same thing is it which S. *Augustine* meaneth, saying: Wee are come into the way of faith,

let

Rom 8.30.

Bern. ser. 5. in dedicat. templi.

Aug Hom. in Ioan. 35.

let vs hold it constantlie, it shall leade vs from degree to degree euen vnto the chamber of the heauenlie King, where all the treasures of knowledge and wisedome beeing hid, wee may learne and behold the reuelation of our election. From hence proceedeth yet another fruite seruing vs for a marke, to assure vs more & more that we are the children of God, when we loue God, and our neighbours for his sake: whereof also followeth the hatred of euill, and an earnest desire to render obedience to God. For if it
1.Ioh.4.19 be so as Saint *Iohn* saith, that our loue to God commeth of this, that he hath first loued vs: The loue that we beare vnto him, is a testimonie that he loueth vs. As also Iesus Christ maintaineth and sheweth, that by the signes
Luk.7.47. of loue, which the sinful woman gaue him, God loued her greatly, and had forgiuen her manie sinnes. So the brightnes of the Moone is a certaine argument that the Sunne ministreth whollie to her, for otherwise she hath no brightnes at all. And in sommer,

the

the heate that is felt in the stones set against the Sunne, is a signe that the Sunne shineth vppon them. Of our owne nature and first generation we are vnprofitable to all goodnes, and inclined to al euill, as Saint *Paule* very largelie setteth forth vnto vs writing to the *Romanes*. If then on the contrarie wee walke in the feare God, giuing our selues to his seruice, and occupying our selues in all good works: is not such a chaunge a testimonie of our regeneration, and consequentlie of our adoption? The tree is knowne by his fruit, saith Iesus Christ: If then wee beare the fruit of iustice, holines and of charitie, wee are trees planted in the garden of God by his holie spirit, and so consequentlie the childen of God. Charitie, saith Saint *Iohn*, is of God, and he that loueth, is borne of God, and knoweth God. As then the heate and light of a coale is a signe that it hath fire: and as the mouing and actions of the bodie are certaine signes, that it liueth, & that the soule is within it: so the testimonie of the

Rom. 3. 10.

Matt 7. 17.

1. Ioh. 4. 7.

holie ghost in our hearts, the peace & quietnes of our consciences before GOD, feeling our selues iustified by faith; this loue towards God and our neighbour, this chaunge of our life, and desire to walke in the feare and obedience of God, are assured tokens of our adoption : as also this, that we are members of the Church of Christ hearing his word, participating with the holie Sacraments, and calling vppen God in the name of Iesus Christ, are testimonies that wee are the children and houshold seruants of God, and heires of eternall life.

How euerie member of the Church ought to applie vnto himselfe the tokens of it, to assure himselfe of his adoption and saluation.

Cap. 3.

Now, although the tokens before mentioned are certaine to assure vs that wee are the children of God : yet there are two

sorts

ſorts of temptations, which aboue all other tend to ſhake vs. The one proceedeth of our ſelues, either for lacke of applying to our ſelues the teſtimonies, which God giueth to the members of his Church to aſſure them of their ſaluation: or through the feeling of a want (as wee thinke) but rather, of the ſmalnes or weaknes of thoſe tokens of adoption here aboue alledged. The other temptation commeth vnto vs frō ſome other where, and cōſiſteth ſpeciallie in two points. To wit, in the reuolt of ſome hauing made profeſsion of the true religion: and in the grieuous and long afflictions which are ordinarie to thoſe that followe the doctrine of the Goſpell. Now, as there is nothing of greater importance than the ſaluation of the ſoule: ſo there is nothing that doth more grieuouſlie afflict and trouble the tender conſciences deſirous of eternall life, than the doubts & feares not to be the child of God, getting to themſelues hereby ſuch ſorowes and anguiſhes, as none are able to comprehend, but those that haue themselues felt and tried them. To helpe then, to the consolation of the soules so daungerouslie, and so mightelie afflicted : first it is to be noted, that this disease cometh to many of this, that they pretend to resolue themselues of their saluation, examining themselues whether they be worthie to be the children of God or no. And as there is none that is, or can bee worthie, so this is at the last to turne doubts into despaire. Other discourse, whether they bee of the number of the elect, and whether their names bee written in the booke of life, to wit, if God loue them, and hold them for his children. But it is not so high, that we must mount, but in the doctrine of the Gospell it is, where we should search the reuelation hereof, and resolue our selues if God hath loued vs, if he doo loue vs, and will hold vs for his childrē in Iesus Christ. For as a man if he be of credite, maketh the hid thoughts of his heart to bee knowne by speaking : euen so

God,

God, who is the trueth it selfe, reuealeth vnto vs, by the preaching of the Gospell, his counsell, and his will touching our adoption & saluation: and confirmeth this reuelation by the vse of the holie Sacraments. But we must note, that this reuelation of the will of God in the Gospel comprehēdeth first two poynts: to wit, that there is perfect & entire saluation in one only Iesus Christ, and that the meane to obtaine it, is to beleeue in him. Moreouer, when this Gospell is preached vnto vs, GOD reuealeth vnto vs yet two poynts more: first, that he will make vs partakers of this saluation in Christ. Secondlie, that he will haue vs to beleeue the testimonie that he hath giuen vs of this his will, to the end that we might bee saued. Now, the difficultie of beleeuing lieth in the perswasiō of these two last points, which notwithstanding are certaine and true. Behold, saith S. *Iohn*, the testimonie of God, which he hath giuen vs of euerlasting life, and this life is in his sonne, he saith not onelie that 1. Ioh. 5. 11

the life is in his sonne, but saith further, that he giueth vs this life, & that the Gospell is the witnes. And hauing protested a little before, that he
1.Ioh.5.10 which beleeueth not this testimonie of God, maketh him a lier: he sheweth sufficientlie that he will that wee should beleeue it. The Apostle to the *Hebrues* passeth further, & saith; that
Heb.6.17. God, willing to shew the immutable stablenes of his counsell to the heires of the promise, interposeth himselfe by an oth, that by two things immutable in which it is impossible that God should lie, wee might haue firme consolation, wee, I say, who haue our refuge to the hope that is set before vs, the which we hold as the ancker of the soule sure & stable, pearcing euen into the sanctuarie of heauen, where Iesus Christ our forerunner is entered for vs. By this he teacheth vs first, that when we heare the Gospell, wee ought to hold for certaine, that the counsell of God which was hid in his heart, touching his will to saue vs, and to take vs for his children, is there

made

made manifest vnto vs. Secondly, that he will that wee beleeue it, seeing he confirmeth it by two things immutable, in which he cannot lie, to wit, his word and his oth, to the end that wee might haue firme consolation, which cannot bee in vs, if we beleeue not. Moreouer, he calleth the reuelation of his counsell, the hope set before vs. Speaking then to vs, he would that we should haue hope: yea and he will that this reuealing of his counsell should be vnto vs a sure anchor of the soule, to shewe, that as a ship is held fast by the anchor, that it might not be carried away of the wind: so God would that this reuealing of his coũsell by the doctrine of the Gospell should hold vs fast, & assure vs against all doubts of our adoption, yea and to pearce euen into the verie heauens with assurance, whereof our forerunner Iesus Christ hath taken possession both for himselfe, and for vs. See then one place shewing very expreslie, that when thou hearest the Gospell, God declareth and reuealeth vnto thee,

 that

that it is his will to saue thee by his sonne Iesus Christ. And to this end he will further, that thou beleeue it And
Ro.10.17. indeed when S. *Paule* saith, that faith commeth by hearing the Gospell, he sheweth that thou canst not beleeue, except that thou heare. Now, faith is a knowledge and certaintie, that it is the will of God to saue thee, & to take thee for his welbeloued child in Iesus Christ. Then it followeth, that the Gospell which is preached vnto thee, and which thou hearest, conteineth the reuealing and testimonie: first, that it is the will of God to saue thee by Christ: secondlie, that thou shouldest beleeue this testimonie which he giueth thee, that thou maiest haue euerlasting life. Who now is he, that ought or can doubt? Seeing also he is not content to say in generall, he
Ioh.3.36. that beleeueth hath euerlasting life: but he commandeth thee to beleeue.
Mar.1.15. Beleeue (saith he) the Gospell. Also, This is his commandement, saith S.
1.Ioh.3.23. *Iohn*, that wee beleeue in the name of his sonne Iesus Christ. Now, to beleeue

leeue the Gospell, or in the name of Iesus Christ, is not onelie to beleeue that there is saluation in Christ, and that he that beleeueth in him hath life euerlasting. For the diuell himselfe beleeueth that, and yet he beleeueth not the Gospell, neither in the name of Iesus Christ. But this is to beleeue, that he hath saluation in Christ for thee, as *Esai* saith: A child is Esay. 9. 5.
borne to vs, a sonne is giuen to vs. And so speaketh the Angell to the shepheards. This day is borne vnto Luk. 2. 11.
you a sauiour. Also, that it is the will of God that thou shouldest be his child, and thou shouldest beleeue it so. The which thing the diuell cãnot beleeue for himselfe: neither is the Gospell offered vnto him. Now, when GOD reuealeth vnto thee his good will and loue towards thee, wherefore doubtest thou? He is true, he neither will, nor can either lie or deceiue. And whẽ he commaundeth thee to beleeue it, must thou examine thy selfe whether thou bee worthie or no? Thou art bound to obey, & so to beleeue, that

he doth loue thee, and that thou art his child by Christ. Call to mind that which is writtē, whosoeuer beleeueth
Ioh.3.16. (what manner a one, or whosoeuer it be) he hath life euerlasting. Neither is it presumption so to beleeue, and that constantly, but it is to him obedience most acceptable. And indeed it is an honour that he requireth of thee to beleeue his word, and so to put to thy seale that he is true. It is verie true that in preaching the Gospell, hee
Ioh.3.39. saith, not, I am come to saue Simon Peter, Cornelius the Centurion, Marie Magdalen, and so of others. He nameth no man by his name that was giuen him by men, either at their circumcision, or at their baptisme, or otherwise: for so might we yet doubt of our saluatiō, thinking that it might be spokē not of vs, but of some other that should haue the same name. But when thou hearest that Iesus Christ is
Matt.9.13. come to saue sinners: either renounce
1.Timo.1.15. the name of a sinner, or confesse that hee speaketh to thee, and that hee is come to saue thee. Make then boldly this

this conclusion: Iesus Christ is come to saue sinners, I acknowledge my owne name, for I am a sinner: therefore he is come to saue me. And also when he saith: Come vnto men all ye that trauaile & are heauilie laden, and I will refresh you: Thou must marke well these words, all ye; for seeing he saith, all ye, he speaketh to all those that trauaile and feele the heauy burthen of their sinnes. Wherfore shouldest thou doubt then, whether hee speake to thee? Conclude rather on this manner, seeing he saith, all ye, he speaketh then also to me, promising to comfort me. And to this purpose saith S. *Paule*, that there is no differēce of men before GOD, but the same who is Lord ouer all, is rich towards all those that call vppon him: Haue thou then recourse vnto him, and beleeue in him, & thou art assured that he will also be rich in mercie euen vnto thee. If there were two or three hundred inhabitants of some towne banished for some offence, and after a generall pardon should be published, that

Math. 11. 28.

Rom. 10. 12.

that all the baniſhed of ſuch a towne ſhould haue free libertie to returne thether, with all aſſurance to enter againe vppon all their goods and honors: ſuppoſe that thou wert one of thoſe baniſhed, and that he that hath giuen the pardon were a faithfull and true Prince: wouldeſt not thou beleeue, that thou wert comprehended in the pardon, although thy name were no more expreſſed, than the names of the other baniſhed, and that returning to the towne thou ſhouldeſt againe bee placed in thy goods? Now, we haue bin baniſhed from the
Gen.3.24. kingdome of heauen by the transgreſsion of Adam. Ieſus Chriſt dying for theſe baniſhed perſons, cauſeth a generall pardon to bee publiſhed by the preaching of the Goſpell, with permiſsion, yea with commandement to returne into heauen. He is a true King, yea the trueth it ſelfe: and the aboliſhing of this baniſhment, & the reentrie into heauē hath coſt him verie deere, euen the ſhedding of his
1.Pet.1.19. **moſt precious bloud.** What occaſion then

then hast thou to doubt of thy pardon,& returne into heauen? For, although thy Christian name bee not expressed; yet if thou be of the number of the banished, he speaketh to thee, behold thy name, thou art there comprehended. Beleeue that he speaketh in trueth, and that his wil is such towards thee, as he declareth to thee by his word. But let vs passe further to the Sacraments, which serue greatlie to resolue vs to beleeue that wee are the children of God. The Sacraments are (as it were) a visible word, representing the grace of the Gospel. But more then that, they are communicated to thee, and thou receiuest the. Is not this to put thee, as it were, into reall possession of thine adoption, and to giue thee assurance of euerlasting life? The Pastour preacheth vnto all, the grace of the Gospell in the name of Christ. But in thy Baptisme he directeth his speach to thee by name, to assure thee of the forgiuenes of thy sinnes, and of thine adoption, as S. *Paule* saith, that those

August. in Ioan. hom. 19.

that

Gal.3.27. that are baptised haue put on Christ,
26. and that so they are the children of God. And it is as if a Prince hauing called backe againe all the banished, amongst whō thou shouldest be one, calling vnto thee by name, amongst the other banished, by a letter sealed of thy pardon, and of reestablishing thee in thy goods. Should not this be to assure thee? As touching the holy supper, Iesus Christ, hauing published by his Minister, that his flesh is meate indeed and his bloud drinke, addeth,
Ioh.6.55. that whosoeuer eateth his flesh and
56. drinketh his bloud, he hath life euerlasting: He calleth thee among others to his table, and giueth thee of the bread and wine, namelie, to assure thy person, that he died for thee, and that he giueth thee his bodie & his bloud, yea himselfe all whole, and all his benefites, that thou shouldest bee with him, the child of God, and an inheritour of life euerlasting. If the diuell or thy conscience trouble thee, to doubt of thine adoption, assure thy soule against such a temptation, by the commu-

munication of the holie ſupper. Say boldlie, Satan, canſt thou denie that I haue been at the holie ſupper, & that I haue receiued bread and wine? I haue ſeen, touched and taſted it, thou canſt not denie it. Further, canſt thou denie that this bread and wine were giuen me for ſeales and ſure pledges of my communicating with the body and bloud of Chriſt? Saint *Paule* ſaith plainlie, that the bread which I haue receiued, is the communiō of the bo- 1. Cor. 10. 16.
die of Ieſus Chriſt. Seeing then thou canſt not denie, but that I haue receiued the bread and wine: and that the bread and wine are the communion of the body & of the bloud of Chriſt, I haue then communion with the bodie and bloud of Ieſus Chriſt, & thou canſt not denie it. True it is that there are ſome, who being outward members of the church, baptiſed in it, hearing the word, and communicating at the holie ſupper, ſhewe themſelues after hypocrites, declaring that they were neuer indeede the children of God. But wee cannot ſay therefore,

that

that the reuelation and teſtimonie of the will of God cõtained in his word, and ſealed by the Sacraments, are doubtfull or vncertaine. For GOD, who offereth his grace in his word, and hath ſealed it by the Sacraments, is faithful and ſpeaketh truelie, reuealing vnto vs and aſſuring vs that he will take vs for his welbeloued children in Ieſus Chriſt. And he can neither lie nor deceaue, as is alreadie said. But theſe are vnfaithfull men, who reiecting the teſtimonies of the will of GOD towards them, depriue themſelues by their incredulitie of
1.Ioh.5.10 the grace which was offered vnto thẽ, doing this diſhonor to Chriſt, to cõpt him a lier. As the Sunne then ceaſeth not to giue light and brightnes, although ſome man ſhutteth his eyes that he may not ſee it, nor bee lightened: and as meate ceaſeth not to bee good and nouriſhing, although it be receiued without profite of a ſtomack euill diſpoſed: So, if manie vnwilling to beleeue that the will of G O D is ſuch, as he hath declared by his word, reiecting

reiecting (by their incredulitie) the grace which GOD offereth them; should their incredulitie make thee call in doubt the trueth of God, and the testimonie of his good will towards thee? If some few among these banished, not trusting the pardon published by a true and faithfull Prince, doo him this dishonor to compt him as a deceiuer or lier: acknowledge thou that iustlie and by good right they remaine banished. But thou, seeing that faithfull Prince Iesus Christ hath sent to pronounce vnto thee a generall pardon, and namelie, hath giuen thee his letters sealed by the Sacraments, commaunding thee to beleeue, and promising thee, that it shall bee vnto thee according to thy faith: Assure thy selfe, that his will is Matt.9.29.
that thou shouldest be his child, and heire of euerlasting life. See how euerie one should assure himselfe, by the preaching of the Gospell, and the vse of the Sacraments, the true markes of the Church: that (being a member of it) he is the child of God: and con-

sequentlie, an inheritour of his euerlasting kingdome. True it is, that faith is the gift of GOD, yea proceeding from the operation of the mightie
Phili.1.29. power of his strength, as S. *Paule* spea-
Ephe.1.19. keth. And this is it which he maketh vs to feele in this difficultie of apprehẽding (by an assured faith) so manie, so cleare and so certaine testimonies of his good will towards vs, touching our adoption. It is therefore needfull that he worke farther with vs by his holie spirit, which (without ceasing) asking of him in the name of Iesus Christ, we are assured by his promise, that he will giue vs, and that, so ioyning with the power and efficacie of his spirit, the preaching of his Gospell, and the vse of the Sacraments, he will giue vs grace to applie vnto our selues (by a true and liuelie faith) the testimonies which he hath giuen vs of our adoption, to our saluation and euerlasting life.

How although the markes of our adoption bee in vs but small and feeble, yet wee ought, and may assure our selues that we are the children of God.

CAP. 4.

I See well (will some say) that I haue iust matter to beleeue it: & therefore am I the more sory that I feele not faith in my self, to assure me without doubt that I am the child of GOD, which thing troubleth mee greatly, so as I feare least by this mine incredulitie, I reiect the grace of God. But vnderstand I pray thee for thy comfort, that there is great difference betweene vnfaithfulnes and weaknes of faith. The vnfaithfull man or infidell careth not for his saluation: or, reiecting the saluation which is in Iesus Christ alone, seeketh saluation other where. Contrariwise, the faithful desire saluation: he knoweth that his

The first temptation proceeding of the small feeling of our faith.

his ſaluation is in Ieſus Chriſt alone:
he ſeeketh it in him, and feeleth a deſire to increaſe in aſſurance, that he
hath ſaluatiō in Ieſus Chriſt, though
he doo not yet feele this peace & ioy
in the holie Ghoſt ſo manifeſtlie as
faith bringeth it forth at the laſt. Alſo
it is not written, he that feeleth, but
Iho.3.36. hee that beleeueth hath euerlaſting
Heb.11.1. life. And indeed, as faith is of things
Rom.8.23. that are not ſeene, ſo the vnderſtanding of it conſiſteth more in certaintie, than in apprehenſiō. In this complaint of *Dauid*, yea and of Chriſt
himſelfe: My God my God, why haſt
Pſal.22.1. thou forſakē me. We heare the teſti-
Mat.27.46. monie of faith by theſe wordes: my
God my God, but without apprehē-
ſion or feeling of fauour or ioy, as this
complaint, why haſt thou forſakē me.
ſheweth. Alſo our faith may bee ſo
ſmall and weake, as it doth not yet
bring forth fruites that may be liuelie felt of vs. But if ſuch as feele themſelues in ſuch eſtate, deſire to haue
theſe feelings: if they aske them of
God by praier. This deſire and praier
are

are testimonies that the spirit of God is in them, and that they haue faith alreadie. For, is such a desire a fruite of the flesh, or of the spirit? It is of the holie spirit, who bringeth it forth onlie in such, as he dwelleth in. He dwelleth then in them. In like manner, is not this praier the worke of the holy ghost in thē? For it is the holy ghost (saith S. *Paule*) which praieth for vs, Rom. 8. 25. and in vs, with grones that cannot be expressed. Againe, none can come to God by praiers, if he haue no trust in him. Then these holie desires and praiers, being the motions of the holie ghost in vs, are testimonies of our faith, although they seeme to vs small and weake. As the woman that feeleth the moouing of a child in her wombe, though verie weake, beleeueth and assureth her selfe that she is with child, and that she goeth with a liue child: so if we haue these motiōs, these holie affections and desires before mentioned, let vs not doubt, but that wee haue the holie ghost (who is the author of them) dwelling in vs,

and consequentlie that wee haue also faith. And we must vnderstand, that the faith of the children of God ceaseth not to bee a true faith, although they feele doubts, feares, & mistrusts. For if they delight not in such infir-
Rom.7. mities, to nourish them; but are sorrowfull and resist them, with desire to feele their saluation in Iesus Christ, behold a battaile in them: and betweene whom? Betweene the spirit and the flesh: betweene faith and mistrust. There is then in them faith assailed with doubts, and the spirit fighting against mistrust, and labouring to ouercome it. These doubts, mistrustings, and incredulities are the fierie darts which Satan throweth against our faith, the which bearing the blowes, as a buckler, as S. *Paule* saith: thrusteth them back and quen-
Eph.6.16. cheth them, so as they pearce not to the heart. What deuises or assaults soeuer the diuel make against vs, saith S. *Augustine*, so he occupie not the place of the heart where faith dwelleth, he is driuen backe. Incredulitie then

then assaulteth vs without, but woundeth vs not deadlie: It troubleth onlie, or so woundeth, as the stroake is yet curable. And such temptations and assaults are common to the most faithfull & excellent seruants of God. If wee consider the continuall course of the life of *Dauid*, there is no mirrour of faith better to bee noted than in him. And yet was not he assaulted with great feares and doubts? What cõplaint maketh he in the 77. Psalm? Hath the Lord forsaken for euer? will he no more shewe me fauour? Is his mercie cleane gone for euer? Is his promise come to an ende for euermore? Hath God forgotten to bee gracious? Hath he shut vp his louing kindnes in displeasure? And to conclude, he holdeth such a course, as a man desperate, saying: This is my death. Where was then in *Dauid*, the feeling of his faith? For al this he had not lost it. And indeed all these words were but representations of feare and dispaire assailing the faith that was in him, and fighting against it: As hee

Psal. 77. 8, 9 10, 11, vers.

ſheweth in other places verie plainly,
ſaying : My ſoule, why art thou caſt
Pſal 42.12. downe, why art thou ſo heauie with-
Pſal.43.5. in me? Put thy truſt in God, for I will
yet giue him thanks, for as much as he
is my manifeſt deliuerance (as it were
before my face) and my God. If theſe
teſtimonies of faith before mentioned ſeeme ſmall: how ſmall and dark
was the faith of the Apoſtles before
the reſurrection of Ieſus Chriſt? They
Mat 16.16 beleeue that Chriſt is the ſonne of
Iohn 6.69. God, the ſauiour of the world : but
Mat.17.23 yet they vnderſtand not that he muſt
Luke 9.45. die, and riſe againe: wherein notwith-
Luk 24.11 ſtãding lieth the principall reſt of our
Act.1.6. faith. Yea, and after his reſurrection
they (acknowledge him for a King)
imagined rather a carnall, than a ſpirituall kingdome. If their faith was
darke in their vnderſtanding : it was
alſo ſmall in their hearts, when they
were offended at Chriſt, and all for-
Mat.26 31 ſooke him : & Peter himſelfe renoun-
Mar.14.27. ced him. And yet we cannot ſay, that
Mar.14.50. they were without faith, though it
Mat.26.70 Mar.14.68. were then verie weake and ſmall. And
alſo

also when the ship being couered with Luk. 22.32
flouds they cried to Iesus Christ: say- Matt. 8.25.
ing, saue vs, we perish: he calleth them
not infidels, but men of little faith, &
fearefull: shewing that they had some
faith in them, though verie small, and
assailed with feare, wherein notwithstanding hauing recourse vnto him,
they were heard, and deliuered out of
daunger. For he came not to breake
the brused reede, nor to quench the
smoaking flax: As *Esay* foretold, shew- Esa. 42.3.
ing therby, that there are some of the Matt. 12.18
children of God, weake as a brused
reede, and hauing as little strength of
faith, as in steed of flaming, it smoa-
keth onlie. This smalnes and beginning of faith is verie aptlie noted by
S. *Paule*, saying: that the righteousnes Rom. 1.17.
of GOD is reuealed by the Gospell
from faith to faith. He sheweth that
there are degrees in faith, and that it
happeneth to vs in the reuealing of
the righteousnes of GOD, by which
we are iustified, as when we see one so
farre off, as with much a do wee know
him: but the neerer we approach, the
more

more cleerelie we discerne him. Manie of the children of God are like to that blind man, whose eyes Christ o-
Mar. 8. 29. pened, but so at the beginning, as he sawe men like trees, forthwith he recouered his sight, but yet troubled at the beginning, but afterward cleared. To bee short, he who in the person of his Apostles hath taught vs to pray
Luk. 17. 5. vnto God to increase our faith, sheweth that he hath children in whom it is weake, and hath neede of increase. Also the chiefe wisedome of the most perfect is to profite. And to this purpose wee must remember, that in all spirituall graces, there is nothing but beginnings and imperfections, in the most perfect, and most highlie exalted in this life. But that the perfection (to the which notwithstanding wee must alwaies tend) and the accomplishment shall be in heauen. To conclude, there are two effects or fruits of faith, to wete, the rest & peace of the conscience before God: and sanctification, which consisteth in the mortification of the workes of the flesh,

and

and newnes of life. Now, as the rest and peace of conscience proceeding frō faith, is a testimonie that it is in vs, so is also sanctification, and the desire to walke in the feare and obedience of God. And indeed, faith is the fountaine of good workes. If then, one of these fruites be languishing, the other sufficeth to assure vs that wee haue faith. As it is knowne that there is true and naturall fire, by the flame & the heate, which are two effects and operations of fire: but if the flame shall become weake, the heate shall suffice to assure vs, that it is naturall, and not a painted fire. In like manner, if this fruit of thy faith be weake, to feele peace and rest in thy conscience, and yet thou feelest the other effect of faith, to wete, a desire to the workes of the spirit, loue towards God, and desire to walke in his obedience: This fruit of thy faith is to thee a sure testimonie that it is in thee, though but smal and weake. But thou wilt say: what comfort or assurance of saluation can a faith so weak

and

and little giue me: I answere; It can assure thee of thine adoption. For so thou haue but one spark of true faith, thou art the child of God. Faith is of such a force, that (following the promise of God) one onelie graine of it,
Mat. 17.20 though neuer so little, laieth hold on Iesus Christ to saluation. Againe, it is properlie Iesus Christ which saueth vs, & not our faith: sauing in so much as it is the instrument, and as it were the hand by which wee take hold on Iesus Christ. Now, faith how little soeuer it bee taketh hold on Christ and receiueth him, not by halfes, but all whole: as an infant taketh and holdeth with his little hand a whole apple, though he doth it not so stronglie or surelie as a man. By the apple of our eye, though merueilous little, we see verie great mountaines, and the verie bodie of the Sunne, much greater than the whole earth: so our faith, though verie little, taketh and receiueth all whole Iesus Christ the sunne of righteousnes. He who (being in a darke tower) seeth not the light of the

the Sunne, but by a verie little hole, may notwithstanding assure himselfe, that the Sunne shineth vppon the tower, as well as he that seeth it by an open windowe, knoweth that it shineth vpon his house. Euen so although we are hindered by the cloudes of mistrust, that we cannot see the Sunne of righteousnes to shine vpon our soules in his brightnes: yet so that wee see but a little beame, wee know that the sunne of life shineth vppon vs, which assureth vs that we are the children of God. Also whosoeuer in this life shall haue the least faith among all the elect, shall yet inioye Iesus Christ all whole, and not a little or halfe saluation, but the full accomplished saluation of eternall life. For whosoeuer beleeueth in Iesus Christ, saith Saint *Iohn*, shall not perish, but haue life e- Iho.3.16
uerlasting. Now, as this ought greatlie to comfort vs in the weakenes of our faith, so ought it to bee a sharpe spurre to inforce vs to growe in faith, that feeling so much the more clearelie and liuelie the peace and ioye of our

our consciences, by the assurance that we are the children of God, wee may the more stronglie resist all temptations, and glorifie our God. There are others, who call their faith and adoption in doubt, saying: That true faith cannot be without good works. Now, I feele my selfe so miserable a sinner, that it maketh me to doubt of mine adoption. Indeed this is a thing greatlie to be lamented, that we render no better obedience vnto God, that there is in vs no greater zeale of his glorie, nor more feruent charitie towards our neighbours: and to be short, no better amendement of life. But if thou hast begun to hate & flee sinne, if thou feelest that thou art displeased at thy infirmities and corruptions: If hauing offended God, thou feele a sorrowe and griefe for it: if thou desire to abstaine: if thou auoidest the occasions: if thou trauailest to doo thine indeuour: if thou praiest to God to giue thee grace: All these holie affections proceeding from no other than from the Holie ghost,

2. Temptation throgh the smalnes of our sanctification.

Ia. 2. 17. 20.

ought

ought to be vnto thee so manie pledges and testimonies, that he is in thee: As also Saint *Paule* teacheth vs, saying: that as those that delight in the workes of the flesh, are of the flesh. So on the other side, those that delight in the workes of the spirit, are of the spirit. These holie desires then to the workes of the spirit, are testimonies of the spirit dwelling in thee. So as being thus led by the spirit of God, thou art the child of God, saith Saint *Paul*: And indeed seeing the children of *Adam* are naturallie inclined to all vices and corruptions, it is a marke of regeneration, & so of being the child of God, when contrarie to nature we are displeased with our infirmities, and fighting against them, wee desire and indeuour to fashion our selues according to the will of our GOD. God hath commaunded vs to loue him with all our heart, with all our vnderstanding, and with al our soule. Now, as we cannot know God in this life, but in part, and darklie, so we can not

Rom. 8. 5

Rom. 8. 14

Rom. 3. 10

Mat. 22. 37.

1.Cor.13. 9.12. not loue him but in part, yea verie little. The perfection is reserued for heauen as also S. *Augustine* saith: All the faithfull ought earnestlie to aspire to this, that they may once appeare before God pure and without spot. But for as much as the best and most perfect estate that we can attaine vnto in this present life, is no other thing, than to profite from day to day: then shall we come to this marke, when, after putting off this sinfull flesh, wee shall cleaue fullie to our God. Therefore also, as the same author saith, when men speake of the perfection of the children of God in this life: to this perfection is required the acknowledging of their imperfection. It is as well in trueth, as in humilitie that the Saincts acknowledge how imperfect they are. God deferreth the accomplishment of our holines and charitie vntill the life to come, to the end that this pride (which taketh force through the increase of vertue) should not ouerthrowe vs, but that walking in humilitie, God might accomplish

Aug. ad Bonif. lib. 3. c. 1. 7.

complish his mercie in pardoning vs, 2.Cor.12.9
his power in sustaining vs, and his truth
in sauing vs. And indeede there is nothing more weake, saith S. *Augustine*,
than the proude, nor more strong than
the humble: For as the proude, trusting
in himselfe, who is nothing but vanitie,
hath God his aduersarie, who resisteth
the proude; so the humble mistrusting 1.Pet.5.5.
himselfe, hath God for his strength and Iam. 4.6.
saluation. God indeede in his lawe requireth a perfect obedience. But that
which he looketh for of vs his children
in this life, consisteth more in the desire
to obey, than in the obedience it selfe. Rom 8.5
According whereunto hee saieth by his
Prophet *Malachi*, I will spare them, as Mal.3 17.
a father dooth his owne sonne that serueth him. If a child take paine to write
well, or to do as he should do anie other
seruice that his father hath commaunded him, although there be great want
both in the writing, and in the other
seruice; yet in bearing with him hee
praiseth him; and saieth, that hee hath
written well, hee had doone his duetie.
Godlines, the loue towardes God, and

the obedience, that we owe vnto him, is often signified by the feare of God, the
Psa.111.10 which also *Dauid* calleth the beginning of Wisedome. And those that haue this feare of God, are acknowledged & called the children of God. Then if thou feel such loue & reuerēce toward God, that thou feare to offend him, thou art
Psa.112.1 the child of God. But then thou fearest to offend God, when thou shunnest the occasions and inticements to sinne, and when hauing offended, thorough ignorāce, ouersight, or other infirmitie, thou feelest sorrow and displeasure, to raise thee vp againe, being resolued to sin no more, and praying to God that he will cōduct thee by his holy spirit, that thou maist walke constantly according to his
1.Iohn 3.9 worde. S. *Ihon* saith, that the children of God sinne not: not that they offend not God euery day, or that they commit not sometimes most greeuous offences,
2.Sam.11 as *Dauid* and Saint *Peter*: And as dai-
Mat.26.74 lie experience dooth too much conuict euerie one of vs. But he saith, that they sinne not, because they loue God, and are afraide to offend him, and doe not willing-

willingly giue themselues to doo euill: but haue sinne in such detestation, that they feele in themselues that conflict, which Saint *Paule* setteth foorth vnto Rom.7
vs in his owne person, in as much as they woulde doo the good which they cannot doo, and doo vnwillingly the euil which displeaseth them: whereof it followeth, as the Apostle concludeth, that if they doo that which they would not doo, it is no more they which do it, but sinne which dwelleth in them: which on the one side ought to giue the occasion to mourne and to crie wyth the Apostle, Alas wretch that I am, who shall deliuer mee from the bodie of this death? But on the other side they ought to feele the comforte which hee addeth, saying, I thanke my God through Iesu Christ. And wherefore? Rom.8.1
Because there is no condemnation to those, who thus fighting against the flesh, walke after the spirit, and consequently are in Iesus Christ. For the rest, when thou feelest a doubt of thine adoption through the want of rendering to God such obedience as thou oughtest,
 know

knowe, that Satan is at hand with thee
falſifying the goſpel in perſuading thee,
that thou ſhouldeſt bee ſaued by thy
workes; or willing to make thee blaſ-
pheme Ieſus Chriſt, in making thee beleeue, that thou mayeſt and oughteſt to
be (at the leaſt) in ſome part, a Sauiour
of thy ſelfe, and ſo a companion of Ieſus Chriſt. Anſwere to this temptatiō,
1.Tim.1. that thou arte a poore ſinner, but that
15 Matt.9.13. Chriſt came to ſaue ſinners, and that
Rom.8.5. there is ſaluation in none but in hym.
Rom 8.1. Furthermore, if thou feel a deſire to the
Rom.7.22 works of the Spirit, thou art of the Spirit, and there is no condēnation to thee,
as is ſaide. If thou delight, as touching
the inward man, in the obedience of the
commaundements of GOD, hee accepteth thee for holie and iuſt, receiuing this deſire to obey him, for an obedience acceptable vnto him. He accepteth his owne worke in thee, and pardoneth thee thine. Continue in this holie
deſire, fighting againſt the fleſh and the
world, ſtrengthening thy ſelf by feruent
praier to the Lord. And behold the certaine teſtimonies of thine adoption.

But

But thou wilt say, I haue of long time asked of God, and do daylie aske his holie Spirite, the encrease of faith and grace to be obedient vnto him; yet I feele no manner of fruite of my prayers. If GOD loued me, and accounted mee for his childe, woulde hee not heare mee? It is the same complaint, that in old time past *Dauid* made, saying: I am wearie of crying, my throat is hoarse, mine eies are failed, while I wait on my God. And in another place, My God, I crie by day, and thou answerest not, and by night, and I haue no rest. Now in saying he had no rest, he sheweth that he did continue in prayer. Also Iesus Christ exhorteth vs to this diligence, by the example or similitude of the importunate widdow, crying still vpon the wicked Iudge to do hir right, and at the last obtaining by her importunacie. And besides that, hee waketh vs vp, saying: Heare what the wicked Iudge saieth: Because shee troubleth mee, I will doe her iustice. And God which is your Father and Sauiour, who is iust and loueth righteousnesse, shall

3. Temptation, because the feeling of the fruit of our prayers is so long deferred, & because of the weakenesse of them.

Psa 69.4.

Psa,22.2.

Luke. 18.1

Psal.11.7

not hee heare the crie of his children
crying vnto him night and day? Verely
I saie vnto you, that hee will doe it,
Luke 11.5. and that quickely. Hee that went by
night to his neighbor to borow bread,
continuing still his request, though the
other alleadged many excuses, yet at
the length he obtained what he would.
Continue then in praying to GOD,
without discouragement. This perseuerance in prayer, is an euident and vehement testimonie of thy faith. For
that is not founde but in the children of
God, guided by his Spirite: especially
Luk. 11.13 seeing thou askest the holie Ghost,
whom Iesus Christ promised thee, thou
askest that, which by his promise is due
vnto thee, without doubt he will giue
it thee. And seeing thou askest the increase of faith, and grace to obey him,
thou askest that which he commandeth
thee to haue, and so that which he liketh
and is pleased withall, Be then assured that thou shalt be heard. Beholde,
Iohn 5. 14. sayth Saint *Iohn*, the confidence that
wee haue with GOD, that if wee
aske anie thing according vnto his wil,

he heareth vs, And if wee know that he heareth vs, whatsoeuer we aske, wee knowe wee shall obtaine the requests that we haue asked. His promises can not faile nor deceiue. Yea, bee thou certaine, that before thou hast ended thy prayer, hee hath heard thee, as *Esay* saith, For our God is a God that hear- Esa,65.24
eth prayers, sayth *Dauid*. But thou o- Psal.65.3
west him this honour to submit thy selfe to his wisedome as touching the time of feeling or receiuing the fruite of thy prayers. If Iesus Christ had healed the daughter of the Cananite Mat.15.22.
at the first petition, her Faith had not beene so kindled in her, nor so commended in the Church vnto the ende of the worlde. The fruites of all trees are not ripe in one daie. In some they doe ripen sooner, and men waite patiently for the other, which ripen in the latter season: *Zacharie* and *Elizabeth* Luke 1,13
thought that they had prayed in vaine, asking of GOD posteritie in their youth. And when they were olde, and without all hope for to obtaine it, the Angell of the Lorde saide vnto *Za-*

charie, Thy prayer is heard: not that prayer which hee made then, for he thought not nowe to haue issue, but the prayer which hee made long time before. That which is more, doe wee not aske of GOD manie graces, the which wee knowe well that wee obtaine, either in part, or in hope onlie? the enioying or full accomplishment whereof is deferred either vntill death, or euen vntill the day of the resurrection. In the Prayer of all Prayers taught by Iesus Christ, wee do aske of

Matth. 6.9 GOD that his name may be sanctified, his Kingdome may come, his will may bee doone in Earth, as it is in Heauen. And when shall wee see the full accomplished effect of this prayer, but in Heauen, when Christ hauing giuen vp his kingdome to GOD his father, wee shall loue him perfectlie, and praise him euerlastinglie? Furthermore, he oftentimes heareth vs, so as Saint *Augustine* saith: not according vnto our will, but as is most for our profite, giuing vs better thinges than those that wee expresselie aske. The

Iewes

Iewes desired the comming of the *Messias*, and asked it of God. He deferred it of long time: at the last hee sent him, but not such a one, as al (as it were) and the Apostles themselues looked for: Act.4.6.
to wete, victorious in battaile as *Dauid*, to deliuer them from the yoake of the *Romans*, triumphing in riches & worldlie glorie, as *Salomon*; but such a *Messias*, as obtaining victorie against the diuell, death, and sinne, hath established a spirituall kingdome in euerlasting life and glorie. Iesus Christ feeling and apprehending the terrible gulphes of the fearful wrath of God vpon him for our sinnes, prayed with strong cries & teares Mat.26.39
to God his Father that he might not enter into the deepe pit of death. The Apostle to the *Hebrewes* saith, that he was Heb.5 7.
heard: and yet notwithstanding he entred, and dranke the Cup of the wrath, and of death which the Father had giuē him. But he was heard, saith the same Apostle, as touching that which (in making his praier) he fered: to wit, frō being swallowed of death. In like manner, S. *Paul* praieth to God oftentimes that he 2.Cor.12.

would

would deliuer him from the Angell of Sathan that buffeted him, but GOD much better (as he himselfe confesseth) gaue him to vnderstand, that the power of God was made perfect in his infirmity: so as he protesteth, as it were enioying the frute of his praiers, thogh otherwise than he thoght, that from that time forth he would reioice in his infirmities, & woulde take delight in them, forasmuch as being weake in himselfe, he was strong in God. So wee will demaund manie times commodities concerning this life, as health, goods, parents, friends, or our country: and God depriuing vs of them, giueth vs spirituall graces, patience, faith, contentment in God, and other like: yea, and our prayer tending onely vnto the preseruation, and enioying such commodities appertaining vnto this life alone: GOD contrariwise depriueth vs of them, to keepe them for vs in heauen, and to giue vs euerlasting enioying of them, as when wee are depriued of them, being persecuted for his name. And that which more is, when wee

feele

feele weakenes in faith, negligence to heare the worde of GOD, coldnesse in charitie, impatience in our afflictions, and we hauing asked of God graces cõtrarie vnto these, feele no amendment: his wil is to make vs feele that these graces are the gifts of God, seeing we haue them not when we will, and that he wil keepe vs in humilitie by the feeling of our infirmities, and trie our patience & faith, in waighting patiently vntill hee make vs feele the fruite of our praiers. I thinke well (wilt thou say) that those that pray vnto God feruentlie and continue constantlie in such praiers, haue therin testimonies that they are the children of God, & are assured to be heard. But what comfort may I take therein, seeing my praiers are so colde, and with so litle feeling of zeale & faith required in them? But is it not in the name of Iesus Christ that thou prayest? And it is for the loue of his welbeloued Sonne, Ioh.16.23. our aduocate and mediatour, that God heareth vs, and not for the excellencie Exo.28.38. of our praiers. It is, as it were, by the mouth of Iesus Christ that we present

our

our praiers to God, to be sanctified by
him, and acceptable to God for his sake,
Mat.17.5. in whom he hath delight. Satan, the e-
nemie of our praiers, by the feeling of
this infirmitie, would make thee leaue
praying to thy God. Resist thē this tēp-
tation. Thinke that it is not a thing indifferent, or left in thy libertv, to pray to
Mat.6.9. God or not. God hath cōmāded thee to
1.Th.5.17. pray; thou owest him obedience; it is an
honour he requireth of thee, thou canst
not denie it him. God cōmandeth thee
Mat 22.37 to loue him with al thy hart. Wilt thou
say, I will not loue God at all, because I
loue him so coldly: I will help the poore
no more, because I cannot doo it with a
feruent charitie. To conclude, what infirmitie or coldnes soeuer thou feelest,
thou art bound to pray, and to continue
Ro.12.12. in thy dutie. In the mean time, acknowledge thy infirmitie, and in thy prayers
aske double pardon, first of thy sinnes
which thou hast committed before, secondly for this sinne, that thou prayest
to God so negligently. See how GOD
(supporting the infirmitie of thy prayers) will smell a sweete sauour of them,

as

as incense offered by our high Priest Iesus Christ, and shall make thee at last feele the fruite of thy praiers. Manie cōplaine of another infirmitie, that hardly they begin their praiers, but in stead of thinking of God, & of that which they aske of him, their minde is wandring otherwhere. And for this they are vexed and troubled: and in truth it is a great infirmitie, for the which we ought gretly to be displeased with our selues. Notwithstanding it is common to all the children of God in general. *Chrisostome* reproouing those of his time for this infirmitie, sheweth quickly the first originall, and after the remedie. Whence commeth this (saith he) that if we talke of warre, of merchandize, or of other things of the world, wee can discourse a great while without thinking of anie other thing, and so soone as wee set our selues to praye vnto God, our mindes wander? It is because the Diuel knoweth well, that in speaking of things of this world, thou doost him no hurt, & therefore he suffereth thee to talk at thy pleasure: but when he seeth, that thou

Psal.141.2.

Chrisost. Homil.of the Canaanit.Mat.15

settest

settest thy selfe vpon thy knees to pray to God, he knoweth that thou goest to procure that, which is against his heart, & to the ruine of his kingdōe. Therfore he thrusts himself in by & by, trobling & drawing thy thoughts hither & thither, to hinder the fruite of thy praiers. Say then to satan, who is hard by thee, and fighteth against thee; go behind me satan, for I must pray to my God. And if hee bee importunate, yet must thou pray to god to driue him away frō thee. So thinking to whom thou speakest, to wete, to the Maiestie of God; and how great things thou askest of him: be displeased with thy infirmity, fight against it, & lifting vp thy hands to heauen cōtinue in praier; and doo it so much the more couragiouslie and constantlie, for that satan feareth nothing more thā the praiers of the children of God; & showeth sufficiently in going about to troble and turn away their mindes to other things, that he feeleth himselfe hindred by their praiers, and that hee feareth the fruite of them. On the other side, if it happen that by affliction either of body

or

or of spirite, thou art so cast downe, that thou cāst not make a framed praier vnto God; bee not discouraged for that, for at the least thou canst desire thine owne health & saluation. There is neither sicknes nor yet tyrant that can let thee to desire: now, desire is praier before God, saith Saint *Augustine*; according whereunto *Dauid* saith, that God heareth the desire of the humble. Say Psal.10.17. thou then with *Dauid*; Lord, all my desire is before thee, and the sighs of my Psa.38,10. thoughts are not hid from thee. *Ezechias* King o *Iuda* in his affliction, could Esai.38.14. not distinctly pray vnto God, but chattered as a Crane or a Swallowe, and mourned as the Doue; yet so lifting vp his eyes on high, hee was heard. What prayer maketh the little Infant to his mother? Hee weepeth and cryeth, not beeing able to expresse what hee lacketh. The Mother offereth him the breast, or giueth him some other thing, such as shee thinketh his necessitie requireth. Much more then the heauenly father heedeth the sighes, the groanes, the desires and

tears

teares of his children: and dooing the office of a Father, he heareth them, and prouideth for them. There are some also that doubt of their adoption & saluation, because they feele not anie comfort or increase of the graces of GOD, neither by reading or hearing the word, neither by communicating at the holie Supper of the Lord. Now, if thou feele thy selfe afflicted and troubled in this respect; vnderstand, that when thou goest to employ thy selfe in these spirituall exercises, satan followeth thee, to make it vnsauerie to thee, yea and to take out of thy minde the word of GOD that thou hast heard. Pray then to GOD, that he driue him away from thee. Secondlie this commeth, forasmuch as thou art not yet much accustomed to the language of the holie Ghost, so as it is to thee as if thou didst heare an excellent sermon, but of one whose language thou didst scarce vnderstand, whereby thou canst neither feele taste nor pleasure, and so thou canst receiue but small pro it. Then thou must cōtinue, & also accustome thy selfe to read & heare the word

The 4. temtation, because of the little increas of grace by the exercises of religion.
Mat. 13. 19.

word of God, thinking alwaies that God ſpeaketh to thee for the ſaluation of thy ſoule, praying him that he will giue thee grace by his holie ſpirit to profite to his glorie and thy ſaluation. And thou ſhalt feele at the laſt that which is ſaid to ſicke men that haue loſt their taſt, that thy appetite will come to thee by eating: And that the word of God, and the participating of the bread and wine in the holie ſupper ſhall be to thee more ſweet, than honie to the mouth, as *Dauid* ſaith. Manie ſicke perſons hauing neither taſte nor appetite, eate notwithſtanding and receiue noriture. So, though in reading and hearing the word of God, and communicating at the Lords ſupper, thou feeleſt not any taſt or appetite: yet in continuing, thou ſhalt receiue ſome noriture for thy ſoule. And if it ſeemeth to thee that thou forgetteſt by & by, that which thou haſt read or heard, practiſe for thy ſoule that which thou dooeſt for thy bodie: becauſe the meates digeſt & abide not in the bo-

Pſalm. 119. 103. Pſal. 19. 11.

die, thou returnest to eate meat again euerie day: So be thou so much more diligent to heare and reade the word, and to communicate at the holie supper without leesing anie one meale for thy soule, when GOD offereth it thee. And as the corporall meate though it passe away: yet there remaineth alwaies some noriture for the bodie: so shall this spiritual meate be to thy soule. Yea it may be that at one sermon thou shalt heare and remember one sentence, which shall serue thee, as it were, for a passeport, a ladder or wings at thy neede to conduct thee by, and by comforting & strengthening thee, to lift thee vp into heauen. If then, when thou goest to reade or heare the word of God, or to communicate at the Lords supper, thou praiest to God (as thou oughtest daylie to do) that he will giue thee his spirit, that thou maiest profite: and so doest continue cōstantlie in these spirituall exercises. This disposition, this holy affection & obedience shal serue thee for sure testimonies of thine adoption,

doption,& thou shalt without doubt, feele increase of thè graces of God.

Finally, there are some, who hauing had liuely feelings of their faith with cófort & ioy in their cósciences, walking besides in the feare of God, are afterwards greatlie troubled, when these graces seem to be dead in them, falling into doubt & mistrust of their saluation, or into crimes & sinnes too vnworthie the childrẽ of God. For satan hereby indeuoureth to perswade them, either that they neuer had the true faith, or that God hath cast them off, taking from them the gifts and graces of his holie spirit: but both the one and the other conclusion is as false, as the author of them is a great lier. And indeede, if the trees which haue flourished & borne their fruite in sommer, are in winter without fruite, without leaues, yea and without apparance of life: dooth it followe therefore either that they had not life in sommer, or that they are dead in the winter. When men go to bed, they rake vp the fire which did

The fift temptation by the interruption of the graces of God.

burne : if thou marke it verie neere, there is no apparance either of heate, nor of brightnes : dooth it followe therfore, that there had been no fire, or that it is then quenched or dead. Contrariwise, hauing been couered ouer night, men kindle againe in the morning the same fire that was hid & couered : and the trees that seemed to be dead in the winter, flourish and beare fruite a while after. If thou seest a drunken man, not hauing for a time the vse of reason, nor anie feeling of it, wilt thou say therefore, that he neuer had a reasonable soule, or that hauing had it, it is now dead? Abide a fewe houres and thou shalt be conuict of the contrarie. And so of that, that thou hast not presentlie the feeling or effects and fruites of faith, can it followe that thou neuer hast had them, or that hauing had them, thou hast

Matt. 26.74 lost them? When S. *Peter* renounced Iesus Christ three times, cursing himselfe, was his faith quenched? On the contrarie, Iesus Christ hauing praied

Luk. 22.31 to God that his faith should not faile, and

and being without doubt heard,faith remained in him,but verie weake and sore beaten, but not destroyed nor quenched. *Dauid* hauing committed adulterie & murther, acknowledged his sinnes and offences, praying to God that he would not take his holie spirit from him. Then he had not lost it; rather it abode in him but as a fire couered with ashes so as it is said; without hauing anie feeling of it to keepe him from such a headlong fall. Faith then may bee in a man without kindling: and being kindled,it is not out,although it be not perceiued for a time. Yea,but (wilt thou say) the Apostle to the *Hebrues* sheweth that there be some,who hauing been lightened, hauing tasted the heauenlie gift,hauing been partakers of the holie ghost,and tasted the good word of God, and the power of the world to come, fall backe and leese these graces, yea without hope euer to recouer them againe. What assurance then can I haue that faith abideth in me, and that GOD will yet make me to

Psal. 51.

Heb. 6. 4, 5, 6.

feele it hereafter? For as he hath shewed mercie vnto *Dauid*, and to Saint *Peter*; so dooth hee exercise his iust iudgemēts vpon other, as vpon those of whome the Apostle spake before. Wee denie not but that there bee reprobates that are greatlie lightened in the knowledge of the mysteries of saluation (which the Apostle termeth here to bee partakers of the holie ghost) and yet that such apprehensions, tastings and feelings as he proposeth followe not thereof. For, reading or hearing the testimonies and representatiōs of the mercies of God toward his Church, of the loue of Iesus Christ towards his elect, and of the excellencie and felicitie of eternall life, they conceaue these things in their vnderstanding, & for the greatnes of them, they are after a sort moued: and when they talke of them, they seeme to be partakers of them. But the difference that there is betweene them & the children of God, lieth chieflie in this, that the apprehensions and feelings of the reprobat

are

are such, as a mã may haue in the reading or telling of an historie, which toucheth vs nothing at all: but the feelings of the children of God are as of a matter that toucheth themselues.

Let vs consider for example the historie of *Ioseph.* Who is hee that reading attentiuelie, how *Ioseph* was sold of his brethren, carried into *Æ-* Gen.37.
gypt, put in prison: and the sorrowe
that *Iacob* had, vnderstanding that he Gen.39.
was deuoured of a wilde beast, that would not bee mooued with compassion towardes *Ioseph* and *Iacob?* Who is hee that reading how *Ioseph*
beeing able to containe himselfe no Gen.45.
longer, made himselfe knowne to his brethren, and how weeping and crying out hee saide vnto them: I am *Ioseph*, is my father yet aliue, and causing thẽ to come neere vnto him, said, I am *Ioseph* your brother whõ ye sold, but be not sorie. Shew to my father al my glorie: Then throwing himselfe vpõ the neck of *Beniamin* his brother, he wept, and in like manner *Beniamin*

wept vpon his necke : after kissing all his brethren hee wept vppon them. Who is he, I say, which is not touched and weepeth not with them ? But because this is a historie of the fact of an other, these motions & feelings soon passe away, so as hauing turned the leafe or talked of another matter, all these feelings are vanished and gone. So is the feeling of the reprobate, hearing or reading the testimonies of so great a mercie of God towards men, and of the greatnes of the happines of the kingdome of heauen : The vnderstanding & apprehension of these things, causeth some motions or feelings in them, as the Apostle saith. But for as much as these good things appertaine not vnto them, neither do the feelings that they haue, take anie seate or roote in their hearts, but are easilie quenched and vanish away. On the contrary, the feeling that the children of God haue, is, as of the good things that appertaine vnto them, & therefore it may well bee colde and drowsie, but not die. As also the feelings

lings that *Ioseph* and his brethren had were ſuch, as although they had thẽ not when they ſlept, yet when they awaked they returned againe. And although that by the death of their father, they were (as it were) interrupted: yet the benefite and the comfort abode by them ſtill. Following this that is aboue ſaid, we ſay boldlie, that what feelings, what illuminations or apprehenſions ſo euer the reprobate haue: ſo it is that they neuer feele the holie ghoſt in them, giuing thẽ teſtimonie that they are the children of God. For according to this teſtimonie, they ſhould be, and ſhould abide the children of God: ſeeing the holie ghoſt can neither deceiue nor lie. As alſo after that God hath made vs once feele by the teſtimonie of his holie ſpirit that wee are his children, wee are certaine that wee cannot periſh, but that wee are indeed, and ſhall continue the children of God. For it is the teſtimonie and reuelation of the ſpirit of trueth. Alſo he that giueth faith, doth not change: & therefore Mal. 3. 6.

fore

Ro.11.29. fore his gifts are without repentance.
Heb.6.4. The second difference may bee taken from this word, tast, which the Apostle vseth: To wete, that the reprobate are like to him who hauing tasted a good peece of wine, making shewe as if he would buy it, vnderstanding the price, & not willing to giue so much, leaueth it there, without buying or drinking of it any more. So the reprobate hauing tasted the heauenlie good things, finding them good, and praising them exceedingly, after they vnderstād the price, that is, that they must renounce themselues, and beare the crosse of Christ, to goe to take possession of the kingdome of heauen, which he hath purchased for thē with his precious bloud. They will none of it at this price, & so renounce these good things without drinking or inioying them. But the children of God on the other side, hauing neuer so little a taste of these heauenlie treasures, desire in such sort to haue the enioying of them, that they make resolution to forsake all, to inioye it.

We

We will adde this third reason: That as those that haue their stomackes charged with euill humours, cease not to eate sometimes for all that, yea and to find tast in some good meates, but are constrained after (through the euill disposition of their stomacke) to cast it vp againe & to vomit: So some reprobates hauing within them an euill conscience, may well taste the good heauenlie gifts, but this euil cõscience, not being able to agree with the true & sure faith of the hart, stoppeth that these gifts take no root to fructifie to saluation, so that finallie they cast it off, or let it wither & come to nothing. And this reasõ with those before, are the principall causes, for the which many, that seemed to bee the children of God, do reuolt, as we will shew hereafter more at large. On the cõtrarie, those who haue faith, are assured, that though the graces of the holy ghost are oftẽ weak in thẽ, & like fire couered with ashes, & trees in the winter, yet it cã neuer come to nought or die: rather they recouer strength

at

at the last, whereby they are certaine to be, and to continue the children of GOD, and heires of euerlasting life. Furthermore, let vs remember that these foule and grosse faults of *Dauid* and of S. *Peter*, & of others are set before vs, first that they should bee to vs as a mirrour of the fragilitie of man, to acknowledge, that if we be exempted, it is by the grace of our God. Secondlie, that wee should so much the more stand vppon our garde. As if in walking thou shouldest see him fall that goeth before thee, thou goest not to fall with him, but thou art to be so much the more circumspect that thou fall not, as he did. Thirdlie, that vnderstanding that faith abideth in them (although very weake & feeble) thou maiest take courage, beleeuing certainlie that faith which was once giuen thee, cannot bee quenched nor die. And therefore continue in assurance that thou art the child of God, raising vp thy selfe by their example, and resoluing with thy selfe to walke constantlie as the child of God in true

holines

holines and righteousnes before him all the daies of thy life. See how wee ought to bee resolued, that although the markes, feelings and testimonies of our adoption set forth here aboue, be in vs but small and weake, and accompanied with great infirmities & conflicts: yet wee may and ought to assure our selues that these marks are truelie in vs, and that therefore wee are certainlie the children of God, & inheritours of euerlasting life. Luke 1.75.

That the Apostacie and reuolt of some hauing made profession of the true religion, ought not to make vs call in doubt neither our religion nor our adoption.

Cap. 5.

WE haue vnderstood here before how we may and ought to resist the doubts of our adoption, proceeding from our selues. Now, we must shewe how wee may ouercome the temptatiōs which come from others. There are two things

princi-

principallie, which trouble the consciẽces of many, to make them doubt whether they be the children of God, and in the way of saluation & of eternall life, or no. First, the horrible offence or stumbling blocke of those which abandon this church, renouncing the doctrine of it, and returning to the puddle of idolatrie: and speciallie when any persons hauing sometimes held any honorable place in the Church do reuolt, and become persecutors of the doctrine which they haue before taught and maintained. For thereof the diuell gathereth two consequences, no lesse daungerous than false: either that our Church is not the true Church, & so that we are not the children of god: or that there is no assurance of perseuerance in the faith, & consequently no certaintie of being the childrẽ of God, which haue had & borne in aparance the markes of adoption. The other offence consisteth in the grieuous & long afflictiõs which we indure: for the prosperitie of the wicked, deriding our miseries, & the apprehension of our own troubles,

bles, giue occasion to doubt whether God care for vs, or whither he loue vs or no. And this ordinarie condition to those that make profession of our religiō, causeth many to condēne it, & haue it in detestatiō, as the mother & nurse of al calamities. As touching the 1. point, cōcerning those that reuolt, it is a small stūbling block to trouble vs: for this was foretold vs, and it is a disease wherwith the church hath alwaies bin afflicted. Many shall be called, saith Iesus Christ, but few chosen. And the parable of the seed falling in diuers sorts of earth sheweth, that with much a doo the 4. part of those that shal heare & professe the Gospel, shall cōtinue to the end. S. *Paule* hath foretold expreslie, that in the latter times many shal fall from the faith. And he aduertiseth the *Ephe.* that euen frō among themselues there should rise vp mē that should teach peruerse things. And the *Cor.* that there shall be in the church not only diuisiōs, but also heresies. Saint *Peter* speaketh yet more largelie: As there hath been (saith he) false prophets among the people of

Of the certaintie of the doctrine notwithstanding the reuolts.

Matt. 20. 16

Matth. 13.

1. Tim. 4. 1.

Act. 20. 34.

1. Cor. 11. 19.

2. Pet. 2. 1.

of Iſrael,ſo ſhal there be falſe teachers amongſt you, which ſhall ſecretlie bring in damnable errours, and manie ſhal follow their damnable waies, by whom the way of trueth ſhall bee blaſphemed. Now, we muſt thinke the accompliſhing of ſuch prophecies ſo much the leſſe ſtrange, because ſuch hath bin the condition of the church
Gen.6. of God at all times. What reuolt was there in the houſe of God before the flood, eight perſons onlie being foūd ſaued in the Arke, and yet amongſt them one hypocrite, who after was
Gen.9.25. caſt off and accurſed. Now, the church of God being inlarged in the poſteritie of *Sem*, againe there was ſeene ſuch a reuolt, that the church of God
Gen.12. was onlie found in the familie of *Abraham*, himſelfe being pulled out of idolatrie. In the time of *Elias* the re-
1.Reg.19. uolt was ſo great in *Iſrael*, that hee
10. thought he had bin left alone. At the comming of our Lord Ieſus Chriſt, the Apoſtacie was ſo generall, that almoſt all the Church, at the leaſt the principal members of it, lift vp them-

ſelues

selues against the Sonne of GOD, and crucified him. When Iesus Christ had gathered manie Disciples, he was forsaken of the most part of them: yea, *Iu-* Iohn. 6.66
das also the Apostle fell from him, sold
him, and betraied him. Iesus Christ Mat.26.14
being taken prisoner by his enemies, all Mat.26.65 Mat.26.69
his Apostles fled away and forsooke 2.Tim.1.
him. Saint *Peter* himselfe denied him 15
thrice. Saint *Paule* complaineth, that all
they of *Asia* had reuolted, And saieth 2.Tim.4.
in an other place, that all had forsaken 16
him. He noteth *Alexander* the Copper Smith, *Hymenæus* and others, who
hauing beene the chiefe members of the 2.Tim 4.
Church, were become heretikes, and e- 14
nemies of the truth. Now it is the same Church, and we must no more be astonished at such reuolts, than at a man hauing rheums all his life (whereby hee casteth out of his bodie aboundance of humours) that shoulde continue in the same disease still euen in his olde age: Herein rather we ought to acknowlege the holines of God, wherewith also he would his Church should be adorned. For he purgeth his Church, not being

able to indure that hipocrits should any lōg time keepe the place and title of his childrē aproching to his Maiestie. And hereunto we may aplie that which *Moses* saith, whē he saw the fire had deuoured *Nadab* and *Abihu* the sonnes of *Aaron*, for offering before the Lorde strange fire: This is it which the Lorde hath spoken, saying; I will be sanctified in those that approch vnto me, & will bee glorified in the presence of all the people: shewing therby, that the nearer mē approch vnto him by honorable offices in his church, and profession of his worde, so much the lesse will hee suffer their corruptions, but punisheth them more sharply, to the end, that as the nearer the peece of wax approcheth to the fire, so much the more the heat of it appeareth in melting it. In like maner the holines of God may better be knowne in the reuolt of hypocrites approching vnto him, & so he may be the more glorified of the people in such iudgements. This is also the cause why manie, who before they had the knowledge of the gospell, seemed in outward apparance

Leuit. 10.3

verie

very good people. Afterward being ioined to the church, become wicked and dissolute in their liues, & very persecutors. It is the vengeãce of god that pursueth thẽ, punishing their ingratitude, their loue of the world and of the flesh, which they brought & nourished in the church, and the contempt of the honor that God did them, when he made thẽ aproch vnto him, receiuing thẽ into his house, speaking to them by the preaching of his word, & presenting vnto thẽ vpon his holy Table, his own Sonne Iesus Christ for the foode of their soules. So farre off is it then, that we should be troubled for such reuolts, that on the contrary, seeing that they are the vengeances of GOD, wee ought so much the more to feare, and to continue the more constantly & holily in the church of GOD. And indeede if wee did at this day see *Dauid* execute that protestation which hee did make of purging his house from vicious and wicked persons, would we (thinke you) depart from it, doubting of the holinesse of it? Shall we not rather be confirmed to Psal. 101.

tarrie there stil, desiring to liue holilie? But more, what damage receiueth the Church in such reuolts? The glorie of it before God consisteth not properlie in the greatnesse of the number, but in the holinesse of them. The health of a man consisteth not in the abundance of humors, which will cause some deadlie disease at the last: for euen they that are laden with them, take medicines to purge them, that they might bee the more whole. This is it which God, hauing spoken of his Church of *Israel*, that her siluer was turned into drosse, & her wine mingled with water, added for a great benefit, that he would take cleane away al her scomme, and remoue al her lead from her: and that hauing restored the Iudges and Counsellers, so as they had bene at the beginning, it shoulde be called the righteous and faithful Citie. Experience sheweth, that in the prosperitie & peace of the church many thrust in themselues, ful of auarice, ambition, pride, and of other corruptions and vanities; to be short it hapneth euen as in a sweet & rainie season, that many weeds

Esay. 1.22

come

come vp amongest the good hearbes, which should bee choaked of them, if the Gardeiner pulled thē not out. Thē, when such people departe from the Church, returning to their vomit, it is as if God gaue a purgatiō to it, to make it more holy, & more acceptable to her bridegrome. Let vs further consider the causes of reuoltes. If this hapned then when the Church was in peace & prosperitie, it shold seeme there were more occasion to call into dout our doctrine: But it is in the time of persecution, that these reuolts are seen; & so, it is feare to leese their goods, their dignities, their parents, their country, their liues, that causeth them to reuolt. It is then the flesh, it is the world, it is the mistrust of God, and not the allowing of the Papisticall doctrine, that maketh them to change their religion. As also S. *Paule* saith, that *Demas* had forsaken him, ha- 2. Tim. 4. 10
uing loued this present worlde. And indeed did this miserable *Iohn Haren* reuolt during the prosperous estate of the towne of *Bruges*, wherein he was minister? By no meanes. But perceiuing the

danger, although he might yet haue exercised his ministerie, he began to seeke the meanes as a hireling, to forsake his flocke. He knoweth what letters I writ vnto him, reprouing his slothfulnes, his crafts and euill conscience in the reasons which he put forth, to haue some colour to withdraw himself. He knoweth also what reproofes he had receyued by the letters of others, that he should not defile his ministerie in intermedling so ernestly in the matters of war & of policie. After the Towne of *Bruges* was redred to the enemy, he withdrew him self into *Zeland* & *Holand*. Where perceiuing that hee began (as good reason was) for many considerations to bee suspected in our churches, and in no reputation, he gote him out of the countrie. So feeling in his conscience small apparance to be established in his Ministery againe, hauing no hope of preferment in any other vocation, and being pursued by the iust iudgement of God falling vpon euil consciences; he reuolted, thinking happilie that hee should receiue some recompence for the offence that

he

he had offered against the holie Ministerie, and at the least to enter againe into the possession of his goods. This then is not the chaunging of doctrine, which mooued him, but (as wee haue saide) it is the flesh, and the world: it is enuie that maketh the Monke. It is ambition the mother of heresie, as saint *Augustine* sayth: It is an euill conscience, the rocke that maketh the shippe-wracke of Faith, as Saint *Paule* sayth, 1.Tim.1.19
which hath made him to chaunge his profession. To be short, GOD could no longer suffer such an hypocrite in his church, nor such a filth in his holie temple: hee woulde bee sanctified in taking vengeance vpon him, who so inordinately approched vnto him. Hee hath set him foorth for an example of his iudgements, that those that make profession of Religion, and chieflie the Ministers of the worde, may study more and more to walke with a good conscience to keepe themselues in their vocation, to renounce the pasions of the flesh, & the illusions of the world, and so with feruent praiers to continue

constantly in the grace of the Lorde. Furthermore, let him make as manie shewes as he wil, let him sweare, let him lift vp his hands, and his eies to heauen, let him weare a great paire of beads, let him goe oft and deuoutlie to the masse; yet shall hee not easily make the Iesuites (who are cunninger than he) to beleue, that hee dooth it indeede and from his heart. For those who among them haue any little more wit than the common sort, vnderstand well enough if they wold confesse it, that the change of the holy Supper into the Masse, the worshipping of bread in it, the fiery purgatory after death, the opinion of meriting paradise by workes, specially those of supererogation; the setting foorth of God the father, who is an inuisible and eternal spirit, vnder the figure of an old man: the worshipping of images, the inuocation of Saints departed, candles lighted at noone dayes, & borne in procession, the great beads hanging at their neckes, and other such idolatries & superstitions, are either so abhominable or so manifestly contrary to the word of God,

God, yea, or so absurd, that he that hath once knowne them by the light of the gospell can neuer allow thē in his heart. But be it, that by the inchantment of satan, and iudgement of God, he were indeed become a Papist, and that S. *Paule* himselfe should reuolt, preaching another gospell; we ought, as he himselfe protesteth, to holde him accursed, and not to be mooued to doubt of our faith. For our religion & faith is not founded vpō the constancie or stedfastnesse of men, but vpon the truth of our God, and vppon the testimonie of the holy Ghost in our hearts. If men be vnfaithfull, saith S. *Paule*, he remaineth notwithstanding faithfull, and can not denie himselfe. When Iesus Christ forsaken of his Disciples, should aske vs, if wee also would leaue him: we are taught to answer with the Apostles; Lord, whether shall wee goe, thou hast the words of eternall life. The faithfull Pastor must (without being astonished at the reuolt of manie) say with *Esai*, Behold I & my children which god hath giuen me, are for signes and wonders. The horrible and fearfull

Gal. 1.

2. Ti. 2. 13.

Ioh. 6. 67.

Esai. 8. 18.

ven-

vengeance, which waighteth on, and followeth these cursed apostates at the verie heeles, should make vs to tremble, & to resolue to renounce all that is vppon the earth, that we may get and hold fast all that is in heauen: & so leauing these poore reuolters to the iudgement of God, to cast our eyes vppon those, who euen in our time haue indured so constantlie the losse of their goods, reproaches, prisons: to be short, who chearfullie haue entered into the flaming fire, & by cruell death mounted into the kingdome of heauen; to the ende that such autentique seales of the heauenlie doctrine, may confirme our hearts to continue constantlie, & chearfullie to follow their steps, and so be their companions in glorie. We ought not to be troubled at these reuoltes, as if we were not assured to continue in the faith, whereby also it shall come to passe, that wee shall be in doubt whether we are, or shal continue the Children of GOD. For as the markes of our adoption set foorth here before are of two sorts: the one inward before God, and the other outward before

Of the assurãce of our adoption, notwithstanding the reuolts.

fore

fore men: they which haue the inward markes, which consist in the testimonie of the holy Ghost in our hearts, in the peace of our consciences, and in the holy desire of our soules, feele these graces, which allureth them that they are the children of GOD, chosen to eternal life: yea more certainly than we are allured by the light of the Sunne that we see, & by the heat that we feele, that the Sun shineth. And in deed they haue the white stone, whereof mention is made in the reuelation, & in that stone Reue.2.17.
a new name of the childe of god writtē, which none can know but he that receiueth it. *The World*, saith Christ, *cānot receiue the spirit of truth, because it hath not seen him, neither hath known him: but ye* Ioh.14.17.
know him, saith hee to his Apostles, *for hee abideth with you, and shall be in you.* As touching the outwarde marke of beeing a member of the visible Church, it is also verie certaine in respect of God, inasmuch as speaking to vs, and sealing his words by the sacraments, he neither wil, nor can deceiue or lie. But if mē hearing his word, & cōmunicating

at the Sacraments, reiect in their hearts the ſpirituall graces which are offered vnto them, and ſo abide vnfaithfull, and wicked within (when notwithſtanding they are helde for faithfull and the childrẽ of god, becauſe of the outward profeſſion:) it is no meruaile if God at the laſt do diſcouer them, & caſt them off: ſhewing therin, that they wer neuer his.
1.Ioh.2.19 And this is it that S. *Iohn* ſaith of ſuch; They went out frõ amongſt vs, but they were not of vs; for if they had bin of vs, they would haue tarried with vs. But this is, that it might appeare that all are not of vs. They that are once grafted in Chriſt, can not periſh: for the giftes of
Ro.11.29. God are without repentance. But euerie plant, ſaith Ieſus Chriſt, which my
Matt.15.13 father hath not planted, ſhall bee pulled
Matt.13. vp. The parable of the ſeede falling into diuers ſortes of earth, teacheth vs two points to this purpoſe. Firſt, that manie ſhal heare the goſpel, but without frute. Secondlie, that it ſhall be their own falt. For if entring into the Church, they bring their cares and loue to the world, without hauing will to forſake them, ſo

as

as it like thornes, choake the good seede of the word. And so hauing no moisture of the grace of God, they wither at the first sunne of persecution; a man may see the cause of their reuolte, to wete, because they were not the children of God. Saint *Paule* hauing said, that God knoweth who are his, addeth: and whosoeuer calleth vpon the name of Christ, let him depart from all iniquitie: shewing thereby, that if there bee anie which ioyne themselues to the Church, calling vpon the name of Christ, and doo not depart frõ iniquity; they discouer thereby that God neuer tooke them for his. Which thing is good to be noted. For manie thinke, that to be of our Church needeth nothing, but to chãge the masse to the preaching, and to the communicating at the Lords supper. And when they vnderstand, that to be the childe of God, is required to renoũce themselues to leaue couetousnes, ambition, drunkennesse, the world, and all pompes: to be short, that they must put off the olde man, and be a new creature: not beeing disposed to do this, they leaue the preaching

2.Tim.2, 19.

ching, and returne to the Masse. Now be these the children of God that reuolt, that they should make those that are in deed and continue to doubt? Nay, rather they are the children of the world, who hauing brought the world in with them, haue also carried the world away with them. They therefore that haue once beleeued, who also beleeuing, feele a desire to liue according vnto god, are assured that they cannot perish. He that

Phil.1.6. beginneth this good work in them, wil accõplish it, euen vnto the day of christ.

Aug.de correct.&gra.ca.12.to.7. And to this purpose saith S. *Augustine* verie wel, He which made vs good, maketh vs also to perseuer in goodnes: but they that fal and perish, were not of the number of the predestinate. It remaineth, that considering in the fall of hipocrites, the double mercie of god toward vs. First, that he hath receiued vs into the number of his children. Secondly, that he will continue this grace towards vs euen to the ende: there remaineth, I say, that we feele our selues double bound to practise the exhortation of S. *Paule*, beseeching vs by the mercies of God, to

offer

offer our selues a liuing sacrifice, holy & Rom.12.1.
pleasing to God, & not to be fashioned
like this wicked world: but rather endeuouring to this, that being transformed by the renuing of our vnderstanding, we may approoue and follow, the good and perfect will of God. And let vs remember that which S. *John* saith, That 1.Iohn 3.3.
they that haue hope to liue with Iesus Christ, and to see him as hee is, do purifie themselues as he is pure.

That afflictions ought not to make vs to doubt of our adoption, but rather confirme vs.

Chap. 6.

LET vs now come to that stũbling blocke and trouble, that proceedeth from our afflictions. What apparaunce is there (saieth the flesh) that wee are the Children of GOD? Our goods are violently taken from vs, our possessions are confiscate, and our Offices and Estates are taken away.

We are driuen out of our Countrey, yea from Countrey to Countrey like vagabonds: wee are hated of father and mother, and of our other kinsfolk & frends: we are drawen and kept in prison: wee are derided and brought into extreame calamities & miseries: we are as sheepe of the shambles, apointed to the sword, to the gallowes and to the fire: To bee short, wee see nothing but the signes of the wrath and the curse of God vpon vs. And that which more is, the Church which wee haue said was the kingdome of Christ, and the house of God, how is it assailed by the mightie men of this world? whome also we see to come to the end of their enterprises, to oppresse, tread vnder foote, rent and scatter this Church, exercising al crueltie against it, as hũgrie wolues vpon a flock of sheep, forsaken of their shepheard. They triumph in their victories, and wee hang down the head & weep, bowing down our necks vnder the yoke of afflictions. They increase in riches, & we consume in pouertie: they are aduaunced to honours and dignities, and we are despised

as

as rebels, & wicked and seditious people. See what the flesh saith: and yet these are but discourses and complaints of great ignoraunce or infirmitie. For what is that which troubleth and offendeth vs in this condition and estate. Euen that whereby wee ought rather to be confirmed, in the assuraunce that wee are the children of GOD, and indeede happie. First, if GOD had promised to entreate his Children in this worlde delicatelie, and to set them vp in riches and high estate, wee might haue some occasion to doubt whether wee were the Children of GOD, all calamities and afflictions quite contrarie falling vpon vs. But seeing it is so, that the Holie Ghost hath foretolde vs both often and manifestlie, that the children of GOD shoulde bee afflicted, and that those that woulde liue faithfullie in the feare of GOD in Christ, shall suffer persecution; this persecution and affliction ought rather to serue vs for a signe that wee are the children of GOD. 2.Tim.3. 12

Moreouer, if the most excellent seruants

uants and children of GOD haue alwayes beene most afflicted. Afflictions ought not to make vs doubt of our adoption and saluation, except wee will call in doubt the saluation and felicitie of those, whom wee confesse to bee the verie blessed children of GOD: Especiallie, if afflictions do serue greatlie to pull our hearts from the Earth, and to lift them vp into Heauen, to purifie our faith as golde in the fire, and to fashion vs into a true obedience of god. Then the vtility and profite which commeth vnto vs thereby, ought to serue vs for a sufficient proofe, that in afflictions GOD sheweth himselfe to be our father, hauing care of our welfare and saluation. And yet more, seeing the taking awaie of our goods temporall, shall bring vs foorth an eternall treasure in Heauen, the mockeries and reproches shall bee turned vnto glorie before GOD, the teares into ioy, our sufferings into comfortes: Who is hee that will not confesse, that such afflictions proceede from the verie loue of GOD towards vs?

vs? To be short, seeing that GOD, strengthening vs in the middest of the fires of tribulations, sheweth in our infirmitie his might and bountie, and seeing (when wee suffer for his name) hee maketh vs witnesses of his trueth: our afflictions are (as it were) stages from whence he maketh his own glory to shine, and giueth increase vnto ours. So farre off is it then, that beeing afflicted, wee shoulde bee troubled or offended, that contrariwise those troubles ought to serue vs for an assurance, that we are the children of GOD: whereof that wee may bee the better resolued, we wil treate of these points more at large.

That the afflictions that happen vnto vs, haue beene foretolde, and therefore they ought to confirme vs in the assurance of our adoption.

CAP. 7.

HE holie Ghost hath at all times foretold and testified by sundry and manifest sentences, that the children of God shoulde be persecuted and afflicted in this life, yea, in such sort, as the first afflictions shoulde bee but the beginnings of greater; and that passing one euill, they shoulde prepare themselues to indure others that should followe as the waues in the Sea. GOD from the beginning of the worlde, hauing pronounced, that hee woulde put enmitie betweene the seede of the woman and the seede of the Serpent, hath aduertised vs, that as long as there shalbe deuils in the world, and children of God, they must vnderstand, that such enemies will imploy

Gen.3.15 Prophecies of the olde testament.

ploy all their strength & means to persecute thē: As this also is represented in the *Reuelatiō* in that which is said by S. *Iohn*, that the olde serpent not being able to deuoure the Sonne of GOD, nor the body of the church, was very angry, and went to make war with the rest of her seede which kept the commaundements of God, and which had the testimonie of Iesus Christ. Likewise God hauing promised seede vnto *Abraham*, and added, that it shoulde bee as the Starres of the Heauen. He tolde him by and by, that it shoulde bee afflicted, saying: Knowe thou for a certayne, that thy seede shall dwell and serue in a Land that is not their owne, and shal be afflicted foure hundred yeeres. And that which is more, hee confirmeth this aduertisement by a vision or notable signe, commaunding him to diuide in peeces, an heifar, a ramme, a hee goate, a turtle, and a pigeon; and sending a flight of Birdes vpon the dead carcases cut in peeces: he shewed him, that his seede (by the greatnesse of afflictions) should be like vnto dead car-

Reue. 12

Gen. 15. 13

cases cut in peeces, and exposed for a pray vnto the Birdes. *Dauid* in a few wordes sheweth this condition to be common to all the children of GOD,
Psal. 34.20 saying, that the afflictions of the righteous are manie. And in howe manie sortes, and in how many places haue the Prophetes foretolde of the afflictions that came vpon the tenne tribes of *Israel* carried after captiues into *Assyria*? In like manner of the kingdome of *Iuda*, the destruction of the Temple, the sacking of the Citie, the massacre of a great part of the people, and the captiuitie of the rest, by the space
Prophecies of the newe testament. of seauentie yeares in *Babylon*. Aboue all, Iesus Christ, who is the wisedome
Mat. 10.16 of GOD, how often hath hee foretolde the afflictions of his faithfull seruants and members of his body? Beholde (saith he) to his Apostles, I send you as Sheepe amongest Wolues. Yee shall bee deliuered vnto the Consistories, and whipped in the Synagogues. Yee shall bee hated of all men for my names sake. If they haue called the Master of the house Beelzebub, how

much

much more his seruauntes. I am not come to bring peace vpon the Earth, but a Sworde. If anie will followe Mat.16.24
mee, let him renounce him selfe, and take vp his Crosse and followe mee. They shall deliuer you to bee punished, and shall slay you. If they haue Per- Mat.24.9
secuted mee, they will also persecute you. Againe, Verelie, verelie I saie Ihon 16.2
vnto you, that yee shall weepe and lament, and the worlde shall reioyce. Yea, hee compareth the faithfull vnto a Woman which trauaileth of Iho. 16.21
childe. True it is, that the wicked are also tormented in their course. But Iudgement sayeth Saint *Peter*, 1.Pet.4.17
must beginne at the house of GOD. And of this iudgement it is that Saint *Paule* dooth speake, saying: That 2.Thes.3.7
wee are ordayned to bee afflicted, which hee dooth confirme by a Sentence full of comforte, saying: That Act.14 22
by manie tribulations wee must enter into the Kingdome of Heauen. Agayne, all they that will liue godlie 2.Tim.3.
in Christ, must suffer persecution. But 12
aboue al, that is to be noted that hee

Col.1.24. saide in an other place: I reioyce, and fill vp in my selfe that which wanted of the sufferings of Christ: meaning by Christ, all the faithfull, with their head, and shewing, that GOD hath ordained a certain measure of pasions for this Christ, and consequently to euery one of his members his portion, which hee must suffer, to accomplish the pasions of Christ. Now this is not without great reason, that the Holie Ghost hath so carefully, and in so many sortes and manners foretolde, that the children of GOD shoulde bee afflicted. It is to this ende, as Iesus

Ihon 16. 1. Christ him selfe teacheth his Apostles, that we shold not be troubled or offended, when we see the faithful to be spoiled, chased away, imprisoned, mocked, & murthered, that then we should remember that it was told vs before. And that it commeth not to passe by fortune or chaunce, nor by the absolute will of mē that we are afflicted. But by the appointment of God the father, and that this is the entertainment which he hath ordained for his seruants and children.

But our flesh doth Iudaize too much in this behalfe. For as the *Ievves* in olde time, looking for a *Messias* triumphing in the world, were offended at his humilitie & base estate, & so at the crosse of Iesus Christ, and therefore reiected both him and his doctrine: euen so our flesh at this day doth still imagine a gospel of veluet agreeable to their desires, and a kingdome of Christ that were of this world. See now why it is troubled and offended, deriding a Christ crowned with thornes, bearing his crosse vpon his shoulders, and laying it vpon all those that will be the children of God with him. But if the Iewes had wel weied that which *Esai* foretold of the *Messias*, That he should grow vp as a roote out of a drie groũd, That he shuld haue Esai.53.
in him neither fashion nor beautie to be desired, That he should be despised and reiected of men; a man so afflicted and accustomed to sorowes, that men shuld hide their faces frõ him, so much should he be contemned; That hee should bee oppressed with iniurie, afflicted, & led to the slaughter as a Lambe. To bee short,

ſhort, that he ſhuld be numbred among the tranſgreſſors. Alſo that which *Zacharie* ſaith; Behold thy king commeth
Zach.9.9 to thee humble, riding vpon an Aſſe. And that which *Daniel* ſaieth, That the
Dan.9 26 Chriſt ſhould be cut off, and ſhould not be. If, I ſay, the Iewes had well weighed theſe Prophecies, and manie other like theſe, touching the abaſement and afflictions of Chriſt: ſo far off is it, that they would haue reiected him, that on the contrarie, they would haue knowen by the accompliſhment of thoſe thinges that were foretolde of him, that he was in deede the *Meſſias* promiſed. In like manner, if we would carefully meditate on that which the holie Ghoſt hath fore ſpoken of our condition, and that wee muſt be conformable vnto the image of
Rom.8.17 Chriſt, ſuffer and die with him: the tribulations which accompanie the profeſſion of the Goſpell, ſhoulde bee vnto vs ſignes and teſtimonies, , that wee are Chriſtians, and the Children of God.

Luk.2 When the Angell ſhewed vnto the Shepards the natiuitie of Ieſus Chriſt, ſaying,

saying, I shewe vnto you great ioy, that this day is borne to you a Sauiour in the Citie of *Dauid*, which is Christ the Lord: Hee addetth, you shall haue these signes, yee shall finde the childe wrapped in swaddeling cloathes, and laid in a maunger. Now, if these shepheards (beeing come to *Bethlehem,*) had found the holie Virgine in an honourable pallaice, and the Childe in a magnificall and royall cradle, had they not had iust occasion to doubt of the tidings of the Angell, this estate not agreeing with the signe that hee had giuen? But hauing found the Childe in poore estate in a maunger, as the Angell had foretolde, they were confirmed to beleeue, that it was the *Messias*.

Euen so, GOD hauing reuealed vnto vs by his Woord, that hee hath chosen vs to be his Children, hauing sealed it in vs by the testimonie and effects of the vnction of the holie Ghost: and hauing also giuen vs the markes in this, that he hath made vs the members

of

of his Church: hee hath foretolde, and hath also giuen one signe more of our adoption, that we shall be reproached & persecuted. If then the world did make much of vs, loued and honoured vs, we might after some sort dout of the word of God, and of our election and adoption. But seeing the accomplishment of that, that was foretolde vs, we ought to bee so much the more confirmed in this assurance, that we are not of the world, but appertaine to our God. And this is it that Iesus Christ tolde his Apostles,

Ioh.15.19. saying; If yee were of the world, the world would loue his owne: but nowe because I haue chosen you out of the world, the world hateth you. If we aske the way to goe to anie place, & that one tell vs (for a signe of the right way) that it is at the beginning durty & afterward full of hils, we wil leaue the other waies which seeme straight, drie, faire and easie: and finding in that way which wee take, durte and hills foretold and giuen vs for a signe, wee will bee so much the more confirmed, that wee are in the right way.

So

So the holie Ghost hauing foretolde, that thorough manie tribulations wee must enter into the Kingdome of heauen, and that the waye leading to eternall life is narrow and difficult: If wee finde the way of the Gospell narrow & full of troubles, let vs acknowledge that we are in the right way to the kingdom of heauen, & that we ought therfore to bee so much the more confirmed in assuraunce that wee are the Children of God.

Act.14.22.

Matt.7.13.

That the Children of God haue alwaies been afflicted, and yet still beloued of God.

Chap. 8.

This that the Holie Ghost hath fore spoken, that the condition of the Children of GOD is to bee afflicted, hath by experience been found to bee true in all ages, whether we consider the people and Church of GOD in the whole bodie, or speake of it particularlie

Examples of the afflictions of the Church during the time of the olde testament.

Exo.1.14.

Exo.1.18

Exo.1.22.

cularly in the members of it. How long and greeuously was the people of *Israel* afflicted in *Ægipt?* *Moses* reciteth, that their life was vexed bitterly, thorough grieuous seruitude, and that all the seruice wherein they serued was tyrannous, *Pharaoh* intending to destroy them, and to roote them out by trauaile and excessiue labour. And not so being able to come to his purpose, neither yet by the commaundement made to the midwiues, to slay secretly all the male children which should be borne: at the last he appointed certeine of the *Ægiptians* his subiects to bee their hangmen openly. Whereby also when *Moses* was borne, his parents hauing hid him some time with great feare, they were at the last constrained (for the auoiding of the furie of these hangmen) to put him out into the brinke of the riuer, as abandoning him vnto death. Could there be anie more barbarous crueltie vsed to anie people? And yet, did they still continue to bee grieuouslie afflicted foure score yeares after the birth of Moses. So that it is not without a cause that the

Lord

Lord called *Ægipt* the house of bond- Exo.20.2.
age, and an iron fornace. The which al- Deut.4.20.
so he confirmeth, appearing to *Moses* in
the middest of a burning bush, saying, I Exo.3.2.
haue seene the affliction of my people.
They were not so soone in the way to
depart out of *Ægipt*, but they wer pur- Exod.14.9.
sued by the Armie of *Pharaoh*, hauing
the sea before them, & the mountaines
on their sides, and so seeing present
death before their eyes. Did they escape the hands of *Pharaoh* in passing o-
uer the sea on drie foote? Then they entred into the horrible and fearefull Deserts, and going three dayes through the
Desertes, they found no water, the first
that they founde was so bitter, that Exo.15.22.
they coulde not drinke it; They were
assayled of enemies, vexed with fierie Serpents, and inflammations vnac-
customed, and wandred vp and downe
fortie yeares in those Deserts, liuing by Num.21.6.
Manna and water.

In the time of the Iudges, how ofte was the people of god broght vnder the cruell tyranie of diuers enemies? Vnder

the

the raigne of *Manasses* King of *Iuda*,
2.King.21. there was such persecution against the
16. faithfull, that *Ierusalem* was filled with
bloud from the one ende to the other.
But aboue all, it was vnkindlie handled
both before and during the Captiuitie
2.King.25 of *Babylon*. The Citie of *Ierusalem* was
taken and sacked, the Temple of God
Ier.39. and spoyled, burnt and destroyed. Hee that
52. escaped the pestilence, famine, and the
sword, was transported into *Babylon*
among the Idolatours their Enemies,
and plunged into all miseries and calamities,
and that by the space of three-
Ier.25.12. score and tenne yeares, as it was foretolde.
The Prophet *Esai* doth sufficientlie
set before vs their miserable e-
Esa.46.7. state, calling the Iewes persons despised,
an abhominable people, seruaunts
to Lordes, wormes of Iacob, the dead
Esa.41.14. men of Israel, people afflicted, ouer-
Esa. 54.11. whelmed with tempests, without anie
comfort. Are they returned out of this
captiuitie into *Iudea*? There they were
vext of their enemies: & aboue al, how
many horrible cruelties did thei indure
by *Antiochus*, *Herod*, and other tyrants.

Let

Let vs also see what complaints the people of God make of the calamities that befell them by the *Assirians*, or (as other thinke) by this *Antiochus*, saying: O God the heathen haue entred into thine inheritance, they haue polluted thy holie temple, and haue brought Ierusalē to a heape of stones. They haue giuē the dead bodies of thy seruants for meat to the foules of the ayre, and the flesh of thy Saints to the beastes of the earth: they haue shed their bloud like water on euerie side of Ierusalem, and there was none to burie them. We haue been a reproach to our neighbours, and a mockerie, and a derision to those that are about vs. Againe, Thou hast put vs (O Lord) farre from thee as sheepe to be eaten, and thou hast scattered vs among the heathen. Thou hast sold thy people without gaine, and doest not increase their price. Thou hast smittē vs downe into the place of dragons, & hast couered vs with the shadowe of death. Also comparing the church to a vine: wherefore (saith he) hast thou broken

Psalm.79. Psalm.44. Psalm.80.

downe her hedges, that all they that go by pluck of her grapes? The boare out of the wood hath destroyed it, & the wild beasts of the field haue eaten it vp. It is burnt with fire & cut down. To be short, we may behold the estate of the Church in these words: Let Israel now say, They haue often times afflicted me from my youth, they haue often times vexed me. The plowers haue plowed vpon my backe, & made long furrowes. In like manner, after the ascension of Iesus Christ into heauen, hath not the Church been, and that continuallie, persecuted, and extreamelie afflicted: as may appeare by the booke of the Acts of the Apostles, and by the Ecclesiasticall histories, in the verie which, a man may note ten general persecutions, which were kindled in al the quarters of the earth, by the publike decrees of the Emperours, besides those that were particular, which were made in diuers places by the Gouernors, or seditious of the people. It is a horrible thing to thinke, and almost incredible, of the bloud

Psal. 129.

Examples of the afflictions of the Church since the time of the newe testament.

bloud which was then shed, & of the desolations of Cities, yea and of some whole Prouinces. For as the Church was then spred ouer all the world, so in all the kingdomes of the earth this furie of persecution was kindled. It was enough for any to confesse that they were Christians, and they should be slaine by thousands. Among other persecutions made by *Hadrian* Emperour of *Rome* in the 9. yeare of his Empire, he caused ten thousand Christians to be crucified in *Armenia*. *Dioclesian* and *Maximinian* hauing enterprised to constraine the Christians, by al manner of torments and cruelties, to renounce their religion, and to sacrifice to the Idols, they forced them after a fashion so furious, that in the space of 17. daies there were 30000. put to death, and as manie or more chained and carried to the mettalls, a torment resembling after a sort, the punishment of the gallies at this day. In those daies such crueltie was excercised at *Trenios* vppon the riuer *Mosel*, that the riuer was red with

Henrie of Ersord.

Oros. lib. 7. chap. 25. Vrsperg.

Vincent. in his mirrour lib. 12. chap. 136.

the bloud of the Christians beeing slaine. The booke intituled *Fasciculus temporum*, witnesseth that the Christians that were in *England*, were all put to death. To bee short, whole townes were burned with their inhabitants, for the hatred of Christian religion. As touching the varietie of the sorts of tormens and cruelties, the diuell surmounted himselfe in deuising them: Some were cut in peeces: Some were tormẽted with stripes of rods euen to the bones: Some were cast to the Lions, to the Beares, and to the Tygers to bee deuoured: Some were couered with beasts skins to be torne in peeces of wolues and doggs: Some were burned quicke: Some were broyled vpon gridirons: Some were crucified: Some had their bodies dropped on with burning pitch and boyling lead: Some were drawne vpon the pauement of the streetes: Some were dashed against the stones: Some were tumbled downe headlong from high places, & into riuers: Some they smothered with smoake procee-

Euse. lib. 8. chap. 11.

ding

ding from a ſmall fire: Some had their intrailes pearced with ſharpe ſtakes: Some were throwne into the Lime kils: Some were ſlaine with the ſtripes of ſtaues and lead: Some had ſharpe reedes thruſt betweene their nailes and their fleſh: Some had red burning plates put vnder their armepits: Some were ſcorched quicke, and then ſprinckled with vineger, or powdred with ſalt: Some were ſet vp quicke vppon forks, and ſuffered to die of hunger or thirſt. And thoſe that could eſcape into the deſerts & mountaines, either they died of hunger, or of thirſt or of cold: or they were deuoured of wild beaſts, or ſlaine of theeues, or caried away ſlaues to the *Barbarians*. Now, although theſe examples ought to ſuffice to make vs vnderſtand what the condition of the Church hath alwaies been, and ſo conſequentlie of the children of God: we will yet notwithſtanding, ſet forth ſome particular examples of thoſe that haue been the moſt excellent ſeruants and children of God. *Abel* hauing offered

Examples of particular members of the Church afflicted in the time of the old testament. Gen.4. Mal.1.2. Gen.28. Gen.31. Gen.32.

vnto GOD a more excellent sacrifice than *Cain*, and so receiuing the testimonie that he was iust, was mischieuouslie & traiterouslie murthered by his brother. Among the Patriarches, let vs consider the afflictions of *Iacob* beloued of GOD: After he had been long time in feare of the threatnings of his brother *Esau*, at the last he was constrained to forsake his fathers house: Being with *Laban* his vnckle, he serued him the space of 20. yeares, feeding his flockes, induring the cold of the night, and the heate of the day: In the meane time he receiued so manie iniuries at the hands of his vnckle, that he resolued with his wiues the daughters of *Laban*, to steale away from him, and to depart without bidding him farewell. He being thus (as it were) fled, he was pursued of *Laban* prouoked to anger, & determining to vse him violentlie, if God (as himselfe confesseth) had not forbidden him. Hauing escaped his hand, he fell into a newe and horrible feare, for the comming and meeting of

of his brother *Esau*, fearing (as he sheweth by the praier which he made to
GOD) least he would slay both him,
with his wiues and children. His el- Gen.35.22.
dest sonne committed adulterie, and
that not with a straunge woman, but
with his fathers owne concubine. His
daughter is rauished and defiled. His Gen.34.
children prophane circumcision the
sacred seale of the couenant of God,
making it to serue to murther, as they
did, al the inhabitants of *Sichem*, who Gen.35.
asked nothing of thē but friendship.
By this crueltie more than barbarous, they exposed their father, themselues, and all their house, to manifest
daunger of vtter rooting out by their
neighbours, if GOD had not held
them backe. His owne children hauing sold their brother *Joseph*, they
made their father beleeue that he was Gen.37.
deuoured of wild beasts. Being pressed with famine, he sent his sonnes into *Ægypt* to get corne: whereby *Si-
meon* being kept prisoner, he vnder- Gen.42.
stood that there was no hope of his
deliuerie, but in sending his yongest

sonne *Beniamin:* which was, as it were, to take away his soule. What manner of life then is this of the good Patriarch, but continuall anguishes and afflictions, as himselfe confesseth, saying vnto *Pharao*, that the daies of his pilgrimage were fewe and euill? Among the Prophets let vs take *Moses*, to whome GOD shewed himselfe more familiarlie. When he was yet a little infant, he was put foorth and abandoned vnto death: beeing after come to the age of fortie yeares, and feeling that God had ordained him to deliuer his people *Israel*, he began to exercise his vocation in slaying the *Ægyptian*: wherevpon he was constrained to forsake the Court of *Pharao*, and to flie. And withdrawing himselfe into the land of *Madian*, he serued *Iethro*, feeding his sheepe the space of fortie yeares: He, I say, that was taken for the sonne of *Pharaos* daughter, that might haue enioyed the riches and pleasures of *Ægypt*. Being after returned into *Ægypt* by the cōmandement of GOD, to deliuer the people

Gen. 47. 9.
Exod. 2.
Act. 7. 25.
Exod. 2.

people of *Israel*, incontinently so soon as he began to exercise his charge in speaking to *Pharao*, the *Israelites* being more afflicted than before, tooke occasion to murmur against him. Hauing conducted the people to the red sea, againe they rose against him with dangerous complaints. And finallie, hauing retired themselues into the desert, he was in continuall trouble, anguish and torment, for the plaints and murmuring of the people, for the enuie of his owne brother and sister: but aboue all, for the vengeances that God executed vpon his people, and speciallie for their sinnes, as whē they made the golden Calfe: And this hauing continued the space of 40. yeres, at the last he died in the desert without entring into the land of promise. Wee may to this purpose set downe many other notable examples, as of *Iob, Dauid*, and others. But as euerie one may note their great and sundrie afflictions by the reading of the sacred Histories, so it shall suffice to set foorth this which the Apostle writeth

Exod. 14. 1

Num. 12. 1.

Exo. 32. 19.

Deut. 34.

to

Heb.11.35. to the *Hebrues*, ſpeaking of diuers of the faithfull, and ſeruants of GOD: Some (ſaith he) were racked, & would not be deliuered, to the end that they might obtaine a better reſurrection. Other were tried with mockings and ſtripes: yea and by bands and impriſonment. They were ſtoned, they were hewen aſunder, they were tempted, they were ſlaine with the ſword, they wandered vp and downe in ſheepe skinnes and in goates skinnes, being deſtitute, afflicted and tormented, of whome the world was not worthie, wandering in deſerts and in mountaines, and in deepe pits and caues of the earth. As touching the examples of the children and ſeruants of God, which haue been ſince the comming of Chriſt in the fleſh, he alone maie and ought to ſuffice, for as much as wee muſt bee faſhioned like to his image, and followe his ſteps. Now, this Prince of glorie making his entrance into this world, created and maintained by him, found no place in the Inne, it pleaſed him to bee borne

Examples of the children & ſeruants of God afflicted vnder the newe Teſtamēt.

in

in a stable, and to be laid in a manger Luk.2.
in stead of a cradle. By and by after
Herode sought to slay him: for the Matth.2.
which cause he was carried into *Æ-
gypt* by *Ioseph* and *Marie*. And what
pouertie (trow ye) indured he there?
Is he returned into *Iudea*? there he Mark.6.3.
passed his life vntill he was 30. yeares
old, in the abiect and base estate of a
Carpenter: Did he begin his charge? Matth.4.
after hee had fasted fortie daies and
fortie nights, he was hungrie, and had
not whereof to eate in the desert.
During these fortie daies and fortie
nights, he was assailed of Satan and
tempted, and finallie indured those
three mightie assaults recited of the
Euangelists. Hee suffered pouertie, Luk.9.58.
not hauing one pillowe to rest his
head on, and liued by almes.

Hee was violently pressed with in- Luk.8.3.
iuries, being called glutton, drun-
kard, deceiuer, and one possessed
with diuells. He was carried violent- Mat.11.19
lie to the top of a mountain to throw
him downe headlong. Hee was be- Mat.27.63.
traied of one of his owne Apostles:

He

Ioh.7.20. He was taken prisoner, spet on, buffe-
Luk.4.29. ted, beaten, mocked, scourged, crow-
Matth.26. ned with thornes. He was condem-
&.27. ned to die, and hanged vpon a crosse betweene two theeues. And besides these persecutions and outward torments, what anguishes did he feele, when he swet bloud and water for distresse and feare? When hee cast his face vpon the earth, & when he cried on the crosse, My God, my God why hast thou forsaken me? let vs adde to
Act.9.16. this example, that of S. *Paule*, that vessell of election. When he was conuerted, Iesus Christ said vnto him, that he would shewe him what he should suffer for his name. And so it came to passe, as he himselfe doth brieflie recite, making comparison of his owne person, with some of the false Apo-
2 Cor.11. stles: Are they the ministers of Christ?
23. I am aboue them, in trauailes more aboundant, in stripes more than they, in prisons more, in deaths often. Of the Iewes I haue receiued (saith he) fiue times fortie stripes sauing one. I haue been three times beaten with rods,

rods, once I was stoned, three times I suffered shipwracke: night and day haue I bin in the deepe sea, in iornies often, in perills of floods, in perills of theeues, in perills of mine owne nation, in perills of the Gentiles, in perills in the Citie, in perills in the deserts, in perills in the sea, in perills among false brethren, in labour & trauaile, in watching often, in hunger & in thirst, in fasting often, in cold and in nakednes: besides the things that happen to me without, there is that which combereth me euerie day, euen the care that I haue of all the Churches. Now, let vs applie these exāples to our purpose. When the Church is persecuted, and the members thereof afflicted, the flesh calleth in doubt, whether we bee the true Church and children of God, or no. But what afflictions indure we, that the most excellent seruants and children of God haue not suffered before vs, as it appeareth by the examples here before alledged. And where is it that we find, that troubles & the crosse are markes

The vse of the afflictions of the church, and of the members thereof.

of

of the falſe Church, and of the children of the world, and not rather the
contrarie, as it hath been ſhewed a-
boue? The people of *Iſrael* beeing ſo
grieuouſlie afflicted in the captiuitie
of *Babilon*, and that for their ſinnes,
God by *Eſay* calleth them, his welbe-
Esa.41.8. loued one, and his elect: and prote-
& 49.15. ſteth that hee can leſſe forget them,
than the mother her child. And that
he had them grauen in his hands, hauing them alwaies before his eyes.
And ſpeaking of them to *Ezechiel*,
Ezec.11.15 he ſaith: Thy brethren, thy brethren,
the men of thy kindred. He conten-
teth not himſelfe to call them once
his brethren, but doubleth the word,
ſaying: Thy brethren, thy brethren,
and addeth, men of thy kindred, that
he ſhould not thinke, becauſe they
were in this miſerable condition, that
they were caſt off of GOD, but that
he ſhould acknowledge them for his
brethren. In like manner, the Holie
ghoſt ſpeaking of thoſe that were
murthered and caſt to wild beaſtes,
Psalm.79.2 calleth them the ſeruants of God and
his

his faithfull ones. The Apostle to the Hebrues speaking of the faithfull which were tormented and afflicted after sundrie manners, and cruellie put to death, saith: That the world was not worthie of them. It is as if he should say, that they being the welbeloued children of God, and brethren of Iesus Christ, the world full of abominable people, was not worthie that they should be conuersant and be any more among them. And so farre off was it that S. *Paule* entred into doubt of himselfe for his troubles, that contrariwise he alledged them to prooue that he was a more excellẽt seruant of Christ thã the others, hauing indured more than they al. And if this sentẽce pronounced by the father touching Iesus Christ: This is my welbeloued sonne in whom I am well pleased, bee true, euen then when he swet bloud & water for distresse, and then when he thought he was forsaken of GOD, so as being in this hell, he continued still the dearelie beloued sonne of GOD: what occasion haue we then, when wee are afflicted with our head, to

Heb. 11. 38.

2. Cor. 11. 23.

Mat. 17. 5.

Luk. 9. 31.

to doubt of our adoption? Let vs set before vs the great number of faithfull which were before the throne & in the presence of the Lambe, clothed with lōg white robes, holding palmes of victorie in their hands: and let vs vnderstand by the testimonie of the
Reue.7.9. holie Ghost, who they be. These are they (saith he) which are come from great tribulation, and haue washed their long robes, & haue made them white in the bloud of the Lambe. Therfore are they before the throne of God, and serue him day and night in his temple. And he which sitteth vppon the throne will ouer shadowe them: they shall neither haue thirst nor hunger, and the Sunne shall beate vpon thē no more, neither any heate: for the Lambe which is in the midst of the throne shall gouerne them, and leade them to the fountains of liuing waters, and God shall wipe away all teares from their eyes. When S. *Peter* exhorted his disciples to constancie,
1.Pet.5.9. saying: That they knew well, that the same afflictions were accomplished in

the

the companie of their brethren which were in the worlde. And when Iesus Christ said to his Apostles: ye are happie when you suffer iniuries and reproches, for so haue they persecuted the Prophets which were before you. The intention neither of Christ nor of Saint *Peter* was to set before them the comfort of miserable persons, as it is saide, to haue companions in their miseries, but rather to shew them, that the afflictions which they indured were proper to the seruants and children of GOD, and that therefore they ought to comfort themselues, beeing honoured with the liuerie of their other brethren and members of Christ, yea, the most excellent seruaunts of God, as the Prophets were. And indeede seeing those whom God had foreknowne, those hee hath predestinate to be fashioned like vnto the Image of Christ. Let vs not doubt (for so Saint *Paule* saith) that it is a true saying, that if we die with him, we shall liue also with him, and if wee suffer with him, wee shall also raigne with him. Let vs remember the saying

Mat.5.12

Rom.8.29

2.Tim.2.11

Iho. 15.20 ing of Christ to his Apostles: The seruant is not aboue his Master, If they
haue persecuted mee, they will also persecute you, if the world hate you, know
that they haue hated mee before you.
And this should be a thing monstrous
Iho. 15.18 to see, vnder a head crowned with
thornes, members handled delicatelie.
Shall wee doubt then of our adoption,
beeing called vnto the same condition
which the welbeloued Sonne of GOD
tooke vpon him going to the inioying
of his glorie? Will wee refuse to follow
him, ascending vp by the crosse into his
Kingdome? Hee hath suffered (sayth
1.Pet 2.21. Saint *Peter*) Leauing vs an example
that wee should followe his steps. Let
vs not then thinke it strange, as he saith
1.Pet 4.12. in an other place, when wee are as in a
fornace, for our triall, as if an vnwonted
thing had come vnto vs. But rather in
as much as wee communicate with the
afflictions of Christ; Let vs reioyce, that
when his glorie shall appeare wee also
may reioyce with gladnes. Now let vs
vnderstand how he addeth, that suffering iniurie for Christes sake, wee are
happie,

happy, forasmuch as the spirit of God, which is the spirit of glory resteth in vs, and the feeling which we haue, causeth vs to glorifie him, though of the blinde worlde he is euill spoken of. Seeing then the heauenly father hath vouchsafed vs such loue, that wee are called the sons of God, although the world persecute vs, because it knoweth neither the Father, nor vs: Let vs saie boldlie with S. *Ihon*, We are now the children of God: And although it dooth not yet appeare what we shal be, yet we knowe (as hee also addeth) that when Christ shall appeare we shall be like vnto him. for we shall see him as hee is. Let vs be contented to be dead in this worlde, and to haue our life hid with Christ in God, beeing assured, that when Christ our life shall appeare, we shall also appeare in glorie. If the Diuell will gather of our afflictions, that we are not the children of GOD; let vs say boldlie that he is a lyar, or let him first plucke out of the ranke of God his children, the Martyres, the Apostles, the Prophets, and other of the best and most approo-

1.Ihon.3.1

Col.3.3.

ued children and seruants of GOD, which haue beene afflicted as well as wee, and more than wee: Euen the holie Virgine and Christ himselfe. But rather seeing that wee beare their liuerie, let vs acknowledge our selues the children of GOD with them, and let vs say (with a holie resolution) with
Rom.8.38. Saint *Paule*, that there is neyther death, nor life, nor Angells, nor principalities, nor powers, nor thinges present, nor thinges to come, nor heigth, nor depth, nor anie other creature which can separate vs from the loue of GOD, which he beareth vs in Iesus Christ our Lorde.

That the faithfull haue the common afflictions of the children of Adam, because of the excellent fruites of them, testimonies of their adoption, and of the loue of God toward them.

Cap. 9.

TO bee yet better confirmed in this trueth, let vs now consider how the afflictions themselues, euen those that are common to the childrẽ of *Adam* serue for our profite and saluation. First, for as much as the reliques of sinne abide still, euen in the most perfect in this life, which maketh them hardened in their faults, and inclined to offend God: We haue neede of helpes, to be waked, to be humbled, and drawen from our sinnes, to keep vs in the time to come, and so to dispose vs to a perfect obedience, holie, and acceptable vnto God. And to this ende tend the afflictions of the children of God, which for this cause are called chastise-

1. Fruit to awake vs out of our sinnes.

stisements, corrections, and medicines of our soules. The children of *Jacob* hauing committed a detestable crime
Gen.42.21 in selling their brother *Joseph*, but they neuer thought of it, vntill that beeing in *Aegypt* pressed with reproches and imprisonment, they called to minde their sinne, saying one to the other, surely we haue sinned against our brother: for we saw the anguish of his soule, when hee besought vs, and wee woulde not heare him, and therefore is this trouble happened vnto vs. *Manasses* King of *Iuda* hauing set vp Idolatrie againe, persecuted those that woulde purelie serue
2.Chro.33 the Lorde, so as *Ierusalem* was full of blood; and hauing shut his eares to the admonitions of the Lorde, at the last was taken by the army of the king of the *Assyrians*, bound with manacles, fettered in chaines, and carried prisoner into *Babylon*. Then, being in afflection, he was exceedingly humbled before God, hee prayed to the Lord, and was heard, and caried backe vnto *Jerusalem*. Then hee pulled downe all Idolatrie, reformed the seruice of God, and comman-

ded

ded *Iuda* to serue the Lorde the God of *Israell*. Yea, the poore pagane marriners, of whom the historie of *Ionas* maketh mention, seeing the continuaunce of the tempest, concluded to cast lots to know who was the cause of that affliction; and God making it to appeare that it was the sinne of *Ionas*; thereof is Ion.1.7
come a common Prouerb in a daungerous tempest; that there is some *Ionas* in the ship. And this procéedeth of a feeling and apprehension of the prouidence and iustice of GOD: this little sparke yet still remaining in man of the image of God, whereby we thinke, that it is hee that afflicteth, that he is iust, & doth nothing but iustice, and so, that afflictions are corrections of our sinnes. Therefore *Ieremie* iustly reproueth the blockishnesse of the people of *Israel* in this, that being afflicted, no man saide Ierem.8.6
what haue I done? See now why God, to make vs more liuelie feele his iudgements, & to the intent to wake vs vp, & to conuert vs vnto him, sendeth vs oftētimes afflictions, which after a sort answere, & haue some conformitie to our

 sins.

sins. As for example, *Ezechias* king of *Iuda* sinned by ambition or vain confidence, in shewing all his treasures to the Embassadors of the king of *Babel*: and GOD tolde him by the Prophet *Esay*,

Esa.39 that all his treasures should be transported into *Babel*. *Dauid* offended God

2.Sam.11 in committing adultery, and in putting to death *Vriah*, and GOD chastised

2.Sam.13 him in this, that *Amnon* his sonne defiled his sister *Thamar*; and that *Amnon* was slaine by his brother *Absolom*,

2.Sam.16.22 that *Absolom* laie publikely with his fathers Concubines, according to that

2.Sam.12.11 which God had saide vnto him: Thou hast done it in secrete, and I will doo it in the sight of all the people. The child

2.Sam.12.10 borne in adultry died, & he was threatned, that the Sword should not depart from his house. Now as the afflictions

2\. Fruit, amendment of life and first in workes. bring vs to the feeling of our sinnes, to wake vs vp, and to humble vs; so therof riseth the resolutions and protestations to fall into them nô more, but to amend them. And this is it that is seene in those that by tempest of sea, or some grieuous disease, are in manifest danger

of

of death. They examine their cõsciẽce, their sinnes & infirmities then come before them: they aske pardon, and make protestations to liue better in time to come. The same also we see in children that are beaten of their fathers. This is it which the Apostle to the *Hebrewes* teacheth vs saying, That no chastisement for the time seemeth pleasant, but grieuous: but after it bringeth the peaceable fruites of righteousnes. And before he had said, That God chastiseth vs for our profite, that we might be partakers of his holinesse. The goodnesse of God (saith S. *Augustine*) is angrie with his children in this world, that hee may not bee angrie with them in the life to come: and by his mercie he vseth some temporal seueritie, to exempt thẽ from euerlasting vengeance. According vnto this, S. *Bernard* made this praier vnto God; Lord burne and cut in this temporall life, that thou maist be mercifull to me in the life that is euerlasting. And it is the same that S. *Paule* teacheth saying; When we are iudged and afflicted, we are nurtured of the Lord, that wee might

Heb. 12. 11.

Prosper in sen. ex. Aug. 5.

1. Cor. 12. 32.

might not be condẽned with the world. And to this purpose *Dauid* protesteth,
Psa.119.67 that before hee was afflicted hee went wrong: but now (saith he) I keepe thy commandements. Againe, It was good
Psa.119.71 for me that I was afflicted, that I might keepe thy statutes. Medicines are giuen either to heale diseases, or to preuẽt thẽ, and therefore are verie requisite for the health and life of man. Nowe what bee these afflictions, but medicines of our soules? as also S. *Augustine* saith, This which thou so lamentest, is thy medicine, and not thy punishment. As in a house where there are manie children, the rod is necessarie: & as in a Citie subiect to diuers diseases, & where there is an euill aire, Phisitions are needfull: so in the house of god, where ther are manie children inclined to euill, the rod is many times more necessarie than bread: and in such an hospitall full of diseases and sores, as the Church is (for out of it they are dead) it is a great fault if there be not Phisitions and Surgeons to heale the corruptions of our soules, & to keep vs from offending God, & from falling into death. Many accustomd to delicate

meats,

meats, haue their mouths out of tast, & after falling sick, they take bitter drinks to recouer againe the health of their bodies: let vs chearfully do the same for the health of our soules. And indeede, behold the difference betweene a madd man, and one that is sicke of a corporall disease; The mad man is angry with the Phisition, chaseth him away, and throweth awaye the medicine: but the other sendeth for a Phisition, taketh drinke at his hand, thanketh him, yea and giueth him a reward: So when God the soueraigne Phisition of our soules, visiteth vs and giueth vs wholsome medicines, let vs not be like mad men reiecting the hand of God, but receiuing the medicine, let vs giue him thankes and blesse him, after the example of *Iob*. Furthermore, howsoeuer the goods and other commodities of this life ought to bee helpes to lift vp our hearts to the spring from whence they come, that is to the goodnesse and power of God, to prayse him: our corruption and affection to the world dooth turne them quite contrarie to thornes and hinderances, so as God oftentimes cutteth them off, or taketh

2. In words & affectiō of heart.

keth them away, or mingleth thē with afflictions, to turn vs from euill, to draw vs vnto him, and the better to dispose vs to his seruice. Experience sheweth, that in bankets and feasts men talke of the world: but where sicknesse, death and burials are, they talk of euerlasting life. It is also seene that riches lift vs vp in pride and insolencie, and that pouertie bringeth vs downe and humbleth vs: that in prosperity we triumph, and feele not the force of the spirituall instructions and teachings: but being afflicted with sicknesse or anie other way, thē we are godly people, wee confesse that all flesh is but grasse, and that we haue here no abiding Citie. To be short, our infirmities tending vnto death, make vs to lift vp our vnderstanding and affections to a better life. Then God, who is good, and dooing well vnto men, who taketh not pleasure in our euills, afflicteth vs not, but to wake vs the better, & to sanctifie vs in his obedience, purifying our affections, and by the sorrowes of troubles maketh vs to abhorre our corruptions, the verie cause of them. He

doth

doth as the good keeper of a vine, who John 1.
cutteth his vine, that it may beare more and better fruite, not suffring it to grow wilde, in leauing too manie boughes on it. And as we cut the winges of hennes and other birdes, that they should not flie away and be lost: so God cutteth off from vs the commodities of the flesh to keepe vs downe, that we lift not vp and destroy our selues with vain confidence & pride. We see also that the corne shut within the chaffe commeth not foorth, if the eare be not beaten: and that it tarieth stil in the chaffe if it be not fanned. The like hapneth to the childrē of god if they be not beaten and fanned by tribulations, to be seperated frō the chaffe of the world, and the pleasures & impediments that be in it. The Prophet *Osea*s when he would shew how God wold Hose. 2. 6.
turne away his people from following idolatrie. I will hedge (saith he) thy way with thornes: wherein hee giueth vs to vnderstand, that as the beasts that go by the way, & see on the side of them faire fields, assaying to goe to thē, & running vpon the hedges of thornes, if they feele the

the sharpe prickes, they goe backe and return into the way: So, when the children of God goe out of the right waye to heauen, to goe to the fieldes of this world & o: the flesh; God maketh thē to come vpon the thornes of afflictions, to the ende that by their prickings they may turne backe againe. When a Mother willing to weane her childe shal say vnto him night and day, My childe, it is time to weane thee; thou art growen great inough, and I am with childe, my milke is corrupt, it will make thee sick; yet he is so fond of the breast, that he cā-not forsake it: but if the Mother put wormwood or mustard vpō the breast, the childe sucking it and feeling the bitternesse, hee quite forsaketh it, without sucking anie more. Euen so, though the preachers preach vnto vs, and exhort vs to forsake the corrupt milk of the world and of the flesh, yet we seeme deafe still and are alwaies backward, vntill God put vppon these cursed teates the mustard and wormwood of afflictions to weane vs.

We haue also of our owne nature too much

much confidence in our selues, & in humane meanes, so as we know not what it is to hope in God against hope, & to trust to him without gage in the hand. So the riches, estates, traffiques, the leaning vpon men, on the husband to the wife, on the father to the children, on the good Prince to the Subiects, are vnto vs as vayles, that keepe downe our sight vppon the earth, and as staues for vs to leane vpon. Now, our God takeing away these vayles and carnall leaning stocks, maketh vs to feele the weaknesse of our faith to humble vs, and to constraine vs to looke vnto him with a pure eye, to cleaue vnto him alone, and wholly to depende vppon him. According to that Saint *Paule* saith, That hee had receiued the sentence of death in himself, that he might haue no confidence in the flesh, but in him that raiseth vp againe the dead.

3. In confidence.

2. Cor. 1. 9.

This is it also which Saint *Peter* teacheth by the similitude which hee proposeth in the first chapter of his first Epistle and the seauenth verse, comparing the afflictions to fire, & faith to the golde, for as golde is put into the fining pot and furnace, not to consume it, but to trie and purifie it: so our faith is tried and purified in the fire of tribulations. For as it hapneth to him that is quiet and at his ease, that he falleth soone asleepe, and hauing an apple or anie other thing in his hand, it falleth, or is easely takē frō him: so the ease of the flesh bringeth vs a sleep in the world, & causeth vs to leese the spiritual good things and to suffer them to fall to the ground. On the contrarie side, the more one forceth to take away a staffe which I holde in my hand while I am awake: so much the faster I shut it in, & hold it the harder, that it may not be taken away from me. Euen so the more the diuell indeuoureth to take faith from vs by tribulations, so much the more doo wee meditate on the promises of God to holde it fast: and the more he thrusteth at vs to ouerturn vs, so much the more strongly we leane vpon the staffe of faith, to ouercome his assaults. From hence also proceedeth this excellent fruite of inuocation of the name of God.

4. In Inuocation and praiers.

And

And surelie in the time of prosperitie, when we are at our ease wee pray not ordinarilie, but of custome and for fashion, but being pressed with necessitie, being assailed on all sides, finding no comfort in the earth, and feeling that we perish if God doo not strengthen, aide and deliuer vs: Then it is, that with all our hearts, wee crie vnto the Lord, that wee protest that he is our father and sauiour, and that our trust is in him: as the feeling of our diseases is it that maketh vs runne to the Phisition. The historie of the booke of Iudges sheweth by manie examples that the people of Israel being in peace grewe corrupt, but after beeing afflicted they had recourse to GOD, asking of him deliuerance. When God slewe them (saith *Dauid*) Psal.78.34.
then they sought him, & turned them selues, and rose earlie in the morning to seeke after God, and then they remembred that God was their rocke, and that the high and mightie GOD was their redeemer. I will goe (saith the Lord by his Prophet *Osee*) and re- Ose.5.15. & 7.1.

turne to my place, vntill they confesse their fault, and seeke my face: They shal seeke me diligentlie in their trouble, saying: Come, let vs returne vnto the Lord, for it is he that hath spoiled vs, and he wil heale vs, he hath striken vs, and he will cure vs. So long as the
Luk.15.11. prodigall sonne had meanes, he continued in his disorders: but beeing brought to extreame pouertie, he remembred his fathers house, and returned vnto him. Furthermore, our
5. In patience and hope. patience is prooued and augmented by troubles, as S. *Paule* teacheth: and
Rom.5.3. by the experience of GOD his assistance, our hope groweth, in so much as making vs (in the time of need) to feele his goodnes, his power, and his trueth, in strengthning and sustaining vs in assaults and conflicts, and in deliuering vs out of our afflictions: he sealeth in vs the assurance of this his
Ioel.2.32. promise, that whosoeuer calleth vpon him shall be saued. And he that shall put his trust in him, shall neuer be cō-
Ro.10.13. founded. For this cause S. *Paule* teacheth vs to reioyce in our tribulatiōs:

adding,

adding, that tribulation bringeth pa- Ro.10.11.
tience, and patience experience, and Rom.5.3.
experience hope. And S. *Iames* exhor- Iam.1.2.
teth vs, to compt temptations for
matter of great ioy, forasmuch as the
triall of our faith ingendreth patiēce.
By the same meanes he trieth our o-
bedience and fashioneth vs. For when
God intertaineth vs in prosperitie ac- 6. In obe-
cording to the flesh, it is easie to sub- dience, be-
mit our selues to so sweete handling, cause he
and to frame our selues according to that affli-
his will, with acknowledging of his cteth vs, is
goodnes and loue towards vs. But first our
when he afflicteth vs with sicknes, po- creatour.
uertie, reproach and other calamities.
Then to feele that he loueth vs, to like
this handling, to subiect our selues
to this his will: herein consisteth Rom.12.1.
true obedience. Then, he afflicteth vs
to trie vs and to fashion vs in this o-
bedience, in as much as working in vs
his children by his spirit, he maketh
vs to cōmit our selues to his gouernment, to depend vpon him, & to suffer
our selues to be guided by his hand,
offring our selues as a liuing sacrifice,

holy and acceptable vnto God, considering that it is reasonable, that wee being his, by right of creation and redemption, he may dispose of vs as it pleaseth him. And herein there are two things to be considered. First, in as much as hee is our creatour, wee ought to practise that which *Dauid*
Psal.39.10. saith: Lord I haue held my peace, and haue not opened my mouth, because it is thou that hast done it: shewing thereby, that whether he tie vs to our bed by sicknes, or bring vs to pouertie, or driuing vs from place to place, he bring vs to many discommodities, or euen make vs to languish in prison, or passe through the sword or fire, we must thinke and say, Lord I hold my peace and will not murmure against thee: but render thee obedience, because it is thou that hast done it: for thou hast all authoritie ouer me, in as much as I am thy creature. And indeed if after the similitude of a potter, who is able to make of the selfe same lumpe of earth, some vessells of honor, and others of dishonor, Saint

Paule

Paule sheweth, that God hath authoritie to chuse some to saluation, and to reiect others, so as they that are reiected to be damned eternallie, haue no cause to replie or murmur: how much more ought wee to hold our peace & obey, when he disposeth that we shall be afflicted but for a little time, and that in the bodie onelie? But that in this obedience wee may feele indeed that we are happie, we must marke an other poynt: that he which doth afflict vs, is not onelie our creatour, but also our redeemer: not only God, but also our GOD and father. And that same assureth vs, that according to the loue that he beareth vs, and according to his infinite wisedome, hee will dispose nothing of vs, which shall not be to his glorie, and to our benefite and saluation. It is well knowne that fathers & mothers take no pleasure to afflict their children, and to make them to weepe. And although they haue power to beate them, to appoynt them their diet, and to put them abroad, either to schoole, or to

Rom. 9. 20.

2. Because he is our father and redeemer.

ſerue ſome other, yet when they doo this, men doo not onlie confeſſe that they haue authoritie ſo to do: but alſo euerie one beleeueth, that it is for the benefite of the children, whoſe duetie alſo it is to like well of it, and to render vnto them willing obedience. Now, properlie God onlie is our father, as Ieſus Chriſt ſaith: Call ye no
Mat.23.9. man father vppon the earth: ye haue but one father, which is in heauen. What iniurie then doo we to this onlie true father, that we being afflicted by his hand, after what manner ſoeuer, doo not ſanctifie his name, conforming our ſelues to his will, thinking and confeſsing, that all proceedeth from his goodnes and loue, to his glorie, and our benefite and ſaluation? See how, in the ſchoole of affliction, we learne what it is properlie to obey God: and that is verie neceſ-
Heb.5.8. ſarie for vs. For, if Ieſus Chriſt being the ſonne, notwithſtanding learned obedience, by the things which he ſuffered: how much more had wee neede to learne to ſubmit our hearts

and

and our neckes by afflictions, to the guiding of our God, as children yeelding themselues peaceablie to the gouernment of their father, saying with *Iob:* The Lord hath giuen, the Lord hath takē, his name be blessed: Iob.1.21.
And with *Dauid* persecuted of *Absalom:* If God say to me, thou pleasest me 2.Sam.15.
not, behold I am here, let him do vn- 16.
to me whatsoeuer pleaseth him. And beeing readie to sacrifice our owne children with our owne hands vnto God, when he shall commaund vs, as *Abraham* did in olde time. To bee Gen.22.
short in following GOD, as the old prouerbe is, in what condition or estate soeuer it shall please him to call *Sen. de vita*
vs. If then afflictions serue, to awake *beata. cap.*
vs out of sinne, to humble vs, to cor- 15.
rect the infinite corruptions that are in vs, to pull vs from the world, to cleaue vnto God, & to draw our harts from the earth, to lift them vp to heauen, to fashion vs in the obedience of GOD, to giue vs increase in patience and faith. To be short, to make vs so much the more feruently to pray vn-

to God; it resteth that wee conclude, that indeede they proceed from the loue of God toward vs, & of the care that he hath of our saluation, and so, that in afflicting vs, he sheweth himselfe indeed our father: as the Apostle to the *Hebrues* doth also teach vs, saying: That God chastiseth those whom he loueth, and correcteth euery child whom he receiueth: If you indure (saith he) chastisement, God offereth himselfe vnto you, as vnto his childrē. For what child is it whom the father doth not chastise? Then, if ye be not vnder chastisement, whereof all are partakers, yee are bastards and not sonnes. Rods then are testimonies, that he accōpteth vs his lawfull children, and not bastards. And nature it selfe teacheth it vs. For, if wee see two children striue together, and a man comming by, taketh the one of them and beateth him, leauing the other, we will iudge by and by that this man is the father of him that he did beate, and that the other appertained not vnto him. And this is it that S. *Peter* meaneth,

Heb. 12. 6.

meaneth, saying: that iudgement beginneth at the house of God: shewing that they are his children and houshold seruants, which are afflicted in this life. The which thing a good auncient father did thinke and well expresse, calling his afflictions, bitter arrowes shot from a sweet and amiable hand. Therefore as, when we see the Carpenters strike with their hatchets vpon pieces of wood to pare it, or plane it: and Masons to polish stones with the strokes of an hammer; wee gather that these are stones and timber, which the master would imploy to some building: Euen so let vs conclude of our selues, that if God lift vp vpon vs the hatchets and hammers of afflictions to polish vs: It is a manifest and sure testimonie, that he hath chosen vs to put in the building of his temple. And that so, we are his children both welbeloued and happie. But let vs passe to another consideration of singular comfort.

1.Pet.4.17.

Grego. Nazian.

Of

Of the afflictions for the name of Christ, and of their fruites.

CHAP. 10.

Rue it is that God being iust, doth neuer afflict vs vniustlie, which thing we ought alwais to think and confesse, to humble our selues, and to giue glorie vnto God. Neuerthelesse, GOD doth not alwaies take occasion of our sinnes to punish vs, but often times hee sheweth this fauour to his children to dispose that the cause and title of their afflictions should bee honorable, calling them
Matt.5.10. persecutions and sufferings for righ-
Mar.10.29. teousnes sake, for the Gospell, for the
Col.1.24. Church, for the name of our Lord Ie-
Matth.5.11 sus Christ, and for the loue of GOD.
Rom.8.35. And this commeth when we are per-
What are the afflictions for Christ. secuted of men, because wee will not approue iniquitie, or false doctrine, nor defile our selues with idolatries and

and superstitiõs, but serue God purelie and holilie according to his word. To be short, when we will liue in the feare of God in Iesus Christ, as Saint *Paule* speaketh, who speaking of these afflictions saith: To you it is giuen of God not onlie to beleeue, but also to suffer for his name: wherein he shew- eth, that such afflictions are the gifts of GOD proceeding from good will & loue towards vs: And see why Iesus Christ said, Blessed are they which are persecuted for righteousnes sake: Also, Blessed are you when men shall reuile you, and persecute you, & speak all manner of euill against you, lying of you for my sake: reioyce ye, and be glad. Whereunto Saint *Peter* agreeth, saying: If ye suffer wrong for the name of Iesus Christ, ye are happie.

2.Tim.3. 12.
Phil.1.29.
They that suffer for Christ are happie.
1 By the testimonie of the word of the God.
Mat.5.10.
1.Pet.4.14.

Now, if we haue no other foundation than the onelie testimonie of Iesus Christ to assure vs, that being persecuted for his name, God loueth vs, and will make vs blessed, were it not an vntollerable impudencie for the diuell, and an incredulitie inexcusable

ſable for vs, to call that in doubt, which he, who is the trueth it ſelfe, doth affirme? Notwithſtanding, to the end that we may the more liuelie feele this felicitie than when wee are perſecuted for his name: let vs conſider the reaſons which the holie ghoſt giueth vs. Firſt, when Ieſus Chriſt had ſaid: bleſſed are they which ſuffer for righteouſnes ſake, he addeth as a rea-

2. For the promiſes. 1. Of the kingdome of heauen. Mat. 5. 10.

ſon: For theirs is the kingdome of heauen. They that through zeale and charitie imploye themſelues to maintaine the innocencie and right of an other, and aboue all the trueth of God, incurre ordinarilie the hatred of the world, lifting vp it ſelfe againſt them, to bring them to ruine. But let them comfort themſelues: for what can they leeſe, seeing the kingdome of heauen is theirs, and cannot bee taken from them? Yea farther, ſeeing theſe perſecutions aſſure them, and prepare them to come thether, Ieſus Chriſt addeth that wee are bleſ-

Mat. 5. 12.

ſed, and that wee ought to skip for ioye when anie iniurie is offered vs,

either

either in word or deed,lying on vs for his names ſake.For your reward(ſaith he) is great in heauen. Note that he ſaith in heauen : for it ſhall be ſpeciallie in the life to come, that we ſhall receiue it. Yet notwithſtanding,in an other place he promiſeth recompence in this preſent life. For marke what he ſpeaketh to his Apoſtles : Verelie I ſay vnto you,that there is none that ſhall forſake houſe, or brethren, or ſiſters, fathers, mothers, or wiſe, or children,or lands, for the loue of me, and of the Goſpell, which ſhall not now in this world receiue an hundred folde as much,houſes,brethren, ſiſters,fathers,mothers,children and lands with perſecution, and in the world to come life euerlaſting. Now, the purpoſe of Ieſus Chriſt is to teach vs, that when by perſecution it ſhall happen that wee ſhall be conſtrained to forſake father, mother, brothers, ſiſters,and lands, he will giue vnto vs, in that poore,vile and baſe eſtate cauſed through perſecution, more ioye, contentment and happines, than if

2.For the reward:

1.In this life.

Mar.10.29.

we

wee had recouered an hundred fathers for one, and an hundred times as much lands and possessions, as was taken from vs. And experience maketh the faithfull to feele the trueth of this promise. And we should feele it much more aboundantlie, if the mouth of our faith were greater. But yet in this weakenes of faith, doo not we knowe, that the wicked in their aboundance are poore, and wee in our pouertie are rich. Their couetousnes is insatiable, and like vnto fire, which, the more wood you put on, the greater it is. As for vs, wee finde contentment and rest in the prouidence of GOD, which neuer forsooke those that put their trust in him. In the time

1.King.17. of *Eliah*, manie had greater store of foode than the widdowe of *Sarepta*, vnto whom he was sent: but she hauing this blessing of the Lord, that the oyle failed not in the cruse, nor the flowre in the barrell, she had more than the richest in the countrie: As he that hath a spring of running water in his house, may say, that hee is more

more assured, and hath more plentie of water, than he that hath it in a cesterne, and that all broken. Besides, this great happines that we feele our selues to be the children of God, that being pilgrimes in this world, the end of our voyage is to come to heauen, which also wee see open, and Iesus Christ reaching out his hands vnto vs to gather vs into his glorie, giueth vs more contentment without comparison, in eating of bread, and drinking of water, than the vnfaithfull haue in all delicates, hauing nothing in their hearts but the world and the earth; and liuing, or rather languishing in continuall feare to be sodainlie depriued of all that, wherein they set their whole felicitie.

This is it which *Dauid* noteth, saying: A little that the righteous hath is more worth, than the great aboundance of the wicked. Yea, the verie ordinary experience teacheth vs, that GOD prouideth for our necessities both more aboundantlie than euer we looked for, & also by such meanes Psal.37.16.

as we neuer thought, accomplishing in his children persecuted, that which Saint *Paule* saith: That godlines hath
1.Tim.4.8. the promise of this present life, and of the life to come. If then (as it is said) the contented bee rich, and that it is not the aboundance which giueth this contentment, but the feeling that wee are the children of a father that is almightie, which loueth vs with a loue incomprehensible, in his beloued sonne, who hath taken vpon him to make vs happie. It must needes followe, that euen in this life we recouer an hũdred times as much, as we haue lost through persecution. And who is he that can doubt if he carefullie meditate this sentence of
Rom.8.31. Saint *Paule*? He that hath loued vs so much, as he gaue his owne and onlie sonne vnto the death for vs, much more shall he giue vs all other things with him. And indeede, seeing wee are the members & brethren of him, whom God hath appoynted the vniuersall heire of all things: let vs not doubt but that all things are ours.

As

As alſo the goods of the houſe appertaineth to the pupils, although the Tutor gouerne it, and giueth it them by portion: and that which is more, hee ſhall ſometimes appoint to euery one his diet, according to that which by the coũſell of the Phiſition ſhall bee thought fit. And indeede if wee ſeeke firſt the kingdom of God and his righteouſnes, Let vs not doubt, following the promiſe of Ieſus Chriſt, but that all other things ſhall be added. In the meane time we muſt eſpecially lift vp our vnderſtanding to the reward promiſed in the life euerlaſting. For true it is, that beſides this contentment whereof wee haue ſpoken: God (to ſhew that it happeneth not for lacke of power to enrich his children, that pouertie and other afflictions do often follow and accompanie the profeſsion of the Goſpell) dooth oftentimes diſpoſe, that they which haue forſaken father, mother, & their worldly goods for the name of Ieſus Chriſt, finde afterwardes many, which ſerue them for fathers and mothers, and obtaine after greater poſſeſ- Mat.6.33

ſions in ſollowing the Goſpell, than they had before. Alwayes this is not the purpoſe of Chriſt to haue vs to reſt vpon ſo bare recompence, as to giue vs goods which are common to the wicked and the infidels. Saint *Paule* propoſeth to the bondſlaues of men, for re-
Col.3.24 compence of their faithfull ſeruice, the inheritance of Heauen. The children then of the houſe of God, ſhold do thēſelues great wrong, to looke for at the hands of a Father, ſo mightie, ſo rich, & ſo liberall, earthlie and tranſitorie riches, & other commodities of the fleſh. Hee eſteemeth it not agreeable to his greatnes, nor to the anguiſhes and trauailes of thoſe which haue forſaken father, mother, their goods and their life for his ſeruice, to giue them things ſo vaine: to the ende, that they ſhould not ſet their mindes thereon, thinking that their felicitie lay in them. The Maſter of a houſe, who keepeth his inheritance for his Sonne, doth not thinke that he doth any thing for him, to clothe him with the liuerie of his ſeruants: as alſo when any one ſhall be receiued for a

Prince

Prince into any countrie, he may well cast some peeces of golde or siluer, amongst the people, to shew his liberality, but the honors and dignities are distributed among his fauourits. GOD wil not feast our bodies with the seruice of our soules. He is liberall and iust, & therefore will recompence Spirituall conflicts with Spirituall Crownes, and accept our labors, not according to the vilenes of our harts, but according to the dignity of his greatnes: seeing also, that he crowneth not in vs, our workes, but properly his owne. Of one and the selfe same seruice, there is one recompence of a King, and an other of a Merchant; so as when we would content our selues with earthly goods, God might answere with better reason than (in old time) *Alexander* the great, that it were enough in regarde of vs that shoulde receiue it, but not in regard of him that should giue it vs. They that knowe the vanity of worldly thinges, haue no contentation but in heauenly things, yea, and will say with Saint *Augustine*; Lorde, if thou shouldest giue

August.

Manuel.
Aug. cha.

mee all that thou hast created in the world, that shoulde not suffice thy seruant, except thou gaue mee thy selfe. As also he saith in another place, All aboundance, which is not my God, is to me scarcitie. Wee must then set before

2. In the life to come

vs the reward promised in the eternall life, wherwith (without al doubt) *Moses* was liuely touched in his hart, when he refused to be called the son of Pharaohs daughter, choosing rather to bee afflicted with the people of GOD, than to enioy for a small season, the pleasures of sin, esteeming the reproch of Christ greater riches than al the treasures of *Ægypt*. For (saith the apostle) he had respect to the reward, which also he receiued, not in this present life, wherin he was afflicted vntil his death; but in heauen, whither hee lifting vp his eies, feared not the furie of the King, but held fast, as if hee sawe him, that is inuisible. The same Apostle writing to the *Hebrevves* that beleeued, sheweth very well, that they also did vnderstand this reward. For he beareth them

Heb. 10. 34

witnesse, that they had taken ioysullie the

the ſpoyling of their goods, knowing, that they had a better riches in heauen, which abideth for euer. Wherein alſo he confirmeth them, adding this exhortation: Then caſt not off your confidence, which hath great reward. Now although, as touching our ſelues, we can not comprehend what this reward ſhall be, yet ought we certainly to beleeue it, that it is moſt certaine, becauſe Ieſus Chriſt hath promiſed it; and moſt excellent: ſeeing that Saint *Paule* affirmeth, that the ſuffrings of this preſent life are not woorthie of the glorie to come, which ſhall be reuealed in vs. As alſo he ſayth in an other place: That our tranſitorie afflictions which indure but a ſmall time, and are gone in a moment, ſhal bring forth in vs an eternal waight of glorie maruelous excellent. And to giue ſome taſte in waighting for the ful reuelation, and inioying of it, let vs note in this laſt ſentence of Saint *Paule*, the compariſon that hee maketh of our afflictions that are ſwift, and paſsing in a moment, and the eternall waight of glorie maruellous excellent, which

The fruite in the life to come incomprehenſible: firſt, for the greatneſſe.

Rom. 8. 18

2. Cor. 4. 17

they bring foorth. For true it is, that our outward man decayeth, as hee said, meaning thereby the losse of health, of riches, honours, friendships, aliances, and other such aides and commodities of this life, and the life it selfe: but in the meane time the inward man is renued euery day, by an happy and excellent chaunge, in goods and honours that are spirituall, heauenly, and eternall. And indeede what is all that which we suffer and lose here for Iesus Christ, in respect of the infinite and incomprehensible good things, which we shall recouer in heauen, whereof also we haue a feeling in this present life? Are we constrained to forsake a fleshlie father? Beholde the heauenly father which offereth himselfe at hand, who alone properly is our Father, as is saide before. What lost the
John 9. man borne blinde beeing cast out of the Synagogue, and refused of the Scribes and Pharisies, when Iesus Christ met hym and receyued hym? If any spoyle our worldly goods, God offereth vs the Kingdome of heauen. If the earth will not beare vs, the heauens open to receiue

receiue vs. If the people of the worlde driue vs away, the Angells offer their presence, acknowledging vs their companions in glory: If men curse vs, those wordes are but winde; and God in the meane time doth blesse vs, & turneth euen the curses of our enemies into blessings as *Dauid* speaketh. If we be thrust 2.Sam.16
out of our offices or dignities, Iesus 12
Christ giueth vs things more excellent, making vs kings and priests to God his Reue.1.6
father: If our parents disdaine vs, & wil not know vs, Christ is not ashamed to auow vs, and call vs his brethren. If we Heb.2.12
be depriued of the succession & inheritance of our parents, Christ acknowledgeth vs the heires of God his father, and fellow heirs with him. Do any make vs weep for sorow? Christ presenteth him selfe to wipe away our tears, & to turne our sorows into perfect ioy. Are we not receiued into any town to be an inhabitant there? God giueth vs freedome in heauen, to dwel in that heauenly *Ierusalem*, the streets whereof are paued with fine gold, the wals are made of pretious stones, the gates are pearls, whereof the

son of god is the temple & the sun. Are we put to death? it is to enter into a better life, ful of ioy and glorie. And indeed let vs consider here the wõderful goodnes of God. As he knoweth that we are too much tied to goods, dignities, and other commodities of the flesh, that in stede of willingly laying vp our tresure in heauẽ, we lay it vp in earth: he so disposeth that we shalbe persecuted for his name, & doth therin, as a good & faithful Tutor, who takyng the mony of his pupill, putteth it out to profit, or buieth for him good rents with it. And hereunto tendeth that which *Dauid* sayeth:

Psal. 56. 9 Thou hast nũbred my fleetings, do thẽ put my tears in thy bottle, are they not noted in thy register? This beeing true, how much more wil he put the drops of blood which we shed for his name into his barell, and in his Register the reproches, the flittings, the losses of father, mother, lands and other goods, the imprisonments, the other afflictions; and aboue all, the deaths which we indure for his seruice and glorie? As also it is

Psa. 116. 15 written, Right deare in the sight of God is

is the death of his Saints. And to what ende serue these registers? They shalbe laid before, not onely the persecutours, to make thē feele so much the more horrible iudgement and vengeance: but especially before vs, to make vs feele an incomprehensible increase of glorie and of ioy, in shewing vs what we haue suffered for his name, and in accepting vs before his Angels. But let vs now consider how our afflictions are of small cōtinuance, and passing away as in a moment, in respect of the weight of the eternall glorie which they bring. And first let vs say boldly, that our troubles are short, because our daies are short; & that the glorie is of long continuaunce, because there shall be no ende of it. But for the better vnderstādіng of the shortnes of our afflictions, we must consider according to the instruction of S. *Paul*, the things inuisible, that are eternal. For in respect of them, wee shall finde, that the visible things which concerne this life, are temporall, that is to say, during a little time. The Patriarch *Iacob* being demaunded of *Pharao* of his age, he answered

2. Because of the eternitie.

2. Co. 4. 18.

Gen.47.9. swered, that the yeres of his pilgrimage
had been few and euill. And how were
they few, seeing he had liued 130.yeres?
surely in comparison of 8.or 900. yeres
which his forefathers had liued, as also
he addeth, that his yeres had not attained to the yeres of his fathers. How then
are not our daies short, not comming at
the most but to 70. or 80. yeres, & that
in those that haue the strōgest or migh-
Psa.90.10. tiest bodies, as the song of Moses importeth. God speaking of the captiuitie of
Babylon which cōtinued 70.yeres, saith
Esai.54.8. thus: I haue for a little while as in a moment of mine indignation hid my face
from thee. How? 70.yeares, are they a
little time, is that but a moment of indignation? yea, in respect of the comforts and euerlasting happinesse, which
he would communicate to his people:
as he addeth, That he would haue compassion on them with euerlasting mercie. This also is the cause why S. *John*
calleth the time folowing Christs com-
1.Ioh.2.18 ming in the flesh, the last houre: as if he
wold diuide the cōtinuāce of the world
into 3.or 4.hours, wherof the last shuld
be after this cōming of Iesus Christ vntill

til the end of the world: so this last hour should now haue cōtinued 1587. yeres, and these 1587. yeres should not be yet a whole houre finished. This seemeth strange to vs. But let vs set before vs 2. eternities of times: that which was before the foundation of the world, & that is an infinite time (if a man may cal that time) and a swalowing vp of the vnderstanding of man: and the eternitie of time which shal be after the ende of the world, and behold againe an incomprehensible infinitenes of time. Now let vs consider the continuance of the world betweene these two eternities. When it shall continue 7. 8. or 9000. yeares, this should not be, in respect of these 2. eternities, 2. or 3. houres, no not one houre: it should bee yet lesse than one graine in respect of all the sand in the world: for, as touching the sand the nūber is finite, but in eternitie there is no end. And here vnto tendeth that which S. *Peter* sayth, That before God, 1000. yeres are but as one day, and a day as 1000. yeres, forasmuch as before the eternitie of GOD, there is no numbring of time; for there is no time at all. According vnto this, 1. Pet. 3. 8.

Moses

Psal.90.4. *Moses* saith, that 1000. yeres before god are as a day that is past. If then 1000. yeres are but as a day past, or an houre, 60. or 80. yeres are but as one minute of time: so the longest continuance of our afflictions should be but one minute; & yet there are some that accomplish not that. And when doo we begin this minute of tribulations? seeing that a great part of our life passeth before we suffer anie thing for the name of Christ; & yet there is some intermission in them, if it were but in sleeping. Then, we doo now see how true it is, that S. *Paule* saith, that our afflictions passe in a moment. And what is that which this moment of afflictions bringeth vs? An eternal waight (saith he) of glorie, as wee haue largely

In the first chapter. shewed here before. And in deede there shall be no ende saith the Angell, of the

Luk.1.33. kingdome of Christ. And wee are the house of *Jacob*, ouer whom he shal raign for euermore. And S. *Paul* saith, that be-

1.The 4.17 ing risen againe, and ascended into heauen, we shalbe with Iesus Christ euerla-

Joh.3.& 6. stingly. For whosoeuer beleeueth in him hath euerlasting life. If God for the

full

full measure of our felicitie shalbe all in 1.Co.15.28
al, when we haue him in vs, who is eter-
nall and immortal, we shall enioy a glorious immortalitie: as also S. *Paul* saith,
That hee hath brought to light, life and
immortalitie by the gospel. To be short,
S. *Matthew* hauing set forth vnto vs the
last iudgement, saith, That the sheepe Mat.25.46.
that shall bee at the right hand of Iesus
Christ, shall goe into euerlasting life. E-
uen so, when he promiseth vs a perfect
ioy, he addeth, that it shal neuer be takē Ioh.16.22.
from vs. Now, what comparison is there
betweene one moment of affliction, &
a glorie, a life, and a ioy, that shal last e-
ternallie and without end? Then when
we thinke that our crosse is long & heauie to beare, let vs set before vs the excellencie and the eternitie of the incomprehensible glorie, wherunto we ascend
by it, whereof also wee feele the earnest
pennie & beginnings in our hearts, waiting for the full feeling, and thorow enioying of this felicitie, when we shall be
lifted vp, and put in possession of the
kingdome of heauen. Now this reward
is certaine and assured to al those which
shall

ſhall ſuffer for the name of Ieſus Chriſt. Such afflictions then are ſeales of the loue of God towards vs, & teſtimonies that he taketh vs into the number of his beſt beloued children, and that he will make vs indeed & euerlaſtingly happie.

Other fruites of the afflictions for the name of Ieſus Chriſt.

Chap. II.

1.Fruit, honor to be a Martyr of Chriſt. BEſides theſe, both excelent & eternal good things, which the ſufferings for the name of Ieſus Chriſt doth bring vs, there is yet the honor that he doth vs, to bring vs foorth to be witneſſes of his truth. In regard whereof, although all they that preach the Goſpell are called witneſſes of Ieſus Chriſt, yet this title of Martyr or witnes, is after a more particular maner, and by excellencie attributed vnto ſuch, as to maintaine the truth of the doctrine of the Goſpell, ſuffer conſtantlie perſecution, and eſpecially vnto death. So we read that S. *Paule* gaue to S. *Ste-* Act. 22. 20 *phen* this title of honor, calling him the

Mar-

Martyr of Iesus Christ. And S. *Iohn* maketh mention of *Antipas*, whome hee calleth a faithful Martyr of Christ. And in the same booke of the Reuelation, he saith, that he saw the great whore drunk with the bloud of the Saints, & with the bloud of the Martyrs of Iesus. In like manner the apostle to the *Hebrues*, hauing recited how many faithful had bin mocked, scourged, cut in peeces, stoned, & otherwise persecuted, he addeth, that in them wee haue as it were a cloude of martyrs or witnesses cõpassing vs round about, and exhorting vs to follow constantly their exãple. The Apostles did well vnderstand and confesse this honor, who after they had been publikelie whipped for the name of Iesus Christ, they went before the councel, reioycing that they had this honour to suffer reproach for his name. And indeed when when we indure persecution, to maintaine the glorie, the authoritie, and the truth of Christ, against Antichrist and his supposts, it is as if Iesus Christ shuld borrowe our goods, our renowme, our bloud, our life, to serue for autenticall

Reu. 2. 13. Reu. 17. 6. Heb. 11. & 12. Act. 5. 40.

seales

ſeales, & moſt ſure witneſſes that cannot faile,of the right and the glorie that appertaineth vnto him. And what are we poore wormes of the earth, that the eternall Sonne of GOD, the King of Kings, and Lord of Lords, ſhall doo vs this honor, to put his glorie (as it were) into our handes, to bee the keepers and defenders of it, againſt thoſe that would ſpoile him of it? And heere let vs conſider the incomprehenſible wiſedome and goodnes of God towards vs. The moſt perfect offend God daylie, and one onely ſinne, be it neuer ſo little to our iudgement, deſerueth death, and euerlaſting condemnation, then it is yet more than the loſſe of our goods, & the corporall life. Now in ſtead of exerciſing his iuſt iudgements vpon vs, hee doth vs this honour, that it which wee endure (which is not the thouſand part of that wee haue deſerued) chaungeth the nature, and in ſtead of beeing the puniſhment of ſinne, God imputeth it, as a moſt excelent ſeruice for the main-

2.Frute,the glorie of God,decla-

tenance of his glorie. But yet there is more. For what are wee to ſuffer wil-

linglie?

lingly? The loue of riches, ambition, the pleasure of fleshly commodities, the affectiō toward father, mother, wife, children, & aboue al to this life, is so strong and vehement in vs, that in stead of renouncing them for Christ, we renounce Christ, and his Kingdome to entertaine vs. And experience sheweth this too much. We are also so very impatient and daintie when there is any question of suffering, that if we should but onely snuffe a candle with our fingers, we wet them with our spittle, that wee might not feele the fire of that small snuffe, which yet we throw from our fingers in al haste: and how then should we abandon our bodies to the death, entring quicke into the fire to be there consumed, if God did not strengthen vs supernaturally? Howe shoulde wee maintaine his trueth against the supposts of Antichrist, if the spirit of his father, the which he promised vs, did not worke mightily in vs? Then when we see these vessells so fraile and weake, to surmount the threatnings of kings, the apprehension of fire, the assaults of Antichrists

claring and accomplishing his power in our infirmitie, and shewing his goodnes, and the trueth of his promises: first toward euery faithfull.

Mat. 10. 19
20

tichrists supposts, and the temptations proceeding from father, mother, wife, and children; are not these so many testimonies of a wonderfull and mighty grace and power of God, which fortifieth them, and maketh them victorious against Sathan, the worlde and the flesh? I can doo all things (sayth Saint *Paule*) through Christ who strengthe-
Phil.4.13 neth me. And in an other place, I re-
2.Cor.12 ioyce (sayth he) in infirmities, in iniu-
10 ries, in necessities, in persecutions, in anguishes for christ. For whē I am weake, then am I strong, euen thorough the might and power of Christ, which shewed it selfe, and was made perfect thorough his weaknesse, as hee had saide before. So then this constancie, this faith, this zeale, & other vertues which God communicateth (by his free goodnes) to his elect, are manifest by persecutions, which otherwise shoulde bee hid. As in running the course, the agility or swiftnes of the horse is known, the strength of a mā in the combat, the sauour of many drugges, in rubbing, or brusing of them, or casting them into

the

the fire, as we see in the incense. The Starres (saith Saint *Bernard*) which appeare not by day, shine in the night, so the vertue that is hid in prosperitie, sheweth it selfe in aduersitie. Now, this which wee haue saide of the power of GOD, shewing it selfe in the infirmitie of his children to his glorie, is seene also in the bodie of the Church, which ordinarily is so poore, so weake, so little holpen, at the handes of men, that if GOD did not sustaine it, it shoulde quickly be swallowed vp. Then when we see it so mightelie assailed, by the potentates of this worlde, conspiring her ruine, by so many forces and slights, and by so many heretiks, doth not God in the guiding, deliuering and preseruing of it, shewe that it is hee himselfe, and he alone, which maintaineth and defendeth it? And that his power and wisedome is woonderfull, in preseruing it against so many enemies, and that his truth is certaine, in accōplishing that, which he hath promised vs, of being with his Church vntill the end of the world? And that it is he which is

Bern. tr. in Can.

2. Toward the body of the church.

Mat.28.29 the stone cut out without hand, which,
Dan.2.34 hath broken, and dooth still breake the great image representing the empires, and kingdomes of the worlde: Which to shew vnto vs more liuely, oftentimes he so disposeth, that leaning vpon the strength of men, she hath beene throwen downe, and being throwen downe, God hath lift her vp againe without meanes, and beyond all hope of man, that all men may know, that the preseruation of the Church is not the worke of Man, but indeede the very worke of God. As also the Lord declareth to
Iudg.7.2 *Gedeon* this his intent, commaunding him to abate his army. There is too many people with thee (sayth the Lord) that I shoulde giue *Madian* into their handes, least peraduenture *Israel* would glory in themselues against mee, saying: My hand hath deliuered me. See also howe it commeth to passe, that when the Deuill thinketh quite to ouerthrowe the Church by persecution, God quite contrary, hath aduanced and increased it: Saint *Luke* hauing recited that the high Priestes and the chiefe ruler

3. Fruit, the aduancement of the church.

lers of the Temple, & the Sadduces lay- Act.4
ing hands vpon the Apostles, put them
into prison, he addeth by and by, that
many of those that heard the word, beleeued. and the number was about fiue
thousand persons. When Saint *Ste-* Act.8. &
phan was put to death, the Church at 11
Ierusalem was quite dispersed: but by 19
the faithfull dispersed, there were as
many more newe Churches set vp. And
it is as if GOD tooke, at the handes
of his enemies, corne into his Garner to
sowe, whereof should follow a goodlie
and plentifull haruest. It is a fruit that
Saint *Paule* noteth in his. afflictions,
saying, Brethren, I woulde haue you to Phil.1.12
vnderstand, that the things which hapned to mee, came to the aduauncement
of the Gospell: so as my bandes were
made famous in Christ, through all the
Iudgement hall, and in all other places: And many of the brethren (made
bolde by my bandes) durst speake of
the worde more freely. *Iustine* in his
communication with *Triphon* writeth
that the same thing hapned in his time.
It may appeare (sayth hee) euery day,

that wee which beleeue in Christ, cannot be astonished nor daunted of any, if they cut off our heades, if they crucifie vs, if they cast vs vnto wilde beasts, or into fires, or vnto any other torment; the more they torment vs, so much the more increaseth the number of the christians, neyther more nor lesse, than as men cut their Vines, to make them the more fruitfull. So the Diuell is greatly beguiled. For in persecuting those which professe the Gospell, hee thinketh to stoppe men from beleeuing in Iesus Christ, to be saued. But it falleth out quite contrarie. For the poore ignoraunt men seeing the constancie of the Martyres: gather twoo pointes, first, that there is no hypocrisie in them, nor any fleshlie pasion which maketh them to followe this doctrine, which to maintaine they vtterly abandon all the commodities of the flesh, the honours of the world, and life it selfe. Next, they are induced to thinke, that the doctrine for which they suffer, is of GOD, seeing it is by no humane, but by very diuine power, that they suffer constantly and willingly so many reproches, discommodities and cruelties. And so is this Sentence so famous verified: That the blood of the Martyres is the seede of the Church. In like manner those that haue alreadie the knowledge of the doctrine, are confirmed as wel to perseuere in it, as to take corage and strength to suffer in like manner for the maintenance of it. For, seeing that GOD forsaketh not his seruants in the conflict, but is with them, and in them, making them victorious: we take thereof assuraunce, that GOD will also ouercome in vs all temptations, threatnings and torments: And beholding them, thorough death to enter into life, and by the Crosse to ascend into the Kingdome of Heauen, wee feele our selues inflamed with desire to be their companions both in the troubles, and in the triumph of glorie. The which thing maketh vs to perseuere constantly in the trueth of the doctrine, which setteth (as it were) before our eyes this soueraigne felicitie, euen the heauens open, and Iesus Christ stretching out his hand, to drawe vs vp into the fellowshippe of his ioye, and glorie incomprehensible and eternall.

The people of the world cannot vnderstand these so excellent fruites of the afflictions for the name of Christ, which we haue set downe heere aboue, being therein like to the Philistins the companions of *Sampson*, which coulde not comprehend this proposition that
Iudg.14. hee made them; Out of the eater came
14 meate, and out of the fierce came sweetnesse: But wee, that are taught in the Schoole of Christ by his Spirite, wee vnderstand and beleeue that as *Sampson* hauing vanquished the Lion, found in the bodie of it honnie, so we hauing constantly ouercome all the persecutions and troubles of this life, which are like vnto fierce and cruell Lions, readie to deuoure vs, wee shall finde this honnie so excellent of the fruites of the crosse of Christ, which shall make vs blessed for euermore. Seeing then, that the persecutions and afflictions that we suffer,

suffer, serue so abundantly and so manie waies and manners to the glorie of god, and the edification of our neighbors, & doo also turne to so great good and honour vnto vs: let vs conclude boldlie, that we beeing so afflicted for the name of Iesus Christ, ought to bee confirmed in the assurance that wee are the members of the true Church, and that God compteth vs for his welbeloued Children.

An exhortation to perseuere constantly in the truth of the Gospell in the time of persecution, not to feare death, to keepe vs from apostacie and dissimulation, to vse the holy Ministerie, to walke in the feare of God, and to pray to him.

Chap. 12.

BY this, that is said aboue, it appeareth that it is so far off, that we haue anie matter to complaine or to be offended at our afflictions, that rather wee haue iust

1.*Cor*.9. iust argument to reioyce, & to comfort
To perse- our selues. And indeed, behold the cou-
uer constāt sel of God, who hath ordained that such
ly in the do should be the way which leadeth vs to
ctrine of glorie. When anie runne in a race, all
the truth, runne, but hee onely beareth away the
with con- prize, which shal runne best. They then
stancie and runne vncertainly, but wee runne with
hope vnder assurance to obtaine the prize, although
the crosse, other runne better than we: onelie let vs
for the as- runne constantly vnto the ende. Like-
surance of wise we striue, not in doubt as those that
of the feli- beate the aire, but it is with the good
citie & ho- fight of faith, assured of the victorie, &
nour of it. by the victory of a crowne, not of leaues
1.*Tim*.6.12 that fade in three daies, but incorrupti-
1.*Cor*.9. ble for euer. And we be not as they that

are mad or superstitious, suffering at all aduenture without knowing wherfore. Wee knowe that it is for the truth, wee know that this truth appertaineth vnto vs, we know that God hath created and lightened vs, to maintaine this truth and grace of God to his glorie. How manie Martyrs hath there been in olde times past, that had not so much knowledge as wee. If wee goe backe, they shall be

our

our Iudges: their zeale and constancie shall condemne our careles knowledge, and vnthankfulnesse vnto God. God hath not called vs to fight and to suffer, leauing vs wandring without a captain: Iesus Christ himselfe is our head, Captaine & guide, bearing his crosse before vs & crying, He that loueth me, let him followe me. Himselfe hath not refused this condition, but hath beaten & made the way, to draw & lift vp his owne into his kingdome. All the Prophets, Apostles, Martyrs, and blessed seruaunts and children of GOD are gone thether before vs. The worke it selfe of our saluation calleth vs thether, and the glorie of God requireth it. Ought we to dispute, whether we ought to obey? Shuld we doubt whether we will be fashioned like his Image, and weare the liuerie of the children of God? Let vs boldly enter into this streight waye, at the ende whereof we shall finde the gate of heauen. Let vs giue our neckes to Iesus Christ to receiue his yoake, and the honour of his order.

How manie great Lords of the world

trauaile

trauaile all their life to come to this honour, to be Knights of the Order of any Prince? And hauing attained to it, they accompt themselues happie men. And what bee the ensignes of such Orders? The one shall haue a Fleece, the other a Garter: and the ensigne of the Order of Christ, is prison, bannishment, losse of goods, reproaches, beatings, death. This is the Order that Saint Paule receiued, and whereof he gloried, saying, I beare
Gal.6.17. in my bodie the markes of Iesus Christ. Now although that a Fleece & a Garter, are in themselfes vile or base things, yet are they honorable and to be desired in the world, because princes take them for the ensigne of their Order, acknowledging and calling them brethren that weare thē. The ensigne then that Christ the King of kings hath taken for his order, shall not it be honourable? Shal we not accompt our selues happie to attain vnto it. Let vs folow cheerfully this glorious troupe marching before vs with triumph; honoured with this Order of the Prince of Glorie, IESVS Christ.

Let

Let vs suffer our selues to be guided by him, who is infinitely wiser than we, and loueth vs better than wee loue our selues. And let vs receiue this fauour of GOD, that so seruing his glorie, our glorie may also be aduaunced. Let vs not be troubled nor shaken with feare, whē we see the persecutors come to the ende of their enterprises, and the children of GOD afflicted. That is to them (sayth Saint *Paule*) a manifest token of destruction, and to vs of saluation. There is no greater curse (sayth Saint *Augustine*) than the prosperitie and felicitie of the wicked, because it is as a strong wine to make them drunke in their iniquities, and to make a heape and tresure (as it were) of the wrath of GOD vpon them. It seemeth to vs that the worlde goeth to confusion and disorder, when the wicked triumph, and the children of God weepe. But on the contrarie, that is to vs a manifest token of the iust iudgement of GOD, as Saint *Paule* sayth, That wee are also made worthy of the kingdome of GOD, for which also wee suffer.

Philip.1.28

2.Thess.1.5

suffer. For it is a iust thing (saith hee) with God, to render affliction to those that afflict vs, and to vs that are afflicted, deliueraunce; then, when the Lord Iesus shall shewe himselfe from heauen with the Angels of his power, and with the flame of fire to doo vengeance vpon those that did not know God, & obeyed not the Gospell of our Lord Iesus Christ, the which shal be punished with an euerlasting punishmēt from the face of the Lord, and from the glorie of his power, when he shall come to be glorified in his Saints, & to be made wonderfull among all the faithfull. Wee are so impatient, so hot, or so foolish, that wee consider nothing but the beginning of the workes of our God: but wee must ioyne them together, and consider the accomplishment of thē, as S. *Iames* teacheth vs, Ye haue heard the patience of *Iob*, and haue seene the ende which the

Ia.5.11. Lord made, and that the Lord is verie mercifull and full of pitie. He that shall set himselfe to consider in his minde how poore *Ioseph* was handled, & sold of his brethren, & how (refusing to consent to

the

the shamefull and detestable request of his Mistres) he was cast into prison, and kept there 2. yeres, surelie a man would take pitie on him, as on a miserable person: but let vs see the accomplishment of the worke of God: let vs cōsider him (by this meanes) exalted to the gouernment of al the Kingdome of *Ægipt*, & then we shall count him happie. Aboue all, if we behold Iesus Christ, mocked, scourged, crowned with thornes, crucified between 2. theeues, who would not be offended, that the Prince of glorie & Sauior of the world shuld so be hādled? But let vs behold him risen againe, ascēded into heauen, & sitting at the right hand of God, aboue al principalities & power, inioying a glory incomprehensible, and we will admire and praise the worke of God. So if we behold his mēbers persecuted, banisht, mocked, spoiled, imprisoned, entering into the fire: what (will we say) is this a father, which handleth his childrē in this sort? But if we ioyne to the crosse the glorie, & the resurrection to the death: to bee short, if wee beholde them in that estate, where-

Gen. 37. 38.

wherein we shall be, when Iesus Christ meeting vs in his maiestie & glory shal lift vs vp aboue al the heauens, into the house of GOD his father, to liue with him euerlastingly, and that the Crosse shall be to vs as a ladder to go vp vpon, to the inioying of such a glory. Who is he then amōg vs that would not shout out for ioy, seing this wonderful worke of God? Who is he that wold not count himselfe happie? Who is he that would haue bin more daintily hādled? Who is he that would not be rauished with the bounty, wisedome & loue of God towards his children? He that neuer saw a haruest, seeing the plowman taking so much paine to till the earth, to spread it with dung, and after to cast faire wheat into the field so tilled, he would thinke that this man were mad, & that a childe were to be whipt that should do such a thing: but seeing after the haruest that should come of it, he woulde chaunge his minde, and acknowledge, that the husbandman had doone an excellent worke. Now, this is the time to til, to dung & to sowe, the haruest shal folow.

Let

Let not vs change the course of the seasons : neither yet let vs seperate them the one from the other, but let vs ioyne the time of the death with the day of the resurrection : and let vs assure our selues, as it is written in the Psalmes, that hauing sowed with teares, wee shall reape with ioye. He that in old time had seene poore *Lazarus* full of sores at the gate of the rich man, &. the rich man at the table in all delights and pleasure, he would not haue chosen to bee *Lazarus*, but the rich man. But if tarrying a while, he, sawe the soule of *Lazarus* carried straight, by the Angels, into heauen, and the rich mans soule goe to the fire of hell, he would change his mind and would desire to be *Lazarus*. Let vs then detest the glistering state of cursed riches, and let vs compt, the poore and afflicted condition of the Lazarusses of our time, waighting to be carried vp into euerlasting glorie, happie. The wicked haue nothing in heauen, nor we in the world. Blessed is the man (saith *Dauid*) whom the

Psal. 126 6

Luk. 16. 19

Psal. 94. 12.

Lord instructeth by the power of his spirit, and by the doctrine of his lawe, to haue contentment and rest in the time of aduersitie, while the graue is digged for the vngodlie, for an end of his felicitie. Yea, if we were called to suffer death for the name of Iesus
2. Not to feare death. Christ. What other thing is this death, but (after a long conflict) the day of victorie, the birth of a blessed soule after a great trauaile, the hauen desired after so furious tempests, the end of a dangerous and troublesome voyage, the healing of all wounds and sicknes, the deliuerance from all feare and terrour, the accomplishment of our sanctification, the gate of heauen, the entrance into paradise, the taking possession of the inheritance of the father, the day of our mariage with the Lambe, the inioying of our desires? Who is it then among vs, who feeling with S. *Paule* the bondage of sinne, would not crie out with him:
Rom. 7. 24. Alas wretched man that I am, who shall deliuer me from this bodie of death? And feeling the good that

death bringeth vnto vs, will not also say with him, I desire to be dissolued, and to be with Christ. If death wherewith God threatned our first parents is a feeling of the wrath of God in the soule, & in the body because of sinne. Wee may well say that death and life are two twinnes vnited and knit together, vntill the separation of the soule and the bodie: and this separation, which is cōmonlie called death, is rather the deadlie stroke of death, the bodie beeing then exempt from paine, and the soule from vice & corruption, waighting vntill the rest of death bee swallowed vp in victorie at the day of the resurrection. It is then an abuse to call life a continual death, and to call that, death, which is the end of a thousand deaths, and the beginning of the true life. It is then also against reason, that wee haue horrour of that which we ought to desire, and desire the continuance of that, the onlie end whereof bringeth vs to eternall felicitie And to this end Saint *Chrisostome* saith verie well, that it,

Phil.1.23.

Gen.2.17.

which is called life and death, haue deceaueable visours. Life deformed, and accompanied with manie miseries & calamities, hath a faire pleasant visour which maketh it to bee desired: and Death, so faire, happie, and to be desired, hath one deformed and fearefull. Let vs put off then, saith he, these visours, & we will change our minds, when wee shall finde vnder the faire visour of life, nothing but matter of heauines and displeasure, and vnder the foule & hideous visour of death, such a beautie and felicitie, as we shall incontinently be taken with her loue. So long as we liue we haue cruell enemies, which neuer cease making warre with vs, whome wee can neuer vanquish, but by death. And indeed wee cannot make the world to die in vs except we die our selues. Sinne which is in vs, liueth in vs, and fighteth against vs, vntill wee, dying, it also die with vs. And by death alone, the deadlie assaults of Satan our chiefe enemie, die foorthwith. But yet why should we feare it, which cannot come

vnto

vnto vs,but by the will of him who is
our heauenlie father, yea and at such
a time as he appoynteth? As *Dauid*
said: Lord my times, that is to say,all Psal.31.16
the minutes of my life are in thy
hands. There is no creature more e-
nemie to man,nor more able to hurt,
than the diuell. And indeed he is called, the enemie, the murtherer, and Mat. 13.39
the roaring Lyon seeking whome he Iho.8.44. 1.Pet.5.8.
may deuour. But the historie of *Iob* Iob 1.& 2.
sheweth plainlie, that GOD holdeth
him brideled, so as hee can attempt
nothing, nor goe either forward or
backward, more than GOD will permit him. And this which is more, he
hath not power to enter so much as
into the swine, without the leaue of Luk.8.32
Christ. What is this then that wee
should feare men? Are not they also
vnder the prouidence,power and gouernment of our GOD? It is GOD,
saith *Hannah* the mother of *Samuel*, 1.Sam.2.3
who weigheth their enterprises, so
as they cannot passe one ounce of the
waight ordained of GOD. It is he

1.Sam.2,6. that ſlaieth and maketh aliue againe:
which bringeth downe to the pit, and
lifteth vp againe: he maketh poore,
and maketh rich: he abaſeth and ex-
alteth. To bee ſhort, It is he alone, as
Pſal.115.3. *Dauid* ſaith, which doth whatſoeuer
he will. Now, wee doubt not, but he
will do that which he hath promiſed
vs, and wee knowe that he hath promiſed vs, yea and that he hath taken
vpon him to make vs happie. If then,
the doctrine of the prouidence of
God importeth, that he hath not onlie ordained in his eternall counſell
the end and iſſue of his worke (which
is his glorie, and the ſaluation of his
elect) but alſo the fit meanes, according to his infinite wiſedome, and re-
quiſite for the execution and accompliſhment of it: let vs be aſſured that
there is no creature that can let or alter his wil, as Saint *Paule* ſaith: If God
be for vs, who ſhall bee againſt vs. Let
Rom.8,30. vs alſo bee aſſured, that whatſoeuer
happen vnto vs, is the way whereby
he hath ordained to leade vs to life
and

and euerlasting glorie. Saint *Paule*, speaking of Iesus Christ, saith, that all creatures are of him, stand by him, and are for him. As also he saith in an other place, that of him, and by him, and for him all things are. Wherefore then doo wee feare our enemies, seeing euen this, that they are, is by the power and will of him, who is our head and sauiour; for asmuch as they can neither enterprise, nor consult, neither yet bee aliue one moment without the will of Christ? And besides this, seeing their life and being, is for him, and for his seruice, that they might be to his members, as fire to purifie them, a rod to correct thē, medicines to heale them, a bridge for them to passe vpon ouer the desert of this world, into the land of promise, ladders to helpe them to ascend into heauen, instruments to glorifie them, & as a knife that cutteth the cords by which we are held in the earth, & hindered to go vnto God, & to be where Iesus Christ our head is? Also, what threatning can the most mightie

Col.1.16.

Ro.11.36.

of the world threaten vs with more horrible, to make vs turne from the seruice of God, than those wherewith God threatneth all those that turne
Mat.10.28 away from him? Feare not, saith Ie-
Luk.12.24 sus Christ, those that can kill the bodie (and yet so, and when GOD will, and the bodie, which within a verie little after must needes die) and can doo nothing more: but feare him, who after hee hath killed the bodie, hath power to throwe both soule and bodie into euerlasting hell fire: him I say vnto you, feare indeede. In like maner, what promises can the world make vs greater, or more certaine, to draw vs vnto it, than those which our God hath made vs, to keepe vs in his seruice, and in his house, promising vs euerlasting life? Now, the Church is his house, and this good GOD hath called you (my brethren) thither, and hath receiued you. He hath nourished you in it sometime. He hath there giuen you the seale of your adoption. He hath begun to clothe you with the liuerie of his children, and hath

fashioned you like to the image of Iesus Christ. A great part of your way is
past. In this your trauaile of child-
hood you haue passed manie torments. If the greatest tormēts come,
the happie deliuerance approacheth.
He that shall continue vnto the end, Mat. 14.13
shall be saued. They that are reuolted,
and doo reuolt, make you to feele in
their vnhappines, how happie you
are, to be the children of God elected
to eternall life. For it is vpon this e- 3. To keep our selues from apostacie and dissimulation.
lection, and so, vppon the good plea-
sure of God, that your perseuerance
doth depend. Acknowledge in it both
his infinite mercie, supporting you,
and pardoning you daylie so manie
faults and sinnes, and also his incomprehensible goodnes leading you, as
it were by the hand, to the inioying
of eternall life. Abhorre you and detest that miserable, yea cursed and vn-
happie state of these Apostates, that
ye may also hate and detest the ambition and the pride, the euill conscience, the despising and abuse of the
gifts of G O D, the loue of the world
and

and thoſe other vices, which threwe them headlong into ruine. And on the contrarie, loue, ſearch and follow all that which God hath ordained to nouriſh godlines, faith, charitie, humilitie in vs, and other gifts and graces which proceed from the election, and are meanes ordained by the prouidence of GOD, to guide vs to the happines promiſed to thoſe which ſhall continue vnto the end. Keepe your ſelues hereafter from theſe falſe *Nicodemites*, who to auoid the croſſe, will abandon (by a ſacrilege vntollerable) their bodies to idolatrie, and ſo conſequentlie to the diuell, in reſeruing, as they ſay, their hearts vnto God. Will the moſt careles husband among them, content himſelfe, if his wife, giuing ouer her bodie to whoredome, ſhould ſay vnto him, that ſhe keepeth neuertheleſſe her heart vnto
1.Cor.6.19 him? Ye are not your owne, ſaith S. *Paule*, yee are bought with a price: Then glorifie God in your body and in your ſpirit, which both appertaine
2.Cor.7.1 vnto God. Againe, Clenſe your ſelues from

from all filthines both of bodie and ſpirit, finiſhing your ſanctification in the feare of God. Perſeuer conſtantlie in the Church, which is your mother, that you may bee the heires of the father. It ſufficeth not to keepe your ſoules from poyſon, ye muſt nouriſh them, that they may liue. Rather than we will ſuffer our bodies to die of hũger, wee will ſell all to get bread: and wee would runne through the fire in ſuch a caſe to ſaue it. At the leaſt, let vs followe thoſe that in the time of famine, forſake their Countries to finde foode. The ſoule is more precious than the bodie. And therefore muſt wee labour more to haue the bread abiding vnto eternall life, than for it that periſheth. Alwaies thinke with your ſelues our ſoules muſt liue, and it is to tempt G O D to deſire to liue without foode. Therefore wee muſt ſeeke foode, that wee maye liue.

4. To vſe the holie miniſterie.

Ioh. 6. 27.

Now, true it is, that to reade and meditate the worde of G O D in the houſe, and to keepe there the familie,

is

is a holie exercise,and very profitable
Col.3.16 for the noriture of the soule. It is cō-
Psa.1.2. maunded of GOD, and such as are
Act.17.11 negligent in this duetie, shewe that
Deut.6 Psa.119 they haue no care of the lite of their
Act.2.42 soules : yet this doth not suffice. Wee
must confesse the name of God, and
call vpon him in the assemblie : Wee
1.Tim.3. must heare the sermons,and commu-
15. nicate at the holie Sacraments : wee
must ioyne and keepe our selues vnited with the Church, which is the pil-
ler and sure ground of trueth,and the
mother of the children of God. This
Gal.4.26 onelie title of mother giuen to the
Church, teacheth vs, that there is no
entrance into the life that lasteth e-
uer,except wee bee conceiued in the
wombe of this mother, that she beare
vs,and bring vs forth, & giue vs sucke
of her breastes : finallie , except shee
hold and keepe vs vnder her conduct
and gouernment,vntill(being vnclothed of this mortall flesh)we be made
like vnto the Angels. In ancient time
Act.11.26 the faithfull were called disciples. For
the Church is also called the schoole

of Christians, wherein (according to the infirmitie that is in vs) we must be the disciples of Christ all the daies of our life. This Church is also often signified by a Temple: and the holie ministerie is ordained of GOD to build it. Therefore whosoeuer despiseth it, 2.Cor.3.6
cannot be builded in this Temple to be there a liuing stone. This Church 1.Tim.3 15
is the house of God: the faithfull, his Heb.3.6
houshold seruants & children. Therfore whosoeuer doth not enter, and Ephe. 2.19 2.Cor.5.8
abide in the Church, cannot call himselfe the child or houshold seruant of God. The preaching of the Gospel is the ministerie of the holie ghost, of life & of glory: whosoeuer refuseth to heare it, hath not the spirit of Christ, and consequentlie pertaineth not Rom.8.9
vnto him, & so abideth in death and euerlasting shame. See how ye must thinke in your selues of the benefite, vtilitie, yea and the necessitie of the holie ministerie, to say with *Dauid:* O Psal.84.2
Lord of hosts how amiable are thy tabernacles? My soule desireth greatly, yea and longeth after the courts of the

the Lord. My heart and my flesh reioyce in the liuing God. Blessed are
they which dwell in thy house, and
praise thee continuallie. Let the tast
and need of this spirituall food cause
those that are now depriued of it, to
say with *Dauid:* Like as the Hart desireth the water brookes, so longeth
my soule after thee O God: My soule
Psal.42.1. is a thirst for God, yea euen for the liuing God, saying: Alas when shall I
come to appeare before the presence
of God? When we shalbe depriued of
our countrie, wife, husband, traffick,
goods, dignities, and other thinges
pleasant to the flesh: let all these bee
nothing to vs: but let vs say with
Dauid, I haue asked one thing of the
Lord, which I will still require, that I
Psal.27. may dwell in the house of the Lord
all the daies of my life, to behold the
faire beautie of the Lord, and carefullie to visite his temple. If *Dauid*, a man
excellent in faith and all vertue, a prophet, and as an Angell amongst men,
confesseth so roundlie, and so often,
the neede that himselfe had to bee in
the

the Temple of the Lord, feeling himselfe as it were rauished with a most feruent desire of this benefite, what ought wee to feele in our selues, who are yet so ignorant, so weake, so corrupt, in the middest of so manie dangers? Say then from the heart with the same *Dauid*: O Lord I loue the habitation of thy house, & the place where thine honour dwelleth: And that good God and almightie father, who hath care to nourish our bodies, yea and prouideth for the nourishment of the little birds, will without doubt heare your desire, and wil prouide for the nourishment of your soules. Psal.26.8.

Moreouer, (accomplishing his promise made by *Esay*, of powring out of waters vpon the drie ground) hee will make you to growe as the grasse, and as the willowes by the riuer sides, for the ioye and comfort wherof, one shall say, I am the Lords, another shall call himselfe by the name of *Iacob*, an other shall subscribe with his hande, I am the Esay.44.

Lords,

Lords, and ſhall call himſelfe by the
5. To walk in the feare of God. name of Iſrael. But vnderſtād farther,
that the Goſpel wherof ye make pro-
feſsion, is a doctrine not to flie about
in the vnderſtāding, but to take ſeate
in the hart; not in the tongue to talk
onlie, but in the life and holie works.
Then be ye doers of the word, & not
onlie hearers deceauing your ſelues.
Iam.1.22 God hath adopted you for his children, but on this condition; that the
image of Chriſt may ſhine in you. God
hath choſen and called you to be his
Temples, and to dwell in you by his
1.Cor.6.19 holie ſpirit: Remember yee that the
1.Cor.3.16 temple of God is holie, and that it is
not lawfull to defile it, nor to put holie things to prophane vſes. God hath
created you for his glorie, and Chriſt
hath redeemed you, that ye might be
his: Remember then that you muſt
bee conſecrated and dedicated vnto
God, neither to thinke, ſay nor doo a-
nie thing but to his glorie. Ye are
Rom.6. dead to ſinne, but liuing to GOD
by Ieſus Chriſt: Applie not then
your members to bee inſtruments of
iniquitie

of iniquitie to sinne, but applie you vnto God, as being of dead, made aliue, and your members to be instrumēts of righteousnesse to God. Yee are made free from sinne by Christ, but it is to bee seruants to righteousnes. Remember that which S. *Paul* saith, that if ye liue according to the flesh ye shal dy: but if by the spirit ye mortefie the deeds of the flesh, ye shal liue: they that are of christ, haue crucified the flesh with the concupiscēces of it. If ye liue in the spirit, walke also in the spirite. As out of fire proceedeth inseperablie heate and brightnes: in like manner if ye haue receiued Christ for iustification, ye must haue him also for sanctification If yee haue hope to see Christ as hee is, purifie your selues as he is pure, following peace with al men, and holinesse, without which none shall see God. Remember what the faithful soule saith, I haue washed my feete, how shall I file them againe.

Rom.6.18
Rom.8.13.
Gal.5.24
Gal.5.25
1.Cor.1.30
1.Iho.3.2.3
Heb.12.14
Can.5.3

The band betweene GOD and vs is holinesse, inasmuch as it appertaineth to his glorie, that hee which is holie, haue no acquaintance with ini-

1.Pet. 1.15 quitie and vncleannes. Be ye then ho-
2.Cor.6 lie, for I am holie saith the Lord. What
participation is there, saith Saint *Paule*,
of righteousnesse with vnrighteousnes?
what fellowship hath light with darkenesse? what agreement hath Christ
with *Belial*, or what part hath the beleeuing with the infidel? or what agreement hath the Temple of GOD with
Idolls? For yee are the Temple of the
liuing God; wherefore depart from a-
mongst them, and separate your selues,
sayth the Lorde, and touch not anie vncleane thing. The ende of our regeneration is, that there may appeare in our
life, an holy melodie and consent betweene the righteousnesse of GOD
and our obedience. Yee haue vnder-
stoode here before, that the desire
of the heart to consecrate your selues to
God, is a marke of your election and
adoption. But see yee that this desire
may shew it selfe by the workes of godlines and charitie. If you make professi-
Ephe.4.20 on that ye know Christ: know ye according to the doctrine of S. *Paul*, that yee
haue not knowne him as ye ought, if ye

mortifie

mortifie not the olde man, and put on Col.2.13
the newe, walking in righteousnesse
and true holinesse. God hath drawne
you out of the power of darkenesse, and
hath transported you into the kingdom
of his beloued Sonne. Walke ye then,
as the children of light: Renounce this
cursed bondage of Sathan: Shew that
ye are faithfull and not traytours to Iesus Christ: Be ye without reproch and Phil.2.15
single harted. The children, I say, of
God vnreproueable in the midst of this
crooked and peruerse nation. Among
whom ye shine as lightes in the worlde,
which beare before you the worde of
life. Shew your selues to feele the whol- Tit.2.11
some grace of God, which teacheth you
to renounce all infidelitie and worldlie
lusts, to liue soberly, iustly, and godly.
Thinke in your selues, that the friendship of the world is enmity to God. And
that ye cannot be friendes to the world, Iam.4.4
but that yee must needes be enemies to
God. Haue no fellowship with the vn- Ephe.5.11
fruitful works of darknes, but rather reproue them, so as your holy conuersation may serue for a reproofe and checke

Iob.28.28. to ſuch as walk diſorderly. Remember,
Eſay.33.6 what God ſaid to man, The feare of the
Lord is true wiſdom, & to depart from
euil is vnderſtanding. Let the fauour of
God be our treaſure: walke, as it were,
Gen.17.1 before him, as he cōmanded *Abraham*.
Think that ye are not your own, to liue
for your ſelues according to your owne
wiſdome & pleaſure, but that ye appertaine vnto God, that ye might liue vnto him, and according to his wiſdome and will reuealed vnto vs in his word. That man hath much profited, who knowing that he is not his owne, hath taken away from himſelfe, and his owne reaſon all lordſhip & dominion, to reſigne it to God, & to ſuffer himſelfe quietlie to be guided according to his pleaſure. There is no vice more common, more pernicious, or more hard to cure than the loue of our ſelues: and therefore there is no leſſon more neceſſary than it, which Ieſus Chriſt taught his apoſtles: That to
Mat.16.14 be of the nūber of his diſciples, we muſt
renounce our ſelues. Renouncing then your ſelues, hate ye that which is euill, and cleaue vnto that which is good, inclined

clined by brotherly charity to loue one
another. Procure things that are good, Col.3.12
not onely before God, but also before
men. If it be possible, so much as in you
lieth, haue peace with al men. Be yee as
the elect of God, holy and beloued, clad
with the bowells of compassiō, of kindnes, of humility, of meeknes, of longsuf-
fering, forbearing one another: and for-
giuing one another, if any man haue a
quarel with another, euē as Christ hath
forgiuen you Loue one another, as God 1.Ihon 10
hath loued you. For herein is the difference betwene the children of God, and
the children of the deuil, & wherein ye
may be knowne to be the true disciples
of Christ. Ye are al members of one bo- Iho.13.35.
dy, let there be no diuision or parts-ta-
king among you, but feele the afflicti- 1.Cor.12
ons of those that weepe, to weepe with 25
them, and to comfort them, & reioyce
with those that reioyce, to praise God
with them. If yee be the Citizens of the
City *Ierusalem*, & wil haue a sure dwelling in it, walke in integritie, labour to Psal.15
deale iustly, speake the truth from your
harts, keepe you from slandering, couetousnes, and all other corruption. Ac-

knowledge in al men the image of God, whereunto you owe honor & loue: and in your brethren acknowledge the re-
Gala.6.10 nuing of this image, and the brotherly coniunction in Christ, in doing good to al men, loue, honor, and help especially,
1.Pet.4.10 those that are of the houshold of faith. Ye are debtors to your neighbors of all
1.Pet.4.8 that ye haue, or are able to do, to be dispos ers of it with condition, that ye ren-
Iam.1.19 der to God an account. Honor the graces of God in your brethren, and couer their infirmities by charitie, be quicke to heare, but slowe to speake, and slow to wrath. For the wrath of man worketh not that which is righteous in the sight of God. Do not desire, hope, or imagine any other means to prosper by, thā by the blessing of God. And do not looke, that hee should aduaunce by the ayde of his blessing, that which he hath accursed by his mouth. So go forward in the amendment of your liues, that this day may passe yesterday. Seale to the puritie of the doctrine, with the holines of your life, that the ignorant seing
1.Pet.2.12 your blameles conuersatiō, & esteming

you

you by your good workes, may glorifie
God, and imbrace the gospel with you, Luke 7.1.
when it shall please GOD to call them.
Haue mind of that great curse pronoũ-
ced by the high Iudge, against such as 2.Cor.13
offend any of the very least. Further- 11
more, reioyce in the Lord, indeuour to
be perfect, be comforted, be of one consent, liue in peace, and the God of loue Phil.2.13
and peace shall be with you. But as it is
God which worketh in vs both to will,
& in worke to accomplish according to
his good pleasure. So aboue all thinges 6. To pray
imploy your selues to pray feruently & to God.
continually. Prayer (saith *Chrysostome*)
is the soule of our souls. For it also is the
soule which quickneth al the actions of
the children of God. It was the lifting
vp of *Moses* hands to heauen, which Exo.17.11
strengthned *Iosuah* & his army, & gaue
him victorie ouer the *Amalekites*. And
in deede, without the grace of God, the
which we obtaine by prayer, all that we
do is but vanitie. Faith is the key that o-
peneth the coffers of the treasures of our
God. Prayer is the hand to draw it out
to inrich our selues. Prayer lifteth vp

our hearts from earth to heauen; it renueth the memorie of the promises of God to confirme vs; it allureth vs against all that wee can feare, it obtaineth all that we can desire. It giueth rest and contentment to our soules. It keepeth and strengtheneth the feare to offend God. It increaseth the desire to go vnto him, whom in praying we feele to be the spring and heape of all good things. It ingendreth in vs a stedfast despising of the world, and renouncing of the flesh: it representeth vnto vs the heauenly and euerlasting felicitie, that we may aspire to the inioying of them. There is nothing to bee more desired, than to be conuersant with him, without whome we can not be happy. But he that wil alwayes be with GOD, he must alwaies eyther pray or reade. For when we pray we talke with God: and when wee reade, God talketh with vs. *Aug. in Psal. 85.* The more we are exercised in prayer to God, the more we increase in godlines. Therefore also we may not be weary or faint-hearted in prayer, although the Lord deferre to make vs feele the fruite

of

of our prayers, For we haue a promise of him that can not lie, that whatsoeuer we aske of GOD in the name of Iesus Christ, it shalbe giuen vs. If he deferre, for some time, to make vs feele the fruit of our praiers, it is for our greater benefite. Let vs continue still and waight, knowing assuredly, that he, who according to his fatherly loue & bounty, desireth our good, can (according to his infinite power) giue that which we aske of him, and according to his truth will hear vs: he also according to his wisdōe knoweth the fittest time, as is before said, and the meanes most apt to make vs feele the fruite of our praiers. When we aske of God (saith S. *Bernard*) euen those thinges that concerne this present life: our praiers are not so soone gone out of our mouth, but they are written in his booke: and we ought (saith he) to be assured, that hee will either giue the thing it selfe which we haue asked, or other things which hee knoweth to bee more profitable for vs. To conclude, Praier is the most mightie and fruitfull worke of charitie, seeing by it we helpe

out

our neighbors present & absent, knowen and vnknowen, great and little, and that both with spirituall and corporall good things, drawing by our praiers the blessing of God vpon them. And in this confidence my very deare and worshipfull Brethren, I will continue in this dutie and office of charitie, earnestlie to pray to God for you, and particularlie I will water with my praiers to God this Exhortation, which I haue directed vnto you, beseeching him with all my heart, that beeing comforted and strengthened thereby, in the doctrine of the truth, which yee haue receiued, yee may continue constantly in it, sealing it by the works of godlinesse and charitie, comforting your selues in the Lord, in that yee are his welbeloued Children in Iesus Christ: and surmounting al temptations and assaults, to the ende, that by the power of the holy Ghost departing Conquerors out of all conflicts, ye may attaine at the last, to the crowne of glorie, which God hath prepared to all his childrē, through Iesus Christ our Lord.

1. Thess. 5. 23 Now the GOD of peace sanctifie you through-

throughout, and preserue your whole spirit, and soule, and bodie blamelesse, vntill the comming of our Lord Iesus Christ. He that hath called you is faithfull, who also will doo it. I also beseech you (my brethren) to imploy your selues more and more in feruent and continuall praiers, for the preseruation, prosperitie and aduauncement of his Church, so mightelie assailed on all sides; and particularlie to bee mindfull of mee in your prayers, that it may please the Father of light, from whence all good gifts doo come, to continue his mercies towards mee, and to guide mee alwaies with his holie spirit, with the increase of his giftes and graces to accomplish the rest of my life, seruing faithfull and holilie to his glorie, & the aduauncement of the Kingdome of our Lord Iesus Christ. *Amen.*

Holie

Holie meditations and praiers.

Chap. 13.

Lord God almightie, al good and all wise, we are confounded before thy holy maiestie, not (ô Lord) for the troubles and extreame calamities wherewith we are oppressed in these daies full of tribulations, anguishes and teares: but forasmuch as we haue offended thee, & for asmuch as our sinnes, our ingratitude, & rebelliōs haue kindled thi wrath against vs: and chiefly forasmuch as the wicked and infidels, take occasion by thy iust iudgemēts & corrections to blaspheme thy holy name. Alas Lord, wee yeelde our selues guilty before thee, confessing that we are inexcusable, and vnworthie to be named thy children: yea, wee are worthie to bee reiected of thee, wee are worthie of hel, & to be creatures accursed for euer. For (ô our good God) whē we were the children of wrath, thine enemies, abādoned to all euil, thou hadst

pitie

pitie vppon vs poore and abhominable sinners. Thou hast cast the eyes of thy fauour vppon vs. Thou hast giuen thy welbeloued Sonne Iesus Christ to the shameful and cursed death of the crosse for vs. Thou hast giuen vs thy holy gospell, that blessed and ioyfull tidings of our saluation: Thou hast accompanied it with thy spirit to lighten vs, to draw vs vnto thee, to make vs partakers of the treasures of thy Kingdome & of eternall life. Thou hast stretched out thy hand from heauen to the depth of hell, to pul vs backe, and to make vs thy happie children. Thou hast done according to the good pleasure of thy will, inasmuch as thou shewest mercie on whom thou wilt shewe mercie. Alas Lord, ought not we to acknowledge the daye of thy visitation, and the time of saluation? Ought not we to feele the abundant riches of thy incomprehẽsible grace towards vs, to loue, serue, praise, and adore thee? to renounce our selues, the world and the flesh, and all that which is contrarie to thy glorie: yea to abhorre all that doth displease thee? to walke as

the

the children of light, and to consecrate our selues vnto thee, to bring foorth fruites worthie of thy Gospell, and becomming the Children of such a Father: to be as bright lights in this darke world, to giue light to the poore ignorãt ones, to draw thẽ with vs into the way of saluation. But alas, ô Lord our God, we (quite contrarie) hauing brought into thy Church the world and the flesh, haue kept in our selues these enemies of thy glory, these plagues of our soules, & haue serued them. Our infidelitie & our flesh haue made vs loue the earth more than the heauen, the world more than thy kingdome, the filthines and dust of vaine riches, more than the treasures of heauenlie and eternall good things, the smoke of humane honors, more thã the glorious estate to be thy childrẽ, & brethren of thy sonne Iesus Christ. Couetousnes the roote of all euill, hath hardened our harts to despise thy poore ones, euen Iesus Christ in his members. Wee haue slaundered thy holy Gospell by fraudes, deceipts, & robbings: occupying our traffique and doing our affaires, as people hauing no knowledge of thee.

The

The aire in the Cities where thy word hath bin preached, hath bin stinking & infected, with the whoredomes, adulteries, and other infamous acts that there haue bin committed. Gluttonie & drūkennes haue made brutish those, that for thy blessings and bountie ought to haue praised thee. Euerie man thinking onlie how to profit & aduance himselt in this world, to the despising of thy holy seruice, & the building of thy Church. The profession of thy holy religion hath serued many, but for the cloke of their iniquities. Wee haue put our trust in the arme of flesh, & in brokē reeds, seeking cōfort for thy Church of the enemies of it, in forsaking the fountaine of liuing waters, and the almightie. Crimes, trespasses, blasphemies and iniquities haue bin winked at & supported, in defiling the seate of thy iustice, without punishmēt: thy threatnings & promises reiected as vanities, the holy Ministerie of thy Word despised, the chastisements which thou hast exercised on our brethren neglected, without thinking what our selues haue deserued. Wee haue not felt sorow for the afflictions of thy children, to mourne with them, and to feare thy iudgements. And what shal we say more, ô Lord? Our iniquities are as mountaines, our ingratitude and rebellions, as the great deepe, our whole life, before thee, being nothing else but a cõtinuall sinne and despising of thy holy Maiestie. If they who neuer heard speak of thy sonne Iesus Christ, and that haue not knowen thy will, are iustly punished in thy wrath; what iudgement, what condemnation, what hells and cursses haue we deserued, hauing so villainously, so long, so obstinately, despised thy holy instructions, thy promises, thy threatenings, and the examples of thy iudgements, which thou hast exercised before our eyes. Also the voyce of our ingratitude is ascended before thee: our iniquities haue, and doo crie vengeance against vs. These are the procurers and aduocates of thy iustice, soliciting these iudgements against vs. Our sinnes haue strengthned our enemies, & haue made them conquerours ouer vs. We haue sowen iniquitie, and we haue reaped afflictions: as thou seest, ô Lord our God,

that

that thy children are baniſhed, ſpoyled, and impouriſhed, that they are cruellie dealt withall, trodden vnder foote, and expoſed to the laughter of thine enemies. Our perſecuters make a ſcorne of thoſe, ouer whō thy name is called on, & they make their boaſt of the euill that they doo: They ſcatter thy flockes: They throwe downe the ſcepter of thy ſonne Ieſus Chriſt: They depriue thy children of the paſture of thy word. Thoſe temples (O Lord) thoſe temples where not long ſince, thy praiſes did ſound, in which thy holie Goſpell was preached, the Sacraments purelie miniſtred, thy name religiouſlie called on: Theſe temples, O Lord, are now defiled with Idols and idolatrie, the abominable Maſſe is eſtabliſhed againe, falſe tales and lies are preached. Theſe temples where thy people aſſembled in ſo great number to praiſe thee, and to behold thy louing countenance, are now filled with people blaſpheming thy holie name, and treading vnder their feete the bloud and glorie of thy sonne Iesus Christ. This youth of orphanes, fondlings, and others that went to schoole, being brought vp in the knowledge of thee, & nourished in thy feare, is now giuen vp to the enemies of thy trueth, to be instructed in the damnable doctrine and seruice of Antichrist. O good God, our sunne is turned into darknes, the Moone into bloud, our health into sicknes, our life into death: And yet, if thou shouldest punish vs yet more rigorouslie, than hetherto thou hast done, & that for one stripe wee should receiue an hundred. If thou shouldest transport the kingdome of thy sonne from vs, to the Turkes, and the Iewes: If thou shouldest send such a famine of thy word, as running through the forrests to haue some refreshing, and finding none, our soules should faint: Yea Lord, if thou shouldest throw vs down into hell: we confesse that it were verie right, and yeeld our selues guiltie, acknowledging that we haue well deserued it. Notwithstanding, O good God and father, there is mercie with

thee,

thee, yea thy mercies are infinite to ſwallowe vp the multitude and grie-uouſnes of our ſinnes. Thou art a God gracious & pitifull, ſlowe vnto wrath, abounding in mercie and trueth, kee-ping mercie for thouſands, pardo-ning iniquitie, tranſgreſsion & ſinne. Thou haſt ſaid that thou wilt not the death of a ſinner, but rather that hee turne and liue. Conuert vs then, O Lord, that we may be conuerted, and that we may liue before thee. We are poore ſinners, we confeſſe it: but yet thy ſonne Ieſus Chriſt came into the world to ſaue ſinners. Behold vs then, O Lord, not in our ſelues (for wee are vnworthy of thy grace) but behold vs in the face of thy ſonne Ieſus Chriſt, and for his ſake, bee at tone with vs, and be mercifull and fauourable vnto vs: that in the multitude of our ſinnes the greatnes of thy grace may ſhine: if thou regard our iniquities, who is he that is able to ſtand before thee? Wee haue been vnfaithfull, but thou remaineſt ſtill faithfull. Thou canſt not renounce thy mercie and goodnes; we haue forsaken thee, but thou hast promised not to forsake vs. Wee haue forgotten thee, but thou hast said, that though a mother should forget her childe, yet wouldst not thou forget vs. Thou hast made a couenant with vs, wherein thou hast promised to pardon our sinnes, and to remember our iniquities no more. Thou hast promised, that though our sins were as red as scarlet, thou wouldest make them as white as wooll: if they were as red as crimson, that they should be made as white as snowe. We are heauie laden, and labour with our iniquities. But Iesus Christ hath called vs to him, and hath promised to refresh vs. Haue pitie thē on vs, O Lord, haue pitie vpon vs. Let our miseries moue the bowells of thy mercie. Forgiue vs (O our GOD) forgiue vs for thine owne sake, for the glorie of thy name, and for thy sonne Iesus Christs sake: Impute vnto vs the goodnes that is in him, that the euill that is in vs may not be imputed. Thou hast punished the iust, that thou mightest

pardon

pardon the wicked: Accept thou the merites of his death and paſsion, for ſatiſfaction of all that is in vs, worthie of thy wrath and indignation: and make vs to feele the fruites of our reconciliation with thee. If thou wilt afflict our bodies, haue yet pitie of our ſoules. If thou wilt impouriſh vs on the earth, depriue vs not yet of the riches of heauen. If thou wilt take away the bread of our bodies, yet leaue vs the ſpirituall bread of our ſoules. Though wee bee in reproach among our enemies, yet let not thy name be blaſphemed. Though we bee accurſed of the world, yet let vs bee bleſſed of thee. Though the world hate vs, yet let thy loue abide vpon vs. O Lord we are thine, forſake vs not. Thou haſt ſaide, I am the Eternall, this is my name, I will not giue my glorie vnto Images, nor my praiſe vnto another. For thine owne ſake then, euen for thine owne ſake haue mercie vpon vs. For why ſhall thy name bee blaſphemed for our ſakes? Not vnto vs Lord, not vnto vs, but vnto thy name giue glorie and honour, in shewing foorth the riches of thy graces, of thy truth, and of thy might. Thou art the God of glorie, sanctifie thy name, in drawing light out of our darknes, and life out of death, making perfect thy power in our infirmitie, and thy great grace in our vnworthines, to thy praise and glorie. Heare the blasphemies of thine enemies, boasting them selues in their counsels and their forces, triumphing and reioycing in our confusion: as if we were not thy people, thy children, thy Church: as if wee were cast off of thee: as if thou were not able to helpe or keepe vs. Neuerthelesse, thou art our creatour, and wee are the worke of thy hands: Thou art our shepheard, wee are thy flocke: Thou art our father, wee are thy children: Thou art our God, wee are thine inheritance: Thou art our redeemer, wee are the people whome thou hast bought. It is thou also (O our God) who by thy word alone, hast created the heauen and the earth, the sea and al that is in them: it is by thee that all things liue, be, and haue their mouing: it is of thee, by thee and for thee, that all things are. It is thou which doœst whatsoeuer thou wilt. And there is neither counsell, wisedome, nor strength against thee. Represse then, O Lord, the rage and furie of thine enemies, breake their forces, dissipate their counsels, confound them in the bold enterprises which they haue taken in hand against thee, and thy sonne Iesus Christ. Maintaine the rest of thy flocke, which thou hast kept vntill this day. Establish againe the Churches that are ruined and dispersed. Suffer not the memorie of thy name to be abolished from the earth: rather let thy word sound, and thy Gospell bee preached, where it hath not yet been heard, to gather thine elect vnto thee, and to magnifie thy name: And that so wee may see it florish more & more, and the kingdome of thy sonne Iesus Christ our Lord to bee aduanced for euer more. *Amen.*

The necessitie and benefite *of affliction.*

Great trouble and vexation
the righteous shall sustaine
By Gods determination,
Whilest heere they doo remaine:
Which grieuous is and irksome both
for flesh and bloud to beare.
Because by nature we are loath
to want our pleasure heere;
And eke because our enemie
that auncient deadly foe
Satan, with cruell tyrannie
the worker of our woe,
Doth still prouoke the wicked sort
in sinne which doo delight,
To please themselues & make great sport,
to vexe vs with despite.
Yet doo the righteous by the crosse
moe blessed things obtaine,
Than anie waie can be the losse,
the dolor, or the paine.

S The

The losse is that, which in few daies
would passe, fade and decay
Euen of it selfe: the gaine alwaies
can no man take away.
All earthly estimation
the crosse may cleane deface,
But heauenlie consolation
the soule dooth then imbrace.
Afflictions worldly pleasures will
abandon out of minde:
Then is the soule more earnest still
the ioyes of heauen to finde.
These worldly riches, goods and wealth,
by troubles may depart:
Then inward ioyes and sauing health
may wholly rule the heart.
In trouble friends doo start aside,
as cloudes doo with the winde:
But Gods assistance doth abide
to cheare the troubled minde.
If we should feele these losses all,
at once, by sudden change:
We may not be dismaid withall,
though it seeme verie strange.
Iob *lost his frends, he lost his wealth,*
and comfort of his wife:

He lost his children and his health,
yea, all but wretched life.
When all was gone, the Lord aboue
did still with him remaine,
With mercie, kindnes and with loue
asswaging all his paine:
Teaching him by experience,
that all things fickle be
(Which subiect are to humane sence)
and yeeld all miserie.
But godlinesse within the heart
remaineth euer sure.
In wealth and woe, it is her part,
true comfort to procure.
Affliction turn'th these worldly ioyes
to greater paine and woe,
Because the loue was linck'd with toyes:
religion is not so.
For when mans heart doth most delight
in pleasure, wealth, and pride:
Religion then will take her flight,
she may not there abide.
Whereby our soules in wofull plight
continually remaine:
Yet haue not we the grace or might
from such lusts to refraine.

In which estate most willingly
(though tending right to hell)
We compt our chiefe felicitie,
and loue therein to dwell.
Therefore the Lord which is aboue,
regarding vs below
With mercie, pitie, grace and loue,
that alwaies from him flow,
Doth mix with griefe these earthly things
wherein we doo delight:
Which to our soules all sorow brings,
or else remoou'th them quite.
Then dooth the holie word of God
most comfortable seeme:
Which we (before we felt the rod)
mere follie did esteeme,
The world which earst most pleasant was
now loathsome seem'th to be:
It doth appeare (as in a glasse)
all fraught with miserie.
Then feare we hell, then flie we sinne,
then seeke we heauen the more:
To vse good meanes we then begin,
which we despisde before.
Then can we pray, then can we call
to God for strength and grace:

Which

Which things before might not at all
With vs haue anie place.
Then heare we with attentiuenes,
then read we with all care:
Then pray we with great feruentnes,
no trauaile then we spare.
Then shall we see, feele and confesse
the state wherein we dwelt,
To be nothing but wretchednes:
though worldly ioyes we felt.
Because the soule by godlinesse
more comfort doth receaue
In one day, than by worldlinesse,
for euer it can haue.
Then we with David *shall confesse,*
that God from heauen aboue
(By humbling vs) doth well expresse
his mercie and his loue.
For ere we felt the scourging rod,
we er'de and went astray:
But now we keepe the law of God,
and waite thereon alway.
Then for religion loue the crosse,
though it doo bring some paine:
The ioy is great, small is the losse,
but infinite the gaine.

FINIS.

A Way of Reconciliation of a good and learned man, touching the Trueth, Nature, and Substance of the Bo
and Blood of Christ in the Sacrament (*STC* 21456) is reproduced here, by agreement, from the copy in th
Folger Shakespeare Library. The size of the text-block is 161 × 92 mm at sig. G3r.

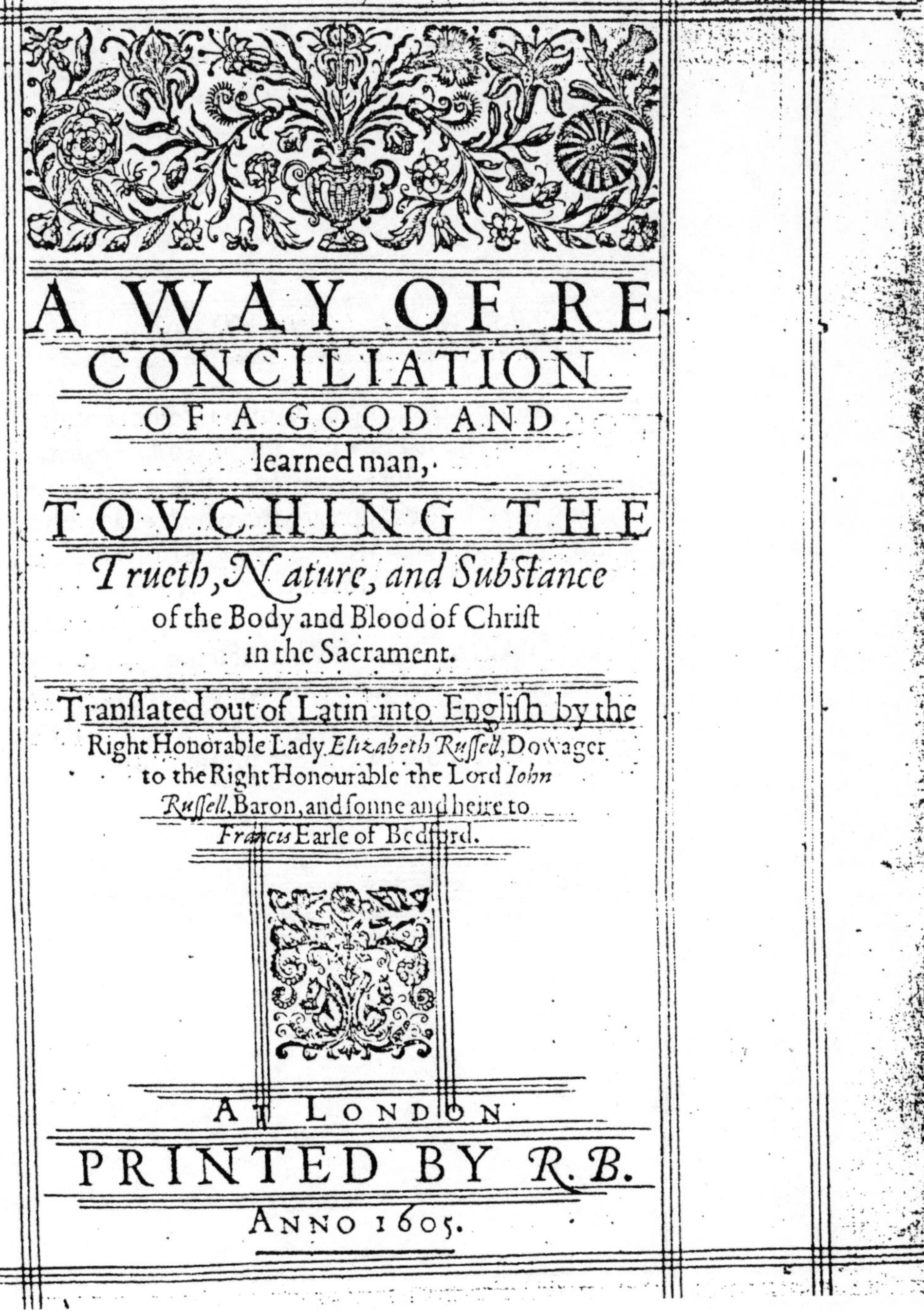

A WAY OF RE-CONCILIATION

OF A GOOD AND learned man,

TOVCHING THE *Trueth, Nature, and Subſtance* of the Body and Blood of Chriſt in the Sacrament.

Tranſlated out of Latin into Engliſh by the
Right Honorable Lady *Elizabeth Ruſſell*, Dowager
to the Right Honourable the Lord *Iohn*
Ruſſell, Baron, and ſonne and heire to
Francis Earle of Bedford.

AT LONDON

PRINTED BY *R.B.*

ANNO 1605.

The Author to the Reader.

TO seeke the attonement of men is to be commended, and it hath a sure promise of God: *Blessed bee the peace-makers.* But I feare me, lest in greedily following the same, it happen to me which chanceth to them that part fraies, while they seeke others safetie, they beare the blowes themselues. And I, while I study to make enemies friends, perhaps shall haue small thankes of them. Which if it happen, the example of him shal comfort me, which said: *If I should please men, I should not be the seruant of Christ.* Farewell, and indeauour thy selfe to please Christ.

TO THE RIGHT HONOURABLE MY MOST ENTIERLY BELOUED AND ONELY DAUGHTER, THE LADY ANNE HERBERT, WIFE TO THE LORD HENRY HERBERT, SONNE AND HEIRE APPARANT TO EDVVARD THE MOST NOBLE EARLE OF WORCESTER.

**

Ost vertuous and woorthilie beloued daughter, Euen as from your first birth and cradle I euer was most careful, aboue any worldly thing, to haue you sucke the perfect milke of sincere Religion: So willing to ende as I beganne, I haue left to you, as my last Legacie, this Booke. A most precious Iewell to the comfort of your Soule, being the woorke of a most good,

learned, and worthy man; Made aboue fiftie yeeres since in Germanie, After by traueile a French creature, Now naturalized by mee into English like to his learned Author, to whom from my part most Honour and seruice is due. Surely at the first I meant not to haue set it abroad in Print, but my selfe onely to haue some certaintie to leane vnto, in a matter so full of controuersie, and to yeeld a reason of my opinion. But since by my lending the Copie of mine owne hand to a friend, I am bereft thereof by some; And fearing lest after my death it should be Printed according to the humors of other, and wrong of the dead, who in his life approued my Translation with his owne allowance: Therefore dreading, I say, wrong to him aboue any other respect, I haue by Anticipation preuented the worst. I meant this to you, good daughter, for a New-yeeres gift, but altered by griefe for your Brothers broken arme. Farewell my

good

good sweet Nanne. *God blesse thee with the continuance of the comfort of his holy Spirit, that it may euer worke in you, and perseuere with you to the ende, and in the ende.*

In Annam Filiam.

Vt veniens Annus tibi plurima commodet Anna,
Voce pia Mater, supplice mente precor,
Vt valeas, pariterque tuo cum Coniuge, Proles,
Officijs iunctis, vita serena fluat.

Elizabetha Russella,
Dowager.

¶ A CERTAINE MAN

wisheth to all Christians the health and peace of our Lord IESVS CHRIST.

HE question of the Supper of IESVS CHRIST, *and Sacrament of Thankesgiuing, hath brought foorth to vs, aboue other things, a cruel and pernitious contention. For the other Authors of sects,* Anabaptists, *and* Suencfeldians, *be neither learned nor of our family. But this is a ciuill and domesticall euill, a bloody and deadly wound hidden in our bowels. Surely it is a lamentable and horrible matter, that the thing which was first instituted for the confirmation of mens minds in loue, and concord, and fellowship of the body of Christ, which is the Church, is now wrested to variance, and confusion. And if there haue bene any good in this broile, it hath bene in the silence and sorrow of good and learned men: of whom aswell the misliking sheweth that there is somewhat in both parts that might be amended, and prayer and earnest desire may percase somewhat obtaine at Gods hand, that contention taken away, the agreement of minds may againe ioyne in one. But this booke which is made tou-*

ching

ching this question, whose soeuer it bee, sure it seemeth to be the worke of a good, learned and modest man, and one that hath bene long, much, and well exercised in the Monuments of our Fathers and Elders. Neither doeth it moue mee, that he would not be named; for because there is no bitter word in this disputation, and he doth reason of the matter learnedly, well, and truely, neither doth seeme willing to craue thankes at mens hands, nor to haue taken this Treatie in hand, either for desire of praise or greedines of Honour, but to be mooued thereunto by the common sorrow and hurt, to make an entry to that thing, the which many men greatly desiring the peace of Christs Church, haue wished with earnest and continuall prayers: namely, the remembrance of the Christian peace, and the forgetting of deuilish debate.

Bucer, (*whom I with honour speake of, and for remembrance sake*) *had found and made a way to this concord, and there was great agreement of minds betweene him and* Luther: *and hee pacified the Churches of the* Heluetians, *and while hee liued there was peace and quietnesse: but when they were both dead, beholde againe bitter bookes on both sides. And surely they be to be pardoned which write vnwillingly: but those which without cause haue renued this wound, (if there be any such) these surely seeme to me little to feare what men iudge of them, or to esteeme the peace which Christ gaue and left vnto vs. But I returne to this Booke, which pleaseth me best aboue other in this kinde of argument; not that I will altogether allow it to the Congregation,*

but

but because it seemeth to come neerest to the taking away of this contention. For which cause he that cannot inuent a better, if he be not content with this, and cannot defend his owne, let him take heed that hee doe not that for mans sake, which he ought to leaue vndone for Christes cause: namely, that he nourish not contention, which is the greatest enemie the Church can haue. I see nothing concluded in this disputation, that either is repugnant from the nature of our Religion, or not honourably ynough spoken of this so great & singuler mysterie; both which things if both the parts had retained or followed, we should haue had quietnesse long ere this. I blame neither part, I beare good will to both, I loue both. And if that were done in writing that is done, and that of many, with good conscience in the leading of our life, and retaining and esteeming the friends on both sides, men should both haue written and disputed of this question on both sides, with lesse offence and bitternesse. But now wee write in such sort, as though wee did defend the persons, and not the cause, and apply the trueth of the cause, not to the ordinance of Christ, but to the interpretation of men. Iesus Christ restore to vs his peace, which he gaue and left vnto vs when hee departed hence, which we haue lost by these our contentions: Iesus Christ, I say, whose Victory, Triumph, Honour, Praise, and Glory, be for euer and euer. Amen.

¶ Away

¶ A way of Reconciliation touching the trueth, nature and substance of the Body, or of the Flesh and Blood of CHRIST in the *Sacrament.*

Hat good man doeth not sorrow, or what man zealous in Religion, doeth not often bewaile the pitifull and vnluckie contention about the LORDS SVPPER, which hath now many yeres troubled the Churches of CHRIST which haue imbraced the pure doctrine, whereby not onely brotherly Loue is broken, but also cities and whole countreys be thereby brought in danger? For whereas after the expelling the darkenesse of Ignorance, and the happy restoring to the Church the gift of tongues, a certaine new Light was restored to the world, and the Gospel had begun to take so great roote, that thereby hope of very great fruit was offered to ensue.: By and by this sharpe and vehement contention, bursting in among the chiefe champions of the Word, hath miserably troubled these very good beginnings. For looke what weapons they had valiantly vsed, in setting foorth the trueth, & in ouerthrowing the enemies of the Gospel, the very same, after this strife was risen, did they bend one against another. So that the happie course of the Gospel that began to flourish is not only hindered, but also by factions & discords, the matter is come to that passe, that vnlesse the mighty Right-hand of the Lord do resist, the trueth doeth seeme to appaule and decay againe, yea, and to returne to the former confusion.

For if we will iudge the matter truely, no force hath so much withstand the inlarging of the Gospel, no not the deceits and inchantments of the idole of *Rome*, not the crueltie of Princes against the flocke of CHRIST, not the troublesome motions of breeders of Sects, as this onely rash contention hath done hurt, which bringeth to the minds of godly men sorrow, to the enemies cause to reioyce, and to the weake and vnlearned, offence and falling. And surely there is no doubt, but that our owne wickednesse hath bene the originall of this so great an euil, as it hath bene of many other: For wee not regarding, or rather contemning the light offered vs, are iustly thought vnworthy of so great a benefit. Which thing also is the cause, that albeit many learned & good men vnderstand what profit it should be for the Christian common wealth speedily to pacifie this quarrell, and to ende the contentions, few notwithstanding doe earnestly traueile about this matter; And if any haue attempted it, it seemeth to fall out as vnluckily taken in hand to the contrary part. For my part, when I saw no end could be made of strife, nor any hope in any one of better sequele, I thought best to commit the matter to GOD by prayer, and with silence to looke for helpe in season at his hands. Yet in this meane space I thought it my part, not to neglect a matter of so great waight, but after examination had of the

chiefe

chiefe points of this controuersie, to bolt out what was trueth, and what not; and then to determine vpon a sure grounded opinion, both by authoritie of holy Scripture, and by the vndoubted testimonies of the Fathers, aswell to satisfie my selfe, as to yeeld a reason thereof to any that should perhaps demand it of mee: that the minde should not wauer continually to & fro, tossed as it were with the contrary violence of winds.

While I take this worke in hand, & diligently tread the steps of the old Interpreters, me thinketh I perceiue (vnlesse my opinion deceiue me) that this controuersie is not so intangled, nor darke, as most men suppose, and that these sharp cōtentions haue come rather by mens fault, then by the nature of the matter; and that the way of Reconciliation shall not bee so hard with men, desirous rather of the trueth then of quarrelling.

❧ Wherefore albeit I took in hand this worke, whatsoeuer it be, priuately to my selfe, yet because among my friends certaine good men and well giuen were so desirous, I did not greatly passe to haue it come to the eares & eyes of other, that if there be herein any profit, it may also do them good. The cause I haue thought good so to diuide, that briefly it may bee brought to three especial points: First wil I shew the trueth of the body of CHRIST in the Sacrament to be giuen to the faithful, and that these termes *Nature* and *Substance* are not to be shunned, but that they of old time disputing of the Sacrament vsed them: Then will I declare the difference betweene the Lords proper body, and that which is in the Sacrament, and that the olde Fathers were of that opinion: And lastly I will set foorth at large, what maner of Body that is which is receiued in the mysterie, & why it is called by that name; after the opinion of the selfe same Fathers. Which things once expounded, a man may easily iudge of the whole controuersie. First, it is manifest ynough by the declaration of the Euangelists *Matthew*, *Marke* and *Luke*, that our Lord IESVS CHRIST, when he should depart out of this world, and leauing the earth, should goe vp to the Father, did ordeine the Sacrament of his Body and Blood in the presence of his disciples at Supper; and so when he had taken the bread, he blessed, brake it and gaue it to them, saying, *This is my body*: After the like maner the Cup also, saying, *This Cup is the new Testament in my Blood, Doe this in remembrance of me.* Paul also writeth to the same effect to the *Corinthians*, in his first Epistle the 11. chapter, rehearsing in a maner the very same words, & in the tenth chapter, *The Cup* (saith he) *of blessing which we blesse, is it not the partaking of the Blood of Christ? The bread which we breake, is it not the partaking of the Body of Christ?* By these words of the Euangelists, and the Apostle, they of old time were of that opinion that CHRIST our Lord, which is Trueth it selfe, spake these things truly, and did in deed performe those things that he spake, so that no place of doubt might any more be left, concerning the trueth of the matter.

Matth. 26. c. Matth. 14. c. Luke 22. c.

1. Corinth. 11.

Et cap. 10.

Moreouer those words which in the sixt chapter of *Iohn*, the Lord spake, *My flesh is meat in deed, and my blood is drinke indeed, &c. The bread which I will giue you is my flesh. And vnlesse you eate the flesh of the Sonne of man, and drinke his Blood, &c.* The Fathers with great accord, as well Grecians as Latines, doe apply to the *Sacrament of Thankesgiuing*; And that they haue interpreted those places so, both in *Iohn*, and the rest of the Euangelists and *Paul* to the *Corinthians*, the testimonies that follow taken out of the authors themselues, shal happily proue.

Iohn 6. c.

First, *Iustin Martyr* in his second Apologie writeth thus,

Iustin Martir Apol. 2.

thus, *And this meate is called with vs, that is, Thankesgiuing, &c.* whereof none other may be partaker but he, which both beleeueth those things to be true which we say, & also hath bene purified with the washing, which is giuen for the remission of sinnes, and regeneration, and also so liueth as CHRIST hath appointed. For wee take not these things to be common and wonted bread, and accustomed drinke, but euen as the word of God IESVS CHRIST our Sauiour was made man, and had both flesh and blood for our saluation: Euen so in like maner wee haue bene taught, that the meate which is hallowed by the prayers of the word that we receiued of him, and by which our blood and flesh, by a change made are nourished, is both the flesh & blood of the same CHRIST which was made man. For the Apostles in their Commentaries, which be called the Gospels, haue left in writing, that CHRIST did so command them, and that he said, when he had taken bread and giuen thankes, *Doe this in remembrance of me, This is my body.* And that when he had taken the cup and giuen thankes hee said, *This is my Blood.* Partly the other words of this testimoniall doe affirme the trueth of his body: and chiefly because by a similitude taken of the two natures in CHRIST, he declareth that there be also two natures in the Sacrament, namely of the outward signe, and of the flesh & Blood of IESVS CHRIST.

Alike vnto this is spoken in *Irenæus* in his 4. booke: For how say they againe that the flesh commeth into corruption, & doth not receiue life which is nourished of the body and Blood of the Lord? Therefore let them either change their opinion, or else abstaine to offer the things which are aforesaid: but our opinion is agreeing to the Sacrament of thankesgiuing, and this Sacrament againe confirmeth our opinion: For wee offer those things that be his; preaching agreeably the partaking and trueth of Flesh and Spirit. For euen as the bread which is of the earth receiuing the calling vpon God, is now no more common bread, but a Sacrament of thanksgiuing, made of two things, earthly and Heauenly: so also our bodies receiuing the Sacrament of thankesgiuing, be not now corruptible, because they haue the hope of resurrection. The same man in his fift booke; and because wee be his members, and are nourished by the creature, & he giueth vs the creature, making his Sonne to arise, and raining as he listeth, the same Cup which is a creature, he confirmed to be his Body, by which he increaseth our bodies. When therefore both the Cup mixed, and the bread made, receiueth the Word of God, it is made the Sacrament of the blood and body of CHRIST, whereof both the substance of our flesh is increased, & consisteth: how then doeth he denie, that the flesh is able to receiue the gift of God which is life Euerlasting, seeing it is nourished with the blood and bodie of CHRIST?

These words of *Irenæus* albeit not very dark, yet wil they be more plaine if we adde certaine things to them out of *S. Augustine.* He in his booke of the *Sentences* of *Prosperus*, and is found *De consecratione distinct. 2.* writeth thus, This is it that we say, and that by al meanes we labour to proue, that the Sacrifice of the Church is made two maner awayes, that it consisteth of two things, Of the visible forme of Sacraments, and the inuisible flesh and blood of our Lord IESVS CHRIST: of the Sacrament, and of the substance of the Sacrament, that is the body of CHRIST. As the person of CHRIST consisteth of God and man, since CHRIST himselfe is very God and very man, because euery thing conteineth in it selfe the nature and trueth of those things whereof

August. tit. de consecr. st. dist. 2.

it is made; But the sacrifice of the Church is made of two things, of the Sacrament, and of the substance of the Sacrament, that is, the body of CHRIST. There is therefore the Sacrament, and the substance of the Sacrament the bodie of CHRIST. S. *Augustine* repeateth that comparison betweene the person of CHRIST, and the Sacrament of thankesgiuing, and therein hee saith plainely, that the trueth and nature of the bodie is conteined. The same man *De consecrat. distinct. 2.* Whether is this mysticall Sacrament of the Cup made in figure or in trueth? The trueth saith, *My flesh is verily meat, and my blood is verily drinke*; Else how can it bee a great matter, *The bread that I shall giue, is my flesh for the life of the world*, vnlesse it bee very flesh? But because it is not godly that CHRIST should be deuoured with teeth, the Lords will was to haue this bread and wine in mysterie to be by his power made his flesh and blood, in veritie by the consecration of the holy Ghost, and to be daily offered mysticallie for the life of the world. That like as his true flesh is created of the Virgin by the holy Ghost without the companie of man, so by this same Spirit the same bodie mystically, is consecrated of the substance of bread and wine. The body of CHRIST is both trueth and figure; Trueth, in that the bodie and blood of CHRIST by the power of the holy Ghost, is made by the strength thereof of the substance of bread and wine: And the figure is that which outwardly is perceiued. *Idem ibidem.*

The same man in the same title: They that eate and drinke CHRIST, eate and drinke life. To eate him is to be refreshed; to drinke him is to liue. That which is visiblie taken in the Sacrament, is eaten and drunke spiritually in very trueth. The same man in his booke of the *Sentences* of *Prosperus* in the same title saith: But we *Idem ibidem.* *Idem ibidem.*

in

in the forme of bread and wine, which we see, do honor inuisible things, namely, flesh and blood. Neither doe we alike take these two formes, as we did take them before the consecration, seeing that we faithfully confesse that before the consecration, they be bread and wine which nature hath framed, but after the consecration, they be the flesh & blood of CHRIST which the blessing hath hallowed. He againe vpon the 54. Psalme, Vntill the world come to an end the Lord is aboue, yet for all that the Lords trueth is also here with vs: For it is fit that the body in the which he rose againe, should be in one place, but his trueth is spred euery where. He also in his Epistle to *Irenæus:* CHRIST is bread of the which hee who so eateth, liueth for euer; whereof hee himselfe saith thus, *And the bread which I will giue is my flesh for the life of the world.* And he expoundeth it how it is bread, not onely according to the word whereby all things liue, but according to the flesh that hee tooke for the life of the world. For mans flesh which was dead through sinne being knit to pure flesh incorporat, made one with it, doth liue by his spirit euen as one bodie by his owne spirit: But he that is not of the body of CHRIST, liueth not of the Spirit of CHRIST. Hitherto *Augustine* hath plainly inough proued the trueth and nature of the body of CHRIST in this Sacrament.

Hilar. de tri. lib. 8.

Hilarie in his 8. booke of the *Trinitie:* I would know now of them that alledge vnitie of wil between the Father and the Sonne, whether CHRIST nowadayes be in vs by trueth of nature, or by agreement of will. For if the Word be verily made flesh, and wee receiue the word, verily flesh in the Lords meate: how should a man not suppose him to remaine naturally in vs, which being borne man, tooke to himselfe an vnseparable nature, now of our flesh, and hath mixed the nature of his

owne

owne flesh with the nature of eternitie vnder the Sacrament of his flesh to be partaked among vs? And a little after: Therefore whosoeuer wil denie the Father to be naturally in CHRIST, let him first denie either himselfe to be naturally in CHRIST, or CHRIST to be in him, because the Father in CHRIST, and CHRIST in vs, do make vs to be one thing in them. If CHRIST therefore did verily take the flesh of our bodie, & if the same man which was borne of the Virgine *Mary* be verily CHRIST; and we verily take vnder a mysterie the flesh of his body, and thereby shal become one, because the Father is in him, and hee in vs: How is the vnitie of will alledged, seeing the naturall propertie (by meanes of the Sacrament,) is a Sacrament of perfect vnitie? Also a little after; For those things which wee speake of the naturall trueth of CHRIST in vs, vnlesse we learne of him, we speake foolishly and wickedly. For he saith, *My flesh is meat in deed, and my Blood is drinke in deed: Hee that eateth my flesh and drinketh my blood, remaineth in mee, and I in him.* There is no place left of doubting of the trueth of Flesh and Blood: For now it is verily Flesh, and verily Blood, both by the confession of our Lord himselfe, and also by our Faith; and these things being receiued by eating and drinking, doe worke that effect, that both wee be in CHRIST, and CHRIST is in vs. Is not this trueth? Let it happen vnto them not to bee true, which denie IESVS CHRIST to be very God. And soone after: And so by a Mediator, the perfit Vnitie should be taught, when as wee abiding in him hee should abide in the Father, and he abiding in the Father should abide in vs, and so should we clime to the vnitie of the Father, when hee is naturally according to his birth in him, we also should be naturally in him, so long as he abideth naturally in vs. And that this natural vnitie is in vs, he hath thus witnessed, *He that eateth my flesh and drinketh my blood, abideth in me and I in him.* And by and by he addeth, This is truely the cause of our life: for that we haue CHRIST remaining in vs carnal men according to the flesh, whereas wee shall liue hereafter by him, after the same sort as he liueth by the Father. If we therefore liue naturally by him after the flesh, namely hauing taken vpon vs the nature of his flesh, how hath he not the Father after the spirit naturally in him, since he liueth by the Father? And he concludeth: To this end be these things rehearsed by vs, because the heretiks affirming falsly the vnitie of wil onely betweene the Father and the Sonne, vsed for the example of our vnitie with the Lord, as though we were vnited to the Sonne, and by the Sonne to the Father, only by obedience and will of Religion, and no propertie of naturall fellowship were granted to vs by the Sacrament of his flesh and blood: whereas in deed the mysterie of the true and naturall vnitie should be taught, both for the honour of the Sonne of God that is giuen vs, and for the Sonne carnally abiding in vs, and wee knit corporally, and vnseparably in him.

Hilarius doeth manifestly teach the true and naturall partaking of the flesh of CHRYST in the Sacrament; And as plainely doeth *Cyrillus* witnesse the same in the 10. booke chap. 13. when he saith, Yet wee denie not that wee be ioyned spiritually in CHRIST by a right faith, and sincere loue: but that wee haue no maner of ioyning with him according to the flesh, that truely we vtterly denie. And soone after; But doth hee happily thinke that the vertue of the mysticall blessing is vnknowen to vs? which when it is wrought in vs, doth it not also make CHRIST to dwell corporally in vs, by the partaking of the flesh of CHRIST? For why be the

Cyrillus lib. 10. cap. 13.

members of the faithfull the members of CHRIST? *Know ye not* (ſaith he) *that your members be the members of Chriſt? Shal I therefore make the members of Chriſt the members of an harlot?* Our Sauiour alſo ſaith, *He that eateth my fleſh and drinketh my blood, remaineth in me and I in him;* whereby it ought to be conſidered, that CHRIST is in vs, not onely by that accuſtomed qualitie which is perceiued by loue, but alſo further by a naturall partaking. For euen as if a man ſhall melt waxe by the fire, and mingle it with other waxe which is likewiſe melted, ſo that one lumpe may ſeeme to be made of both; So by the communion of the body and blood of CHRIST he is in vs, and wee in him. For this corruptible nature of the bodie could not otherwiſe be brought to vncorruption and life, vnleſſe the body of naturall life ſhould be ioyned thereto. The ſame man alſo in his 4. booke vpon *Iohn* the 14. chapter doeth witneſſe: For truely it behoueth that not onely the ſoule ſhould aſcend into bleſſed life by the holy Ghoſt, but alſo that this rude and earthly body ſhould be brought againe to immortalitie, by a taſte, feeling, and meate like vnto it. The ſame man in his 11. book vpon *Iohn cap. 27.* The Sonne, as man, is made one with vs corporally by the myſtical bleſsings, but ſpiritually as God. And a little after; For we receiuing corporally and ſubſtantially, (as it hath bene ſaid) the Sonne of God which is made one by nature with the Father, be made pure and glorified, being partakers of the nature that is from aboue. The ſame man in the ſame book vpon the 26. chapter: For to the end therefore ye might knit euery one of vs among our ſelues and God, although wee differ both in body and ſoule, yet hath he found a meane agreeable to the determination of his Father, and his owne wiſdome. For he bleſsing with his owne body (through the myſtical

Idem in Io. lib. 4. cap. 14.

Idem in Io. lib. 11. cap. 27.

Idem eodem lib. cap. 26.

communion) them that beleeue, doth make vs one bodie, both with himselfe, and also among our selues. For who wil thinke those distant from this naturall vnion, which be vnited in one CHRIST by the vnion of one CHRISTS bodie? *For if all we eat one bread, we be made all one body.* And within few wordes after: But that this bodily vniting to CHRIST is attained by the partaking of his flesh, *Paul* himselfe againe doeth witnesse, disputing of the mysterie of godlinesse: *the which* (saith he) *hath not bene knowen to the sonnes of men in other generations, as it hath bene reueiled now to his holy Apostles and Prophets in the Spirit, that the Gentiles be coheires and ioyned in body, and equall partakers of the promise in Christ.* The same man to *Calosyrius*: For that wee should not be afraide of the flesh and blood set vpon the holy Altars, God submitting himselfe to our frailtie, putteth a force of life into those things that bee offered, turning them into the trueth of his owne flesh, that the body of life as it were a certaine quickning seed, may bee found in vs: whereupon he addeth, *Doe this in a remembrance of me.* Hitherto *Cyrillus*.

Idem ad Calosyrium.

Cyprianus de cœna Domini.

Cyprian of the Supper of the Lord; This bread not in outward apparence, but in nature changed by the mightie power of the Word, is made flesh, which the Lord did reach to his disciples. And in the same place; Who euen to this day createth, and sanctifieth, & blesseth, and diuideth, to those that take it godly, this his most true and holy bodie. *Hierom* vpon *Matthew, De consecrat. dist. 2.* He tooke bread, which is the comforter of man, and passed to the true Sacrament of Passeouer. That as *Melchisedec* for a figure therof before had done when he offered bread and wine, he should represent it in the trueth of his bodie and blood.

Hieron. in Matth. de consecrat. dist. 2.

Chrysost. in Io. Hom. 45.

Chrysostem vpon *Iohn, Hom. 45.* But that not onely by loue,

loue, but euen in very deed wee should be turned into that flesh, he worketh the same by the meate which hee hath giuen vs. For when he ment to bring his loue vpon vs, he ioyned himselfe to vs by his body, and made himselfe one with vs, that the body might be knit with the head. The same man *Homil. 61.* Therefore that we should be this not only by charitie, but in very deed should bee mingled with that flesh, this is brought to passe by the meat which hee hath giuen vs. *Chrysostom* hath also many other sayings to the same meaning. *Idem Hom. 61.*

Those things that *S. Ambrose* writeth in his 6. booke the first chapter of the Sacraments, do agree with these: Euen as our Lord IESVS CHRIST is the true Sonne of God, not as men be by grace, but as a Sonne of the substance of the Father; so is that which wee take, the very flesh of CHRIST, and they drinke his very blood as he himselfe said. And a little after; Then when his disciples could not away with the talke of CHRIST, but hearing that he would giue them his flesh to eate, and his blood to drinke, they went away: But *Peter* alone said, *Thou hast the words of eternall life, and whither should I goe from thee?* Lest therefore any moe should say this, as though there should be a kinde of lothsomnesse of blood, but that the grace of redemption might remaine, therefore receiuest thou the Sacrament in a similitude, but thou obteinest the grace and vertue of the true nature. The same man in his 4. booke the 4. cap. Thou seest therefore how effectuall in operation the word of CHRIST is. If then there be so great efficacie in the word of our Lord IESVS CHRIST, that that should begin to bee, which was not; How much more is it of effect, to make those things to be that were before, and to be changed into another thing? And so that which was bread before the consecration, the *Ambros. lib. 6. de sacra. cap. 1.* *Idem lib. 4. cap. 4.*

same is become the body of CHRIST after the consecration, because the word of CHRIST doeth change the creature; And so of bread is made the body of CHRIST, and the wine mixed with water in the cup, is made blood by the consecration of the heauenly word. But perhaps thou wilt say, I see not the forme of blood, But it hath a likenesse. For euen as thou hast taken the likenes of his death, so also doest thou drinke the similitude of his blood, that there should be no abhorring of blood, and yet the price of our redemption wrought. Also before the wordes of CHRIST the cup is full of wine & water: after the words of CHRIST haue wrought, there is the blood made which hath redeemed the people. Therefore marke how the word of CHRIST is able to make alteration in all things. Beside, CHRIST himselfe doeth testifie, that wee doe receiue his bodie and blood, of whose fulnesse and testimonie we ought not to doubt. Likewise peraduenture thou saiest, I see another thing, How prouest thou that I do receiue the bodie of CHRIST? This remaineth yet for vs to proue, that this is not it which nature hath fashioned, but it, that blessing hath hallowed; and that there is greater force of the blessing, then of nature: because nature it selfe is also changed by the blessing. Also: But if the blessing of man was of such force that it could turne nature; What doe we say of the very heauenly consecration, whereas the very wordes of the Lord our Sauiour do worke? For this Sacramẽt which thou receiuest, is wrought by the words of CHRIST. But if the word of *Elias* was of such force that it could bring fire from heauen; Shall not the word of CHRIST be of power to change the kinds of elements?

Eusebius Emyssenus de consecrat. dist. 2.

Eusebius Emyssenus likewise, who was in yeeres before *Ambrose*, doth witnes in these wordes, the opinion which

which was then had of the Sacrament, and it is had *De consecrat. dist. 2.* Whereupon the heauenly authoritie confirmeth, *That my flesh is verily meat, and my blood is verily drinke.* Let therefore all doubt of misbeliefe be laid aside, because hee that is author of the gift is likewise witnesse of the trueth. For the inuisible priest doeth turne with his word, by a secret power, the visible creatures into the substance of his bodie and blood, saying thus, *Take ye, eate ye, this is my body*, and the hallowing being repeated, *Take ye, drinke ye, this is my blood.* Therefore euen as the height of the heauens, the depth of waters, and largenesse of earth had their being of nothing, suddenly at the becke of the Lord that commanded: so with the like power in the spirituall Sacraments when power commandeth, effect obeieth. How great therefore and wonderfull benefits the force of the heauenly blessing doeth worke. How it ought not to seeme a new & vnpossible matter to thee, that earthly and mortal things bee turned into the substance of Christ, aske thy selfe that art borne anew in Christ. Hee againe in his oration of the bodie of the Lord: Let not man dout but that the chiefe creatures at the becke of power by the presence of Maiestie, may be turned into the nature of the Lords bodie. *Leo* the bishop and the Synode of *Rome* as is there declared; In what darknesse of ignorance, in what bodie of slouthfulnes haue they hitherto lyen, that they would neither learne by hearing, nor know by reading that which is so agreeable in the congregation vvith the confession of all persons, that the trueth of the bodie and blood of Christ, among the Sacraments of the communion cannot be kept in silence, no not of the tongues of Infants, because in that mysticall distribution of the spirituall food, this is giuen, and this is receiued, that wee receiuing the strength of this heauenly

Leo & Syn. Rom. de consec. dist. 2.

heauenly meat, doe become his flesh, which was made our flesh.

Gregor.hom. Pasch. ibidem.

Gregorie homilia paschali, and it is there rehearsed. For he is daily eaten and drunke in trueth, but yet he remaineth vvhole and one, and vnspotted. And it is therefore a great mysterie, and to be reuerenced with feare, because there is one thing to the sight, and another to the vnderstanding. *Euthymius* vpon *Matthew cap. 64.* Therfore euen as the old Testament had sacrifices and blood, so also hath the Nevv, namely the bodie and blood of the Lord. For hee said not, These be signes of my body, but he said, *These be my body & my blood.* Therfore vvee must not take heed to the nature of those things that bee set before vs, but to the vertue of them. For euen as aboue nature hee did deifie the flesh that vvas taken of the Virgine (if it bee lavvfull to vse this phrase) so also doeth hee vnspeakeably change these things into his very liuely bodie, and into his very precious blood, and into the grace of them.

Euthym. in Matth. cap. 64.

Theophil. in Matth. cap. 26.

Theophilactus vpon *Matt. 26.* In saying *This is my body*, hee declareth that the bread vvhich is sanctified vpon the Altar, is the very body of the Lord, and not a figure ansvvering vnto it; for he said not, This is a figure, but *This is my body.* The bread is transformed by an vnspeakable working into the body of Christ; albeit it seemes bread to vs that bee weake, and abhorre to eate raw flesh, especially the flesh of man. For that cause truly bread appeareth, but it is flesh. The same man vpon *Marke cap. 14.* When he had blessed it, that is, vvhen he had giuen thanks, he brake the bread, which thing also we do, adding thereto prayers, *This is my body:* this I say which you take. For the bread is not a figure and example onely of the Lords body, but it is turned into the very bodie of Christ. *Damascenus* doth also vvrite almost

Idem in Marc. cap. 14.

most the very same things *lib.4.cap.14.* The bread and vvine is not a figure of the body and blood of Christ to the right faith; for God forbid wee should beleeue so: but it is the very deified bodie of the Lord by his owne saying, *This is my body*; not a figure of my bodie, but my bodie, *This is my blood*, not a figure of my blood.

Damas.de fide. Orth.lib.4. cap.14.

Many other places also may be brought forth here, taken out of the Fathers, vvhich agree with the rehearsed, by al the vvhich vve may easily perceiue, what vvas the opinion of them al, asmuch as apperteineth to this part of our diuision, namely, that the Sacrament of Thankesgiuing is not only a figure of the Lords body, but also comprehendeth in it the trueth, nature & substance of the same. For it cannot be a doubt to any man that will read their writings, that they oftentimes vsed these termes, Truly, Naturally, & Substantially, & the coniugates of them. And although our faith dependeth not vpon men, but vpon the word of God: yet since they defend their opinion with the authoritie of the Scripture, it is very profitable for godly minds & desirous of the trueth, to cōsider how so many notable men both for godlinesse and learning, haue vnderstood the words of the Scripture, and with great agreement left their interpretations to their succesion; neither shall he auoid the blame of rashnesse (whosoeuer he be) that dare despise so great authoritie.

Now let vs take in hand our second part. Whether they of ancient time haue thought that there is any difference between the body of our Lord, which is distributed in the Sacrament, and that which was taken of the Virgin mother, vvhich ascended into heauen, and from thence shall come at his time to Iudgement. That is, whether the body of Christ bee in the Sacrament of Thankesgiuing, according to the proper signification of a mans body, or otherwise, differing somewhat from a proper body. When I speake of a proper body, I meane a body properly vnderstand, which shall suffice to haue once admonished. Then vvhether these termes, Trueth, Nature, Substance ought to be vnderstand after the common sort in this matter, or after a more peculiar maner, and more fit for the Sacraments. Finally, whether there be any æquiuocation in these termes or no. For there is not onely heed to bee taken with vvhat words the fathers haue spoken in old time, but also what they ment when they so spake. And that is not to be proued by our ovvne or other mens inuentions, or light coniectures, but by the assured testimonies of the Fathers themselues. But that wee may haue the easier entrie to this matter, wee must perceiue that the body of Christ is called not after one maner vvise in the Scriptures, but sundry vvaies. First, as that bodie as vvas taken vpon him, and borne of the Virgin, vvhich also rose againe, and ascended into heauen, of the vvhich this vvas spoken, *Mee truely shall ye not haue alway*. And this, *I leaue the world, and go to my Father*. And this, *Feele and behold, for a spirit hath not flesh and bones, as you see me haue*. Secondarily, as the Church is called the body of Christ, according to this saying, *You are Christs body*. And this, *And he gaue him to be a head ouer all things to the Church which is his body*. Thirdly, as the Sacrament of the body of Christ is called the body of Christ, wherof Christ himselfe said, *This is my body*. And *Paul, The bread which we breake, is it not the partaking of the body of Christ?* And this, *Making no difference of the Lords bodie*. Which places be vnderstood of the Sacrament of his body, vvhereby it commeth to passe, that the bodie of Christ is called properly and vnproperly. Properly that bodie taken of the Virgin; Vnproperly, the

Sacra-

Sacrament and the Church. That the Church is not properly the bodie of Christ, no man doubteth. It remaineth that vvee prooue the same of the Sacrament. This is especially to bee marked, as oft as they of old time treat of the Sacrament, they all apply to the Sacrament the vvords of our Lord, vvhich are spoken in the sixt chapter of *Iohn*, *My flesh is verily meat, & my blood is verily drinke. The bread which I will giue is my flesh, and vnlesse you eate the flesh of the Sonne of man*, &c. Which things shalbe proued by their ovvne sayings before alledged, and also by those that shall follovv. Neither are they to bee allovved, that deny this chapter of *Iohn* to be referred to this Sacrament, seeing so great a troupe of vvitnesses be against them. But the opinion of them seemed more probable, vvho as they iudge this Euangelist to set forth the humanitie of Christ lesse then the rest, and his diuinitie more amply: so doe declare that these things vvhich are rehearsed by the other Euangelists concerning the institution, and outvvard ceremonie of this Sacrament, are not at all mentioned of *Iohn*; but that he openeth & expoundeth more plainly vnto vs the true and right vnderstanding of them. And it is plaine that the mindes of the *Capernaites* vvhen the Lord said, *My flesh is verily meat; And vnlesse ye eat the flesh of the Sonne of man*, &c. vvere much offended and troubled, and therefore leauing him departed, for they vnderstood him too grosly, and after the common sort. But his Tvvelue Apostles that taried by him being admonished, and lift vp to a more higher meaning, and of more Maiestie, heard of him, *The words which I haue spoken be spirit and life.* Vpon this it commeth to passe, that all the old vvriters do flie the common iudgement and vsuall vnderstanding in those vvordes, *This is my body*, and vvhich the Lord spake of eating his flesh, and follovv a more diuine vvay of vnderstanding them, and more agreeable to the Sacraments, as they themselues affirme.

Chrysost. in Matth. cap. 26. Hom. 83.

Chrysostom vpon *Matthew 26 hom. 83.* expounding the vvords of the Supper, *Take ye, eate ye, this is my body*, &c. doth aske this question, Why were they not troubled vvhen they heard this? And he ansvvereth, Because he had taught them alreadie many and great things concerning this point before: Wherefore also hee did not confirme that vvhich they had often before perceiued. And not long after hee addeth, Hee himselfe did also drinke of it, least at the hearing of those vvordes, they should say, What? do vve then drinke blood, and eate flesh? and vpon that might be troubled; For at the first also when he spake of these matters, many vvere offended onely for the wordes. Lest therefore this should therr also haue happened, he did this first himselfe, that hee might bring them to the partaking of these mysteries vvith a quiet minde. We be taught here by *Chrysostom*, that the Apostles were not troubled when they heard the Lord say, *Take ye, eat ye, this is my body*; Because they had bene alreadie taught before, hovv that which vvas spoken ought to be vnderstood, namely where others were offended, as it is in *Iohn*, & said, *This is a hard saying*, they abode and had learned, *It is the Spirit that giueth life, the flesh profiteth nothing; The wordes that I haue spoken vnto you, are spirit & life*: that is to say, as the same *Chrysostom* in the same place expounded it, they are spiritually to bee vnderstood: which selfe thing the Lord himselfe confirmeth by his owne deed, vvhen hee did eat the same bread, & drinke the vvine vvith them, lest they should thinke vpon any base or common matter, but should be brought to the partaking of the mysteries With quiet minds. It is no hard matter to perceiue by this

this that *Chrysostom* vvriteth in this place, that it is one way a body, that Christ himselfe called his body when he said, *Take ye, eat ye, this is my body*, the which he also receiueth himselfe together with his disciples; and another vvay to bee his proper body which was fed vvith the other. The one did eat, the other was eaten, & after a diuers sort either of them is called his body.

To this purpose maketh also that vvhich *Clemens Alexandrinus* schoolemaster to *Origen*, teacheth in his booke, intituled *Pædagogus*, when he saith, διττὸν δὲ τὸ αἷμα τοῦ χριστοῦ: τὸ μὲν σαρκικὸν, δι' οὗ ἐλυτρώθημεν: τὸ δὲ πνευματικὸν, ᾧ κεχρίσμεθα. The blood of Christ is two maner of wayes: the one fleshie whereby vve are vvashed, the other spirituall vvherevvith we haue bene anointed. Whom *Hierom* follovving vpon the Epistle to the *Ephesians* the first chapter saith, The blood and flesh of Christ (saith he) is vnderstood tvvo maner of vvayes: that is, either that spirituall and heauenly, whereof he himselfe spake, *My flesh is verily meat, and my blood is verily drinke; And vnlesse you eate my flesh and drinke my blood, you shall not haue euerlasting life:* Or else the flesh and blood that vvas crucified, that was shed vvith the speare of the souldier. There bee tvvo things that *Hierom* teacheth in this place, That those vvords in the 6. chap. of *Iohn*, do appertaine to the Sacrament, euen as *Chrysostom* doth: and that the flesh that vvas crucified, doeth differ from that vvhich is in the Sacrament, vvhich he calleth Spirituall & Diuine. The same man vpon *Leuiticus*, and is to be seen *De consecrat. dist.* 2. Of this sacrifice vvhich is by miracle vvrought for the remembrance of Christ it is lavvfull to eate: but of that which Christ offered vpon the Altar of the Crosse, it is of it self lavvful for no man to eat. A plaine and manifest distinction.

Augustin in lib. senten. Prosperi. It is his flesh vvhich couered

Clemens Alexand. lib. inscrip. Pædagogus.

Hierom. in Epi. ad Ephes. ca. 1.

Idem. in Leuit. de consecrat. dist. 2.

August. in lib. Sent. Prosperi.

uered with the forme of bread, we receiue in the Sacrament, and his blood which vnder the forme and tast of wine we drinke, that is to say, the flesh is the sacrament of flesh, and blood is the sacrament of blood. By flesh and blood being both inuisible, spirituall, intelligible, is betokened the visible & sensible body of our Lord Iesus Christ, full of the grace of all vertues & diuine Maiestie. Who seeth not hovv plainly *Augustine* putteth a difference between the proper body of Christ which he termeth visible and sensible, and that flesh which we receiue in the sacrament, vvhich he affirmeth to be inuisible, spirituall, intelligible, and a signe of the other body? The same man in his Epistle to *Irenæus*; You shall not eat this body which you see, and drinke that blood which they that shall crucifie me shall shed. The same truely, and not the same; The same inuisiblie, and not the same visibly. He putteth a difference when hee saith, Not this body: and againe, The same, & not the same. The maner of the difference is, the same inuisibly which hee termeth before the inuisible body, namely the Sacrament of the body: and not the same visibly, or the visible body, which is referred to the proper body: for this body wheresoeuer it be, is visible. The same man in his booke *Sent. Prosperi:* Christ was once offered in himselfe, yet is hee daily offered in the Sacrament, which is thus to be vnderstood. That, in the outward shewing foorth of his body, in the distinction of all his members, very God, and very man, did but once hang vpon the Crosse, offering himselfe a liuely sacrifice to the Father. The body which is in the Sacrament, hath neither outward shewing forth of the body, nor distinction of members, but his proper body neuer wanteth his distinction of members.

Idem in Epist. ad Iren.

Idem in lib. Sent. Prosperi.

Idem in Ps. 33.

The same man vpon the 33. Psalme: And he was caried

ried in his owne hands. But my brethren, who can vnderstand how this might be done in a man? For who can be caried in his owne hands? A man may well be caried in other mens hands, in his owne hands no man is caried. How it may be vnderstond in *Dauid* himselfe, according to the letter, we shall not finde, but in Christ wee shall finde it. For Christ was caried in his owne hands when he commending his owne body, said, *This is my body*; for that body was caried in his hands, and afterward expounding himselfe better he saith, And hee was caried in his own hands. How was he caried in his owne hands? Because when he ment to cōmend that body and blood of his, hee tooke into his hands, that which the faithfull knew, and he caried himselfe after a sort, when he said, *This is my body.* In saying that body was caried in his hands, and he tooke into his handes that which the faithfull knew, and he bare himselfe after a sort; he doeth declare that this saying is not to be vnderstand simply of one selfe body, but that body that did carie was one, namely his proper bodie, and that which was caried another, to say, the Sacrament of his body.

The same man vpon the 98. Psalme, It seemed a hard saying to them, when he said, *Vnlesse a man do eate my flesh, hee shall neuer haue euerlasting life.* They tooke it foolishly, imagined of it fleshly, and thought that the Lord would haue cut certaine pieces out of his bodie to giue them, and they said, *This is a hard saying.* They themselues were hard, not the saying: for if they had not bene hard, but humble spirited, they would haue said within themselues; He speaketh not this without a cause, there is may hap a certaine hid Sacrament in it; They would haue taried with him meeke spirited, not hardned, and haue learned of him that which those

Idem in Psal. 98.

that

that remained did learne when they were gone. For when his Twelue disciples abode with him after their departure, they seemed to bewaile to him the death of them, because they were offended at his wordes, and gone backe. But he instructed them & said vnto them, *It is the Spirit that quickeneth, for the flesh profiteth nothing; The words that I haue spoken to you, are Spirit and life*, Vnderstand you that spiritually which I haue spoken to you. You shall not eate this bodie which you see, neither shall you drinke the blood which they shall shed that crucifie me. I haue commended to you a certaine Sacrament. If it be spiritually vnderstood, it will giue you life. Although of necessitie it must be ministred visiblie, yet must it bee vnuisibly vnderstood, where hee saith, Not this bodie which you see, &c. And I haue commended a certaine Sacrament vnto you; hee maketh a plaine distinction betweene the two bodies, whereof one is properly his body, the other the Sacrament of his body.

Idem de doct. Christ. lib. 3.

The same man, *De doctrina Christiana lib 3. Vnlesse you eate the flesh of the Sonne of man and drinke his blood, yee shall haue no life in you.* Hee seemeth to command a hainous and wicked thing; therefore it is a figure commanding that wee must communicate with the passion of the Lord, & sweetly and profitably lay vp in remembrance that his flesh was crucified and wounded for vs. If we following the letter do vnderstand it, as the words doe properly sound, Hee seemeth (saith he) to command a hainous thing: therefore (hee saith) it is a figuratiue speach, and ought not to be vnderstood of the eating of his proper body, but of the Sacrament of his body, which is after a spirituall sort the body of Christ.

Idem ad Boniface. Epist. 23.

The same man to *Boniface* in the 23. Epistle; For so wee speake, as when Easter draweth nie, wee say, To

morrow

morrow, or the day after is the pasion of Christ, whereas indeed he suffered so many yeeres before, and that pasion hath not at all bene made but once. For vpon very Easter day we say, This day the Lord rose againe. whereas so many yeres are past since he rose againe, Why is none so foolish to reproue vs, & say we lie in so saying? but because we call these dayes according to the similitude of those in which these things were done, so that it is called the same day, which is not the same, but by the course of time is like that, and it is said to bee done that day for the ministring of the Sacrament, which was not done that day, but long before. Was not Christ once offered in himselfe? and yet in the Sacrament not onely at all the solemnities of Easter, but euery day he is offered to the people. And hee lieth not, that being asked the question, doeth answere that he is offered: For if the Sacraments should not haue a certaine likenesse of those things whereof they be Sacraments, they should be no Sacraments at all. And of this likenesse, they take the names oftentimes also of the things themselues. Euen as therefore after a certaine sort, the Sacrament of the body of Christ is the body of Christ, and the sacrament of the blood of Christ, is the blood of Christ: so also the sacrament of faith is faith. We see also in this place, that the proper body of Christ which was once offered, is discerned from that sacrament which is daily offered, and after a sort is the body.

The same *S. Augustin*, as it is to be found *De consecrat. dist. 2.* Whether is this mysticall sacrament of the cup vnder a figure, or vnder the trueth? The trueth saith, *My flesh is verily meat, and my blood is verily drinke*, else how shall it be a great matter; *The bread which I will giue is my flesh for the life of the world*, vnlesse it be very

Idem de consecrat. dist. 2.

E flesh

flesh in deed? But because it is not lawfull to deuoure Christ with teeth, the Lords will was that this bread and wine should be made potentially in a mysterie, his flesh and blood verily by the consecration of the holy Ghost, and should be daily offered mysticallie for the life of the world: That euen as very flesh was made of the Virgin by the holy Ghost, without the company of man; so also by the same through the substance of bread and wine, the same body is mysticallie consecrated. The body of Christ is both trueth and a figure; Trueth, while the body and blood of Christ, by the power of the holy Ghost in power of the same, is made of the substance of bread and wine: but the figure is that which is outwardly seene.

Here also *Augustin* doeth put a difference betweene the very flesh taken of the Virgin, and the trueth of the flesh that is made of the substance of bread and wine: for this (saith he) is daily created his very flesh, and offered in mysterie, which thing is not lawfull to be spoken of the very proper body of Christ. The same author in the same booke, Vntill the end of the world the Lord is aboue: but yet the trueth of the Lord is for all that here with vs. For it is fit that the body wherein hee rose againe should bee in one place, but the trueth thereof is spread euery where. Doeth he not plainely teach, that the body wherein hee rose againe is one, which necessarily must be contained in one place, and that the trueth of his body is another, which is so farre spred abroad, as the sacrament is rightly ministred?

Here is moreouer to be noted, that the trueth of the Lords body is spoken two wayes, and ought two maner wayes to bee vnderstood; for one maner of trueth of his body is required in mysterie, another simply and without mysterie.

Those

Those words also of *Augustin* in the same place, *De consecrat. dist. 2. Vtrum sub figura, &c.* doe make for this purpose; That because we do now take the similitude of his death in our Baptisme, so also wee may take the similitude of his flesh and blood, so that the trueth should not be wanting in the sacrament, and yet be no laughing stocke to the Infidels for drinking the blood of a man slaine. He affirmeth the likenesse of flesh and blood to be coupled with the trueth in the sacrament: yet so as if one would vnderstand it properly to be the blood of a man slaine, wee drinke it not: for so might the infidels laugh vs to scorne. *Idem ibidem.*

He againe in the same title, *Hoc est quod &c.* Euen as therefore the heauenly bread, which is the flesh of Christ after his sort, is called the body of Christ, wher-as indeed it is the sacrament of Christs body, namely of that which was to be seene, handled, mortall, set vp-on the Crosse; and the sacrifice of the flesh which is made by the hands of the Priest, is called the pasion of Christs death and crucifying, not in very deed, but by the signification of the mysterie: so the sacrament of faith which is meant Baptisme, is faith. Againe he tea-cheth plainely, that the body of Christ which is to be seene and felt is one thing, and that another, which af-ter his sort is called the body of Christ, whereas indeed it is a sacrament of that body of his which is to be seen and felt. *Idem ibidem.* Whereupon the Glosse vpon the same place hath thus, The heauenly bread (that is to say) the hea-uenly sacrament which doth truely represent the flesh of Christ, is called the body of Christ, but vnproperly; and therefore it is called after a peculiar maner, not in the trueth of the matter, but by the signification of the mysterie. *Glossa ibidem.* And a little before, the same Glosse saith in the same place; The heauenly sacrament which is vp- *Idem ibidem.*

on the Altar is vnproperly called the body of Christ, euen as Baptisme is vnproperly called faith.

August. ad Dard.

To this agree those wordes that the same *Augustin* writeth to *Dardanus* in this wise: Keepe faithfully the Christian profession, That hee rose againe from the dead, He ascended into heauen, Sitteth on the Right-hand of the Father: Neither shall he come from any other place then from thence to iudge the quicke and the dead; And so shal he come, (the voice of the Angel being witnesse) as hee was seene to goe into heauen, namely in the same forme and substance of flesh: vnto the which flesh hee hath assuredly giuen immortalitie, and not taken away the nature. After this forme he is not to be thought that he is euery where spred abroad: For we must take heed that wee affirme not so the diuinitie of his manhood, that wee take away the trueth of his body.

Idem ibidem.

Afterward in the end of the same Epistle; Doubt not that Christ our Lord the onely begotten Sonne of God, equall to the Father, euen that Sonne of man which is lesse then the Father, is both altogether present euery where as God, and also in some certaine place of heauen, for the measure of his true body. The trueth of Christs body, which in another place he said is euery where spred abroad when hee speaketh of the sacrament of his body, here where he entreateth of his true body indeed properly vnderstood, he denieth that according to that maner of body it is euery where spred abroad, but that so the trueth of his body is cleane taken away.

Augustin is not contrary to himselfe, but sheweth plainely ynough that the body, and the trueth of the body is to be taken two waies. Peraduenture I seeme to haue rehearsed ouer many places out of *Austin*, but

yet

yet this one place doe I thinke not to bee ouerpassed, which he hath left in writing vpon the Gospel of *Iohn tract. 50. The poore haue ye alwayes with you, but me shall you not haue alwayes.* Let good men receiue this also, and not bee troubled: for hee spake of the presence of his body. For according to his Maiestie, according to his prouidence, according to his vnspeakeable and inuisible grace, that is fulfilled which was said by him, *Beholde I am with you euery day, euen to the ende of the world.* But according to the flesh, which the Word tooke vpon him, according to that that he was borne of the Virgin, according to that, that hee was taken of the *Iewes*, that he was nailed to a tree, that hee was taken downe from the Crosse, that he was wrapped in linen clothes, that he was layed in the graue, that hee appeared in his resurrection, ye shall not alvvayes haue him with you. Why? Because according to the presence of his body, hee was conuersant vvith his disciples fourtie dayes, and they being in company vvith him, by seeing him and not follovving him, he ascended into heauen, and is not here, for he is there, he sitteth on the Right-hand of the Father: and here hee is also, for the presence of his Maiestie did not depart. After another sort according to the presence of his Maiestie, we haue Christ alwayes. According to the presence of his flesh it vvas rightly said to the disciples, *but mee shall you not haue alwayes:* for the Church had him a few dayes according to the presence of his flesh, and now keepeth him by faith, and seeth him not with eyes. Thus much out of *Augustin.*

Idem in Ioan. tract. 50.

Where *Augustin* speaketh of that which is properly called Christs body, he denieth that it is simply present here, and doeth refuse such a presence of his body: but when he speaketh of the Sacrament, hee doeth affirme that his body is verily present, and a true presence of his body, yet not properly, but, as he himselfe doeth instruct vs, according to his Maiestie, according to his vnspeakeable & inuisible grace, whereof we wil speake more at large hereafter. It is plaine therefore, that the body of Christ in the sacrament is to bee vnderstood one way, and that an other way which of necessitie must be in some place of heauen, for the fourmes sake of a true body, as hee saith. Now let vs goe forward to other.

Gregor. Nazianz. oratione de Pasch.

Gregorie Nazianzene in his Oration of the feast of Easter, saith thus, But let vs be made partakers of the Passeouer, but yet still figuratiuely, albeit this Passeouer be more manifest then the old. For truly the Passeouer of the Law (I speake boldly) was a more darke figure of a figure: but within a while wee shall enioy it more perfect and manifest, when the Sonne the Word it selfe, shall drinke it new with vs in the kingdome of his Father, opening and teaching vs those things which he hath now shewed sparingly. Here *Nazianzene* called the sacrament of Thankesgiuing a more manifest Passeouer then the Passeouer of the Law: yet still for all that a figure, namely of that which wee shall enioy more perfit and manifest in the kingdome of his Father. This Passeouer therefore which is performed in mysterie, doeth differ from that which remaineth for euer, wherewith wee shall bee satisfied in the world to come.

Gregor. in hom. Pasch.

The other *Gregorie* in his Homily of the Passeouer: This wholesome sacrifice doeth renew to vs by a mysterie the death of the onely begotten Sonne: which although he rising againe from death dieth no more, nor death shall haue any more dominion ouer him, yet hee liuing immortally, and vncorruptibly in himselfe, dieth

againe

againe in this mysterie, and his body is also receiued euery where, and his flesh for the health of the people, his blood is not now shed into the hands of the vnfaithfull, but is powred out in the mouth of the faithfull. By this therefore we may iudge what maner of sacrament this is, which for our absolution doeth alwayes represent the Pasion of the onely begotten Sonne. For what faithfull man can doubt, that in the very houre of the sacrifice, at the voyce of the Priest, the heauens open, and the company of Angels be present in the mysterie of Iesus Christ? This *Gregorie* maketh a difference betweene this sacrifice, and the other, and doeth also shew that this death, this pasion, this body, which things be done in this mysterie, doe represent and imitate those things which were done long agoe. For if you follow the letter, his body is not spred out euery where, nor his flesh suffereth, nor dieth any more, although these things be said to be done in mysterie.

The same opinion had *Eusebius Emissenus*, whose wordes are rehearsed *De consecrat. Dist. 2.* as followeth. Forasmuch as hee would take away from the eyes the body taken of the Virgin, and would place it aboue the starres; it was necessary that in the day of his Supper, the sacrament of his body and blood should bee consecrated vnto vs, to the end that that might be worshipped continually by a mysterie, which was once offered for a ransome: that seeing a dayly and vnceasing redemption did runne for the saluation of all men, there might be a continuall oblation of redemption, and that continuall sacrifice might liue in memorie, and might euer be present in grace, a true, perfect, and onely sacrifice to be esteemed in faith, not to bee iudged by forme nor by outward sight, but by the inward affection. Whereupon the heauenly authoritie confirmeth, that

Euseb. Emis. de consecrat. dist. 2.

My

My flesh is verily meat, and my blood is verily drinke.

Let all doubt therefore of vnfaithfulnes depart, seeing he that is the author of the gift, the same is witnes of the trueth: for the inuisible Priest by his word and secret power, turneth the visible creature, into the substance of his body and blood, saying, *Take, eate, this is my body*, and after the blessing being repeated, *Take and drinke* (saith he) *this is my blood.* Therefore euen as at the becke of the Lord commanding it, suddenly, and of nothing the hie heauens, the depth of the waters, and largenesse of the earth was made: so by the like power in spiritual sacraments, where power doeth command, effect doth obey. By plaine words doth *Eusebius* teach vs, that the proper body which he termeth taken vpon him, is not in the sacrament, but withdrawen from the earth, placed aboue the starres: and therefore is ordained the sacrament of the body, wherein is contained the substance of the body, yet in a mysterie and by grace, not that substance which hee said before was taken away, which if it were present, the sacrament were not needfull; but a spirituall substance, and fit for the sacraments, whereupon hee also calleth the sacraments spirituall. And lest we should imagine it a more grosse substance then is fit, hee alledgeth foorthwith the example of regeneration, saying, How great benefit therfore, and worthy to be praised, the force of the heauenly blessing doeth worke, and how it ought not to bee a new and vnposible matter to thee, that earthly & mortal things be changed into the substance of Christ, aske thy selfe that art new borne againe in Christ. Lately farre from life, a stranger from mercie, and inwardly a dead man, from the way of health thou wast banished; and suddenly professing the Lawes of Christ, and by wholesome mysteries renewed, thou hast leapt into the body of the Church, not by sight, but by beleefe, and of the childe of perdition wast thought worthy by a secret purenesse, to be the Sonne of God by adoption, abiding still in the visible measure, and made inuisibly greater then thy selfe, without increase of quantitie. For although thou wast the very selfe-same man before, yet by augmentation of faith, thou art become much otherwise: for in the outward man nothing is added, and all in the inward man is cleane changed, and so man was made the sonne of God, and Christ was formed in the minde of man. Euen as therefore without corporall feeling (the former basenesse set apart) thou hast suddenly put on a new dignitie; and as in this point that God hath healed those things that were amisse in thee, put away thine infections, wiped away thy spots, thy eyes are not trusted vvithall, but thy inward senses: so when thou goest vp to the holy Altar, to be fed with the spirituall meat, behold in thy faith the holy body and blood of Christ, honour it, marueile at it, touch it with thy minde, take it in the hand of thy heart, and especially receiue it, whole Christ, with the thirstie draught of the inward man.

Eusebius declareth by this similitude, what maner of change is made in the sacrament, how earthly things be turned into the substance of Christ, and what maner of substance that is: without doubt, like vnto that change wherewith wee be altered in our Baptisme, and such a substance as wee put on in the bath of Regeneration, when we be borne the children of God, and made a new creature, and new men, when we passe into the body of the Church, where in our outward part nothing is changed, but all inwardly, and for that cause calleth he it spirituall food, which we behold in faith, touch with minde, take with the hand of our heart, and receiue with the thirstie draught of the inward man.

Ambros. in Epist. ad Hebr. de consecrat. dist. 2.

With this agreeth that that *Ambrose* writeth vpon the Epistle to the *Hebrewes*, and is repeated *De consecrat. dist.* 2. In Christ was once a mighty sacrifice offered for an euerlasting Redemption: vvhat doe vve then? doe vve not dayly offer him? yes, but in remembrance of his death: and it is but one sacrifice, not many: for Christ vvas once offered, and this sacrifice is a paterne of that. *Ambrose* saith plainely, that that true sacrifice vvas once offered, but this sacrifice is offered euery day: and hee declareth in vvhat sort it is one sacrifice, and not one, vvhen he saith that this is a paterne of that. The same man in his booke of Mysteries saith, In that sacrament is Christ, because it is the body of Christ: it is not then a corporall, but a spirituall food, vvhereupon the Apostle also saith of the figure of it, *That our fathers did eate the same spirituall food*: for the body of God is a spiritual body, the body of Christ is the body of the diuine spirit. These things cannot be said of Christes true and proper body, namely, that it is a spirit: for a spirit hath not flesh and blood, vvhich that body hath, as the Lord himselfe did vvitnesse before his disciples, *Feele yee, and see you* (saith he) *for a spirit hath not flesh and bones, as you see me haue.* Wherefore the same auctour *De sacramentis lib. 4.* saith thus: Thou seest therefore hovv mighty in operation the vvord of Christ is. If then there be so great force in the vvord of the Lord Iesu, that those things should begin to be which were not: hovv much more is it of force, to make those things remaine which were, and yet to change them into another thing? The heauen was not, the sea was not, the earth was not. But hearken to him that saith, *He spake the word and they were made, he commanded and they were created.* Therefore that I may ansvvere thee, it was not the body of Christ be-

Idem in lib. de Myst.

Idem de Sacr. lib. 4.

fore

fore the conſecration; but after the conſecration I tell thee it is now the body of Chriſt. *He ſpake the word and it was made, he commanded and it was created.* Thou waſt thy ſelf, but thou waſt an old creature; after thou waſt conſecrated, thou didſt beginne to be a new creature. Wilt thou know how new a creature? Euery one is (ſaith he) a new creature in Chriſt. *Ambroſe* taketh his argument *à maiore*, By the word of God new things are made: then is it no maruelle, if things which now be, and remaine, are changed into another thing by his word, vvhich thing is done in Sacraments. Examples of the firſt are Heauen, the Sea, the Earth: of the later, man, which before he be regenerate is an old creature, but after regeneration, by force of the word, albeit he be the very ſame he vvas before, namely a man ſtill, yet he receiueth an invvard change, and of an old, is made a new creature.

Like vnto this he affirmeth the change in the ſacrament to bee, when as both bread remaineth, and yet getteth to it ſelfe a nevv ſubſtance (that is to ſay) a new dignitie. That ſame thing doth hee yet more fully expound in his ſixt booke, writing thus: Peraduenture thou mayeſt ſay, How is it very fleſh? for I ſee a ſimilitude, I ſee not the trueth of blood in deed. Firſt of all, I told thee of the vvord of Chriſt, that it worketh as of force, to change and alter the appointed kindes of nature. Moreouer, when the diſciples of Chriſt could not away with his talke, but hearing that hee vvould giue them his fleſh to eate, and his blood to drinke, went their way; yet *Peter* alone ſaid, *Thou haſt the words of eternall life, whither ſhall I goe from thee?* Leaſt therefore any moe ſhould ſo ſay, but the grace of Redemption ſhould remaine; Therefore thou takeſt the ſacrament in a ſimilitude, but thou doeſt attaine the grace

Idem de ſacrament. lib. 6.

and vertue of the true nature. At the last he addeth to make vp the matter; And thou which receiuest bread, art made partaker in that spirituall food, of the diuine substance.

We learne by the authoritie of this so great a man, that that which we take in the sacrament, is a spiritual, not a corporall food; neither that that flesh is to be taken after the maner of his proper flesh, as the *Capernaits* did, and vvith offence went backe, but together with the outvvard signe we obtaine the grace and vertue of the true nature, and receiuing the bread are partakers of his diuine substance. And here also we see that *Ambrose* was of the same opinion that *Emissenus* was, and far otherwise vnderstandeth both the alteration which is made in the sacraments, and also the very terme of substance, then it is either taken in proper speach, or as Philosophers do naturally speake.

Idem de offic. Lib. 4. cap. 48.

To the same purpose serueth also that which he writeth in his booke *De officijs lib. 4. cap. 48.* Here is the shadovv, here is the image; there is the trueth: the shadow in the Lavv, the image in the Gospel: but the trueth in heauen. In time past the Lambe was offered, the calfe vvas offered; Novv is Christ offered: but he is offered as man, as taking his Pasion, but hee as a Priest doeth offer himselfe here as in an image, but there in trueth, where hee maketh intercesion for vs, as an aduocate vvith his Father. Hee putteth a difference in the one oblation from the other. And albeit both (after their maner) be done in deed, yet this vvhich is solemnized in the Church, is done in an Image, but the trueth it selfe remaineth as an Aduocate for vs vvith the Father.

Origen in Psal. 38.

And this place of *Ambrose* doeth seeme to be like to that place of *Origen* vpon the 38. Psalme, vvhere he intreateth of that saying of ***Paul***, ***For the Law hauing a shadow***

dow of those good things to come, hath not the very Image of the things &c. And thus he vvriteth: But if any man can passe from this shadovv, let him come to the Image of the things, and see the comming of Christ made in the flesh; Let him behold that hie Priest, both novv offering sacrifices to the Father, & that shall hereafter offer; And let him vnderstand all these things to be the Images of spirituall things, and that heauenly things be noted by corporall Offices. It is therefore called an Image vvhich is receiued for the present time, and may be discerned by the nature of man. If thou canst vvith thought and mind pearce the heauens, and follovv IESVS vvho hath pearced the heauens, and is novv present before the face of God for vs, there shalt thou find those good things of vvhich the Lavv had a shadovv, and Christ shevved the Image in the flesh, vvhich are prepared for the blessed, vvhich neither eye hath seene, nor eare heard, nor ascended into the heart of man: vvhich things vvhen thou shalt see, thou shalt vnderstand that he that vvalketh in them, and continueth in desire and earnest affection after them, such a one vvalketh not novv in an Image, but in the very trueth it selfe. *Origen* writeth to the learned and practised, and therefore not easie to be vnderstood of all men. Notvvithstanding, he shevveth plainely that the sacrifices vvhich be here offered, be Images of that trueth vvhich pearced to heauens, and abiding before the face of God is intercessor for vs: And therefore that the Images of the trueth be one thing, and the very trueth another. And that although these Images haue also their trueth, yet this differeth from that proper trueth vvhich vve shall there indeed attaine to, vvhen vve follovving Christ, shall pearce the heauens vvhere hee abideth; the vvhich after a sort vvee also enioy here,

 vvhile

while in our deuout meditations our mindes being lift vp to heauen, we behold those secret good things. He also vpon *Matthew cap. 15.* saith: Neither is it the material bread, but the Word that is spoken ouer it, that profiteth to him that eateth not vnworthily of the Lord. And these things are spoken of the figuratiue and mysticall body.

Idem in Mat. cap. 15.

Many things beside may be said of the Word which was made flesh. Here **Origen** doeth declare, that the true flesh, (that is to say) the true nature of man, which Christ being the Word tooke vnto him, to bee one maner of flesh, and an other thing to bee his figuratiue and symbolical body, with which words he calleth the Sacrament. To this purpose serue the wordes that he writeth *Contra Celsum lib. 8.* We obeying the Maker of all things for his great benefits bestowed vpon vs, when we haue giuen Thankes, are fed with the loaues set before vs, which by intercession and prayers are made a certaine more holy body. These words, A certain more holy body, do not agree to the proper body of Christ, but they agree to the sacrament of Thankesgiuing, which after a certaine maner is his body. The same man vpon *Leuiticus Homil. 7.* expoundeth the same matter more plainely, saying: But you if ye be the children of the Church, if you bee indued with the mysteries of the Gospel, if the Word made flesh dwelleth in you; acknowledge you these things which we speake, that they be the Lords, lest peraduenture he that is ignorant, be ignorant still: Acknowledge that they be figures which be written in the holy Volumes, & therefore examine them as spiritual, & not carnall men, and vnderstand those things which bee spoken: For if you take those things as carnal men, they hurt you, and doe not nourish you. For there is also in the Gospel a let-

Idem contra Celsum lib. 8.

Idem in Leuit. Homil. 7.

ter that killeth: The killing letter is not onely found in the olde Testament. There is also a letter in the nevv Testament that can kill him which will not spiritually marke those things that bee spoken. For if thou follow this that hath bene spoken, according to the letter, *Vnlesse ye eat my flesh and drinke my blood*, this letter slayeth. Seeing then the Authors euery where referre these wordes to the sacrament; and *Origen* commandeth so much to flee the letter, as to say that it killeth: Who seeth not, that Christes flesh is in the sacrament one way to bee vnderstood, and another according to the letter, and in proper speech?

Epiphanius in Anchorato is of the same opinion, where he saith: For wee see that our Sauiour tooke into his hands, as the Gospel cōtaineth, that he rose in the Supper, and tooke these things, and when hee had giuen Thankes, he said, *This is mine, &c.* And we see that it is not equal, nor like, neither to the Image that is in flesh, nor to his inuisible Godhead, nor to the features of his members: for this is of a round fashion and without sence, as much as to the povver of it selfe appertaineth. And therefore his will was to speake by grace, *This is mine, &c.* And euery man beleeueth his saying: for he that beleeueth not that he is true as he hath said, hee is fallen from grace and health. But that which we haue heard wee beleeue that it is his: for vve know that our Lord is altogether sence, all indued with sence, all God, all mouing, all working, all light, all incomprehensible; but yet he, that hath giuen vs this with grace. *Epiphanius* doeth in this place endeuour himselfe to proue, that man being made after the Image of God, hath in deed the Image of God, not according to the proper nature of diuinitie, but after grace; and vseth the similitude taken of the Sacrament of Thankesgiuing.

Epiphanius in Anch:or..to.

uing, the which according to the proper nature of a body, he denieth it to be the body of Christ, since it hath neither the forme of a true body, and lacketh feeling and mouing, and yet it is verily beleeued to be his body by grace.

Cyprian de Cœna Domini.

Cyprian also in his sermon of the Supper of the Lord, doeth very godly and plentifully reason to the same effect, out of the which I haue thought sufficient to touch these fevv places. For none of the Fathers haue more extolled the dignitie of the Sacrament, and shutting out all carnall sence, more plainely declared the true vnderstanding of so great a mysterie. An vnconsuming meat (saith hee) the Master did set before his disciples: neither were the people bidden to a sumptuous and cunningly dressed Banquet, but there is giuen an immortall food differing from common meates, retaining the shape of bodily substance, but prouing by inuisible vvorking, that the diuine vertue is present. Againe, There did sometime arise a question (as it is read in the Gospel of *Iohn*) of the noueltie of this word, and at the doctrine of this Mysterie were the hearers amazed, vvhen the Lord said, *Vnlesse you eate of the flesh of the Sonne of man, and drinke his blood, you shall not haue life in you*: Because certaine, for that they did not yet beleeue, nor could vnderstand, went backe, for that it seemed to them an horrible and hainous thing to feed vpon mans flesh, thinking hee had spoken this after that sort, as though they should haue bene taught to haue eaten his flesh sod, or rosted, and cut in pieces: whereas the flesh of his person, if it should bee deuided into morsels, could not haue bene sufficient for all mankinde, which being once spent, Religion should seeme to perish, vvhich should not haue aftervvard a sacrifice remaining any longer. But in such like thoughts flesh

and

and blood profiteth nothing, because as the Master himselfe hath expounded, *These words be Spirit and life:* neither doth the carnall sense pearse the vnderstanding of so great a depth, vnlesse Faith be added too. The Bread is food, the Blood is life, the Flesh substance, the Body the Church. A body, because of the agreeing of members in one; Bread, for the conformitie of nourishment; Blood, for the effect of life giuen; Flesh, for the propertie of the humanitie taken. Also hee sayth, This common bread beeing changed into flesh and blood, doeth procure life and encrease to the bodies, and therefore by the accustomed effect of things, the weakenesse of our faith is aided, and taught by a sensible argument, that the effect of eternall life is in the visible Sacraments, and that we be knit to Christ not so much by corporall, as by spirituall passage. Also this bread which hee reached to his disciples, beeing changed, not in forme but in nature, by the omnipotencie of the Word is made flesh; and euen as in the person of Christ the humanitie was seene and the diuinitie hid, so into the visible Sacrament vnspeakeably doeth the diuine substance powre it selfe. Also the Master truely of this Institution sayd, that *Vnlesse wee should eate and drinke his blood, we should not haue life in vs:* instructing vs by a spirituall lesson, and opening our vnderstanding to so hidden a matter, that wee should knowe that our eating is an abiding in him, and our drinke as it were a certaine incorporation, by submitting our seruice, and ioyning our willes, and vniting our affections. Also hee sayth, Among the guests of the Lords table the natural man is not admitted; whatsoeuer flesh and blood doeth appoint is shut out from this company, it sauoureth nothing, it profiteth nothing, whatsoeuer the finenes of the sence of man doth goe about. *Cyprian* hath these and many other places to the same purpose. The very words of *Cyprian* doe sufficiently declare that which belongeth to our purpose: How the Letter is not to bee followed in these things which be spoken of this mysterie; how the vnderstanding of the Flesh is vtterly to be shunned, and all things to be referred to a spiritual sense: That there is the presence of the diuine power in this Bread, the effect of euerlasting life, and that the diuine substance is powred thereinto; that the words are spirit and life, that a spirituall lesson is giuen; that this Body, this Blood and Flesh, this substance of body, ought not to be taken after a common sort, nor as mans reason doth appoint, but to be named, thought of, beleeued for certaine excellent effects, powers and properties ioyned thereto, which be euen within the body and blood of Christ by nature; namely, that it doeth both feede and reuiue our soules, and prepareth our bodies to resurrection and immortalitie.

Cyrill. in Ioan. lib. 4. cap. 14.

The same opinion hath also *Cyrillus*, who though he affirme in many places, the trueth and nature of the body of Christ to be in the Sacrament; yet hee is in opinion, that it is a spiritual and diuine matter, and not to be vnderstood after the manner of men. For first he declareth, that the same maner of eating is set foorth in the words of the Lords Supper, which the Lord himselfe signified when he said, *Vnlesse you eat the flesh of the Sonne of man, &c.* For so he writeth in his 4. booke vpon the 14. Chap. of *Iohn:* Where after he had spoken somewhat of them that did say, *How can this man giue his flesh to be eaten?* hee addeth these words; Therefore they ought first to haue set the rootes of faith in their minde, and then to seeke for those things that are to be sought for of man: but they, before they would be-

leeue,

leeue, did seeke importunately. For this cause therefore, the Lord did not open, how it might be, but exhorteth to seeke it by faith. So to his disciples that beleeued, he gaue the pieces of bread, saying, *Take ye, and eate ye, this is my body.* The cup also in like maner he caried about, saying, *Drinke yee all of this: This is the cup of my blood, which shall be shed for many for the remission of sins.* Thou seest manifestly, that by no meanes he would declare the maner of the mysterie to them that sought it without faith: but to them that did beleeue, and did not seeke it, he plainely declared it. Likewise in cap. 21. vpon these words, *This is a hard saying*, thus he saith: And such as want sharpenesse of wit, are wont to abhorre knowledge, which should be sought with great study, and much labour: but yet the spirituall man accustomed to the Lords doctrine, as to great dainties, doth continually sing, *How sweet be thy words vnto my throat! yea aboue hony to my mouth.* But the naturall Iew doeth thinke this spirituall mysterie full of foolishnesse; and where by the Lords words he is stirred to an higher vnderstanding of things, yet he falleth still to his accustomed madnesse. Likewise in his cap. 22. expounding these words, *Doeth this offend you? &c.* hee writeth on this sort. For ignorance, many which followed Christ, not vnderstanding his words, were troubled: for when they heard him say, *Verely, verely, I say vnto you, vnlesse ye eate the flesh of the Sonne of man, and drinke his blood, you shall not haue life in you*, they thought Christ had called them to the cruel maners of beasts, and stirred them to eate the rawe flesh of a man, and to drinke blood, which be euen horrible to heare. For they had not yet knowen the maner of this mysterie, and the godly ministration thereof. Also in the 24. chapter. The words therefore that I haue spoken to you bee spirit, that is:

Idem in cap. 21

Idem in cap. 22

Idem cap. 24.

spirituall, and of the spirit, and life, that is to say, they be of the liuely and naturall life. The same mans words are rehearsed to *Calosyrius*, which follow. For least we should abhorre flesh and blood set vpon the holy Altars, God fauouring our frailty, powred into the things offered the power of life, turning them into the trueth of his owne flesh, that a body of life, as it were a certaine seed that giueth life, might be found in vs.

Idem ad Calosyrium.

By these and many other places in *Cyrillus*, we be lift vp from the letter to the spirite, from the sence of the naturall man, to a more hie vnderstanding of a spirituall mysterie. It must not be thought here, that we eate the rawe flesh of a man, or drinke his blood, but that the words bee spirituall, and spiritually to bee vnderstood, that they be termed flesh and blood, but ought to be vnderstood of spirit and life, that is to say, of the vertue of the Lords flesh that giueth life: And therfore saide hee that the povver of life was put into the outward signes, and called it by an apt signification the body of life. The same man vpon *Iohn lib. 11. cap. 26.* doth expound somewhat more plainely, how wee be coupled corporally both with Christ and with our selues, and that by the partaking of the sacrament, although we be seuered both in body and soule. It must be considered, saith he, whether to the vnitie of consent and will wee may also finde a naturall vnity, by which we shall be lincked among our selues, and we all vnto God. For peraduenture we are ioyned also with corporall vnion, although we be seuered one from another, that ech one apart hath his being and distance of place. For although *Peter* and *Paul* be one by vnity in Christ, yet *Peter* is not *Paul*. Afterward within few words hee thus concludeth; The originall therefore, and the way whereby wee bee partakers of the holy

Idem in Ioan. lib. 11. cap. 26.

Ghost, and vnited to God, is the mysterie of Christ, for we bee all sanctified in him. Therefore, that hee might vnite vs one to another, and euery one to God, although we bee seuered both in body and soule, yet hath hee found a vvay agreeable to the counsell of his Father, and to his ovvne wisedome. For hee blessing those as beleeue, with his body, through the mysticall communion doeth make vs both with himselfe, and also among our selues, one body. It is plaine that *Cyrillus* spake not of the same kind of body, when he saith, Although they bee seuered in body and soule, yet they which beleeue, through the body of Christ, and by the mysticall communion be made one body with Christ, and betvveene themselues. For euen as the faithfull, being ioyned in that spirituall body, are one body, although their proper bodies remaine seuered: Euen so also wee being ioyned with Christ in that spirituall body, are made one body with him, although his ovvne proper body bee farre distant from our bodies. Let vs adde one place more taken out of this Father, which is in his booke *Ad Euoptium Anath. 11.* where he speaketh thus of *Nestorius*. Doeth not he pronounce this mysterie to be ἀνθρωποφαγίαν, that is a deuouring of mans flesh, and violently driue the mindes of the faithfull, without conscience, into false interpretations, and with mans inuentions take those things in hand, which are receiued by an onely pure, and vnsearchable faith? *Cyrillus* doth in this place obiect against *Nestorius*, That to maintaine this error, he did speake too grosly of the Sacrament, as though the faithfull doe properly therein eate mans flesh, which by the Greeke word hee calleth ἀνθρωποφαγίαν: But such kind of thoughts hee termeth ἐξιτήλως, that is to say, as *Budæus* doeth interpret it, counterfeite, not right, not sincere: For so much as here is

Idem in lib. ad Euop. Anat. 11

 no

no place for such kinde of worldly and common imaginations.

We ought to thinke the like of *Theophylactus*, who although in some place he may seeme to haue followed a more grosse opinion, as vpon *Matthew* the 26. Chapter, whose words wee haue aboue rehearsed, wherein he seemeth to denie, that the bread of the Sacrament of thankesgiuing, is a figure of the Lords body, but the very body indeede; yet when he saith, It is no figure, he meaneth that it is not onely a figure, as in another place, where vpon *Marke* and *Iohn* it is read: for else hee should haue repugned against all the olde Writers (and that is not likely) who throughout, terme this Sacrament a figure, an image, a signe and patterne. Besides, in that he said it was the body in very deede, his meaning was not to haue it taken after a worldly and common sort, as it shall manifestly appeare by those things that follow: for he writing vpon these words in the sixt Chapter of *Iohn*, *The Iewes therefore did striue among themselues, saying, How can this man giue vs his flesh to eate?* saith thus: It behoueth vs therefore, after that wee heare, *vnlesse yee eate the flesh of the Sonne of man, yee shall haue no life*, in taking the heauenly mysteries to keepe stedfast and vnwauering faith, and not to be inquisitiue how. For the naturall man, that is, hee that followeth mans carnall and naturall thoughts, is not apt to conceiue such matters as bee aboue nature and spirituall, and euen so he doth not vnderstand the spirituall eating of the Lords flesh, whereof who so bee not partakers, shall not bee partakers of euerlasting life. And by and by hee expoundeth thus these words, *Hee that eateth my flesh, &c.* In this place we learne the Sacrament of the communion. For he that eateth and drinketh the Lords flesh and blood,

Theophylac. in Ioan. cap. 6.

abideth

abideth in the Lord himselfe, and the Lord in him: for there is a new mixture made, and aboue reason, so that God is in vs, and wee in God. Here the Author teacheth, that faith must be had in the mysteries, and not to be inquisitiue how: and therewithall he remoueth apart mans carnall or naturall thoughts, and requireth onely a spirituall meaning, and commendeth a more hie maner of eating. For he addeth not long after vpon these words, *This is a hard saying, who can heare him? &c.* But see their folly; For their duetie had been, to haue asked, and learned those things whereof they were ignorant. But they drew backe, and did expound nothing spiritually, but all things as they outwardly appeared. For in as much as they heard of flesh, they thought he would compell them to be σαρκοφάγους, that is, deuourers of flesh and blood. But because we vnderstand it spiritually, neither wee bee deuourers of flesh, and yet be we sanctified by such meate. By and by also expounding this, *It is spirit that quickeneth*, thus he writeth: Because, as we haue often sayd, they that carnally expounded such things as Christ spake, were offended: he sayth, When those things that I speake are spiritually vnderstood, that onely bringeth profit: but the flesh, that is to say, to expound them carnally, profiteth nothing, but is occasion of offence. So therefore such as heard carnally those things that Christ spake, were offended. He addeth therefore, *The words which I speake are spirit*, that is to say, they be spirituall, *and life*, (hauing nothing that is carnall) and bringing euerlasting life. Let vs adde hereunto those things which he writeth vpon Marke 14. cap. 1. For the bread is not onely a figure, and a certaine patterne of the Lords body, but it is turned into the very body of Christ. For the Lord sayth, *The bread which I will giue, is my flesh.* And againe, *Vnlesse ye eate the flesh of the Sonne of man, &c.* And how, saith he, is not the flesh seene? O man, this is done for our infirmitie. For since the bread and wine bee of those things which we be acquainted withall, we abhorre them not: but if wee should see blood and flesh set before vs, we could not abide it, but should vtterly abhorre it. Therefore God of his mercie fauouring our frailtie, retaineth still the forme of bread and wine, but he altereth the element into the power of flesh and blood. By all these places it is most certaine, that *Theophylactus* followed the steps of the ancient fathers, set aside all carnall imaginations in this Sacrament, & called vs to such as be hie and spirituall, that it is not only a figure of the Lords bodie, but rather is verely his body, & yet they that be partakers are not σαρκοφάγοι, that is to say, flesh eaters: And he addeth the cause, for that we vnderstand it not carnally but spiritually, that is to say, that they remaine the formes of bread and wine, but yet do passe into the power of the Lords flesh and blood, and, as he tearmed it, be transelemented, in which tearme there is no cause why we should faine to our selfe any Popish Transubstantiation as they cal it. For writing vpon the 6. Chapter of *Iohn*, he vseth the same terme, saying thus: Therfore euen as I, saith he, liue for the Father, that is, as I am borne of the Father, which is life: euen so also, he that eateth me, liueth by the meanes of me, while he is after a sort mixed with me, and is transelemented into me that can quicken. By this terme of transelementatiō he meant to signifie nothing els, but the same change that is fit for the Sacraments: wherof *Ambrose*, *Emissenus* and others make mention, as before we haue repeated: for otherwayes wee cannot be transelemented into Christ. And no maruell that *Theophylactus* so tearmed

Idem in Ioan. cap. 6.

it, since *Chrysostom* himselfe vpon the sixt chap. of *Iohn*, *homilia 45.* vseth these wordes: But that we should not onely by loue, but also in very deed bee turned into that flesh, hee hath wrought it by the meate which hee hath giuen vs. Behold, *Chrysostome* saith, we are turned into the flesh of Christ really, as I may so terme it: But yet who seeth not that turning to be spirituall, not carnal? Euen so is bread turned in very deede, and transelemented into Christes flesh, but by a spiritual and no carnall turning, because the bread doeth get to it the power of the flesh. And these things which haue bene thus cited out of *Theophylactus*, albeit he be not so ancient an authour, yet because hee is chiefly alleaged of such as followe the carnall sence in the sacrament of thankesgiuing, though hee doth very manifestly expound himselfe, and teacheth nothing repugnant to holy Scriptures and writings of old Authors, I meant to shew the true opinion of so learned a man, and not to discredit his authoritie as a late writer.

Chrysost. in Ioan. cap. 6. homil. 45.

Damascenus is yet vnspoken of, whom the aduersaries vse as it were a chief champion: but in case they would not snatchingly picke out such sentences as serue the humor of their affections, but marke well the through drift of his writing; he helpeth not so much their cause as he doth ouerthrow it. Albeit (that I may frankely admonish the reader and vtter mine opinion) he is but a very slippery and an vncertain author in expounding of this mysterie, and none, I dare say, among the olde writers, shall be found, that hath reasoned of this matter so obscurely and doubtfully. Truely I gather by him, that vvhen hee had determined to write a breuiat of the true faith, hee vvould neither leaue this sacrament vnspoken of, nor yet vvist how to intreate of it plainely enough: The vvhich of his ovvne vvords the

Damaſ. De fide Orthod. lib.4. cap.14.

indifferent reader ſhall eaſily iudge. He vvriteth *De fide orthod. lib.4. cap.14.* of Chriſt in this vviſe: It behooued, not onely that the firſt fruits of our nature ſhould come into the partaking of a better, but that all perſons, as many as would, ſhould both be borne by a ſecond natiuitie, and nouriſhed with a nevv meat, meet for that natiuity, and ſo preuent the meaſure of perfection. And a litle after: And becauſe he is a ſpirituall Adam, it behoued the natiuitie alſo to be ſpirituall, and likewiſe the meate. For ſince vvee haue a double and compound nature, it is fitte that the natiuitie bee alſo double, and the food likevviſe compound. The natiuitie therefore is giuen vs by vvater and ſpirit, I meane by holy Baptiſme: but the meate is our Lord himſelfe Ieſus Chriſt, vvhich came dovvne from heauen. Then after alleaging the vvordes of the Lords Supper, and proofes of vvhat force the vvord is, he addeth: Euen as all things vvhatſoeuer God had made, he hath made them by the vvorking of the holy Ghoſt: ſo novv alſo the ſame force of the holy Ghoſt bringeth to paſſe thoſe things that be aboue nature, the vvhich no thing can comprehend but onely faith. And a little after: But bread and vvine bee taken: For God knovveth mans vveakenes: For commonly thoſe things vvhich it is not acquainted vvith, it ſhunneth vvith loathſomneſſe. Therfore he humbled himſelfe after his wonted maner, and bringeth to paſſe by the accuſtomed things of nature, ſuch things as bee aboue nature. And euen as in Baptiſme, becauſe it is the maner of men to bee waſhed vvith vvater, and anointed vvith oyle, he coupled vvith oile and vvater the grace of the holy Ghoſt, and made it to be the vvaſhing of regeneration: After the ſame ſort, becauſe men are vvont to eate bread and drinke vvine and vvater, he coupled therevvithall his

Diuinitie, and made them his body and blood, that by matters vsuall and agreeable to nature, we may be caried to those things which passe nature. Hitherto hee seemed to agree with the rest; for such as the second natiuitie is, such, saith he, is the meate: He termeth the natiuitie spirituall, likewise also the meat: The natiuitie to be double, through water and the holy Ghost, the meat also double: but how it is double hee alleageth not forthwith, as hee did in the natiuity, but the meate, saith he, is the very bread of life which came downe from heauen: yet after a few wordes he declareth howe it is done, saying, As the water is coupled with the grace of the holy Ghost, and is made the washing of regeneration: so is the diuinitie coupled with the bread, and is made the body & blood of the Lord. And this hee affirmeth to be the working of the holy Ghost, and that the bread and wine be taken for mans infirmitie, and by matters vsual to nature, those things bee wrought that passe nature, which onely faith can comprehend. None of these things be contrary to the opinion of the other Fathers: but those things that follow be not so. It is verely his body, saith he, that is knit with the diuinitie, that body taken of the holy Virgin. This before him no man had said. If his meaning be of the proper body, the authoritie of the Fathers that were before him cryeth out against him, which plainely affirme that body to be taken from the earth, caried aboue the starres, and not to be here: who also with manifest difference doe separate that body from the sacrament of the bodie, vnlesse peraduenture we may so interprete it, as that saying of *Augustine*, The same body, and not the same body: the same by grace and power, and not the same according to the proper maner of a body: the which it may seeme that this Authors meaning was when he writ this. For by and by there followeth: Not that the body that was taken of the Virgin, should come down from heauen, but that the very bread and wine is chaunged into the body and blood of the Lord. By which woords hee himselfe testifieth, that this body which is receiued in the Sacrament, is to bee vnderstood one way, and that body which was taken, which hee denieth to come downe from heauen, another way. For if it abide in heauen without comming downe hither; and if bread be made of the very same body that was taken; sure the bread must be in heauen, and the faithfull shall here receiue neither the bread nor yet the body, which thing no man in his right wits can affirme. But if wee leaue the body that was taken in his place in heauen, as our faith doth require, and say notwithstanding that the same is present in the sacrament by grace and power, as the rest of the Fathers do pronounce, and therefore this bread may be called and beleeued for the naturall propertie of a body that is coupled with it, to be the body of Christ, not properly as that body that he tooke vpon him, but after a spirituall sort, as the sacrament of that body; the matter is not intricate, but plainely opened, neither shall there bee any neede to frame crooked mazes that be cleane contrary to our faith, or to knit vaine ropes of sand, or to shun the similitudes that the former Fathers vsed, and to inuent other similitudes grosse and strange from mysteries, as *Damascenus* doth in this place. For euen as (saith hee) the bread in eating, and the wine and water in drinking, are naturally turned into the body and blood of him that eateth and drinketh them, and be made another body, then that they had before: so the Shewe bread, and the wine and water by inuocation and

comming

comming of the holy Ghost, bee changed aboue the law of nature, into the body and blood of Christ, and be not two but one and the same. What other thing doeth hee by this similitude, but open a way to σαρκοφαγίαν and ἀνθρωποφαγίαν: that is, the eating of mans flesh, which thing *Cyrillus*, *Theophylactus* and other Fathers do detest? How much better haue *Cyprian*, *Ambrose*, *Epiphanius*, *Emissenus*, and other said, which affirme a like change in the sacrament of thankesgiuing, as that which is made in Baptisme? whereby it commeth to passe, that the signes do remaine the same, and by grace they get to themselues a new substance in like maner, as one selfe man being not yet regenerate doeth belong to the olde Adam, and after regeneration becommeth a new man, and a new creature, not by a fleshly meane, which agreeth not to sacraments, but after a spirituall sort.

But *Damascenus* forgetting himselfe, who had before affirmed this meate to be spirituall, as the regeneration in Baptisme; now teacheth it to be carnall, if this bread must passe into the body of Christ, as common bread doth into the bodies of those that eate it: vvhereby it happeneth, that he falleth also into another errour: for he denieth this bread and wine to bee a figure. This bread and wine (saith he) is not a figure of the body and blood of Christ, God forbid, but the very deified body of the Lord. And no marueile it is that he denieth this, if he be in opinion that this bread is so changed as common bread is into the body of the feeder. But all they of old time throughout be repugnant: and surely hee iarreth with himselfe: for after those wordes cited out of the sixt Chapter of Iohn, *Vnlesse yee eate the flesh of the Sonne of man, &c.* And *My flesh verely, &c.* by and by he bringeth another similitude of a coale, farre diuerse from the former. A coale (saith he) is not simple wood, but coupled with fire: so the bread of communion is not simple bread, but coupled with the diuinitie. How diuers is the maner of these two similitudes? before he said, that the Shewbread was turned into the body of Christ, beyond nature, as the common bread is naturally changed into the body of him that eateth it, but that is not done vvhile there remaineth bread: here he saith, that the bread of communion is not simple bread, but bread coupled with the diuinitie. The bread therefore remaineth: to what is it coupled? to the diuinitie. Where is then that grosse transmutation? Againe a litle after: This is that pure sacrifice without blood, which God hath commanded by the Prophet should be offered to himselfe, from the rising of the Sunne, to the going dovvne of the same. If hee speake of the body that hee tooke vpon him, how is it without blood? if hee speake of his spirituall body and blood, he saith trueth. Againe he saith: This body is not consumed, it is not corrupted, nor cast into the draught. If his meaning be of his spirituall and better substance of the sacrament, vvee confesse it: if of the outward signe, *Origen* farre better learned then *Damascenus* saith, As touching to that material part that it hath, it goeth into the belly, and is cast into the draught. *Damascenus* goeth yet further and saith, The bread is the first fruites of the bread to come, which is ἐπιούσιος, but *epiousios* doth signifie either the bread to come, that is of the world to come, or els that which is taken for the consecration of our substance. But vvhether it be this way or that way, it is aptly called the body of Christ. For the Lords flesh is a spirit giuing life, because it was conceiued of a quickening spirit. For that which is borne of spirit, is spirit. But this I speake not, to take away the nature of a body, but willing to shew

his

his quickening and diuinitie. How changeable is this ſpeach? ſometime one and the ſelfe bread is one and ſelfe body, another time it is the firſt fruits of the bread to come: otherwhile fleſh: at another time ſpirit: At laſt, about the end he ſaith, For albeit ſome named the bread and wine patternes of Chriſts body and blood, as that holy man *Baſill*; yet after the ſanctifying they called it not ſo, but before the ſacrifice was ſanctified. But in that which is commonly called the liturgie of *Baſill*, it is plaine otherwiſe, and the reſt of the Fathers do oftentimes the like. And *Damaſcenus* himſelfe ſhutteth vp his oration with this concluſion: And they be called the patterns of things to come, not becauſe they be not verely the bodie and blood of Chriſt, but becauſe now by them we be made partakers of the diuinitie of Chriſt, and then ſhall be by vnderſtanding, by ſight onely. What ſhall we do with this man, who a little before denied that they were called patternes after ſanctification, and now he himſelfe doeth plainely call them patternes after ſanctification? what maner inconſtancie is this? This is not a teaching of myſteries, but in ſaying ſomewhile one thing, and another while another, it is to wrap all things in blind darkeneſſe. Truly I thinke in my mind, that *Damaſcenus* knew not how to determine this matter certainely, but did heape together haſtily and confuſedly thoſe things which hee had read, and which were written wiſely of the olde Fathers, and when hee could not winde himſelfe out, hee floteth to and fro, and as the Grecians terme it, πτερυγίζει that is to ſay, wafteth with his wings. For that hee was perſwaded that there ſhould be a carnall (as they terme it) tranſubſtantiation, that is not likely, ſince that the very Greeke Church vnto this preſent day hath not admitted that opinion. And indeede no marueile, if in this mysterie he saw the lesse, or had no sound opinion, if those things be true which be reported of him in his life, that after hee was made a Monke hee fondly became a basketseller in the market place, that he fained foolish miracles, that he was a superstitious worshipper of Images, and a most earnest maintainer of the same.

The authoritie of them of old time ought to bee of more credit with vs, whose iudgement commended to vs with learning and vnfained godlinesse, is of much more weight: vvho for the vnderstanding of this so great a mystery, exclude all sence of the flesh, and cal vs backe to a spirituall maner of vnderstanding. Wherefore wisely and learnedly doth *Bertram*, which was no long time after, seeme to haue obserued this distinction in the ancient Fathers, and agreeable also to the scriptures, and to haue set foorth in a worke of his, though not long, yet clearely and truely, what ought to be thought of this controuersie: and if wee gather thereout a few places fit for our purpose, it shall not be amisse; for he is neither a very new Author, seeing hee liued about seuen hundreth yeeres past, and beside, he was no lesse famous for his life then for his learning. With many arguments hee proueth this proposition, That the flesh of Christ taken of the Virgine, and that which is taken in the sacrament, differ one from another. For he writeth in this maner, expounding these wordes of *Ambrose:* That is the vndoubtedly true flesh of Christ, that was crucified, that was buried. Therefore it is verely a sacrament of that flesh. The Lorde Iesus himselfe cryeth, *This is my body*. How diligently, saith *Bertram*, hovv wisely is this distinction made? Of the flesh of Christ vvhich was crucified, which was buried, that is, by the vvhich Christ vvas both crucified

Bertramus de corp. & sang. Christi.

cified and buried, he saith, It is his very flesh indeed: but of that which is receiued in the sacrament, he saith, It is therefore verily the sacrament of that flesh: making a distinction betweene the sacrament of his flesh, and the trueth of his flesh, in that he said, That in the trueth of his flesh which he tooke of the Virgine, he was both crucified and buried, and therefore said that the mysterie that is now ministred in the Church, is verily a sacrament of that flesh wherein he was crucified: manifestly instructing the faithfull, that that flesh in which Christ was crucified and buried, is not a mysterie, but the trueth of nature. But this flesh which now conteineth in a mysterie the similitude of that other, is not flesh in forme, but in Sacrament: so that in forme it is bread, in sacrament the true body of Christ, as the Lord IESVS himselfe crieth, *This is my body.* Whose minde that we may the better vnderstand, it is to be marked (the which we did also note before) that as he meaneth the body of Christ two maner of wayes, so doth he alledge also two maner of truethes of the same, namely the one trueth properly, which he termeth the trueth in forme, and the trueth of nature, which he doth attribute to the flesh that was crucified and buried; the other a spirituall trueth, which he termeth the true body in the sacrament.

The same man repeating the saying of *Ambrose*, The food then is not corporall but spirituall, saith: Thou mayest not therefore bring the sense of the flesh: for according to that, there is nothing here determined. It is indeed the body of Christ, but not corporall, but spirituall: It is the blood of Christ, but not corporall, but spirituall. There is nothing therefore to be vnderstood corporally, but spiritually. It is the body of Christ, but not corporally: and it is the blood of Christ, but not corporally. Note when he saith, Not corporally, he meaneth not properly corporally, (for by the spirituall eating also in the sacrament we are corporally annexed with Christ, as *Cyrillus* and *Hilarius* doe witnes,) but mystically, not properly. The same man saith of the same *Ambrose* a little after: He hath taught vs very plainely, how we ought to vnderstand the mysterie of the Body and Blood of Christ. For after he had said that our Fathers did eate spiritual food, and drinke spirituall drinke, when as for all that there is no man that doubteth, but the *Manna* which they did eate, and the water which they did drinke, were corporall; he applieth it to the mysterie which now is ministred in the Church, defining after what sort it is the body of Christ. For in that he saith, The body of God is a spirituall body, Christ vndoubtedly is God, and that body vvhich he tooke of the Virgine *Mary*, which suffered, which was buried, which rose againe, was vndoubtedly a true body, the same that continued visible, and able to be felt: but that body which is called the mysterie of God, is not corporall but spirituall. But if it be spirituall, then is it not visible, nor able to be felt: and therefore S. *Ambrose* addeth, saying, The body of Christ is the body of a diuine Spirit. But a diuine spirit is nothing that is corporall, nothing that is corruptible, nothing able to be felt. But this body which is solemnized in the Church, as touching the visible forme, is both corruptible and to be felt. Soone after also he concludeth vpon the words of *Ambrose*, in this wise: By the authoritie of this great learned man, we be well taught, that there is a great difference betweene the body wherein Christ suffered, and the blood which he shed hanging vpon the Crosse out of his side, and this body which in the mysterie of Christes pasion is daily solemnized of the faithfull, and that blood also which is receiued in the mouth of the faithfull, is a mysterie of that blood wherwith the whole world was redeemed. Hee confirmeth that also by the authoritie of *Hierom*, and after rehearsall of this place, The blood and flesh of Christ is vnderstood two maner of wayes; either that spirituall, &c. thus he concludeth: With no small difference hath this doctour made a distinction of the body and blood of Christ. For in that he saith, that the flesh or blood which are daily receiued of the faithfull are spirituall, and yet that the flesh that was crucified, and the blood which was shed with the souldiers speare, are not said to be spirituall nor diuine; he doeth manifestly signifie, that they differ as much one from another, as do spirituall things and corporall, visible and inuisible, diuine and humane, and that those things which differ from themselues, are not all one. But the spirituall flesh which is receiued in the mouth of the faithfull, and the spirituall blood which is daily giuen to the faithfull to drinke, doe differ from the flesh that was crucified, and from the blood that was shed with the souldiers speare, as the authoritie of this man doth witnesse. Therefore they be not all one: For that flesh which was crucified, was made of the flesh of the Virgin, framed together of bones and sinevves, and seuered with the features of the members of a man, quickned with the spirit, of a reasonable soule, indued with reason into a life proper to it selfe, and motions agreeable to the same. But on the other side, the spirituall flesh which feedeth spiritually the people that doe beleeue, after the forme that it beareth outwardly, is made of the graines of corne, by the handes of the workeman, framed together of no sinewes and bones, seuered with no varietie of members, quickened with no reasonable substance, nor can exercise any proper motions. For whatsoeuer giueth the substance of life, it is of a spirituall force, and of an inuisible working, and of a diuine power. Againe, of the wordes of *Augustine* he concludeth in this maner: By authoritie of this doctour intreating of the Lords wordes of the sacrament of his body & blood we be manifestly taught, that those wordes of the Lord be to be vnderstood spiritually, and not carnally, as hee himselfe sayeth, *The words which I speake to you, bee spirit and life,* Namely the words of eating his flesh and drinking his blood: for he spake it vpon that occasion, whereat his disciples were offended. Therefore that they should not bee offended, the heauenly Master calleth them back from the flesh to the Spirit, and from a corporall sight to inuisible vnderstanding. We see therefore the food of the Lords body, and the drinke of his blood, are after a sort his very body, and his very blood, namely in that they be Spirit and life. Hee addeth againe after the matter proued: Therefore we see, that there is a great difference betweene the mysterie of the body & blood of Christ which is now receiued of the faithfull in the Congregation, and that body which was borne of the Virgin *Mary*, which suffered, which was buried, which rose againe, which ascended into heauen, which sitteth at the right hand of the Father. For this that is ministred in the way, is to be taken spiritually: For Faith beleeueth that which it seeth not, and spiritually feedeth the soule, and doth reioyce the heart, and giueth euerlasting life, and incorruption, while that is not minded which feedeth the body, which is crushed with teeth, which is broken in pieces, but that which by faith is spiritually receiued. But that body wherein Christ suffered and rose againe, is his owne proper body taken of the Virgin *Maries* body, able to be felt and seene, euen after his resurrection, as he himselfe said to his disciples, *Beholde my hands and my feet: for I am euen he, handle me and see, for a spirit hath not flesh and bones, as ye see me haue.*

Bertram writeth many things to this purpose; but let it suffice that wee haue touched thus much. Which mans exposition, and manner of disputing vpon the Sacrament, is (in mine opinion) diligently to be wayed and imbraced, for tvvo respects: First, because hee sticketh to the authoritie and testimonie not onely of those fathers of whom he hath repeated a few, but also many moe, I might say of all the most auncient: Secondarily, because that where the credit of the man was so much that he was prouoked to write by a most famous Prince, and his writing published abroad, and in sight of all men, he was praised of many, reprehended of none, or noted of any one spot of erronious doctrine, whereby it came to passe that before these new grosse and naturall transubstantiation makers sprung vp, the doctrine of *Bertram* touching the Sacrament, was allovved by the iudgement of euery man that was best learned: Albeit this terme of transubstantiation being indeed new & not necessarie, yet perhaps might haue some place, as the word Trans-elementation, if they had not brought in another change of the substances then a sacramentall, and that which the auncient fathers did vnderstand, which is brought to passe the former substance remayning still. But they not satisfied with the noueltie of the terme, haue inuented a monstrous interpretation. For they appoint the very proper body of Christ to be in the Sacrament, and plucke from it the true properties of a mans body, whereas it should seeme that *Aquinas* himselfe was not ignorant of the distinction aboue mentioned. For he writeth *3. part. Sum. q. 76. art 3.* on this manner: Christ is whole vnder ech peece of the formes of Bread and Wine, not onely when the hoste is broken, but also when it remaineth whole: neyther is there distance of parts one from another, as the eye from the eye, or the eye from the eare, or the head from the feete, as there is in other bodies organicall: for such maner of distance is in the true body of Christ, but not as it is in this Sacrament. He affirmeth the true body of Christ to bee one, which is organicall, and hath difference of members, which also hee denyeth to bee in the Sacrament; and that to be another, which is in the Sacrament, and wanteth varietie of members: which thing if he meant of the spirituall body as the old writers did speake, he iudged right; but if hee meant to signifie any masse of flesh without forme, it is a great absurditie, and contrarie to the opinion of all the old writers.

Aquin. 3. parte. Sum. q. 76. art. 3.

Lombardus also Author of the sentences, concerning the verie and proper flesh of Christ *lib 3. Sentent. Dist. 3.* saith thus: Christs flesh that was taken, is neither heauenly, nor of the aire, nor of any other nature then of such as all mens flesh is. Since therefore the manner and nature of the flesh of Christ is common with the flesh of other men, as *Lombardus* saith, and such flesh as *Aquinas* affirmeth commeth not into the Sacrament; it followeth by their testimonie, that these two kindes of flesh differ much. And that this may the better appeare, and bee laide vp in memorie, I thought it not without profit to adde, of such things as we haue spoken of before, a certaine distinction which the Greekes call διάκρισις by comparison.

Lombardus.

1 The proper bodie of Christ, hath the naturall forme of a mans body: The mysticall bodie hath not.

2 The-

2 The proper body hath a head, breast, members seuered: The mysticall hath not.

3 The proper body hath bones, vaines, & sinewes: The mystical hath not.

4 That may bee seene and touched: This can neither be seene nor touched.

5 That is indued with the true sences of a body: This is without sence, as *Epiphanius* saith.

6 That is organicall: This is not.

7 That is no figure: This is a figure of his proper body.

8 That is not in mysterie: This is in mysterie.

9 That, of his owne nature, is humane and bodily: This is heauenly, diuine, and spirituall.

10 The matter of that is not subiect to corruption: The materiall part of this is bread, and is corrupted.

11 No man may eate that by it selfe: This, both a man may and ought to eate.

12 That is contained in one place: This, wheresoeuer the Sacrament is ministred, is present; but not as in a place.

13 That is not a Sacrament of another body: This is a Sacrament of another body.

14 That being taken of the virgin *Maries* bodie, was once create: This is not taken of the Virgin, but daylie by the mysticall benediction is create potentiallie, by the testimonie of *Augustin* and *Cyprian*.

15 That is a naturall body: This is aboue nature.

16 Finally, that is simply: This is after a sort.

17 That properly & perfectly: This is a bodie vnproperly.

Hitherto wee haue spoken of the difference which the auncient Fathers haue godly and diligently obserued, betweene Christs proper bodie, and the Sacrament

ment of the same bodie: In the which although many things haue beene spoken, which doe not only declare that there is a difference (which in this place we meant to doe) but also doe admonish vs vvithall, what manner of bodie that is in the sacrament: Yet because wee haue not hitherto so fully expressed this point, as the weightines of the matter requireth, We haue thought good from hence-forvvard to intreate of this part more fullie; Namely, in vvhat sort this Sacrament is the Lords bodie, and wherefore our Lord himselfe at the first, as the Euangelists make mention, aftervvard *Paul* the Apostle, lastly all they of old time, following the authoritie of them, haue left in writing that it is so called, and is so indeed; not that this manner which is a spirituall and hid thing, can be found out by mans reason, or that wee goe about to search out curiously such things as bee forbidden and denyed, but that all mans inuentions set apart, we may follow those things that haue bene left vs by the authoritie of Scriptures, and auncient Fathers that agree with them, and that manner which the Lord himselfe would wee should know, and the Church instructed by him and his Apostles, hath receiued, not to depart from that. This is to bee holden fast which wee proued before, that not onely the Lordes wordes, which be spoken in the 6. Chapter of *Iohn*, *Vnlesse yee eate the flesh &c.* And *My flesh is verily meate*, and the rest that followeth in the same place, but also these wordes of the Lords supper, *Take ye, eate ye, this is my body*, and *This is my blood*, are to bee vnderstood spiritually, not carnally, and that one maner of eating is meant in both places. When I say, Not carnally, I meane, Not according to the letter, nor as the words doe properly sound: for this is to vnderstand carnally, as *Chrysostome* witnesseth vpon *Iohn*, of these

these words, *The flesh profiteth nothing*. What is it, saith he, to vnderstand carnally? To vnderstand the things simply as they be spoken, and nothing else. For those things that be seene, are not so to be iudged, but all mysteries are to be considered with inward eyes, that is to say, spiritually. Let not this rule of *Chrysostome* go out of our minds. But these two, Carnally, and Spiritually, are contrary; when the one is forbidden, the other is commanded, and contrarywise. And that carnall sense hath no place in this mysterie, not onely *Chrysostome* is the Author, as we recited euen now, and *Cyprian*, where he saith, Neither doth carnall sense pearse the vnderstanding of so great a depth, and *Theophylactus* writing thus, But because we vnderstand it spiritually, we be neither deuourers of flesh, and yet be sanctified by that meat. But to be short, I may in maner say, that all the ancient Fathers with one voice do forbid vs to vnderstand the wordes of the Lords Supper carnally, and command a spirituall meaning: The which by many testimonies repeated in this peece of worke, euery man may readily perceiue. Neither is this sufficient, if we auoyd one maner of vnderstanding carnally, and fall into another. For he that doth vnderstand the eating of Christs flesh after the letter, and as it were a proper kinde of speech, he is a carnall *Capernaite*, whether he suppose it to be done properly one way or another. That is plaine by these wordes of *Augustin* vpon the 98. Psalme: It seemed a hard matter to them that he said, *Vnlesse a man eate, &c.* They tooke it fondly, and imagined of it carnally, and thought that the Lord would haue cut out peeces of his body, and haue giuen to them. And a little after: That which I haue spoken, vnderstand ye spiritually. You shall not eate this body which you see, I haue commended to you a certaine

Chrysostom. in Ioan. Hom. 46.

Augustine in Psal. 98.

taine sacrament, if it be spiritually vnderstood, it will giue you life. Here *Augustine* calleth carnall vnderstanding foolishnesse, and appointeth spirituall vnderstanding as necessary. And his meaning is not that this is onely a carnall sense, if a man should imagine of the cut pieces of the Lords body, albeit he rehearseth but this one carnall way of vnderstanding, but also of all other the like. For it is a likely matter, that euen all the *Capernaites* did vnderstand it carnally, and yet not all after one way. For one maner is rehearsed of *Cyprian* writing thus: It seemed to them a horrible and wicked matter to feed of the flesh of man, imagining that this had bene so spoken, as though they should haue bene taught to eate his flesh either sodden, or rosted, or cut in gobbets. And *Cyrillus* doth impute to them another kinde of carnall vnderstanding: for he saith, For after they had heard, *Verily verily I say to you, vnlesse ye eate the flesh, &c.* they thought Christ had called them to the cruel maner of wilde beasts, and that they were prouoked to an appetite to eate the raw flesh of man, and drinke blood, which things bee horrible euen to bee heard. Wherefore if we beleeue that the flesh of Christ properly so called is there present, whether we thinke it raw, rost, or sodden, either whole or cut in gobbets, open or couert, the sense is vtterly carnal, & the words be carnally vnderstood. For it is not therefore to be thought a spirituall sense, because they say the flesh of Christ is present inuisibly: For if their meaning be of the proper flesh, we cannot say that we eate him not therefore carnally, because we see him not. The blinde see not those things which they eate, and men many times in pottage and brothes eate egges and flesh, which neither they see, nor otherwhile feele in taste. But none of all these is a spirituall sense, or doth con-

Cyprian.

Cyrillus.

taine

taine a more hie meaning, but as the wordes simply do signifie, eate egges and flesh, which *Chrysostome* termeth carnall vnderstanding.

Since therefore, all carnall meaning of the words set apart, a spirituall must be had and retained therein; we ought godly to seeke, and reuerently to search out, what maner of vnderstanding that is, that hath bene set foorth and commended vnto vs; the which we also wil indeauour our selues to doe, not departing from the footsteps of the very same Fathers. Euen as there be two parts, whereof the sacrament doth consist, that is, the outward signe, and inward vertue: so is that spirituall sense which is here required, taken of both these parts. The carnall vnderstanding doth follow the letter, as *Nicodemus* when he had heard, *Vnlesse a man bee borne againe of water and the spirit, &c.* hee asketh this question: *How can a man be borne againe? Can he returne againe into his mothers wombe?* The spirituall man departeth from the letter, and so are we borne againe in Baptisme. And the washing is of two sorts: Outward and inward; carnall and spiritual: the one according to the letter, and is made by water; the other doth shunne the letter, and is performed in spirit. Either of them is said to be truely done, but after a diuers maner. The first maner of speaking is proper, the other figuratiue; and the figure hath otherwhile relation to the outward similitude, otherwhile to the vertue inwardly hid. It is figuratiuely spoken, *All flesh is grasse.* For the withering grasse hath a certaine similitude of a man that soone perisheth. *Beware of the leauen of the Pharises.* This is taken of the proper strength of leauen, which spreadeth the taste therof thorowout the whole lumpe; very like whereunto is the infection of ill doctrine. Now in this sacrament the Fathers of old time haue noted tvvo things, for either of the which it may well be called and accompted the body of Christ, but especially when it comprehendeth them both. For both because the Bread is a figure of the true body, it is iustly called his body, and much more because it hath the liuely force of the same ioyned thereto, but in especiall, because it comprehendeth both. And that the figure of any thing hath by good reason the name of the same, and is called the thing it selfe, indeed *Esay* sheweth where he saith, *The people bee verily hay*, and *He verily hath borne our iniquities.* By a similitude is the people called hay, and the Lord vpon the Crosse had in him a similitude of a sinnefull man, although he himselfe was without sinne: after which maner also Christ is said to be the true Vine. *I am the true Vine*, saith he: and other places which a man shall often finde in the Scriptures. *Iohn Baptist* spake the trueth when he said, *Behold the Lambe of God.* The Lord himselfe said the trueth when he said of *Nathaniel, Behold an Israelite in deed in whom is no deceit.* That word Verily, or Indeed, is not to be referred to the outward, but to the inward circumcision: for the people of God also vvhich is gathered of the Gentiles is now more truely called Israel, then the Ievves themselues, according to the saying of *Paul, We be the Circumcision which worship God in spirit.* And this, *He is not a Iew which in outward appearance is a Iew, but he is a Iew which is a Iew in secret.* Yet be we not for all that properly Iewes, but we are called so by a figure, & all these figuratiue speaches for the outward similitude of the things. Wherefore it ought to seeme neither a new thing, nor yet a marueile, if the Lords bread be said to be verily the body, where it is a figure of the body.

August. ad Bonif. epist. 23. Hereupon *Augustin* to *Boniface* in his 23. Epistle saith:

For

For thus wee ſpeake oftentimes: As when Eaſter is at hand, we ſay, The Lords paſsion ſhal be to morrow, or the next day, where hee ſuffered ſo many yeeres agoe, and that paſsion hath neuer been done but once. Likewiſe vpon the very Eaſter day wee ſay, To day the Lord roſe againe, when ſince hee roſe againe ſo many yeeres are paſt. Why is none ſo fooliſh to reproue vs, and ſay we lie in ſo ſaying, But becauſe wee vſe to call theſe dayes according to the ſimilitude of them in which theſe thinges were done? So that it is called the ſame day which is not the ſame, but by courſe of time is like vnto it, and it is ſaid to be done that day for the miniſtring of the Sacrament, which was not done that day but long agoe. Was not Chriſt once offered in himſelfe? yet in the Sacrament, not onely in all the ſolemnities of Eaſter, but euery day hee is offered to the people. Againe he lieth not, that being asked the queſtion, doth anſwere that he is offered: for if the Sacraments ſhould not haue a certaine likeneſſe of thoſe things whereof they be Sacraments, they ſhould be no Sacraments at all: and of this likenes alſo many times they take the names of the things themſelues. Euen as therfore after a certaine manner, the Sacrament of the bodie of Chriſt is the bodie of Chriſt, and the Sacrament of the blood of Chriſt is the blood of Chriſt: ſo alſo the Sacrament of faith is faith. By this place of *Auguſtin*, and many other both of his & other fathers, we ſee that the figures and ſimilitudes of things bee often called by the name of the thinges themſelues, and that this is one cauſe, though not the onely, why this ſacrament is called verily Chriſts bodie.

To this agree thoſe things that we commonly finde amongſt olde writers, who tearme this Sacrament otherwhile a figure, as *Tertull. cont. Mart lib. 4. This is my body,* Tertull.

body, ſaith he, that is to ſay, a figure of my bodie. And *Nazianzene*, which ſaid the old Paſſouer was a figure of a figure. And *Auguſtin*, The bodie, ſaith hee, of Chriſt is the trueth, and a figure. Sometime a ſigne, as *Auguſtin contra Adimant cap. 12.* The Lord put no doubt to ſay, *This is my body*, when he gaue the ſigne of his bodie. And *Chryſoſtome* vpon the 26. of Matthew *Homilia 83.* For if Chriſt be not dead, whoſe figure & ſigne is this ſacrifice? Finallie, of ſome it is called a figure, and a badge, as of *Origen* and *Chryſoſtom*; of ſome other, an example, patterne, and image, as of *Ambroſe*, *Baſill*, and *Origen*: wherefore not without cauſe, it hath alſo the name of that thing, whoſe figure, badge, and patterne it is. Wherefore it is the more to be maruelled what commeth into their mindes, that cannot abide to haue it called a figure, nor doe acknowledge any figure in the words of the Supper, but doe reprochfully call them that doe acknowledge it, figure framers: whereas it is plaine for all that, that all old writers did ſo call it, and that by thoſe words of the Lords ſupper, the Lorde did conſecrate the Sacrament of his body: this being manifeſt alſo, that after the letter & proper manner of ſpeech, the bodie of Chriſt ſignifieth one thing, and the Sacrament of his bodie another. And if it ſhall not be a figure, it ſhall neither be a ſigne nor a ſacrament, And ſo ſuch as be ready to call other men ſacramentaries, they themſelues doe take away the ſacraments altogether. Therefore let no man doubt but this ſacrament is both a figure, and therefore doeth alſo take the name of that thing whereof it is a figure.

Nazianzene. *Auguſtin.* *Chriſoſtome.*

We ſaid there was another thing which the auncient Fathers acknowledging in this ſacrament, would haue it verily to be the Lords body, and that is the vertue of the body it ſelfe that is of force, and giueth life, which vertue by grace and mysticall blessing is ioyned with the Bread and Wine, and is called by sundry names, where the matter it selfe is all one. Of *Augustin* an intelligible, inuisible & spirituall body: Of *Hierom*, diuine & spirituall flesh: Of *Irenæus*, a heauenly thing: Of *Ambrose* a spirituall foode, and body of a diuine spirit: Of other, some such like thing. And this also doth make much the more, that the sacrament is most worthy to haue the name of the true body and blood, seeing not onely outvvardly it showeth forth a figure and image of it, but also inwardly it draweth with it a hid and secret naturall propertie of the same bodie, that is to say, a vertue that giueth life: so that it cannot now be thought a vaine figure, or the signe of a thing cleane absent, but the very body of the Lord, diuine indeede and spirituall, but present in grace, full of vertue, mightie in operation. And it hapneth often, that the names of the thinges themselues be giuen to their vertue and strength. We say leauen is in the whole lumpe, wheras a small quantitie of leauen cannot spread so farre abroad, but the strength and sharpenes of the leauen. We say that the fire doth warme vs, when the heate of the fire doth it, we being a good way off from the fire. Likewise that the Sunne is present, doth lighten, burneth, nourisheth, when indeede the heat of the Sunne doth it, and the Sunne himselfe cannot goe out of his spheare. So is a King said to be in all his realme, because of the power of his dominion. Neither doth the scripture want these examples: for we often meet with them. Wee will at this time bee content with one of them, but very manifest. Christ spake of Iohn, saying, *He is Helias*, because he was indewed with the vertue or power of *Helias*; the angell vnto *Zacharie* witnessing the same and saying, *Hee shall goe before him in the spirit and power of Helias*. Likewise therefore as *Iohn* was *Helias*, because he had the spirit and power of *Helias*; So the Lords bread is the body of Christ, because it hath his grace and liuely power ioyned therewithall.

But that this is not a fained or a lately sprung opinion, but was receiued, and allowed of the auncient writers, we wil confirme it by their open testimonies, partly reciting some of the forenamed places, and partly adding other. *Augustin* vpon *Iohn tract. 27. If therefore yee shall see the Sonne of man where hee was before*: What meaneth this? by this hee answereth that which had troubled them: by this he openeth the cause why they were offended: by this plainely, if they would vnderstand. For they thought that hee would haue giuen among them his body: but he said that he would ascend into heauen euen whole. When ye shall see the sonne of man ascend where hee was before, surely euen then shall ye see, that hee giueth not his body in such sort as ye imagine; surely euen then shall yee vnderstand that his grace is not consumed by biting, nor perisheth by eating. The same man out of the sermon of the words of the Lord, and it is rehearsed *de consecrat. Dist. 2.* The faithfull doe know how they do eat the flesh of Christ: Euery man taketh his part, whereupon the parts bee called the grace it selfe: by parts hee is eaten, and he remayneth all whole: by parts he is eaten in the sacrament, and remayneth all whole in thy heart. The same man vpon *Iohn, tract. 50.* Thou hast Christ both at this present, and in time to come; presently by signe, presently by the sacrament of Baptisme, presently by the meate and drinke of the Altar. Thou hast Christ presently, but thou shalt haue him alway: for when thou shalt goe from hence, thou shalt come to him that said to the thiefe, *This day shalt thou be with mee in Paradise*.

dise. And soone after: *The poore shall yee alway haue with you, but mee shall yee not alwayes haue.* Let good men receiue this also, and not be troubled: for he spake of the presence of his body. For according to his maiestie, according to his prouidence, according to his vnspeakeable and inuisible grace, that is fulfilled which he hath spoken, *Behold I am with you daily, euen vnto the end of the world.* But according to the flesh which the Worde tooke vpon him, according to that that hee was borne of the Virgin, according to that that hee was taken of the Iewes, that he was fastned to the tree, that hee was taken downe from the Crosse, that he was wrapped in linnen clothes, that he was laid in the graue, that hee appeared in his resurrection, yee shall not haue him alwaies with you. Why? Because according to the presence of his body he was conuersant with his Disciples fortie dayes, and they being in his company, and seeing him, and not following him, he ascended into heauen, and is not here: for he is there, hee sitteth on the right hand of the Father. These be *Augustins* words. Whereas he said before that Christ is present with vs by faith, and by the sacraments; afterward he said that he is present with vs by Maiestie, by vnspeakeable and inuisible grace, and so that is fulfilled by him which hee spake, *Behold I am with you to &c.* But according to the proper presence of the flesh, that he is not here, which proper nature of the flesh also he hath dilated plentifully by a *Periphrasis*, to exclude altogether such a manner of presence, & to establish his presence in the sacraments by grace & power. *Augustin* teacheth vs by the Lords words, that his true and proper body is ascended into heauen euen whole, but the grace of that body we receiue by the sacraments, which is neither consumed by biting, nor perished by eating.

To this agreeth that the same Author writeth vpon the 65. Psal. The murtherers dranke the same blood by grace, which they shed through madnes. The same man vpon the Gospel of *Iohn tract 26.* Giue eare to the Apostle: *I would not* (saith he) *haue you ignorant, brethe-ren, that our Fathers were all vnder a cloud, and all did eate one maner spirituall food:* Spirituall truely all one, but corporall, another: for they did eate *Manna*, we another thing, but the same spirituall meat that wee doe. And they all dranke the same spiritual drinke: yet they one thing, we another in outward appearance, which not withstanding did signifie all one in spiritual power. He calleth the sacrament spirituall food, for the spirituall power ioyned therewith, which power also was in the sacraments of the old testament, albeit our outward signes and theirs were diuerse. The spiritual power was all one in both: That of a body to bee borne at his time; This of a body alreadie borne, suffered and raysed againe. So *Manna* was to them the bodie of Christ, as the sacrament of thankes-giuing is now to vs. For this spirituall power, *Augustin* also called it, as we said before, a spirituall, inuisible, and intelligible body, wherby is signified the visible body of the Lord, and able to be felt. Hereunto also belongeth that saying of the same Author: The body of Christ is both trueth, and a figure: Trueth, while the body & blood of Christ, by the power of the holy Ghost, in power of the same is made of the substance of bread & wine: but a figure is that which is outwardly seene. The meaning of these words be, that the substance of bread & wine be made the body of Christ, for the power of his body giuen to them by the holy Ghost. The same man in *Psalme 77.* Their meate and drinke therefore in mysterie was all one with ours; yet in signification, not in out-

Idem in Psal. 65.

Idem in Ioan. tract. 26.

Idem in Psal. 77.

outward appearance: for the selfe same Christ was figured to them in the rocke, but to vs he was made manifest in flesh. But hee saith, That *God was not well pleased with them all.* In that he saith, *not with all*, there were some then there in whom God was pleased. And albeit the sacraments were common to all, yet his grace, which is the power of the sacraments, was not common to all. This place of *Augustin* if it bee well weighed, doth much helpe to vnderstand how Christ is present in the sacraments. For he ioyneth together these two, Signification and Grace, which hee affirmeth to be the strength of the sacrament.

To these agree those things which *Ambrose* writeth *lib. 6. de Sacramentis:* Afterward, when the Disciples of Christ could not away with his talke, but hearing that hee would giue them his flesh to eate, and his blood to drinke, went their way; yet *Peter* alone said, *Thou hast the words of eternall life, whither shall I goe from thee?* Least therfore any moe should so say, as though there should be a kind of loathsomenes of blood, but that the grace of redemption might remaine, thou therefore takest the sacrament in a similitude, but thou doest obtaine the grace and vertue of his true nature. *Ambrose* doth plainely teach, how it is true flesh. For hee hath noted both: The figure, where hee saith, thou takest it in a similitude; and the inward strength, because vndoubtedly it giueth the grace and vertue of the true nature. Which place being diligentlie marked, the residue which be found of his, may easilie be expounded. The same man in his booke *De ijs qui initiantur mysterijs:* Christ is in that sacrament, because it is the bodie of Christ. Therefore it is not a corporall, but a spirituall food: whereupon the Apostle speaketh of the figure of it, that our fathers haue eaten spirituall meate, & haue

Ambros. de Sacra. lib. 6.

Idem de ijs qui initiantur mysterijs.

drunke spirituall drinke; For the body of God is a spirituall body. The body of Christ is the body of a diuine spirit. By these words of *Ambrose* we be admonished, what manner of body this is, and why it is so called, because it hath the spirituall vertue of the true bodie. For these termes, Not a corporall but a spirituall food, and The body of the heauenly spirit, bee most aptly applied to the grace and vertue of his true bodie. Which thing also *Eusebius Emißenus* confirmeth *de consecrat. Dist.2.* Seeing hee meant to take from our eyes the body taken of the virgin, and would place it aboue the starres; it was necessary, that in the day of his supper the sacrament of his body & blood should be consecrated vnto vs, to the end that that might bee worshipped continually in mysterie, which was once offered for a ransome for vs; that seeing a daylie and vnceasing redemption did runne for the saluation of all men, it might be a continuall oblation of redemption, and that continuall sacrifice might liue in memorie, and might euer be present in grace, a true, perfect, and only sacrifice, to be esteemed in faith, not to be iudged by forme nor outward sight, but by the inward affection. It is manifest by the wordes of *Emißenus*, that the body that was taken of the Virgin was taken from vs, and was placed aboue the starres, and therefore that the sacrament of the same was necessarily ordayned, that that true, perfect, and onely sacrifice which vvas once offered vpon the Crosse, might liue continually in memory, and might alvvay be present in grace, that vve should not cease to remember continually the benefit of our perpetuall redemption, neither haue any cause vvhy vve should require the presence of his flesh, seeing vve feele the presence of the same by grace to be of no lesse efficacie, vvhich is to bee esteemed by faith,

Eusebius Emissenus.

not

not to be iudged in forme, or outward appearance, but in the inward affection. And that which he writeth immediatly after in the same place: For the inuisible priest doth turne with his word, by a secret povver, the visible creatures into the substance of his body & blood, saying thus: *Take ye, eate ye, this is my body &c.* And least we should imagine it a more grosse substance, or that called againe which he said before was taken avvay, he alledgeth foorthvvith the example of Regeneration, saying, Hovv great benefit therefore the force of the heauenly blessing doth worke, and hovv it ought not to be a nevv and vnpossible matter to thee, that earthly and mortall things bee changed into the substance of Christ, aske thy selfe, that art nevv borne againe in Christ. Lately thou wast farre from life, a stranger from mercy, and being invvardly dead, banished from the way of health: and suddenly professing the Lawes of Christ, and by vvholsome mysteries renued, diddest passe into the body of the Church, not by sight, but by beleefe, and of the childe of perdition wast thought worthy by a secret purenesse to be made sonne of God by adoption, abiding stil in thy visible measure, and inuisibly made greater then thy selfe, without increase of quantitie. For although thou wast the very selfe-same man before, yet by augmentation of Faith thou art become farre another; in the outvvard man nothing is added, and all is changed in the invvard man, and so man was made the Sonne of Christ, and Christ was formed in the minde of man. Euen as therefore the former basenesse set apart, thou hast suddenly put on a nevv dignitie; and as in that God hath healed those things that were amisse in thee, put avvay thy imperfections, vviped avvay thy spots, thy eyes are not trusted withall, but thy senses: so when thou goest vp to the

Idem ibidem.

reuerend Altar to bee fed with the ſpirituall meat, behold in thy faith the holy Body and Blood of thy God, honour it, marueile at it, touch it vvith thy minde, take it in the hand of thy heart, and eſpecially receiue it whole, vvith the thirſtie draught of the invvard man.

Euſebius Emiſſenus declareth by this ſimilitude, what maner of change is made in the ſacrament; how earthly things, namely bread and wine, be turned into the ſubſtance of Chriſt, and what maner of ſubſtance that is: ſurely like vnto that change wherewith wee be changed in Baptiſme, and ſuch a ſubſtance as we put on in the waſhing of regeneration, when we paſſe into the body of the Church, where nothing is changed in our outward part, but all in our inward man, which is called a new man and a new creature: and for that cauſe doeth *Emiſſenus* terme this ſubſtance, A ſecret pureneſſe, and new dignitie. In like maner alſo he calleth the bread of the Lord, which hath gotten a nevv ſubſtance, that is to ſay, a ſecret power and nevv dignitie, Spirituall food, which we behold with faith, touch in minde, take in the handes of our heart, and receiue with the thirſtie draught of our inward man. If it be well and diligently weighed, how *Emiſſenus, Ambroſe*, and the other fathers haue vſed the termes of Nature and Subſtance, it may eaſily be vnderſtood how vainely they trouble themſelues, which appoint a carnall eating of the fleſh, and doe not apply the wordes to the matter intreated of. For that which we ſee done in other diſciplines, that the words do change their ſignifications, according to the matter that euery kinde of learning treateth of, as *Genus, Species, Figura*, and other ſuch like, do ſignifie one thing with the Grammarians, another with the Logitians, and another thing with other writers; the ſame alſo ought we to obſerue in diuinitie,

uinitie, when they intreat of the Sacraments. The fathers make mention of Nature and Substance, not φυσικῶς but θεολογικῶς, that is, not as naturall Philosophers speake, but men disputing of diuine matters, do apply the terme of Nature and Substance, to grace, vertue, and efficacie, forasmuch as the nature of the Sacrament so requireth.

The like maner of speaking doeth *Chrysostome* vse when he saith: But that not onely by loue, but euen in very deed, we should be turned into that flesh, that is wrought by the meat which he hath giuen vs. We be turned in very deed into the flesh of Christ: but that conuersion is spirituall, not carnall. And thus much by the way of the signification of the words. *Epiphanius in Anchorato*: For we see that our Sauiour tooke into his handes, as the Gospel containeth, *that hee rose in the Supper and tooke this, and when he had giuen thankes, he said, This is mine &c.* And we see that it is not equall, nor like, neither to the image that is in the flesh, nor to his inuisible Godhead, nor to the features of his members. For this is of a round shape, and without sense, as farre as pertaineth to power; and therefore his will was to speake by grace, *This is mine &c.* and euery man beleeueth his word: for he that doth not beleeue that he is true as he said, he is fallen from grace and health. But we beleeue that we haue heard, that it is his: for wee know that the Lord is all sense, all indued with sense, all God, all mouing, all working, al light, all incomprehensible, but yet as one which hath giuen vs this with grace. We admonished you before, that *Epiphanius* doth in this place goe about to proue, that man being made after the Image of God, hath verily the Image of God, not according to the proper nature of diuinitie, but after grace, and vseth the similitude taken of the sacrament

Chrysostome.

Epiphan. in Ancho.

ment of Thankesgiuing, the which, according to the proper maner of a body, he denieth to be the body of Christ, since it hath neither the forme of a true body, neither can feele, or moue, and yet is beleeued by grace to be verily his body.

Idem lib. 3. cont. Hær. To. 2.

He is of the same opinion *Lib 3.* against *Hæresies To. 2.* where he speaketh thus of the sacraments: Christ went downe into the waters, rather giuing then receiuing, rather offering then needing, giuing them light, making them mighty for a figure of those things that were to be wrought in them; whereby they that beleeue on him in trueth, and haue the faith of trueth, might learne that he was verily made man, and was verily Baptized, and that so by his ascension they also might come and receiue the vertue of his comming downe, and might be made lightsome by his giuing light, that the saying of the Prophet may here bee fulfilled, in the change of power that was giuen for saluation, the vertue I meane of the bread that was receiued from *Ierusalem*, and of the strength of the water: so that here the vertue of the bread and strength of the water may be made of force in Christ, that the bread should not be the strength in vs, but the vertue of that bread. And the meat surely is bread, but the vertue in it is it that quickneth; And not that water alone should cleanse vs, but that in the strength of water, by faith and efficacie, and hope, and perfection of mysteries, and calling vpon the sanctification, might be wrought for vs the perfection of saluation. This place doeth make the other somewhat more plaine. There he said, that the bread of the sacrament of Thankesgiuing is the body by grace: here he attributeth vertue to the bread, as strength to the water in Baptisme, often repeating this terme Vertue, and confirming that this vertue and strength doth san-

ctifie

ctifie. The meat (saith he) is bread, but the vertue in it doth quicken: and he declareth that this vertue of the bread doth sanctifie, and strength of the water is made by grace, not naming it with one word; but describing it more fully with many wordes, saying, That these things be done by faith, and hope, and the perfection of the mysteries, and calling vpon of the sanctification for the perfection of saluation. The same Author rehearseth almost the same words in *Anacephaleosis*.

Idem in Anacephaleosi.

The same was also *Cyprians* opinion. There is giuen (saith he) an immortall food differing from common meats, retaining the shape of bodily substance, but prouing by inuisible working, that the presence of a diuine povver is there. Thou hearest the presence of a diuine povver, thou hearest an inuisible working (that is to say) the grace of God. Againe, By the wonted effect of things the weakenesse of our faith being aided, is taught by a sensible argument, that the effect of eternall life is in the visible sacraments. And againe, Euen as in the person of Christ humanitie was seene, and diuinitie hid: so into the visible sacraments, vnspeakeably doth the diuine substance powre it selfe. Againe, These words be spirit and life, neither doth the carnall sense pearce the vnderstanding of so great a depth, vnlesse faith be added. The bread is food, the blood is life, the flesh substance, the body the Church. A body, for the agreeing of members in one; bread, for the conformitie of nourishment; blood, for the working of quickning; flesh, for the propertie of the humanitie taken. In this place *Cyprian* witnesseth, that this sacrament is called flesh and blood, for the working of the quickning, and for the propertie of the humanitie which Christ tooke (that is) the proper vertue thereof, namely spirit and life. And foorthvvith he addeth; Christ

Cyprian. de Cœna Dom.

doth othervvhile call this sacrament his body, otherwhile flesh and blood, othervvhile bread, with the corporal nature whereof, according to these visible things, he hath communicate the portion of euerlasting life. And againe, The sacraments, as much as in them is, cannot be without their proper vertue, neither by any meanes doeth the diuine Maiestie absent it selfe from the mysteries. These termes which *Cyprian* commonly vseth, The diuine povver, The working of quickning, The effect of eternall life, The portion of life, The diuine substance, The diuine Maiestie, what other thing doe they set out to vs, then that which *Augustine* said, that according to his Maiestie, according to his vnspeakeable and inuisible grace, Christ is with vs euen vnto the end of the world, especially since that he shutteth out the carnall sense, and requireth a spirituall, as we haue in another place more fully expounded?

Cyril. ad Calos. Neither thought *Cyrillus* any othervvise, writing in this sort to *Calosyrius*: For that we should not abhorre flesh and blood being set vpon the holy Altars, God fauouring our frailtie, putteth a force of life into those things that be offered, turning them into the trueth of his proper flesh, that a body of life, as it were a certaine quickning seed, may be found in vs. That trueth of body which *Cyprian* calleth The working of quickning, The effect of eternall life, The portion of life, the same doth *Cyrillus* terme the force of life, a body of life, a quickening seed, meaning the spiritual power & grace, Idem in Ioan. lib. 4. cap. 17. as he expoundeth himselfe vpon *Iohn lib 4 ca. 17.* saying thus: Euen as a little leauen (as *Paul* saith) doth sowre the whole lumpe, so a little blessing of God doth draw the whole man into himselfe, and doth fill him with his grace, and in this sort doeth Christ abide in vs, and we in Christ. By this meanes he reiecteth ἀνθρωποφαγία, that is to is to say, the eating of mans flesh, and withdraweth the minds of the faithfull from vntrue meanings & worldly thoughts, and affirmeth to *Euoptius*, that this mysterie is receiued in an onely pure and exquisite faith, as we haue mentioned before. For it is necessary that such an eating be spirituall and made by grace.

Idem ad Euopt.

Athanasius was of this opinion. In his booke of the sinne against the holy Ghost he writeth in this sort: For this cause made hee mention of the Ascension of the Sonne of man into Heauen, that hee might withdraw them from a corporall imagination, & that they might afterward learne, that the heauenly meate that commeth from aboue, and the spirituall food which he giueth, is called the flesh of Christ. For, *the wordes that I haue spoken to you* (saith he) *be Spirit and life.* Which is asmuch as if he should say, The body which is shewed and slaine, shalbe giuen for the food of the world, that it may be spiritually distributed in euery one, and bee made a preseruation for all to the resurrection of eternall life. For this cause (sayeth *Athanasius*) mention was made of the Ascension of the Sonne of man, that he might call vs away from corporall imagining of his presence, and might afterward learne that the grace, or spirituall povver which he termeth the heauenly meat comming from aboue, and spirituall food, and affirmeth that it is spiritually distributed, is called the flesh of Christ.

Athanas. de Pecca. in Spiri. Sanct.

To these agreeth *Chrysostome* vpon *Matthew cap. 26. Hom. 83.* Will ye not see (saith he) with what a chearefulnesse of minde Infants doe snatch the breast, with what appresing do they fasten their lips to the nipples? Let vs with no lesse desire come also to this Table, and spirituall nipple of this cup, yea rather with a greater coueting let vs (like sucking babes) sucke the grace of

Chrysost. in Matth. cap. 26. Homil. 83.

 the

the Spirit: Let vs haue one griefe and heauinesse of heart, if we be depriued of this spirituall food. The same man in the same Homily saith, That it is an insensible thing which is giuen vs in this sacrament, but by things sensible, euen as in Baptisme. These be the words: Since therefore he saith, *This is my body*, let vs haue no doubt, but beleeue, and behold it with our vnderstanding. For no sensible thing is deliuered vs from Christ, but by sensible things, and yet all things which he deliuered be insensible. So also in Baptisme, by water which is a sensible thing, that gift is granted: but that which is wrought in it, (namely regeneration and renuing) is a certaine intelligible thing. For if thou haddest bene without a body, hee would haue giuen thee the gifts barely without body: but because thy soule is ioyned to a body, in sensible, things to be vnderstood are giuen thee. O hovv many do now a daies say, I would I might see his forme and shape, I would I might see his garments, also his shooes I would I might see. Thou doest therefore see him, touch him, eat him; thou desirest but to see his garments, but he giueth thee himselfe, not only that thou maiest see him, but maiest touch him and haue him in thee. *Chrysostom* doth here command vs to beleeue Christ, vvhen he saith, *This is my body*, but to behold it with the eyes of vnderstanding: For he saith, that neither any sensible or bodily thing is giuen in the sacraments, but by those things that be sensible, the very gifts to be vnderstood, and incorporall are giuen vs; and that not onely in Baptisme, but also in the Supper of the Lord. But if Christ do giue vs himselfe in his Supper, and yet no bodily thing is giuen, (for he saith that the gifts be incorporall) It is manifest that *Chrysostome* doth agree with the rest of the Fathers, that Christ is present in the vse of the sacrament

Idem ibidem.

ment by grace and vertue of his body. And although this Author doe vse in some places deuout *Hyperbolicall* speeches disputing of this sacrament, which thing he hath also done here, when hee affirmeth that Christ is set before vs, not only to be seene, but also to be touched: yet an indifferent reader may easily perceiue by this place and some other, what was his right opinion of this matter. The very same thing doth *Theodoritus* plainely teach in his first Dialogue, in this wise; *Theodoritus Dial.* 1.

Ortho. Our Sauiour himselfe chaunged the names, and gaue the name of the figure to his bodie, and the name of his bodie to the figure.

Sodal. Thou saiest true: but I would learne the cause of this change of names.

Ortho. The cause is plaine to them that bee instructed in the heauenly mysteries: for his will was, that they which partake the heauenly mysteries, should giue no heed to the nature of the thinges which bee seene, but by the change of names they should beleeue the alteration that is made by grace: for he which before had called his naturall body meat and bread, and againe calleth himselfe a Vine, the same hath honoured the figures which be seene, with the title of his bodie and blood, not altering the nature, but ioyning grace to the nature. Nothing can bee spoken more plainely then *Theodoritus* doth here expounde, how bread is the body of Christ, that is to say, because the nature of bread remaineth, and yet by grace is made his bodie, in that grace is ioyned to the nature of the bread. The same man *Dial.* 2. For neither doe the mysticall signes, after the sanctification, depart from their proper nature, for they tarie in their former substance, shape and forme, and may bee seene and touched euen as before: but they be vnderstood to be the things that *Idem Dial.* 2.

they bee made ; and so beleeued and worshipped , as though they were the same which they be beleeued. He said before , that the nature of the signes did remaine, but that there was a change made by grace ; that the nature was not changed , but that grace was ioyned. Here doth he plainely say , that the substance , fashion and forme of the outward figures bee the same after sanctification, that they were: but yet they be made other things to our vnderstanding and faith , that is to say, by grace as he taught vs before, singing al one song with *Chrisostome* , That no sensible or corporate thing is here giuen , but that they bee things intelligible, and incorporate, which be giuen by grace and with vertue.

Euthymius in Matth. cap. 64.

Hereunto appertaine the words of *Euthymius* vpon *Matthew chap. 64.* Therefore euen as the olde Testament had sacrifices and blood , so hath the new also, namely the body and blood of the Lord : for hee saide not, These bee signes of my body, but , These bee my body & my blood. Therfore we must not take heed to the nature of those things which bee set before vs, but to the vertue of them. For euen as aboue nature , hee deified the flesh that was taken of the Virgin , if it bee lawful to vse this phrase ; so also doth he vnspeakeably change these things into his verie liuely body, and into his verie precious blood , and into the grace of them. In that hee saith , Wee may not regard the nature of those things that be set before vs , he teacheth that the nature of the bread remaineth: and in that hee addeth, But to the vertue of them , hee sheweth that by vertue they be the body of Christ , and not by any carnall meanes. Finallie he addeth by interpretation, And into the grace of them , that hee might exclude carnall imaginations.

Leo & Synod. Ro. de con. dist. 2.

Leo and the Synode of Rome *de consecrat. Dist. 2.* doe not differ from these : for thus bee the

words:

words: Because in that mysticall distribution of spirituall food, this is giuen, and this is receiued, that wee receiuing the vertue of this heauenly meate, may become his flesh which was made our flesh. You haue almost the very words which *Emissenus* and *Chrysostome* vsed, as we rehearsed before, The distribution of the heauenly food, the vertue of the heauenly meate receiued, and that so we become his flesh. What other thing is this, then that wee be ioyned with his flesh by grace and vertue? For how can we otherwise be channed into his flesh?

To this tendeth also the saying of *Hilary* there brought in among other: For the visible quantitie is not to be esteemed in this mysterie, but the vertue of the spirituall sacrament. Moreouer *Theophylactus*, which is counted as it were a certaine follower and interpreter of *Chrysostome*, doth affirme this most plainely, as we haue aboue more fully set foorth: out of the which I will repeate a few thinges here; the rest, Reader, thou maist thy selfe take out of him. For both he taketh vtterly away carnal imaginations, and affirmeth that the words of this mysterie are spiritually to be vnderstood, as those which haue no things carnall, but bring euerlasting life: and he sheweth the manner and way how to vnderstand them writing in this wise. And how (saith he) is not flesh seene? O man, this is done for our infirmitie: for insomuch as the bread and wine be of those things which we be acquainted withall, we abhorre them not: but if we should see blood and flesh set before vs, we could not abide it, but should abhorre it. Therefore God of his mercie fauoring our frailtie, retaineth still the forme of bread & wine, but he changeth the creatures into the power of flesh and blood. The same man *in Ioan. cap 6.* vpon these words, *This is*

Hilarius.

Theoph. in Mar. cap. 14.

Item in Ioan. cap. 6.

a hard saying, who can away withall? &c. See their follie: for their dutie had been to haue asked & learned those thinges whereof they were ignorant; but they started backe, and did construe nothing spiritually, but all things as they outwardly appeared: For when they heard of flesh, they thought hee would compell them to be deuourers of flesh and blood. But because wee vnderstand it spiritually, neither wee be deuourers of flesh, and yet we be sanctified by such meat. The opinion of *Theophylactus* is certaine, that the faithfull be not in the sacrament σαρκοφάγοι, that is, deuourers of flesh, as I may so terme it, as the letter properly soundeth: but that spirituall sence is required, that is, the forme of bread & wine being retained, the vertue of his flesh and blood is receiued of the faithfull, as it is manifest by his owne words both here and those before rehearsed. Wherefore *Bertram* following the opinion of the old Fathers, hath thus written: For according to the substance of the creatures, they be the same also after, that they were before the consecration. They were before bread and wine, in which forme being now consecrated they seeme to remaine. Therfore is there a thing changed inwardly by the mightie power of the holy Ghost, which faith beholdeth, and feedeth the soule, and ministreth substance of eternall life. Likewise: But now, because faith doeth behold that whole, whatsoeuer that whole is, and the eye of the flesh perceiueth nothing, ye shall vnderstand that those things which be seene, be the bodie and blood Christ, not in forme but in strength. The same *Bertram* when he had rehearsed this saying of *Isidore*: Which thinges for that cause be called sacraments, because vnder the couer of corporall things, the diuine power doth worke more secret saluation, whereupon they be called sacraments

Bertram.

craments also, of their secret and holie vertues, and in Greek it is called μυστήρια because it hath a secret & hid dispensation. And after he addeth of his own this saying: What be we taught therby; but that the body & blood of the Lord be for that cause called Mysteries, because they haue a secret and hid dispensation, that is, they be one thing which they outwardly betoken, and another which inwardly they inuisibly worke? Of this also they be called sacraments, because vnder the couer of corporall things, the diuine power doth more secretly minister the saluation of those that receiue them faithfully. By all these things which haue hitherto bene spoken it hath bene made manifest, that the body and blood of Christ which in the Church be receiued by the mouth of the faithfull, bee figures, according to their visible forme; but according to their inuisible substance, that is, the power of the heauenly Word, they verily be the body and blood of Christ. Whereupon, according to the visible creature they feed the body, but according to the vertue of their better substance, they both feed and sanctifie the minds of the faithfull. These bee *Bertrams* words.

Hitherto haue we declared, what hath bene the opinion of the old true diuines of the Supper of the Lord, aswell Grecians as Latines, euen vnto *Bertrams* time, who in the yeere after Christs birth 840. was a famous man both in life & learning, noted by no man of Heresie, nor found fault with as hauing ill written, but greatly praised by the iudgement of learned and good men. Wherefore that *Iohn*, called *Abbas Trithemius*, doubted not to reckon him in the roule of diuine & famous writers, and to praise him by this his testimony that foloweth: *Bertram* an Elder and Monke very expert in holy Scripture, and notably wel learned in humanitie, quick *Abbas Trithem.*

of wit, eloquent of speech, no lesse famous in life then learning, writ many notable little treatises, whereof a few haue come to my knowledge. He writ one booke of Predestination, a cōmendable worke: To *Charles* the king, brother to *Lotharius* the Emperor, of the body and blood of the Lord, another booke. These things haue I the more willingly rehearsed, to this intent, to reproue that railing boldnes of tongue that some man hath vsed, who in a book newly set forth of this controuersie, when he had nothing wherewith he could answer *Bertram*, thought it sufficient to despise this so famous a man, & to note him with the name of an heretike. *Bertram*, saith he, or what other soeuer was author of that worke set forth in his name, was a crafty and an impudent Heretike. O shameles face and meet to be bridled! *Barnard* also which liued 300. yeere after *Bertram*, doth reiect all carnall vnderstanding in the wordes of the Lords Supper, and acknowledgeth onely a spirituall; whose words, taken out of his Sermon in the day of the Lords Supper, I haue here added: A sacrament is called a holy signe, or holy secret. Many things certainly be done only for themselues: some other also for other things betokened: and they be called signes, and be so. As for example of vsual matters, a ring is giuen absolutely for a ring, & there is no signification: It is giuen to set a man in possession of any estate of inheritance, and it is a token: so that now he that receiueth it, may say, the ring is of smal value, but it is the inheritance that I seeke. After this sort therefore our Lord drawing neere his Passion, was careful to set his disciples in possession of his grace, that his inuisible grace might be giuen by some visible signe. To this intent hee ordained the sacraments. To this end is the partaking of the sacrament of Thankesgiuing. The same man of *S. Martin:*

Idem de S. Mart.

Without

Without faile euen vnto this day is the same flesh giuen vs, but spiritually, not carnally: neither haue we to finde fault that there is denied to this our time, the appearing which was shewed to the Fathers of the olde Testament, or that presence of his flesh which was declared to the Apostles: For certainely, neither of both can be prooued to be wanting to those that consider it faithfully. For the true substance of his flesh is also now present with vs no doubt, but in a sacrament, and there be reuelations, but yet in spirit and povver: so that no part of grace can be prooued to be wanting in the time of grace that now is. In cõclusion, neither the eye hath seene, nor the eare hath heard, neither haue they ascended into the heart of man, which God hath prepared for them that loue him. Notwithstanding, he hath reueiled them vnto vs by his Spirit. Neither marueile thou, that he gaue carnal apparances vnto them which looked for his carnall comming: for it is necessary that we haue the grace so much more of force, & the reuelation of more dignitie, as those things vndoubtedly be more excellent that we looke for. It cannot be hid by these things that we haue spoken, what was *Bernards* opinion of the presence of the flesh in the Lords Supper. First, folowing the old writers, he appointeth two parts of the sacrament: the outward signe, and the invvard matter, which he defineth to be inuisible grace. Againe, the flesh is giuen to vs, but spiritually, not carnally. Finally, that the very substance of his flesh is present, but yet as it is fit for the time of grace, in grace, spirit and povver. As for that other Sermon of the Supper of the Lord, since it is not reckoned among *Bernards* owne works, albeit it be not contrary to these things that we haue now spoken, (if so be the author be thought to agree with himselfe) yet since it is counted another mans worke, & to haue a false title, it ought not to take place in a controuersie of so great a matter. Therefore in this third part of this worke I meant to shew, & I thinke I haue so done, how Christ our Lord ought to be beleeued to be present in the administration of his holy Supper, according to common & agreeable interpretations of the ancient Fathers. First I taught, that a spirituall vnderstanding of eating the flesh of Christ was required by them, and all carnal imagination abolished. Then, that it was no spiritual maner of vnderstãding, if a man folow the letter, and proper signification of the words, such as they fained which brought in Transubstantiation, or doe appoint a grosse presence of flesh with the bread, but that all such imaginations be carnall and humane, & not spirituall. Lastly, what those Fathers deemed spirituall vnderstanding, namely that the body of Christ in the sacrament of Thankesgiuing, is giuen to the faithfull by grace and effectual povver, in a certaine holy signe.

But here a doubt riseth. If we beleeue that the grace and vertue of his true body bee ioyned with the bread and wine, wee shall seeme to attribute too much to the Elements, & therof should come a double euil: for so it shall come to passe, that the worshipping of the sacrament will follow, & the perill of idolatrie; & euill men when they receiue the sacrament should also eate his body, & be partakers of his grace. But that cannot be. *He that eateth me* (saith Christ) *he shall liue for me, and hee that eateth this bread shall liue for euer*: which cannot bee vnderstood of ill men. As concerning the worshipping of the sacrament, I answere, that the ancient fathers receiued the sacrament of thanksgiuing with reuerence and great honor, & yet for all that, were safe from idolatrie; which thing might also happen to vs, if the ancient discipline were reuoked, & the maner of Catechisme restored. For *Augustin* doth euidently teach in *Psal. 98.* when he saith, That the ancient fathers worshipped when they did receiue. He gaue you his very flesh to be eaten for saluation: but none eateth that flesh vnles he haue first worshipped. And we do not only not offend in worshipping, but we offend in not worshipping. The same man in *Sent. Prosperi.* But we in the forme of bread and wine which wee see, doe honour inuisible things, namely flesh and blood. Likewise *Eusebius Emissenus*: When thou goest vp to the holy Altar to bee fed with the spirituall food, behold in thy faith the holy bodie and blood of thy God, honour it, esteeme it greatly. And *Chrysostome 1. Cor. 10. Homilia 24*: For I will shew thee that on earth, which is worthy of greatest honor. For euen as in Kings pallaces, not the walles, not the goulden roofe, but the body of a King sitting in his throne, is the excellentest of al: so is also in heauen, the body of the king, which is now set before thee to bee seene in earth: I shew thee neither Angels, nor Archangels, nor the hie heauens, but the Lord of all them. *Ambrose* vpon the *1. Cor. 11.* The sacrament of thankesgiuing is a spirituall medicine, which being tasted with reuerence doth purifie a deuout mind. And by and by he teacheth, that we must come with a deuout minde, and with feare to the holy Communion, that the mind may know, that it oweth a reuerence to him whose body it cometh to receiue. *Theodorit* also *dial. 2* For neither do the mystical signes after the sanctificatiõ depart from their proper nature; for they remaine in their former substance, shape & fashion, and may be both seene and touched euen as before: but the things which they be made, be vnderstood, and beleeued, & worshipped, as if they were the self things which they be beleeued.

August. in Psal. 98.

Idem in Sent. Prosp.

Euseb. Emiss.

Chrysost. 1. Cor. 10. Hom. 24.

Ambros. 1. Cor. 11.

Theodoritus Dial. 2.

By this and other places, it is easie to perceiue, with what honor, & with what reuerēce the ancient fathers came to the holy Communion. Neyther is it any maruell, since they beleeued that they receiued in that bread, the true nature, and vertue of our Lords true body, and were farre off from idolatrie, being instructed and diligently taught, not to worship the outward signe, but the inward vertue. Which thing *Augustin* declareth by these wordes, *De doctrina Christiana lib. 3. cap. 9.* For he serueth vnder a signe, which worketh or reuerenceth any thing that signifieth, not knowing what it signifieth: but he that either worketh or reuerenceth a profitable signe ordained of God, whose force and signification he vnderstandeth, doth not honor this that is seene and passeth away, but rather that whereunto all such things be referred. And soone after: But in this time, after that by the resurrection of our Lord Iesus Christ the most manifest iudgement of our libertie appeared, we haue not bene laden with the weightie operation of those signes which we now vnderstand: but the Lord himselfe, & the doctrine of the Apostles hath deliuered vnto vs a few in steed of manie, and those verie easie to be done, & most pure to be kept; namely the sacrament of Baptisme, and the celebration of the body & blood of our Lord, which euerie man when he receiueth, being instructed, he knoweth whereto they be applied, so that he doth reuerence them not with a carnal seruitude, but rather with a spirituall liberty. Here wee see with what learning the Christian men in time past were seasoned, before they should come to the vse of the sacraments; and how, albeit they honored or worshipped aswell in Baptisme as in the celebration of the Supper, yet that was done without perill or offence. Perill, as here it is euident,

August. de doct. Christ. lib. 3. cap. 9.

when as they had no respect to that which is seene and doth decay, but to the vertue and signification therof: Offence, because they had a conscience in time past, I will not say to receiue the sacraments before Infidels, and such as were ignorant of the mysteries, but not so much as to talke of so secret matters before them. Of the which thing there be many testimonies: but wee wil for this time be content with this one, taken out of the *2.Dial.* of *Theodoritus*. For *Orthodoxus*, being asked how he before the consecration called that which was offered by the Priest, answered, We must not speake frankely: for it is likely that there be some here present which be not instructed in the mysteries of Christ. *Eran.* Answere mee therefore softlie. By this place it is euident, how warily, and soberly they in time past spake of the mysteries. And this is worth the labour to note, That the ancient writers, when they spake of the sacraments, did vse diuers termes of honoring, reuerencing, or worshipping: By the which notwithstanding either they meant to signifie some other honour and reuerence meet for holy matters, then that which is cōmanded of God when he saith, *Thou shalt worship the Lord thy God, and him onely shalt thou serue.* So that worshipping may be defined to bee of two sorts: the one, wherewith we worship God himselfe: The other, wherewith we worship the prescribed signes & diuine mysteries, according to that saying, *Worship yee his footstoole:* which thing most men vnderstand to be spoken of the arke of couenant: other interpret it to be of the humanitie of Christ. Or admit that there is one manner of worshipping in both places, wee might say, that the flesh of Christ is to be worshipped, though it bee a creature, for the diuinitie ioyned therewith; that the arke of couenant was to be worshipped, for the presence

Dial. 2. Theod.

ſence of the diuine maieſtie, which God himſelfe promiſed ſhould be there preſent. After the which ſort alſo we may worſhip the ſacrament of Thankeſ-giuing for the vnſpeakeable and inuiſible grace of Chriſt ioyned therewith, as *Auguſtin* ſaith, not honouring that which is ſeene and paſſeth away, but that which is beleeued and vnderſtood. This alſo is worthy to be marked, that the worſhip in old time, was not done by the idle lookers on, but by them which did receiue the myſteries, and were made partakers of their grace. For he that worſhippeth & receiueth, to him it is the body of Chriſt; not to him that worſhippeth & receiueth not. For to this intent was that meat ordained, that wee worſhipping ſhould eate, and not that wee ſhould worſhip it when others eate. Thus much bee ſaid concerning the worſhipping. But in that it is denied that euill men can eate the body of Chriſt, which thing ſhould neceſſarily be done, if the ſpirituall vertue & grace be ioyned with the bread; it may be anſwered, That there is a diſtinction to be vſed. For if we haue regard to the very nature of the ſacrament, the diuine povver can by no meanes be abſent from the ſigne, in that it is a ſacrament, & ſerueth to that vſe: but if we regard the manners & inclination of the receiuer, it is not life & grace to him, vvhich othervviſe of the ovvne nature is both, becauſe the vvickedneſſe of euill men cannot be partaker of ſo great a goodneſſe, & ſuffereth it not to bring forth fruit, but contrariwiſe to them is it death & damnation. For euen as diuers kinds of meats bee of their owne nature wholeſome, but if they be put into diſeaſed bodies, they increaſe the euill, and oftentimes ſhorten their time, not through their nature, but through the fault of the receiuer: ſo alſo commeth it to paſſe in the ſacrament, vvhoſe proper vertue is alvvayes preſent

sent till it hath performed the office thereof, although an euil man when he receiueth it, cannot be partaker of so great goodnesse, nor perceiue any fruit thereof.

Cyprian de Cœna Domini confirmeth the very same. The sacraments truely, saith he, as much as in them is, cannot be without their proper vertue, neither by any meanes doth the diuine Maiestie absent it selfe from the mysteries. But albeit the sacraments permit themselues to be receiued or touched of vnworthy persons; yet for all that they cannot be partakers of the Spirit, whose infidelitie or vnworthines doth resist to so great an holinesse. And therefore these gifts to some be a sauour of life to life, and to some a sauour of death vnto death: For it is altogether right, that the despisers of grace be depriued of so great a benefit, that the puritie of so great grace should haue no dwelling in the vnworthy. *Augustin* against the letters of *Petiliane lib. 2. ca. 47.* Therefore remember that the maners of ill men do nothing hurt the sacraments of God, to make that either they be not sacraments at all, or be lesse holy: but the hurt is to the ill men themselues, that they should haue them for a testimony of damnation, and not for a helpe to saluation. The same man in his fift booke of Baptisme *Contra Donatistas cap. 8.* For euen as *Iudas* to whom the Lord gaue a sop, made place for the deuil in himselfe, not by receiuing that which was euil, but by ill receiuing it; So euery man that receiueth vnworthily the sacrament of the Lord, maketh it not euill because he is euill, or that he receiue nothing, because he receiueth it not to his saluation. For it was the body of the Lord, & the blood of the Lord also to them, to whom the Apostle said, *He that eateth vnworthily, eateth & drinketh his owne iudgement.* The same man *contra Crescen. lib. 1. cap. 25.* Albeit the Lord himselfe say, *Vnlesse a man*

Cyprian. de Cœna Dom.

August. cont. literas Petill. lib. 2. cap. 47.

Idem de Bapt. lib. 5.

Idem contra Crescen. lib. 1. cap. 25.

eate my flesh, and drinke my blood, he shall haue no life in him, doth not the same Apostle teach, that this becommeth destruction to them that vse it ill? For he saith, *He that eateth the bread, and drinketh of the cup of the Lord vnworthily, is guilty of the body and blood of the Lord.* Behold, how diuine and holy mysteries do hurt those that vse them ill. Why not Baptisme in like maner? By these & many other places it is euident, that the sacrament of Thankesgiuing, asmuch as pertaineth to the nature of the sacrament, is verily the body and blood of Christ, and is verily a diuine and holy thing, albeit it be receiued of the vnvvorthy: where notwithstanding they be not made partakers of the grace, & holines thereof, but they draw thereout death and damnation. For neither doth so great a goodnes remaine in them, or enter into them, to the intent to remaine, but to condemne them. Neither doeth the touching of the Lords body any more profit them, then it did the *Iewes* that crucified Christ, to touch his body that was hallowed, & alwaies indued with his grace. Wherefore let this be certaine, that the sacraments, as long as they be sacraments, doe retaine their vertue, neither can they be separated from it. For they alwayes consist of their parts, heauenly and earthly, visible and inuisible, inward & outvvard, whether good men or euill, worthy or vnvvorthy receiue them. And also that change of signes and passage of elements into the invvard substance, which wee often find in the old writers, can by no meanes stand, if we separate the vertue from the signe, or would haue the one receiued apart from the other. But this is so to be vnderstood, as long as the signe serueth to that vse, and is applied to that end for the which it was ordained, according to Gods word. For if we apply it to other vses, and abuse it contrary to Christs institution; either it is

no

no sacrament at all, or else it ceaseth from being a sacrament. Therefore they commit no light offence, which do not direct the signes of bread and wine to that end which Christ ordained them for, but do consecrat them for a pompe, farre off from Gods word, and yet notwithstanding doe thrust them to the simple people in stead of sacraments. For although they be ministred orderly, and according to their lawfull vse; yet when that vse and doing of their proper office doeth cease, they retaine no longer neither the name, nor vertue of sacraments, which thing the old custome of the church doeth proue. For when the Communion was ended, men did eat their common supper, and spent together in the Church those things that remained of the sacraments, as *Hierom* doth witnesse vpon the *1. Cor. cap. 11.* And partly those things that remained vnspent, were streightway cast in the fire, as *Hesychius* teacheth *In Leuit. lib. 2. cap. 8.* whereof neither was lawfull to be done, vnlesse they had ceased to be sacraments. Wherefore, neither is that doubt of them that receiue it vnworthily, of any force to subuert this opinion which we haue set forth, but that neuerthelesse remaineth safe, and vnhurt, and worthily to be imbraced of men desirous of trueth and concord. First, because the dignitie & due honour of the sacraments is not hurt, but remaineth whole and vnblemished, whilest we confesse both the trueth of his body, and the nature and substance of the same, to be receiued of the faithfull together with outward signes, which thing the ancient Fathers do testifie to be done. Againe if we receiue that distinction which the same Fathers diligently obserued, betweene that proper assumpt body of the Lord, or that he tooke vpon him, and this figuratiue body, or sacrament of his body, there is no offence committed against the rule of

Hierom in 1. Cor. cap. 11.

Hesych. in Leui. lib. 2. cap. 8.

our faith, which by no meanes is to be wronged, since that we attribute to either body their due. For we say, that his proper and assumpt body is in a place, and limitted within the space of a place, for the maner of his true body, as *Augustine* saith: As the true maner of humane nature requireth, and the true beleeuing fathers against *Marcion, Eutyches,* and other heretikes do stoutly affirme; Which thing they that deny, and appoint that body to be euery where, doe by that meanes deny the true nature of his body, and fall into the errors and heresies of them. And yet there is no let, but the trueth of his mysticall body, because it is a spirituall and diuine matter, is as largely spread & present, as the celebration of the sacrament is spread, according to the opinion of the same true beleeuing Fathers. Furthermore, no absurdities follow this doctrine, as very many doe insue both that grosse Transubstantiation, & also that carnal coupling with the bread; namely, that mise, beasts, desperate men doe gnaw, chew, or swallow that precious body of the Lord which was taken of the Virgine, whereas it is lawfull for no man to eat of that body, no not for a godly man, as *Hierom* witnesseth. Beside, this is no doubtfull doctrine, nor hard to be perceiued, but open, and very cleare, as farre as the nature of the mysteries do permit. And albeit this controuersie doth otherwise seeme to many, intricate, and like a maze; this exposition is easie, no darkenes in it, no wordes of the Scriptures, nor testimony of the Fathers be against it, but all they do agree & friendly accord. Adde hereunto, that this maner of handling this matter, is old, & constantly deliuered to vs frō the ancient Fathers, not new sprung, nor at this time first inuented, as the matter it selfe declareth; & therefore it maketh them more friendly to obtaine the peace and tranquility of the Church, ſince that all men may vnderſtand that it is no new opinion, made out of our owne heads, but the ancient opinion of the true beleeuing Fathers called to memory againe: eſpecially ſince it is of ſuch ſort as can iuſtly offend no part, but moue & exhort all men to be content. There be ſome that take in ill part, that the ſacrament of Thankeſgiuing is called a ſigne or figure, as though it were a bare ſigne or vaine figure. Here they heare that it is not only a ſigne, but the thing it ſelfe, not onely a figure, but alſo the trueth. Not being contented herewith, they vrge the Fathers, they require the nature of his body in the ſacrament. Here alſo they do heare, that the preſence of his nature is taught, and that there is a naturall participation. Yet they goe further, and command vs to confeſſe a ſubſtance of his body. They ſee alſo that the ſubſtance is by vs affirmed to be preſent, and that our communion with Chriſt naturally and (if I may ſo ſay) ſubſtantially, is here ſet out: but yet that theſe termes ought to bee vnderſtood, not as Philoſophers, but as Diuines vſe to ſpeake. Neither would wee ſtriue ſo much about that terme of Tranſubſtantiation, albeit it be barbarous & nothing neceſſary, if ſo be they would interpret it to be ſuch a change of ſubſtance as the ancient Fathers acknowledged, that is to ſay, a ſacramentall alteration; ſuch alſo as is made in a creature that is regenerat by Baptiſme, which is made a new man, and a new creature; and ſuch alſo as is made when wee be turned into the fleſh of Chriſt, which examples the ancient Fathers vſed. We do not ſo much eſchew the termes themſelues, although there is alſo reſpect to be had of them; but we require the ſignificatiõ of them, which the Fathers themſelues taught and earneſtly demaund; And onely that σαρκοφαγίαν that is to ſay, the deuouring of fleſh, which by no meanes they

 allow,

allow, but condemne as foolish and wicked, we reiect, as farre off from the Scriptures, and farre from the interpretation of the Fathers, and finally directly striuing with the true faith: and we iudge, that a spiritual meaning is necessary in the eating of this flesh, followving therein Christ himselfe the Author, and the consent of the best allowed interpreters that we haue. Surely it is a marueilous matter to see, hovv in other controuersies we be *Aristotle*-men, and oftentimes take hold of distinctions more curious then necessary: and in this disputation of Sacraments we admit no difference, we allow no equiuocation, although both the nature of the thing requireth it, and the authoritie of the old writers doe as it were point vs to it with a finger; and seeing that neither the Scriptures, nor the holy Fathers do speake of the diuine mysteries after a naturall sort, but after an high and diuine maner, as becommeth men that treat of diuine matters, and inspired with God, comparing spiritual things with spirituall things. Againe, if there be any man that thinketh that there is here too-much attributed to the elements, it is not so: but their due reuerence is giuen to the outward signes for the holy vse of them. But the invvard povver which commeth by the force of the word of God, is onely that which the mind of the faithfull doth respect, which sanctifieth the body and the minde of him that vseth it. But if there be any that require a miracle, (for some of the Fathers called the sacrament of Thankesgiuing, a notable miracle) surely it is no lesse to be marueiled at, that the bread and wine being earthly creatures, and ordeined to feed the body onely, doe possesse that force in them, and so mighty an efficacie by the vertue of the mystical benediction, that they cleanse, nourish, sanctifie, and prepare to immortalitie both minds and bodies, so that

they

they make vs members of Christ, and one body with him. Yea this miracle hath more weight, more dignitie, greater profit, and more agreeable to the maner of the mysteries, then any grosse Transubstantiation, or naturall and humane flesh-eating can comprehend. Wherefore, the seeds of contention and discord bee now taken away, and there remaineth no cause why, but the Churches of Christ, especially those that professe the desire of the Gospel, may agree in one with quiet minds and coupled affections, which now disagree among themselues with bitter hatred.

These things, my brethren, I haue thought meet to gather together touching this controuersie full of thornes, as it seemed to many: surely at the first not with this intent to set it abroad in print, but to haue some certaintie whereto I may leane, in a matter so full of controuersie, and yeeld a reason of my opinion. But now, that me thinketh I haue taken some fruit of this worke, vvhatcuer it bee, I am not vnwilling if it may bring any profit to others also. This I know in my owne conscience, that I haue sought for no other thing in this Treatie, but godly and modestly to profit my selfe and others.

I beseech the GOD and Father of our Lord IESVS CHRIST to remooue from the mindes of Pastours, Doctours and Ministers of the Church, the greatest confusion of the Church, φιλονεικίαν καὶ φιλαρχίαν, that is, desire to striue and rule, and dispose their mindes to peace and brotherly concord in Christ, that they may not abuse this notable bond of loue, deliuered and commended by the Lord himselfe to his Church, wresting it to the nourishing of contentions and factions: And vouchsafe to inspire with his Spirit the hearts of Princes

Princes and Magistrates, that they may aboue all things regard what doeth most become the rule committed to their charge, and aduance Gods glory, and not respect vvhat may grovv to their coffers by this troublesome time, with the cruell vexation of their Subiects, and common calamitie of their Common-weales.

STC
21456

RECORD OF EXHIBITION

Date	Opening
[illegible]